War, Peace and International Order?

The exact legacies of the two Hague Peace Conferences remain unclear. On the one hand, diplomatic and military historians, who cast their gaze to 1914, traditionally dismiss the events of 1899 and 1907 as insignificant footnotes on the path to the First World War. On the other, experts in international law posit that The Hague's foremost legacy lies in the manner in which the conferences progressed the laws of war and the concept and application of international justice.

This volume brings together some of the latest scholarship on the legacies of the Hague Peace Conferences in a comprehensive volume, drawing together an international team of contributors.

Maartje Abbenhuis is an Associate Professor in Modern European History at the University of Auckland, New Zealand.

Christopher Ernest Barber is a PhD candidate in International History at the University of Auckland.

Annalise R. Higgins is a recent graduate of the University of Auckland and a PhD candidate in World History at the University of Cambridge.

Routledge Studies in Modern History

For a full list of titles in this series, please visit www.routledge.com.

15 Transnational Perspectives on Modern Irish History
Edited by Niall Whelehan

16 Ireland in the World
Comparative, Transnational, and Personal Perspectives
Edited by Angela McCarthy

17 The Global History of the Balfour Declaration
Declared Nation
Maryanne A. Rhett

18 Colonial Soldiers in Europe, 1914–1945
"Aliens in Uniform" in Wartime Societies
Edited by Eric Storm and Ali Al Tuma

19 Immigration Policy from 1970 to the Present
Rachel Stevens

20 Public Goods versus Economic Interests
Global Perspectives on the History of Squatting
Edited by Freia Anders and Alexander Sedlmaier

21 Histories of Productivity
Genealogical Perspectives on the Body and Modern Economy
Edited by Peter-Paul Bänziger and Mischa Suter

22 Landscapes and Voices of the Great War
Edited by Angela K. Smith and Krista Cowman

23 War, Peace and International Order?
The Legacies of the Hague Conferences of 1899 and 1907
Edited by Maartje Abbenhuis, Christopher Ernest Barber and Annalise R. Higgins

24 Black Cosmopolitanism and Anticolonialism
Pivotal Moments
Babacar M'Baye

War, Peace and International Order?
The Legacies of the Hague Conferences of 1899 and 1907

Edited by Maartje Abbenhuis, Christopher Ernest Barber and Annalise R. Higgins

LONDON AND NEW YORK

First published 2017
by Routledge
2 Park Square, Milton Park, Abingdon, Oxon OX14 4RN

and by Routledge
711 Third Avenue, New York, NY 10017

First issued in paperback 2018

Routledge is an imprint of the Taylor & Francis Group, an informa business

© 2017 selection and editorial matter, Maartje Abbenhuis, Christopher Ernest Barber and Annalise R. Higgins; individual chapters, the contributors

The right of Maartje Abbenhuis, Christopher Ernest Barber and Annalise R. Higgins to be identified as the authors of the editorial material, and of the authors for their individual chapters, has been asserted in accordance with sections 77 and 78 of the Copyright, Designs and Patents Act 1988.

All rights reserved. No part of this book may be reprinted or reproduced or utilised in any form or by any electronic, mechanical, or other means, now known or hereafter invented, including photocopying and recording, or in any information storage or retrieval system, without permission in writing from the publishers.

Trademark notice: Product or corporate names may be trademarks or registered trademarks, and are used only for identification and explanation without intent to infringe.

British Library Cataloguing-in-Publication Data
A catalogue record for this book is available from the British Library

Library of Congress Cataloging-in-Publication Data
Names: Abbenhuis, Maartje M., editor. | Barber, Christopher Ernest, editor. | Higgins, Annalise R., editor.
Title: War, peace and international order?: The legacies of the Hague conferences of 1899 and 1907/edited by Maartje Abbenhuis, Christopher Ernest Barber and Annalise R. Higgins.
Description: Abingdon, Oxon; New York, NY: Routledge, 2017. | Series: Routledge studies in modern history | Includes bibliographical references and index.
Identifiers: LCCN 2016043884| ISBN 9781138213678 (hardback: alk. paper) | ISBN 9781315447803 (ebook)
Subjects: LCSH: International Peace Conference–Influence. | War (International law)–History–20th century. | Pacific settlement of international disputes–History–20th century.
Classification: LCC KZ6013 .W37 2017 | DDC 341.6–dc23
LC record available at https://lccn.loc.gov/2016043884

ISBN 13: 978-1-138-33202-7 (pbk)
ISBN 13: 978-1-138-21367-8 (hbk)

Typeset in Sabon
by Deanta Global Publishing Services, Chennai, India

Contents

	List of contributors	vii
	Introduction: unbridled promise? The Hague's peace conferences and their legacies MAARTJE ABBENHUIS	1
1	Justifying international action: international law, The Hague and diplomacy before 1914 WILLIAM MULLIGAN	12
2	Peace through law: the Hague Peace Conferences and the rise of the *ius contra bellum* RANDALL LESAFFER	31
3	Muddied waters: the influence of the first Hague conference on the evolution of the Geneva Conventions of 1864 and 1906 NEVILLE WYLIE	52
4	Reconsidering disarmament at the Hague Peace Conference of 1899, and after ANDREW WEBSTER	69
5	More than just a taboo: the legacy of the chemical warfare prohibitions of the 1899 and 1907 Hague Conferences M. GIRARD DORSEY	86
6	*Sub silentio:* the sexual assault of women in international law SARAH GENDRON	103

7 The duel of honour and the origins of the rules for arms, warfare and arbitration in the Hague conferences   121
ROBERT A. NYE

8 Writing for peace: reconsidering the British public peace petitioning movement's historical legacies after 1898   138
ANNALISE R. HIGGINS

9 The Hague as a framework for British and American newspapers' public presentations of the First World War   155
THOMAS MUNRO

10 Norway's legalistic approach to peace in the aftermath of the First World War   171
MARTA STACHURSKA-KOUNTA

11 Against the Hague Conventions: promoting new rules for neutrality in the Cold War   189
WOLFGANG MUELLER

12 The neutrals and Spanish neutrality: a legal approach to international peace in constitutional texts   207
YOLANDA GAMARRA

Index   225

List of contributors

Maartje Abbenhuis is an Associate Professor of Modern European History at the University of Auckland. She works on a variety of subjects relating to war, peace, neutrality and internationalism in the period after 1815. She is the author of two monographs: *The Art of Staying Neutral: The Netherlands in the First World War, 1914–1918* (Amsterdam University Press, 2006) and *An Age of Neutrals: Great Power Politics 1815–1914* (Cambridge University Press, 2014). At present, she is working on a global history of the Hague Peace Conferences funded by a Royal Society of New Zealand Marsden grant.

Christopher Ernest Barber is a doctoral candidate in history at the University of Auckland. His research focuses on international arbitration and adjudication in the period 1794–1914. His thesis is due for completion in May 2017. His previous publications include 'Nineteenth-Century Statecraft and the Politics of Moderation in the Franco-Prussian War' in the *European Review of History: Revue européenne d'histoire* (2014) and 'The "Revolution" of the Franco-Prussian War: The Aftermath in Western Europe' in the *Australian Journal of Politics and History* (2014).

M. Girard Dorsey is an Associate Professor of History and a core faculty member in Justice Studies at the University of New Hampshire. She earned a law degree from Harvard and a doctoral degree in History from Yale. Under the name Marion Girard she published *A Strange and Formidable Weapon: British Responses to World War I Poison Gas* (University of Nebraska Press, 2008) that included analysis of political, diplomatic, military and cultural reactions to the weapon. She is working on a book project regarding American, British and Canadian restraint regarding chemical warfare during the Second World War.

Yolanda Gamarra is Professor of Public International Law and International Relations at University of Zaragoza (Spain). She has held the post of Coordinator of the International Forum at the Institution 'Fernando el Católico' (Spain). She has been Visiting Fellow at the Lauterpacht Centre for International Law (University of Cambridge), Visiting Researcher (as Fellow

'Salvador de Madariaga' of the Spanish Ministry of Education and the Government of Aragón) at the Institute for Global Law and Policy (Harvard Law School), Fellow at the Royal Complutense College at Harvard and Visiting Fellow at the Max Planck Institute for Comparative Public Law and International Law.

Sarah Gendron is an Associate Professor of Francophone and Genocide Studies at Marquette University, in Milwaukee, Wisconsin. Her publications include *Repetition, Difference, and Knowledge in the Work of Samuel Beckett, Jacques Derrida and Gilles Deleuze* (Peter Lang, 2008), scholarly articles related to genocide in cultural studies and translations of literary works by Simone de Beauvoir and Frédéric Brun. She is currently writing a manuscript on cultural and linguistic propaganda in genocide entitled *Mad Men: Public Relations, Mass Media and Genocide Propaganda*.

Annalise R. Higgins is a doctoral candidate in history at the University of Cambridge. Her research is on environmental diplomatic history. She was awarded a 2016 Gates Scholarship. She earned her MA in history at the University of Auckland with the support of a scholarship from Maartje Abbenhuis' Marsden Grant project, 'A Global History of the Hague Peace Conferences, 1899–1914'. She has worked on the history of neutrality and on British public petitioning in support of the 1899 Hague Peace Conference.

Randall Lesaffer is Professor of Legal History at Tilburg University, Professor of International and European Legal History at the University of Leuven and Visiting Professor of International Law at Catolica Global Law School, Lisbon. He studied law as well as history at the Universities of Ghent and Leuven and obtained his PhD from the latter university in 1998. From 2008 to 2012 he served as dean of Tilburg Law School. He is editor of *Oxford Historical Treaties* and president of Grotiana.

Wolfgang Mueller is Lecturer and Deputy Director at the Institute for Modern and Contemporary Historical Research, Austrian Academy of Sciences. He has been a visiting professor at the Universities of Vienna, Rostock and Leiden and the Nicolaus Copernicus University. His recent publications include *A Good Example of Peaceful Coexistence? The Soviet Union, Austria and Neutrality, 1955–1991* (ÖAW, 2011) and *The Revolutions of 1989: A Handbook*, co-edited with Michael Gehler and Arnold Suppan (ÖAW, 2015).

William Mulligan is Senior Lecturer in History at University College Dublin. He received his doctorate from the University of Cambridge in 2001. He was a member of the Institute of Advanced Study in Princeton and held a EURIAS Fellowship at the Wissenschaftskolleg in Berlin. His most recent publications are *The Great War for Peace* (Yale University Press, 2014) and *The Wars before the Great War*, co-edited with Dominik Geppert and Andreas Rose (Cambridge University Press, 2015).

Thomas Munro is a doctoral candidate in history at the University of Auckland. His main research interests are the First World War and international relations during the nineteenth and twentieth centuries. His thesis examines how the multitude of ideas relating to war, peace, international law and organisation that developed out of the Hague Peace Conferences of 1899 and 1907 remained relevant through the course of the First World War and in its aftermath.

Robert A. Nye is Horning Professor of the Humanities and Professor of History Emeritus at Oregon State University. He has published several scholarly monographs and edited books and sixty articles and chapters. His work covers the history of the social sciences and the history of norms and pathologies in gender, medicine and sexuality in Western Europe and North America. His major books are *Crime, Madness and Politics in Modern France* (Princeton University Press, 1984), *Masculinity and Male Codes of Honor in Modern France* (Oxford University Press, 1993) and *Sexuality, An Oxford Reader* (Oxford University Press, 1999). He has recently co-edited, with Erika L. Milam, *Scientific Masculinities*, Vol. 30 #1 *Osiris* (2015).

Marta Stachurska-Kounta is a doctoral student in history at the University of Oslo. In 2017 she is due to defend her thesis titled 'Norway and the League of Nations 1919–1939. A Small State's Quest for International Peace'. Her research focuses on Norwegian foreign and security policy as well as internationalist thinking around the peaceful co-existence between nations.

Andrew Webster is Senior Lecturer in Modern European History at Murdoch University, Perth. He is the author of numerous articles on the history of the League of Nations, international disarmament and international arbitration during the interwar period. He is currently completing a manuscript on the history of international disarmament from 1899 to 1945.

Neville Wylie is Professor of International Political History and Associate Pro-Vice Chancellor at the University of Nottingham. He is author of 'The 1929 Prisoners of War Convention and the building of the interwar POW regime', in S. Scheipers (ed.), *Prisoners in War: Norms, Military Cultures and Reciprocity in Armed Conflict* (Oxford University Press, 2010), *Barbed Wire Diplomacy: Britain, Germany and the Politics of Prisoners of War 1939–1945* (Oxford University Press, 2010), *Britain, Switzerland and the Second World War* (Oxford University Press, 2003) and editor of *The Politics and Strategy of Clandestine War. Special Operations Executive, 1940–1946* (Routledge, 2006) and *European Neutrals and Non-Belligerents during the Second World War* (Cambridge University Press, 2001).

Introduction
Unbridled promise? The Hague's peace conferences and their legacies

Maartje Abbenhuis[1]

When the *American Monthly Review of Reviews* suggested in 1900 that the 1899 Hague Peace Conference lacked 'full contemporary appreciation', it referred to a sense of unbridled promise that the conference evoked among many, although by no means all, contemporaries.[2] Whether they appreciated its achievements or not, the peace conference held in The Hague in 1899 was nevertheless an extraordinary event. Called in August 1898 by the young Russian Tsar Nicholas II to settle what he called the 'incessant problem' of 'excessive armaments', the conference's agenda grew to cover a range of international issues relating to avoiding and regulating war.[3] From the outset, the Tsar, his rescript and the proposed conference received concerted and on-going attention from the world's media. It also inspired millions of individuals to write to Nicholas II, to petition their governments and to advocate for real progress in advancing international co-operation and global peace.[4]

These efforts bore fruit. Between 18 May and 29 July 1899, more than 100 delegates representing 26 sovereign states met in the city of The Hague to consider disarmament, the international law of war, the principles of international arbitration, mediation and 'good offices' and extending the 1864 Geneva Convention to warfare at sea. That the delegations were willing to negotiate these issues, most of which were key to their states' sovereignty and security, is remarkable. Even more remarkably, the conference did not end in a stalemate or ignominy.

Over the course of ten weeks, the delegations at The Hague authored three conventions, issued three declarations, offered up a resolution and announced six *voeux* (literally 'wishes').[5] These included the Convention for the Pacific Settlement of International Disputes (I), which formalised a comprehensive system of conflict-resolution mechanisms and also established the Permanent Court of Arbitration (PCA). The Convention with Respect to the Laws and Customs of War (II) founded a universal military code for waging war on land. The Convention for the Adaptation to Maritime Warfare of the Principles of the Geneva Convention of 22 August 1864 (III) extended the Geneva rules and, in so doing, legitimised them.[6] The Hague Declarations (IV, 1–3) outlawed three types of weaponry: namely, bombs released from balloons or 'analogous' craft, asphyxiating poisonous gases and dum-dum bullets (hollow-tipped ammunition that expanded on impact). The resolution further noted that the 'conference is of the opinion' that restricting military might was 'extremely desirable for the increase of the material and moral welfare of mankind', thereby legitimising disarmament as a valid subject for further diplomatic negotiation.[7]

The *voeux* suggested that the Geneva Conventions of 1864 be revised, urged a future Hague conference and prioritised the codification of the law of neutrality as a topic for discussion at that conference. The Final Act of the International Peace Conference (1899) also included an essential clause, named after its author, the international lawyer Fyodor Martens. The Martens' Clause stated that the signatory powers:

> clearly do not intend that unforeseen cases should, in the absence of a written undertaking, be left to the arbitrary judgement of military commanders. Until a more complete code of the laws of war has been issued, ... inhabitants and ... belligerents remain under the protection and the rule of the principles of the law of nations, as they result from the usages established among civilized peoples, from the laws of humanity, and the dictates of the public conscience.[8]

The Martens' Clause thereby legislated the expectation that all 'civilised' states would conduct their wars in 'civilised' ways. While it was (and often is) dismissed as haughty rhetoric, the Martens' Clause impacted public perceptions of warfare in the years to come. It also shaped (and continues to shape) the international law of war in fundamental ways.[9]

The articles, clauses and declarations comprising the 1899 Hague Conventions shaped the history of international relations.[10] They established the precedents that all states were responsible for engaging in conflict-resolution mechanisms, that wartime conduct should be limited and that international law held a central place in international affairs. The first set of Hague conventions were foundational to the development of international law and the appearance of human rights and humanitarian agreements through the twentieth and early twenty-first centuries. They also set a notable precedent for the future of international organisation as well as for the rise of international judicial forums.

The second Hague conference, called in controversial circumstances during the Russo–Japanese War by United States president Theodore Roosevelt, made equally large strides in shaping international order. The conference, not held until 1907, looked to further the 1899 conventions. The 1907 Hague event was even more globalised than its predecessor. Representatives from 44 governments attended. As such, the 1907 Hague Peace Conference constituted the first time almost all of the world's governments negotiated their concerns in a multilateral setting. In so doing, they initiated a revolutionary trend in global organisation and transnational interaction.[11]

The 1907 agenda was also enormous.[12] It covered all manner of subjects, including extending the Permanent Court of Arbitration and arbitral procedures. It posited the possibility of a Permanent Court of International Justice (which, in the end, would not be established until after the First World War) along with an International Prize Court (IPC) to adjudicate neutral grievances in time of war. It sought to delineate the international law of neutrality both at sea and on land and looked to augment the laws of war to cover maritime warfare.

The second Hague conference met between 15 June and 18 October 1907. For more than four months its delegations debated and negotiated. The second conference's achievements were substantial, although little progress was made on some key ideas: disarmament was purposely left off the agenda at Germany's insistence, the International Prize Court (Convention XII) was never created because the negotiations on maritime warfare stalled and Great Britain did not ratify the subsequent 1909 London Declaration that sought to regulate contraband issues.

Still, the 1907 Hague Conventions—all 14 of them—were substantive in content and application.[13] They created a powerful set of rules and regulations for the conduct of wars and for conflict resolution that had a long-lasting impact on international affairs. The Convention for the Pacific Settlement of International Disputes (I, 1907), for example, remains in force today, as does the Permanent Court of Arbitration. The Convention respecting the Limitation of Employment of Force for Recovery of Contract Debts (II, 1907) made it illegal for states to use the threat of war or violence to recover private debt, instead referring those disputes to the Permanent Court of Arbitration. The Convention relative to the Opening of Hostilities (III, 1907) ruled that states must formally declare a war before entering into war-like acts, in order to provide ample time for conflict-resolution mechanisms to be initiated. The Convention respecting the Laws and Customs of War on Land (IV, 1907) confirmed most of the 1899 conventions and augmented them where necessary. The Convention relative to the Rights and Duties of Neutral Powers and Persons in Case of War on Land (V) and the Convention concerning the Rights and Duties of Neutral Powers in Naval War (XIII) also remain in effect today and established the world's first comprehensive law of neutrality, bringing centuries of diplomatic bickering and conflict over the limits of neutrality and belligerency to a head.[14] The Convention relative to the Conversion of Merchant Ships into War Ships (VII, 1907) ensured that the delineation between naval warships and private civilian vessels was maintained in time of war to avoid reinstituting the principle of privateering that had been abandoned during the Crimean War.[15] The Convention relative to the Laying of Automatic Submarine Contact Mines (VIII) further aimed to restrict the use of sea mines in order to guarantee the safety of private property and trade in time of war.

For contemporaries, the Hague conferences were controversial events. On the one hand, many internationalists welcomed the conferences and the

Hague conventions. Most peace activists, numerous international lawyers and large numbers of ordinary people did too. From 1899 on, 'The Hague' itself became a prominent idea, permeating media representations of wars and diplomatic crises.[16] On the other hand, the fear that the Hague conventions might limit states' sovereign authority compelled numerous governments, militarists and diplomats to ignore or limit their application. For historians, the conferences remain contested. Historians of diplomacy and international relations tend to dismiss the events either as 'failures' or as 'little more than a footnote *en route*' to the First World War, as N. J. Brailey put it.[17] These historians often look towards the horrors of that global conflagration and to the belligerent governments' willingness to ignore or overrule the Hague regulations to reinforce their interpretations. In contrast, legal historians tend to present the Hague conferences and their legacies in more laudatory ways.[18] They evaluate the conferences' importance in terms of the legal precedents they set and the legal changes they inspired.[19] From yet another perspective, historians of pacifism applaud the peace appeal of the conferences, yet they also tend to underestimate the conferences' attractions for the wider public, both at the time and subsequently.[20] Rarely do these histories meet. This volume attempts to bring the various disciplines together to assess the history and on-going relevance of the Hague conferences, the conventions they brought into being, the institutions they established, the precedents they set, the people they influenced and the ideas they shaped. Altogether, the following twelve chapters argue for a reassessment of the 1899 and 1907 Hague conferences' importance as essential moments in determining the shape of international history in the twentieth and twenty-first centuries.

The fact that the Hague system became a permanent development after 1907 is easily forgotten. A third peace conference was planned for 1915. Unfortunately, the events of the First World War overtook the proposed 1915 event and an official Hague peace conference was never held, despite several attempts. After 1918, a new age of collective security based on the League of Nations' mandate seemed to overshadow the Hague conferences' promise for the judicial and international organisation of the world. Yet even in the 1920s, The Hague's influence continued to radiate. The Permanent Court of Arbitration remained in session. The Permanent Court of Justice, established in 1918, evolved into the International Court of Justice and the International Criminal Court in the aftermath of the Second World War. Both sit in The Hague accommodated within the city's Peace Palace complex, which was built in 1913 as a home for the PCA.[21] The city of The Hague also continues to revel in its connections to the 1899 and 1907 conferences. In 2012, the city's official motto changed to 'peace and justice' (*vrede en recht*) to reflect the importance of the more than 160 international organisations housed there and The Hague's many years of service to the principles of international organisation.[22]

This collection presents a range of chapters dealing with the Hague conferences and their legacies. The chapters cover a range of academic disciplines and investigative approaches. Above all they highlight how essential The Hague has been (and continues to be) to the international arena, to the ways in which people interpret war and state violence, to the development of humanitarian principles and human rights and to understandings of the power of public agency. The chapters do not offer a comprehensive history of the Hague conferences nor do they narrate all of their multifarious historical and contemporary applications. To access those, readers must look elsewhere.[23] What the chapters do attempt is to highlight how relevant the Hague conferences are to shaping the history of the modern world.

The collection opens with an incisive chapter by William Mulligan. The chapter makes a thought-provoking argument for reassessing how contemporaries in the years leading up to the First World War considered the prospect of global industrial war and interpreted the dynamics of international diplomacy. Mulligan argues for a historiographical readjustment away from considering the 1871–1914 era's diplomacy as dominated solely by the normative idea of 'might makes right', and highlights how essential international legal norms were in shaping contemporary understandings of power politics. Comparing the diplomatic discourse circulating around the 1906 Moroccan crisis with that of the 1908 annexation of Bosnia-Herzegovina, Mulligan reveals subtle but important shifts in European public diplomacy. He argues for a decline (or 'fraying') of the language of international law by 1908 and situates that decline in its contemporary context, including that of the second Hague peace conference of 1907. Overall Mulligan suggests that, by 1914, the need for states to be able to publicly justify their involvement in war required a careful balancing act between promoting their sovereign rights and situating those rights within existing legal norms and the sanctity of treaty obligations. He thereby reminds historians that for four decades (from 1871 on) the European powers tempered their military ambitions on the continent. That history is only explicable when considering the wider political context of the time, which acknowledged international law as a powerful normative idea. After all, as Mulligan concludes: 'international law could only gain traction during the war because it had been an important way of thinking about international politics before the war'.

Randall Lesaffer continues with the theme of international law in Chapter 2 by asserting the importance of the Hague conferences in marking the shift from *ius ad bellum* ('right to war law') to *ius contra bellum* ('law preventing war'). Lesaffer argues that international lawyers tend to posit the Hague conferences as making minor improvements to the international law of war. Instead, he offers a strong case for the sophistication of contemporary ideas around *ius ad bellum* and for the regulation of international arbitration in 1899 and 1907. The chapter not only looks back to the roots of *ius ad bellum* in the medieval and early modern periods but also charts the key developments in international legal thinking across the nineteenth century in order to contextualise and explain the establishment of the Permanent Court of Arbitration and the Hague Convention for the Pacific Settlement of International Disputes. Altogether, Lesaffer suggests that the Hague conferences had a long pre-history which legal scholars ought to consider, and that they were essential to shaping twentieth-century legal doctrines.

In Chapter 3, Neville Wylie also highlights the power of legal norms in the international system by analysing the impact of the 1899 Hague Convention (III), which extended the Geneva rules for the alleviation of the care of the sick and wounded in time of war to warfare at sea. When historians write about the first Hague conference, they tend to offer only a sentence or two to the third Hague convention and imply that its creation was as good as guaranteed. Wylie revises our understanding of these negotiations. He also emphasises how diplomatically contested the idea of expanding the Geneva Conventions was at the time and, in so doing, makes a convincing case for the first Hague conference's importance in legitimating the Geneva Conventions' content and spurring their revision (which occurred in 1906). He argues, above all, for the normative power of the Hague law in promoting Geneva law as a set of principles applicable to the conduct of all armed forces. As such, Wylie connects the Hague and Geneva traditions and suggests that to see them as separate developments muddies our interpretation of their origins and their on-going relevance.

In Chapters 4 and 5, Andrew Webster and Marion Girard Dorsey focus on another key ideal promoted and legitimised by the two Hague conferences, namely that of arms limitation. Webster opens his chapter by suggesting that the 1899 conference 'marks the opening of the modern era of efforts towards international disarmament'. His chapter offers a history of the disarmament discussions held in The Hague that year and charts their legacies in 1907, through the First World War and into the interbellum period. Above all, Webster argues that disarmament was a worthy concept promoted by peace activists. It was also considered as a practical step to limiting warfare and establishing a stable international environment. He concludes that while in 1899 'informed observers' considered disarmament a premature development, by the 1920s disarmament—while difficult—was recognised as a legitimate diplomatic ambition.

Girard Dorsey also makes a compelling case for the imaginative power of the delegates at the 1899 Hague conference, who prohibited using poisonous and asphyxiating gases before they were even invented. In so doing, she argues for the normative power of prohibition because almost everyone in 1914 believed chemical warfare to be illegal. That belief ensured that when Germany initiated the world's first military gas attacks in 1915, the global reaction helped to maintain an international taboo on the subject. Dorsey further reiterates that while gas warfare continued as a feature of modern warfare from 1915 on, it always did so on the margins of what was considered 'acceptable' conduct by states. In fact, chemical warfare was further legislated for in three anti-chemical warfare treaties in Washington (1922), in Geneva (1925) and in Paris (1993). The use of gas warfare in the First World War was not a 'failure' of The Hague. Rather, Dorsey makes a convincing argument for the Hague conferences' significance in shaping twentieth- and twenty-first-century expectations regarding the conduct and application of war.

In Chapter 6, Sarah Gendron focuses on the ways in which The Hague's principles shaped understandings about the application of the rules of war and set norms for military conduct against civilians. She focuses on the silencing of women as subjects of The Hague's war rules, and argues that sexual violence against women in time of war has existed as a sub-stratum of the law, largely silenced (*sub silentio*) for too long. The lack of clarity presented by Article 46 of the Hague conventions influenced not only the conduct of warfare after 1899 but also offered reprieve from persecution for soldiers who engaged in sexual crimes against women. Gendron highlights how it took more than a century of sexual assaults for international law to catch up and lift the veil of silence. Yet Gendron also acknowledges the importance of the Hague rules in marking a shift to the recognition of women as legitimate subjects of International Humanitarian Law (IHL).

In a striking contrast to Gendron's chapter on women's rights, in Chapter 7, Robert Nye offers a fascinating connection between the negotiations at the Hague conferences of 1899 and 1907 and the gendered principles that existed around duelling in *fin-de-siècle* European societies. Nye argues that only by situating the conferences within their social and cultural contexts can some of their underlying principles and ideas be fully appreciated. Nye contends that the men who negotiated the Hague conventions considered their world in terms of codes of honour and highly regulated notions of civility. The nature of the discussions at The Hague, the language delegates used and the resulting conventions speak to the importance of chivalry, patriarchy and protection of the weak, concepts that were also prevalent in the codification of duelling. Nye further posits that contemporary concepts of masculinity shaped the delegates' expectations for the conduct of states. He highlights how the integration of ideas of restraint, civilisation and public order, which featured prominently in Europeans' social life, also underwrote arbitration and the regulation of the prevention and alleviation of war. His chapter is particularly important for integrating social and cultural contexts in international history.[24] It also brings out—much like Gendron's chapter—the highly gendered and moralised notions that influenced (and continue to influence) the shape of international affairs.[25]

Annalise Higgins' chapter on W. T. Stead reinforces Nye's point about the wider public and social environments in which the conferences of The Hague and their conventions played out. She highlights not only how essential public agitation for the ideas of the Tsar's rescript and the 1899 Hague conference was among the wider British public, but also shows how historians of the 1899 moment fail to assess the global relevance of the public's agency in advocating for the conference's agenda. Higgins is particular to stress that the conferences' historiography places too much emphasis on the influence of one man, the self-styled sensationalist journalist, W. T. Stead.

By focussing on Stead, Higgins suggests, historians of peace activism have skewed the history of the Hague conferences, and hindered understanding of these conferences as having widespread and global appeal at the time and subsequently.

In Chapter 9, Thomas Munro also focuses on the public appeal of The Hague's regulations by offering an overview of newspaper reporting in the United States and Great Britain at the outbreak of the First World War. He shows how, in both countries, the public debate around the war evolved using the language of 'The Hague' to make a case for the war's morality. By focusing on The Hague as a lens through which to read the war, Munro notes how contemporaries defined ideas of 'civilisation' and 'civilised' conduct in terms of international law and the internationalist ideas underpinning the Hague conventions. In so doing, he adds to a growing body of research that emphasises how essential popular notions of international legal developments were to framing contemporary understanding and expectations of war and state violence.

Marta Stachurska-Kounta analyses another key legacy of the creation of the Permanent Court of Arbitration, namely that of the establishment of the Permanent Court of International Justice (PCIJ) in 1919. In Chapter 10, she shows how important the establishment of the PCIJ was as a medium for neutral countries, such as Norway, to influence the post-war international order. Many neutrals used the legacy of the Hague conferences and their involvement in them to advance their cause as neutrals and non-belligerents in the aftermath of the First World War. As they were largely denied input into the Versailles negotiations, these neutral states looked for other opportunities to influence the international order. Their opportunity came in advancing ideas of judicial organisation, the PCIJ included. Stachurska-Kounta reminds us that the ongoing legacy of that involvement is significant because it legitimated a role for neutrals in the League of Nations' era of collective security.

In Chapter 11, Wolfgang Mueller provides an insightful investigation into the ways in which the Soviet Union attempted to revisit and revise the terms of The Hague's neutrality conventions in the 1950s and 1960s. He argues that, in legitimising communism as an ideology worthy of reworking the international order, the communist bloc had to create a new framework for international law by moving it away from the western capitalist traditions to which it was so intimately tied. The Hague conventions therefore featured in the Soviet mindset as a perpetuator of the western capitalist order. Mueller also shows how important the Soviet reinvention of neutrality law was for the global power balance at the time. In reinventing neutrality, the Soviet government hoped to assign new obligations to the Cold War's non-aligned states (including Switzerland, Austria, Turkey and Sweden). As a result, it posited 'neutrality in peacetime' as a term that imposed binding obligations on long-term and permanent neutrals. In the Hague tradition, neutrality was a concept that applied only to the wartime relationship between neutrals and belligerents. Mueller's chapter reminds us how the Hague rules were, and are, not legal vacuums: they can be (and have been) reinvented to meet a changing global order's needs and the ambitions of states, great and small.

Like Mueller, Yolanda Gamarra also investigates the reinvention of the law of neutrality. In the final chapter, Gamarra presents an extraordinary history of the power of the Hague conventions to shape domestic legal developments. Gamarra charts how Spain's neutrality and adherence to the principles of the Hague conventions through the First World War helped to present the country as a paragon of pacifism and conflict resolution. By the time Spain developed a new constitution in 1931, after the fall of the Rivera government, it embedded the Hague principles in the constitution itself. Not only did the 1931 constitution establish the requirement that Spanish foreign policy avoid the waging of war, it offered a powerful precedent for other states to reframe their constitutions in its wake (including Portugal). These ideas remained so influential that, when Spain reinstituted its democratic foundations in 1978 in the aftermath of Franco's rule, the preamble of that constitution returned to some (although not all) of the ideas present in the 1931 document. For Spain, the Hague conventions continue to have powerful domestic and international repercussions.

On 9 August 1899, the final issue of the *Peace Crusade*, a journal established in the United States with the express purpose of supporting the public momentum behind the peace message of the first Hague conference, surmised that:

> the Conference has achieved so much more than even the most hopeful students prophesied, that the historian of whatever school will be obliged to mention it in the future.[26]

The Hague conferences of 1899 and 1907 are not only mentioned today in a variety of public and academic forums, they also form the basis of significant and on-going discussions and interpretations about the value of war, peace, international law and international organisation. As the chapters in this collection relate, the legacies of The Hague remain substantial and substantive.

Notes

1 With grateful thanks to the Royal Society of New Zealand, the New Zealand Centre for Human Rights Law, Policy and Practice at the University of Auckland and the Faculty of Arts at the University of Auckland for supporting the 'War, Peace and International Order? The Legacies of the Hague Conferences of 1899 and 1907' conference held on 19 April 2016.
2 *American Monthly Review of Reviews*. 22 December 1900, p.643.
3 For the text of the Tsar's rescript and the second circular: J.B. Scott. (1909). *The Hague Peace Conferences of 1899 and 1907. Volume 1. Part 1. A Series of Lectures Delivered Before the Johns Hopkins University in the year 1908*. Baltimore: Johns Hopkins University Press, pp.41–42, 45. Although 'rescript' may be a faulty descriptor for the Tsar's diplomatic invitation, it is the word contemporaries used to describe the document.

4 For more: M. Abbenhuis. (forthcoming). *For the Peace of the World. A Global History of the Hague Conferences, 1898–1915*. Also A. Higgins' chapter in this collection.
5 For the full text of the conventions: J.B. Scott, ed. (1918). *The Hague Conventions and Declarations of 1899 and 1907. Accompanied by Tables of Signatures, Ratifications and Adhesions of the Various Powers and Texts of Reservations*. New York: Oxford University Press.
6 For more see N. Wylie's chapter in this collection.
7 Regardless of the power politics that also defined the moment: S. Keefer. (2006). Building the Palace of Peace: The Hague Conference of 1899 and Arms Control in the Progressive Era. *Journal of the History of International Law*, 8, pp.1–17. See also A. Webster's chapter in this collection.
8 J.B. Scott, ed. (1920). *Proceedings of the International Peace Conference. The Hague, May 18–July 29, 1899*. New Edition. Washington D.C.: Carnegie Endowment for International Peace, p. 208.
9 For more: R. Schircks. (2001). *Die Martens'sche Klausel. Rezeption und Rechsqualität*. Baden Baden: Nomos Verlagsgesellschaft; T. Meron. (2000). The Martens Clause, Principles of Humanity, and Dictates of Public Conscience. *American Journal of International Law*, 94(4), pp.78–89.
10 C.f. R. Sharwood. (2002). Princes and Peacemakers. The Story of the Hague Peace Conference of 1899. In: S. Rosenne, ed., *The Hague Peace Conferences of 1899 and 1907 and International Arbitration*. The Hague: T.M.C. Asser Press, p.455.
11 C.f. C. Reeves. (2005). From Red Crosses to Golden Arches. China, the Red Cross, and the Hague Peace Conference, 1899–1900. In: J. Bentley and A. Yang, eds, *Interactions. Transregional Perspectives on World History*. Honolulu: University of Hawai'i Press, pp.64–93.
12 Scott, *Hague Conventions*.
13 For the full text of the conventions: Scott, *Hague Conventions*.
14 For more: M. Abbenhuis. (2014). *Age of Neutrals. Great Power Politics 1815–1914*. Cambridge: Cambridge University Press, esp. pp.178–218.
15 For more: J. Lemnitzer. (2014). *Power, Law and the End of Privateering*. Houndsmills: Palgrave MacMillan.
16 Abbenhuis, *For the Peace of the World*. See also T. Munro's chapter in this collection.
17 N.J. Brailey. (2002). Sir Ernest Satow and the 1907 Second Hague Peace Conference. *Diplomacy & Statecraft*, 13(2), p.201.
18 Although note R. Lesaffer's perspective on the legal historiography in this collection.
19 As an example: Rosenne, ed.
20 S. Cooper is the leading historian on peace activism and the Hague conferences: (1967). *Peace and Internationalism. European Ideological Movements behind the Two Hague Conferences (1889–1907)*. PhD. New York University; (1972). *Arbitration or War? Contemporary Reactions to the Hague Peace Conference of 1899*. New York: Garland; (1991). *Patriotic Patriotism. Waging War on War in Europe 1815–1914*. Oxford: Oxford University Press. Also useful are: C. Marchand. (1972). *The American Peace Movement and Social Reform 1898–1918*. Princeton: Princeton University Press; D. Hucker. (2015). British Peace Activism and "New" Diplomacy: Revisiting the 1899 Hague Peace Conference. *Diplomacy & Statecraft*. 26(3), pp.405–423; and A. Higgins' chapter in this collection.
21 For more: R. Lesaffer. (2013). The Temple of Peace. The Hague Peace Conferences, Andrew Carnegie and the Building of the Peace Palace (1898–1913). *Preadviezen*.

Mededelingen van de Koninklijke Nederlandse Vereniging voor Internationaal Recht. 140, pp.1–38; J. Joor and H. Stuart. (2013). *The Building of Peace. A Hundred Years of Work on Peace Through Law. The Peace Palace 1913–2013.* The Hague: Eleven.

22 For more: Den Haag. Internationale Stad van Vrede en Recht. *Geschiedenis.* [online]. Available at: http://www.denhaagvrederecht.nl/vrede-en-recht/thema/geschiedenis.htm [Accessed August 2016]; P. van Krieken and D. McKay, eds. (2005). *The Hague. Legal Capital of the World.* The Hague: T.M.C. Asser Press; A. Eyffinger. (2003). *The Hague. International Centre of Justice and Peace.* The Hague: Jongbloed Law Booksellers.

23 The following are useful overview histories: A. Eyffinger. (1999). *The 1899 Hague Peace Conference. 'The Parliament of Man, the Federation of the World'.* The Hague: Kluwer Law International; A. Eyffinger. (2007). *The 1907 Hague Peace Conference. 'The Conscience of the Civilized World'.* The Hague: JudiCap; B. Tuchman. (1966). *The Proud Tower. A Portrait of the World Before War 1890–1914.* Toronto: Bantam, esp. pp.253–322; I. Clark. (2007). *International Legitimacy and World Society.* New York, Oxford: Oxford University Press, esp. pp.61–82; C. Davis. (1962). *The United States and the First Hague Peace Conference.* Ithaca: Cornell University Press; C. Davis. (1975). *The United States and the Second Hague Peace Conference. American Diplomacy and International Organization 1899–1914.* Durham: Duke University Press; J. Dülffer. (1980). *Regeln gegen Krieg? Die Haager Friedens-Konferenzen 1899 und 1907 in der internationalen Politik.* Berlin: Ulstein.

24 For examples: G. Brockington, ed., (2009). *Internationalism and the Arts in Britain and Europe at the Fin de Siècle.* Oxford: Peter Lang; M. Geyer and J. Paulmann, eds. (2001). *The Mechanics of Internationalism. Culture, Society and Politics from the 1840s to the First World War.* London: German Historical Institute; A. Higgins. (forthcoming). The idea of neutrality in British newspapers at the turn of the twentieth century, c. 1898–1902. *New Zealand Journal for Research on Europe.*

25 P. Krebs. (1999). *Gender, Race and the Writing of Empire. Public Discourse and the Boer War.* Cambridge: Cambridge University Press, esp. pp.80–81.

26 *Peace Crusade.* August 1899, n.p.

1 Justifying international action
International law, The Hague and diplomacy before 1914

William Mulligan

In late March 1909, the St Petersburg correspondent of *Le Journal des débats politiques et littéraires* lamented the Bosnian Crisis' international consequences:

> We have legality, the written law, the formal engagements of Austria (the treaty of Berlin), and the rights of peoples, of which one makes such a show today. But in reality, since the Bismarckian era, of which M. Aehrenthal [the Habsburg Foreign Minister] is the principal exponent, what is international law? It is nothing but a prejudice, which modern diplomats like to talk up. From the moment when a powerful country can annex a weaker country, it can do so by the law of the strongest. We are returning to the savage state, in diplomacy as well as politics. In the current generation, anything is permitted. That, it seems, is progress.[1]

The correspondent simultaneously lamented the passing of an era of international politics restrained by legal norms and implied that the right of the strong's triumph harked back to Bismarck's time. The emphasis on power and anarchy in European politics will hardly surprise historians, though the mournful plea to international law should give pause for thought.[2] These kinds of appeals were self-interested and even naïve, but their frequency demonstrated their significance. International law, in its manifold forms, legitimised political action and provided foundations for the European order. The Hague conferences reflected the importance attached to international law, yet they also challenged how political leaders and diplomats had understood the meaning, application and scope of international law.

Integrating late nineteenth- and early twentieth-century diplomats, politicians, journalists and others' sensitivities to international law requires scholars to reconsider assumptions about the workings of international politics before 1914. There is a sophisticated historiography that characterises the period as one of power politics. The wars of the mid-nineteenth century had consecrated the principles that 'might makes right' and that national interest should be unrestrained by wider moral or political considerations. Bismarck's successes in the 1860s owed as much to his grasp of these principles as to Prussian military power. After 1871, the militarisation of European politics continued. Although states shied away from territorial expansion on the continent, the search for security brought in its wake an arms race, shifting alliances, periodic diplomatic crises and imperial expansion. The underlying principles of international politics found expression in social Darwinist ideas and radical nationalist and militarist associations. In this reading, there is little scope for international law and the Hague conferences. At best they provided well-meaning but ill-conceived alternatives to power politics. At worst, they constitute an irrelevance when it comes to answering the big questions, such as why war broke out in 1914.

Yet the Hague conferences in particular, and international law more generally, were central features of international politics between 1871 and 1914. Integrating these into accounts of international politics can contribute to understanding how the great powers maintained a general peace, how assumptions underpinning peace frayed before 1914 and how different actors—diplomats, peace campaigners and lawyers, for example—sought to reconstitute international law as a basis for managing conflict. The Moroccan Crisis, the 1907 Hague conference, and the Bosnian Crisis offer opportunities to explore how these changes in the meaning of international law were worked out between 1905 and 1909.

Studying norms in international politics adds additional layers of complexity to interpretations based on military power, security and geopolitical interests. Before embarking on a discussion of international law as a norm, it is worth remembering that the treaties, conventions, customs and juridical opinion comprising international law were themselves products of power and interests. International law, as historians of empire remind us, reinforced racial hierarchies and excluded states from the international order.[3] Nor was international law a fully consistent body of knowledge. Certain clauses' meaning, the law's underlying principles and the silences in the law gave politicians scope to contest decisions, assert their interests and negotiate. Diplomats, soldiers and lawyers had different conceptions of the scope and application of international law. Even as international law was codified in the Hague conferences and institutionalised in the International Court of Arbitration, uncertainty about the meaning and application of international legal codes reigned.

Yet this uncertainty did not diminish international law's importance. As Isabel Hull argues, the leading powers during the First World War framed their conduct in terms of international law.[4] Its centrality in the war cultures after 1914 reflected deeper roots in European politics. Hull points out that international law is the product of both practice and opinion. Her observation also applies more generally to the establishment of norms in international politics. Repeated practice, in this case acting within bounds framed by legal precepts, creates expectations of future action. It also offers incentives for partners to reciprocate behaviour. The pay-off for restraint in the present is more stable international politics in the future. Opinion also offers a route to the establishment of a normative environment.

Despite the guarded and secretive cabinet diplomacy of the 'long' nineteenth century (1815–1914), diplomatic action—including alliance formation and decisions for war and peace—required justification before domestic and international audiences.[5] Understandings of international law became an important test for foreign policy's legitimacy. Before embarking on an action, decision-makers considered how to justify their policy. Justification was important not merely to gain legitimacy for that political action, but also as a means of signalling future behaviour. The legitimacy of any move was also contested in the press. Newspapers engaged with each other across national boundaries, while chancelleries in Europe were as interested in élite public opinion in other states as they were in public opinion in their own country. The importance attached to opinion and legitimacy reinforced the centrality of the normative environment in the conduct of international politics. Public scrutiny—of issues such as disarmament and the conduct of war—informed negotiations at The Hague, reflecting the requirement for public justification of foreign policy. On the other hand, the Hague conferences sought to codify international law to meet future contingencies in a broader way than many diplomats wished.

*

In the 1860s international lawyers formed associations and started journals. That they did so reflected confidence in the progressive unfolding of history, at least within the so-called 'civilised world'. The Franco-Prussian War undermined the optimism that characterised international lawyers in the 1860s, but by the mid-1870s they had recovered their poise. Between 1870 and 1872, the resolution of both the Anglo-American disputes following the Civil War (the *Alabama* crisis) and the crisis over the remilitarisation of Russian ports in the Black Sea raised international lawyers' hopes. The 1871 Treaty of London stipulated that states could not unilaterally revise international agreements, while the Geneva arbitration to settle the Anglo-American dispute was considered an important gain for the practice of international law. Lawyers held regular meetings and published in learned journals, and universities set up chairs in international law. Following the successful conclusion of the *Alabama* case, Gustave Moynier—a professor of international law at Geneva—suggested to Gustave Rolin-Jacquemyns—a lawyer from Ghent and a veteran of the 1860s associations—that a new institution be set up and devoted to propagating international law. At a September 1873 meeting in Ghent, the *Institut de droit international* was established. It provided a forum for members to develop international law in terms of the 'consciousness of the civilised world'.[6] Although Rolin-Jacquemyns expressed his frustration in the 1880s at the slow application of law to international politics, the Institute's opening marked a renewed confidence in the possibility of mitigating conflict through international law.

The relationship between the academic study of international law and its importance in diplomacy remained relatively distant. Lawyers were employed in chancelleries and embassies around Europe, but their role was to draft texts and to translate diplomatic language into legally binding documents. Unsurprisingly, the main preoccupation of diplomats was the practical application of international law. They received some legal education as part of their general training, but other disciplines were considered more important. The British Foreign Office favoured history or the classics as subjects to broaden the mind of the aspiring diplomat. Although not at the core of the diplomat's training, law was central to nineteenth-century European political culture. The dominant position of lawyers in the French Third Republic, the importance of reforms in civil law for the German *Bürgertum* and the sensitivities of British politicians and officials to the 'rights of free-born Englishmen' were some of the more notable examples of legal sensibilities.[7]

Of course, sensibilities about domestic legal cultures seeped into discussions of international politics even though issues such as the imposition of martial law in colonies were deemed strictly domestic affairs. Richard Haldane, the Lord Chancellor in Asquith's Liberal government, developed a theory of international relations that owed much to his understanding of how domestic society evolved from violent anarchy to the civilised rule of law. At a September 1913 meeting of the American Bar Association in Montreal, he argued that certain habits of thought and behaviour that facilitated cohesion had developed within societies.[8] Each societies' *Sitten* (customs) were enforced by moral and social, not legal, sanction. Indeed, *Sittlichkeit* was more often internalised into individuals' daily behaviour. Within domestic societies this was the product of long-term historical developments, which, Haldane argued, could be replicated in time within international politics. While arms races and 'perils of war' continued to disfigure international politics, Haldane claimed that the 'best people in the best nations' were increasingly judging international political behaviour according to principles rather than a particular national interest.

French ideas about *solidarisme* likewise transposed from the domestic to the international context, offered a different twist. Peter Jackson shows how *solidarisme* shaped the thinking of French internationalists, such as Léon Bourgeois. *Solidarisme* described the development of domestic social relations, in which individuals had debts and obligations to others in society. These were rendered into contracts by law, thereby ensuring social stability, whereas in Haldane's reading, custom could evolve and go beyond law. In international politics, Bourgeois perceived a similar dynamic. Individual states owed their existence to international society and therefore had both an interest and an obligation to uphold that society. In the case of juridical internationalism in France, there was an emphasis on the necessity of enforcing judicial decisions. As Jackson notes, this distinguished French from British and American conceptions of international law, which were more reticent about enforcement.[9]

Similar narratives can be found in unexpected quarters. Kurt Riezler, adviser to Chancellor Bethmann Hollweg, and best known for his elaboration of the 'risk policy', offered an account of state formation in *Grundzüge der Weltpolitik in der Gegenwart* (1913). As tribes developed into communities and then into nations, the legal order evolved and strengthened the state. The state first used force to impose laws but, as the legal order consolidated, force retreated into the background. Laws became a moral value or norm (*Sitte*), so that obedience was self-evident.[10] While Riezler viewed politics as a struggle for power, he also acknowledged the increasing 'cosmopolitanism' of international relations. Trade, cultural exchange and migration had fostered interdependency between nations and international law, which, according to Riezler, provided an important way of organising this cosmopolitan world. Law—expressed in speeches, customary practices and conventions—tamed power politics. 'There is no doubt', he explained:

> that this idealist atmosphere, even if it is only show and soap bubbles, is in itself a real power. ... [It] makes it difficult for most to breach these rules and practices with little cause, and it compels all to cover these breaches and to mitigate their form. In this way the struggle is refined and slowed down, and the predator is tamed.[11]

Riezler pointed to the limits of international law. Most laws and conventions were concerned with the conduct, not the prevention, of war. Arbitration only applied in limited circumstances. Yet arbitration offered a means to prevent 'unwanted wars', often started through isolated incidents. Moreover, the requirement that governments justify their action, Riezler argued, reduced the possible circumstances in which a war could be initiated.

Riezler's analysis reflected the increasing use of arbitration to settle international disputes. The 1899 Hague Convention provided for a permanent court of arbitration. Verena Steller notes that hardly any disputes were submitted for arbitration until 1904. Between 1904 and 1908, 60 cases were the subject of arbitration, with a further 50 cases in 1908 and 1909.[12] Arbitration was used in some sensitive cases before 1914, including one dispute over French authorities arresting three German citizens who had deserted from the French army in Casablanca in 1909, and one arising from Italian authorities' seizure of a French vessel in 1912. Vital national interests and questions of national honour were generally excluded from arbitration, but the latter had a particularly nebulous character. Premier Raymond Poincaré's reaction to Italy's seizure of the French vessel moved the issue into the realm of prestige politics before the process of arbitration provided a mechanism for limiting the dispute.[13]

The Hague conferences seemed to buttress the arguments of Haldane and others about the growing prominence of international law in European politics and the development of an international legal imaginary. Popular expectations about international law's potential to restrain violent conflict shaped the conferences' agenda. Although politicians believed that contentious issues, notably disarmament, could not be settled at the conference, they also considered that public discussion had its own value. 'It was true', Grey noted, 'that some of the subjects we prepared to discuss were not ripe for settlement, but they could only be ripened by being brought into the light'.[14] The suspicions of Wilhelm II and of the Austro-Hungarian Foreign Minister Alois von Aehrenthal that the disarmament agenda was designed to embarrass the two central European monarchies were revealing. Neither power could simply reject disarmament given the widespread public approval of initiatives for disarmament across Europe and indeed the wider world.[15]

The requirement that governments publicly justify major foreign policy initiatives was reflected in the debate about the form that declarations of war should take. It was agreed that declarations of war should either follow an ultimatum, setting out the reasons of the dispute, or should contain a statement of the causes of the war. The report to the Second Commission, dealing with this issue, concluded that:

> we are not to cherish the illusion that the real reasons for a war will always be given; but the difficulty of definitely stating reasons, and the necessity of advancing reasons not well-substantiated or out of proportion to the gravity of war itself, will naturally arrest the attention of neutral Powers and enlightened Public opinion.[16]

In this and others matters, The Hague established legal mechanisms and rules for applying shared norms.

Diplomats remained ambivalent about the possibility that conventions could secure peace, but their ambivalence revealed how international law could work as a restraint. Georg von Münster, the German ambassador to Paris, told Chancellor Bülow before the 1899 conference that 'I will not go into the conference with illusions, as honourable as it is'. Yet he also recognised that the great powers could not afford the collapse of the conference. Théophile Delcassé, the French Foreign Minister, worried that the conference would establish a tribunal which would function as a 'kind of moral constraint'. A great power that refused to submit to arbitration, Delcassé noted, would risk international approbation.[17] It was not so much the laws' specific content that mattered, but the risk of public censure if a state rejected arbitration. The court's establishment created expectations that it would be used and imposed limits on the conduct of power politics. It narrowed the scope for justifiable war.

Yet The Hague also represented a departure from diplomats' understandings of the application of international law. In this context, it is worth bearing in mind the distinction made by H.L.A. Hart between primary and secondary rules. Primary rules direct people to perform or refrain from certain actions; secondary rules enable people to specify how primary rules are established and enforced. By codifying international law and establishing permanent institutions, The Hague represented a step towards the creation of secondary rules in international relations.[18] Diplomats tended to consider international law not in terms of abstract principles and formal institutions, but in terms of specific agreements about discreet issues. These agreements were often territorially bounded—the Treaty of Berlin of 1878 and the Madrid Convention of 1880 were examples of how rights and norms assigned in one region did not have universal application. Solutions and justifications that worked well in one region, such as the principle of nationality, were not necessarily suited to other contexts. That treaties could not be unilaterally revised was a norm of international affairs, but the principles informing one treaty did not necessarily have wider application. The Hague conventions on the other hand created future-orientated mechanisms and general principles to be applied in as yet unforeseen circumstances. This represented a more abstract vision of the operation of international law. Diplomats fretted that specific foreign policy requirements would be subordinated to legal abstractions. Indeed, in creating secondary rules, the Hague conventions also diminished diplomats' power. At around the same time as diplomats, peace campaigners and international lawyers were renegotiating the meaning and scope of international law at the Hague conferences, the specific diplomatic norms concerning the application of treaties and conventions were fraying.

*

Despite the codification of the international law of war, the establishment of legal institutions to mediate and arbitrate disputes and the pressures from the public sphere to eliminate warfare at the two Hague conferences, the normative value of international law—particularly as understood by diplomats—suffered setbacks in the first decade of the twentieth century. Historians often view the Moroccan Crisis (1906) and the Bosnian Crisis (1908–1909) as key staging points on the path to war because they exacerbated Franco-German and Austro-Russian geopolitical rivalries. The crises fuelled national outrage, made the alliance system more rigid and stoked arms races. The costs of compromise in 1906 and 1909 reduced the scope for compromise in future crises. Historians pay less attention to the place of international law in these disputes.

Although these two events were classic great power confrontations, the norms governing the revision of treaties and conventions played a central role in all parties' strategies. These crises weakened international law's normative restraints for two reasons. First, international law was used—to adapt Steller's phrase—as an offensive diplomatic weapon.[19] It was not deployed to defend existing interests alone but, rather, it was used to frame a diplomatic crisis with a view to testing diplomatic alignments. This way of using international law stood in stark contrast to the mechanisms developed at the first Hague conference. Second, and more seriously, legal obligations were simply ignored. Statesmen, aware that they were breaking treaties, resorted to other justifications, drawing on the rhetorical tools and concepts, such as 'the civilising mission', available to them. As the Hague conference codified international law as a means of managing conflicts, some politicians reached for alternative principles to justify foreign policies.

*

By the turn of the twentieth century, Morocco was the last independent state in North Africa. In 1880, leading European powers (though not Russia), the United States and Morocco signed the Madrid Convention guaranteeing the Sultan's independence and regulating the legal status of foreigners and certain Moroccans who enjoyed the foreign powers' protection. During the two decades that followed, Moroccan independence came under intense pressure as France sought to extend its influence in the region. Domestic unrest and an increasing European economic presence offered imperialist powers opportunities in Morocco either to extend informal influence or to establish a protectorate. French governments concluded agreements with Italy, Spain and Britain recognising the primacy of French interests in Morocco and dividing North Africa into spheres.

These 'Ententes' were colonial bargains, but they had implications for the European balance of power. The exchange of notes between Italy and France loosened the attachment of Italy to its Triple Alliance partners—Austria-Hungary and Germany—while the *entente cordiale* moved Britain closer to the Dual Alliance of France and Russia. From Berlin's perspective, these developments, particularly the Anglo-French Entente, were a source of alarm. So, when Wilhelm II landed at Tangier on 31 March 1905 and declared his support for the Sultan's independence, he was not only protecting German interests in Morocco but also testing the Anglo-French Entente. Specifically, German diplomats targeted the Entente's architect: Delcassé.

Friedrich von Holstein, the leading exponent in the German Foreign Office of challenging the Entente, chose the grounds of the dispute with France carefully. He framed the question in terms of international law with several purposes in mind. It placed Delcassé in a difficult position, forcing him to explain why France no longer observed the 1880 Madrid Convention. Holstein also hoped to drive a wedge between France and its partners, who had no immediate interest in Morocco but at the very least had to pay lip-service to international law. Finally, international law offered a means to cultivate support domestically, linking German honour and prestige with broader principles in European politics. But Holstein was largely uninterested in defending broad principles of international law, particularly the inviolability of agreements. Holstein saw the crisis as a trial of strength between Germany and France. As Holstein wrote, 'to pull back, after one had taken a position, would have the same consequences as ducking out of a duel, that means one would face further, greater demands'.[20] He instrumentalised law, rather than seeing it as an end in itself.

Holstein set out his thinking in a number of letters in April 1905. 'The contracting collective of power [the signatories to the Madrid convention]' he told Bülow, 'is the principle on which we can stand fast, without arousing the appearance of aggressive intentions'. If the French government rejected German claims, it would 'put itself in the wrong, ... [and show] a bad conscience and sinister intentions'. Holstein also sought to frame the arguments in the press in terms of international law with a view to providing Delcassé's French critics with ammunition to attack him in the Chamber of Deputies.[21] Holstein was furious that the *Norddeutsche Allgemeine Zeitung* had not published his piece on international law on 1 April. Writing to Josef Neven-Dumont, the publisher of the *Kölnische Zeitung* and the *Straßburger Post*, Holstein explained that his purpose was to place France in the wrong. His understanding of international law was bound up with his understanding of the conduct of power politics. 'And in international relations', he continued, 'as you will have read recently, right and wrong is only without meaning if the miscreant is strong enough to defy all others'.[22] According to Holstein, France (the wrongdoer in this instance) was not strong enough to defy Germany and could not rely on British support. Because Germany had international law *and* power on its side, it could push France to back down and devalue the Entente.

German politicians and diplomats repeated the mantra of international law in private conversations and public speeches until the conference convened in Algeciras in 1906. Paul von Schwabach, an influential banker with links to the German political élite, told Alfred von Rothschild, a member of the London branch of the family, that Germany had the 'right' to protect its interest and acted as a 'contracting power' against France's pretentions to be the 'European mandatory'.[23] Theodor Schiemann, a journalist close to the Foreign Office, echoed some of Holstein's language about the duel:

> It is clear that Germany cannot retreat. It is defending its good right, which France thought it could set aside through a brutal fait accompli; but no state, committed to keeping its shield pure, can tolerate this.[24]

Outlining German policy to the Reichstag in December 1905, Bülow rejected claims that German leaders were looking for an excuse to attack France over a trivial interest: 'In any case the principle "minima non curat praetor" does not apply to affairs, in which the treaty rights and the prestige of a country are in question'. Germany, he suggested, was devoted to peace, but ready to protect its interest, and simply wanted France to return from the terrain of power politics to that of international law.[25]

Most French politicians and the French press rejected these arguments and framed their case in different terms. A week after Wilhelm II's speech in Tangiers, Delcassé told the Chamber of Deputies that France sought to establish order in Morocco—for the benefit of all powers—on the basis of its recent agreements. 'In negotiating in the name of France with the Moroccan government, we are only invoking', he argued

> today as yesterday, the claims which a long common frontier confers upon us, the damages, the sacrifices of all kinds which result from the

constant trouble of the neighbouring Moroccan region, the obvious powerlessness of Maghzen to put an end to it, the necessity recognised by him for our help, his appeal to our propositions and advice.[26]

Initially, the French press and politicians dismissed references to the 1880 Madrid Convention. An editorial in *Le Temps* noted that no other signatory had protested against French policy. Instead, they emphasised the agreements with Britain, Italy and Spain.[27] Two days after Delcassé's speech, *Le Temps* explained in an approving editorial that the 'particular rights' arose from 50 years of sacrifice and a common border. France would act in the interests of all to restore order.[28] The French claims were rooted in broader European notions of 'the civilising mission', not in treaties or conventions, or, for that matter, in international law.

By early June, Delcassé was isolated and resigned. The collapse of Russian power in the Russo-Japanese War was the principal reason for his weak position. However, Holstein's framing strategy had also weakened British backing for the French Foreign Minister. The French press criticised Delcassé on various grounds—his failure to ease German anxieties before embarking on his Moroccan policy and the hesitant character of *pénétration pacifique*—but, in general, journalists continued to dispute the 1880 convention's importance. Its specific terms, governing the rights of protected individuals in Morocco, had little to do with the issues at stake in the 1905 Moroccan Crisis. Referring to more recent agreements, *Le Temps* declared that it was not 'appropriate to subject these to some form of revision'.[29]

In turning down the opportunity to negotiate a bilateral agreement with France and instead pushing for a conference, German leaders miscalculated. The conference's outcome represented a diplomatic defeat for Germany. Concerns about international law retreated into the background. The conference became a trial of strength between Germany and France, backed by Britain. Conferences had traditionally served the purposes of multilateral diplomatic negotiations, which produced international treaty law. On this occasion, the form could hardly disguise the practice of power politics. A few leaders admitted German claims about international law in principle but expressed scepticism about the real importance of German interests in Morocco.[30] Schiemann tried to argue that German negotiators had successfully defended important international legal principles, but the conference's outcome was more often framed in terms of 'prestige', 'honour' and 'dignity'.[31]

The Moroccan Crisis contributed to the erosion of the normative value of international law in two ways. First, Holstein instrumentalised the Madrid Convention and the more general principle of international agreements' inviolability to serve the purposes of power politics by testing the Entente. Initially his strategy worked, but, in stretching the arguments and pushing demands after Delcassé's resignation, German leaders exposed what many suspected: that in this instance the German government were subordinating the principles of international law to suit German interests. Delcassé's response to the German challenge also diminished international law's importance. He ignored the Madrid Convention, and based French claims on the conventional justifications of imperial politics: deals between imperial powers and 'the civilising mission'. The Moroccan Crisis was both a European and an imperial question. The logic of European power politics and the legitimising claims of imperial expansion squeezed the space for applying international law. This pattern was repeated during the Bosnian Crisis.

*

After the Russian victory over Ottoman forces in 1878, the European powers met in Berlin. The resulting Treaty of Berlin produced a legal framework for managing the Eastern Question. Commissions met, diplomats negotiated and reforms were promised, although delivery was often painfully slow. The treaty allowed for the Austro-Hungarian occupation of two Ottoman provinces, Bosnia and Herzegovina. It also set the conditions for Bulgarian statehood. The King remained a tributary of the Sultan, and Eastern Rumelia remained under Ottoman control, but its governor was Christian. The Treaty of Berlin served as the foundational text for the Eastern Question for three decades, until 1908. In that year, the Young Turks' revolt brought the Committee of Unity and Progress (CUP) to power in Constantinople. One of the central ambitions of the CUP leaders was to strengthen the Ottoman Empire against the predatory ambitions of the great powers. This process required internal reform, including elections to a National Assembly on the basis of male suffrage. Austro-Hungarian leaders had long harboured ambitions of integrating Bosnia and Herzegovina more fully into the Habsburg Empire. The prospect of men in these two provinces electing representatives to a parliament in Constantinople threw the Habsburg occupation's problematic character into stark relief. With representatives in Constantinople, the population in Bosnia and Herzegovina—already suspect in Habsburg officials' eyes—could plausibly demand an end to occupation, given that the original justification for the occupation was the despotic nature of Ottoman rule. The Bulgarian king, Ferdinand, also faced the prospect that the ethnic Bulgarian population in Eastern Rumelia would be forever integrated into the Ottoman Empire through the mechanisms of representative politics. Faced with these prospects, Bulgaria and Austria-Hungary acted. On 5 October 1908 Ferdinand declared Bulgarian independence, including Eastern Rumelia. The following day, Austria-Hungary annexed Bosnia and Herzegovina.

The Habsburg Foreign Minister, Alois von Aehrenthal, prepared the ground for the annexation in meetings with the Italian Foreign Minister, Tittoni, and his Russian counterpart, Izvolski. As it transpired, the deals cut at these meetings failed to legitimise the annexation. Not only did Aehrenthal seek diplomatic cover, but he and his colleagues also developed justifications for the annexation throughout the summer of 1908. In 1907, Aehrenthal had argued that Habsburg policy 'rests on the basis of international law, namely the Berlin agreement, and the maintenance of Turkish possessions, as long as this is possible'.³² The following year, Habsburg leaders were clearly aware that the annexation constituted a violation of the Treaty of Berlin. Even if this did not stop the move, it did give them pause for thought. At a meeting of the Common Council of Ministers on 19 August 1908, Aehrenthal told the assembled ministers that 'the Berlin treaty would be torn up by the annexation'. Beck, the Austrian Minister-President, pointed out that although the treaty had many holes, it remained in existence. Annexation meant the 'complete shredding' of the treaty. It was also clearly conceived as an act of power politics. Beck argued that as such, it required no legal justification. 'If one took the step of annexation under the pressure of circumstances (*Zwangslage*)', Beck told his colleagues, 'one would not need a legal title (*Rechtstitel*), as such a situation would have its own inherent justification, and one could appeal to this not only abroad but also in front of one's own legislatures'.³³

Yet, despite this clear understanding of the meaning of the annexation, Habsburg ministers struggled to come up with a different justification that could meet the demands of international legitimacy. On 17 August, two days before the Council of Ministers' meeting, Wekerle (the Hungarian Prime Minister) responded to Aehrenthal's request for his views on the planned annexation. Much of Wekerle's memorandum was devoted to justifying the move. 'Although the annexation is an act of power', he argued:

> it cannot lack legal basis. This is not only to do with the international legal perspective, but would also be contrary to our interests, because it would create a precedent, which could be easily used against us in the formation of states in the Balkans – nor would it be in accordance with hour past or with our conduct up to now.³⁴

He recognised that the Treaty of Berlin provided no legal justification. His solution, based on an argument about Hungarian historical rights in the provinces, was self-serving and tortuous.³⁵ Wekerle's memorandum was testimony to wider discussions amongst the Austro-Hungarian élite about their policy's presentation. In his correspondence, Aehrenthal hinted at two lines of argument that later became central to the public presentation of policy. First, the right to annexation was implicit in the Treaty of Berlin and amounted to only a minor change. The treaty's purpose was to secure stability in the Balkans; if these two provinces slipped from Austro-Hungarian control, the consequences would be destabilising. Second, the Austro-Hungarian mandate in 1878 had rested on its 'civilising mission'. Only by annexing the provinces would the monarchy be in a position to fulfil its duties to the population and complete its work.³⁶

In the days before the annexation, diplomats at the Ballhausplatz prepared notes for the Ottoman Empire and the great powers. They opened with the evacuation of the Habsburg garrison from the Sandjak region in the Ottoman Empire, which was presented as a form of compensation to

Constantinople. The notes claimed that the annexation was designed to fulfil the Treaty of Berlin's general purpose: stability in the region. The spirit (not the letter) of the law was what mattered, according to Vienna. In addition, Austria-Hungary had to complete its 'cultural work' in the region. The provinces had already improved their 'cultural' and 'intellectual level' under Habsburg occupation. These achievements could only be safeguarded by fully integrating the provinces into the Habsburg monarchy.[37]

These justifications fell on deaf ears. In part, the Bulgarian declaration of independence on 5 October—the day before the Austro-Hungarian annexation—compounded the difficulties of justifying the move. The Grand Vizir—the leading Ottoman minister—told Pallavacini that, while the annexation was not of major significance, the Bulgarian move had clearly enjoyed Austro-Hungarian support. Moreover, the Vizir, referring to the Treaty of Berlin, was not prepared to accept a change in the status of the two provinces without prior negotiations.[38] Leading British and French politicians, as well as the unfortunate and duped Izvolski, criticised Austria-Hungary's move. 'The arbitrary tearing up of the Berlin treaty is unacceptable', Metternich (the ambassador to London) summed up.[39] Clemenceau was reluctant to take any military measures, but thought the Triple Entente 'should be very stiff in their language regarding the breach of treaty engagement and the offence to public morality committed by Austria'. Describing the annexation as a 'bombshell', Charles Hardinge (the Permanent Secretary in the British Foreign Office) argued:

> our line of action will be to quote the Protocol of the Treaty of 1871 to which Austria was a party, in which it is stated that no Treaty can be modified without the consent of those who are party to it, except by friendly agreement.[40]

Given that Izvolski had been party with Aehrenthal to a proposal to tear up the Treaty of Berlin, and that the Entente powers signalled from the outset that their response would be limited to verbal protests, why did they make such an issue of the unilateral breach of the treaty? As Paul Schroeder has pointed out, the annexation made little difference in terms of the overall distribution of power in Europe. Habsburg forces had already occupied and administered the region for three decades. The Entente powers wanted a conference to ratify the changes. A conference would have provided Izvolski with a golden bridge to cover his retreat and the possibility of guarantees about future revisions to the regulations governing naval ships' access through the Straits. The revision in international law was linked to form, which in turn had repercussions for domestic politics in various states. 'On the one hand', as Jules Cambon, the French ambassador to Berlin, put it:

> the Ottoman government cannot put itself before the forthcoming assembly, with a treaty sanctioning the diminution of the empire,

without being covered by Europe. On the other hand, the Emperor of Austria can expand his possessions in fact; but Russia will never recognition this expansion in law, if Europe has not consented to it at least in form.[41]

The annexation was a blow to states' domestic and international prestige because it represented a unilateral revision of a treaty.

The press in the Entente states concentrated their condemnations of Aehrenthal's policy on the violation of the Treaty of Berlin. An editorial in the *Journal des débats politiques et littéraires*, referring to the Bulgarian as well as Austro-Hungarian action, warned that in the aftermath of the ripping up of the treaty it was impossible to predict future courses of action.[42] The following day, its editorial demanded a conference, referring to the precedent of 1871:

> When Russia, in 1871, declared its intention to no longer conform to the clauses of the treaty of Paris regarding the Black Sea, a conference was held. Then Austria was the most ardent in demanding the intervention of Europe. It cannot oppose this in the current case. In any case nobody will try to take away the two occupied provinces. Only the official possession must be approved beforehand, subject to further modifications, to the satisfaction of other interests. If a new condition of Balkan affairs is to be established, it is necessary that it conforms to justice, to the law of Turkey, to the legitimate interests of all the states of the peninsula.[43]

The conference represented a cure for various ills: injured pride, the unfulfilled interests of other states and the preservation of the form of international law.

Some of the German press also expressed concerns about Aehrenthal's disregard for treaty rights. The unilateral act represented a further step towards the arbitrary use of force without restraints. Upsetting long-standing norms posed a risk to peace, by making international politics less predictable. The failure to take into account wider European interests and the likelihood that smaller Balkan states would make claims, possibly leading to the Ottoman Empire's dismemberment, alarmed German observers. By tearing up the Treaty of Berlin, Austria-Hungary had opened up the Eastern Question and thrown away the foundational text. Nobody doubted that the German government would support its Austro-Hungarian ally's claims, but criticism of Aehrenthal was thinly veiled. 'The worst result of this week, so full of bad events,' argued Paul Michaelis in the *Berliner Tageblatt*:

> lies in the circumstances that trust in international agreements has suffered a mortal blow. What is the use if agreements about all kinds of details are solemnly written down and sealed, only that they are broken

when one party wishes? One need not fully give up the hope that this time a war of all against all can be averted. But the damage, which will not be repaired, lies in the erosion of mutual trust, which will lead to a latent danger of war and an increased readiness for war. Europe will long suffer from the fatal consequences of this most calamitous week.[44]

Yet the bulk of the press in the Habsburg and German Empires backed the annexation. They rejected calls for a conference. Partly mindful of the experience of 1906, many observers saw a conference as a form of trial, with Austria-Hungary cast as the miscreant facing the judgement of Europe.[45] The striking similarity with the arguments of French politicians and press in 1905 was only enhanced by the 'civilising mission' being adopted as a central justification for annexation. *Die Post* distinguished between King Ferdinand's 'unscrupulous' policy, which disregarded others' rights, and the Austro-Hungarian annexation, which marked the culmination of 30 years' work in Bosnia and Herzegovina.[46] Rights to annexation derived from the claims of the 'civilising mission' rather than from inconvenient treaties. Austro-Hungarian politicians claimed that the population in the two provinces had benefitted and would continue to do so from the education, transport and political reforms introduced under Habsburg rule.

Throughout the autumn of 1908, Aehrenthal refused to countenance a conference. By the spring of 1909 the crisis had escalated. Habsburg forces had mobilised, while opinion in Serbia ran high. Russia supported Serbian claims, but had no means to exert any military pressure on Austria-Hungary or its German ally. In late March, Bülow issued an ultimatum compelling Russia and Serbia to recognise the annexation's legality. The German press denied that Russia had caved in to an ultimatum in an unsuccessful attempt to spare Izvolski's blushes.[47] The French press saw the crisis' outcome as further confirmation of the degrading of international law. 'The law of nations (*droit des gens*) has lost. A sinister precedent has been established', argued the editorial in the *Journal des débats politiques et littéraires*.[48] In 1915 Robert Seton-Watson, the leading British commentator on Balkan affairs, commented on the repercussions of the annexation. Aehrenthal, he wrote:

> felt himself to be merely setting the seal to a document which had been signed a generation earlier. He had failed to reckon with the outcry which this technical breach of international evoked: like Bethmann-Hollweg he had no blind faith in 'scraps of paper', and had no scruple in tearing up the treaty of Berlin on which the whole Balkan settlement had rested.[49]

*

Between the Moroccan and Bosnian crises, the second Hague conference took place. This sequence highlights various threads in the shifting understandings of international law before 1914. First, the 1907 Hague Peace Conference was testimony to international law's growing purchase on the public imagination throughout many parts of the world. The popular support for the Hague conferences was based on the same structures in the public sphere which compelled governments to justify their foreign policy moves in Morocco and Bosnia in terms that went beyond narrow conceptions of national interest. Governments had to forge foreign policy within parameters set by a transnational public sphere. Second, the understandings of international law in the Hague conferences on the one hand, and in the Moroccan and Bosnian crises on the other hand, differed. In part this reflected diplomats' and international lawyers' different approaches to law. The latter had a more rigid conception, whereas the former understood international law primarily as the codification of treaty agreements of relations between states. In the years before the First World War, the assumptions underpinning the functioning of international law shifted towards a more prescriptive understanding. At the same time, diplomats began to both undermine and lose faith in their own particular understanding of international law. This did not mean that war was inevitable, but rather that one of the resources—shared diplomatic understandings of international law—which had restrained power politics was now fracturing. The Hague system represented an attempt to construct a new basis for applying international law.

The *Journal des débats politiques et littéraires* warned that Austria-Hungary would learn the price of its 'miserable success' as future generations of vengeful Serbs grew to maturity.[50] The price the Austro-Hungarians paid in 1908 and 1909 ultimately proved to be a heavy one, and not merely because of the legacies of the Bosnian Crisis in Pan-Slavic circles in Russia and radical nationalist politics in Serbia. Aehrenthal had undermined one of the normative pillars—international law—upon which the Dual Monarchy depended. Facing the challenge of nationalist politics domestically, the irredentist claims of Balkan states and Italy, and Russia's growing power, Austria-Hungary had few tools to manage the inevitable domestic and international conflicts to which it was exposed. After 1908, Habsburg leaders could no longer appeal to international law. During the Balkan Wars in 1912 and 1913, the Treaty of Berlin was barely mentioned. Nationality was the legitimising principle of the tentative settlements following the Balkan Wars. This principle was converted into international legal texts, most notably the 1913 Treaty of London and Treaty of Bucharest. The nationality principle differed wholly from the questions of the balance of great power interests that informed the Treaty of Berlin. As Christopher Clark points out, during the July crisis Austro-Hungarian leaders had few ideological resources to defend their interests. In part, they only had themselves to blame.[51]

The fraying of international law as a means of managing power politics in the early twentieth century did not mean war was inevitable; rather, it deprived diplomats of a useful tool for legitimising foreign policy action and restraining power politics. Granted, in the last resort, international law could never stop a state bent on aggressive war. Yet, for over four decades it contributed to tempering military ambition. The requirement to justify war made it more difficult to initiate conflict without good cause. As German leaders found to their cost during the First World War, there were political penalties to violating treaties. Despite being prostituted to power politics and cast aside as an inconvenience before 1914, the purpose of international law remained clear to political leaders and others after the outbreak of hostilities. International law could only gain traction during the war because it had been an important way of thinking about international politics before the war. The Hague became the touchstone of wartime debates, a set of texts agreed before the war but whose content and meaning was contested during the war. The wartime debates about The Hague completed a transition from one form of understanding of international law to another, a process begun in the early twentieth century.

Notes

1 *Journal des débats politiques et littéraires*, 3 April 1909, p.1.
2 M. Koskenniemi. (2001). *The Gentle Civilizer of Nations. The Rise and Fall of International Law, 1870–1960*. Cambridge: Cambridge University Press.
3 L. Benton. (2010). *A Search for Sovereignty. Law and Geography in European Empires, 1400–1900*. Cambridge: Cambridge University Press.
4 I. Hull. (2014). *A Scrap of Paper. Breaking and Making International Law during the Great War*. Ithaca: Cornell University Press; this was also an important theme in the three-volume J. Winter, ed. (2014). *Cambridge History of the First World War*. Cambridge: Cambridge University Press. See the contributions by J. Horne (chapter 21) and A. Duperchin (chapter 23) in the first volume, and G. Henri-Soutou (chapter 19) in the second volume.
5 W. Mulligan. (2014). The Restraints on Preventive War Before 1914. In: J. Levy and J. Vasquez, eds, *The Outbreak of the First World War. Structure, Politics, and Decision-Making*. Cambridge: Cambridge University Press, pp.115–138.
6 M. Koskenniemi. (2002). *The Gentle Civilizer of Nations. The Rise and Fall of International Law, 1870–1960*. 2nd ed. Cambridge: Cambridge University Press, p.47.
7 M. Johns. (1989). *Politics and the Law in Nineteenth Century Germany. The Origins of the Civil Code*. Oxford: Oxford University Press; R. Kostal. (2008). *A Jurisprudence of Power. Victorian Empire and the Rule of Law*. Oxford: Oxford University Press.
8 Grey to Haldane, 14 September 1913, MS 5910, fo. 104, Haldane Papers, NLS [National Library of Scotland]; R. B. Haldane. (1914). *Higher Nationality. A Study in Law and Ethics*. Washington DC: Government Print Office.
9 P. Jackson. (2013). *Beyond the Balance of Power. France and the Politics of National Security in the Era of the First World War*. Cambridge: Cambridge University Press, pp.65–73.
10 J. Ruedorffer. (1916). *Grundzüge der Weltpolitik in der Gegenwart*. Stuttgart: Deutsche Verlags-Anstalt, pp.12–14.
11 Ruedorffer, pp.164–166.
12 V. Steller. (2011). *Diplomatie von Angesicht zu Angesicht. Diplomatische Handlungsformen in den deutsch-französischen Beziehungen 1870–1919*. Paderborn: Ferdinand Schöningh, pp.319–320.

13 J. Keiger. (1983). *France and the Origins of the First World War*. London: Macmillan, pp.59–61.
14 Grey to Durand, 6 November 1906. In: G. Gooch and H. Temperley, eds. (1932). *British Documents on the Origins of the War, 1898–1914*. Vol. 8. London: H.M. Stationery Office, p.197.
15 Szögyény to Aehrenthal, 23 March 1907. In Wank, ed. (1994). *Aus dem Nachlass Aehrenthal. Briefe und Dokumente zur österreichisch-ungarischen Innen- und Außenpolitik 1885–1912*. Vol. 2. Graz: Neugebauer, p.487.
16 J. B. Scott, ed. (1921). *The Proceedings of the Hague Peace Conferences. The Conference of 1907*. Vol. 3. New York: Oxford University Press, p.44.
17 Steller, *Angesicht*, pp.247, 259.
18 H. Hart. (1961). *The Concept of Law*. Oxford: Clarendon Press; G. Brennan, L. Eriksson, R. Goodin and N. Southwood. (2013). *Explaining Norms*. Oxford: Oxford University Press, pp.41–43.
19 Steller, *Angesicht*, p.336.
20 Holstein to Radolin, 11 April 1905. In: N. Rich and M. Fisher, eds. (1963). *Die Geheimen Papiere Friedrich von Holsteins*. Vol. 4. Göttingen: Musterschmidt Verlag, p.298.
21 Holstein to Bülow, 5 April 1905. In: Rich and Fisher, p.297.
22 Holstein to Neven-Dumont, 20 April 1905. In: Rich and Fisher, p.301.
23 Schwabach to Rothschild, 21 June 1905. In: P. Schwabach, ed. (1927). *Aus meinen Akten*, Berlin: Flemming, pp.73–74.
24 T. Schiemann. (1906). *Deutschland und die Grosse Politik, anno 1905*. Berlin: Georg Reimer, pp.164–165.
25 Die Internationale Lage, 6 December 1905. In: Wilhelm von Mossow, ed. (1914). *Fürst Bülows Reden*. Vol. 4. Leipzig: Philipp Reclam, pp.34–42.
26 *Le Figaro*, 8 April 1905, p.3.
27 *Le Temps*, 7 April 1905, p.1.
28 *Le Temps*, 9 April 1905, p.1.
29 *Le Temps*, 10 June 1905, p.1; C. Andrew. (1968). *Théophile Delcassé and the Making of the Entente Cordiale. A reappraisal of French Foreign Policy, 1898–1905*. London: Macmillan, pp.281–295.
30 Schoen to Auswärtiges Amt, 24 February 1906, R10288, PA-AA.
31 T. Schiemann. (1907). *Deutschland und die große Politik, anno 1906*. Berlin: Georg Reimer Verlag, pp.119–122; Holstein to Pascal David, 13 May 1906. In: Rich and Fisher, p.383.
32 Konzept einer Weisung an Pallavicini, 6 March 1907. In: Wank, pp.470–472.
33 Minutes, 19 August 1908. In Anatol Schmied-Kowarzik, ed. (2011). *Die Protokolle des Gemeinsamen Ministerrates der Österreichisch-Ungarischen Monarchie 1908–1914*. Budapest: Akadémiai Kiadó, pp.185–188.
34 Wekerle to Aehrenthal, 17 August 1908. In: Wank, pp.610–613.
35 Wekerle to Aehrenthal, 17 August 1908. In: Wank, pp.610–613.
36 Aehrenthal to Beck, 7 August 1908; Aehrenthal to Pallavicini, 18 September 1908; Aehrenthal to Tittoni, 25 September 1908. In: L. Bittner and H. Uebersberger, eds. (1930). *Österreich-Ungarns Aussenpolitik von der Bosnischen Krise bis zum Kriegsausbruch 1914* (hereafter ÖUA). Vienna: Oesterreichischer Bundesverlag, pp.23–25, 92–93, 98.
37 Erlaß, 3 October 1908, in ÖUA, pp.123–124.
38 Telegramme from Constantinople, 6 October 1908, in ÖUA, pp.138–139.
39 Metternich to the Foreign Office, 10 October 1908, R1993, fo. 17, PA-AA.
40 Bertie to Hardinge, 4 October 1908; Hardinge to Bertie, 5 October 1908, Bertie Papers, MS 63022, fos. 77–84. British Library.

41 J. Cambon to Pichon, 26 October 1908, doc. 507. In: Alfred Costes, ed. (1950). *Documents diplomatiques francaises, 1871–1914*. 2nd Series, Vol. 11. Paris: Imprimerie Nationale, pp.858–859.
42 *Journal des débats politiques et littéraires*, 6 October 1908, p.1.
43 *Journal des débats politiques et littéraires*, 7 October 1908, p.1.
44 *Berliner Tageblatt*, 11 October 1908, p.1.
45 Holstein to Bülow, 8 October 1908, doc. 1138, pp.518–519; *Die Post*, 21 October 1908, p.2.
46 *Die Vossische Zeitung*, 9 October 1908, p.1; *Die Post*, 5 October 1908, p.1.
47 *Die Vossische Zeitung*, 2 April 1909, p.1.
48 *Journal des débats politiques et littéraires*, 5 April 1909, p.1.
49 R. Seton-Watson. (1915). *The War and Democracy*. London: Macmillan, p.146.
50 *Journal des débats politiques et littéraires*, 23 March 1909, p.1.
51 C. Clark. (2012). *The Sleepwalkers*. London: Penguin, pp.405–412.

2 Peace through law
The Hague Peace Conferences and the rise of the *ius contra bellum*

Randall Lesaffer

In his 29 July 1899 closing address to the first Hague Peace Conference, the Russian diplomat and conference president, Baron Egor de Staal (1822–1907), evaluated the work done at The Hague. According to him the conference's significance did not lie with the First Commission, which had dealt with disarmament and failed, nor with the Second Commission, which had reached agreement over the codification of the laws and customs of war on land, but with the Third Commission, which had produced the Convention for the Pacific Settlement of Disputes. This convention, which Staal said should be labelled 'The First International Code of Peace' inaugurated 'a new era ... in the domain of the law of nations'.[1] Few attendees disagreed with Staal. The ambitions many had cherished for the conference with relation to the pacific settlement of disputes struck at the heart of the fabric of international law because they pertained to one of a state's key sovereign rights: recourse to force or war. They also formed the core of the reformist, moderate side of the international peace movement's 'peace through law' programme.[2]

While Staal did not mince his words in hailing The Hague's work as the beginning of a new era in the law of nations, the rest of his speech betrayed less self-gratification and more realism. Staal reiterated that the conference had not delivered all that some participants and many observers had hoped. He underscored that the conference attained what was possible by steering a middle course between the dictates of existing international law, governmental concerns and the ideals for change. He expressed this opinion with a phrase that has lost little of its currency today: the conference had to conciliate 'the principle of sovereignty of states and the principle of just international solidarity'. He put a twist on the ambivalent feelings of achievement and disappointment when he called the conference a 'first step' and ended with the words: 'The good seed is sown. Let the harvest come'.[3]

Many contemporaries shared Staal's assessment of the conference as a meagre beginning but a beginning nonetheless. Similar ideas accompanied the second Hague Peace Conference of 1907. Few expressed them as well as Elihu Root (1845–1937), the New York lawyer and US Secretary of

State, who years later, when reflecting upon the progress made on the 'peace through law' agenda, stated:

> Not only the conventions signed and ratified, but the steps taken towards conclusions which may not reach practical and effective form for many years to come, are of value. Some of the resolutions ... do not seem to amount to very much by themselves, but each one marks on some line of progress the farthest point to which the world is yet willing to go. They are like cable ends buoyed in mid-ocean, to be picked up hereafter by some other steamer, spliced, and continued to shore ... Each necessary step in the process is as useful as the final act which crowns the work and is received with public celebration.[4]

The ambivalence seen in assessments of The Hague's work persists in the historiography of international law, in general, and of use of force law in particular.[5] International lawyers and international legal historians consider the Hague conferences the two first, modest steps in the incremental process leading to the prohibition of the use of force between states through the Covenant of the League of Nations (1919), the Pact of Paris (1928) and the Charter of the United Nations (1945).[6] In this grand narrative, the smallness of The Hague's contribution to the process is indicated by the argument that after the First World War, The Hague's work, with its focus on arbitration and adjudication, was side-lined in favour of collective security. Although the Covenant of the League established a permanent international court—fulfilling one of the 'peace through law' movement's major aspirations—it was superseded by the principle of collective security.[7]

The traditional historiography of international law posits a stark contradiction between the almost complete lawlessness in relation to a state's right to resort to force and war before 1899 and the gradual restriction and almost complete revocation of this right between 1899 and 1945. Even today, many international lawyers hold that late nineteenth-century use of force law was a veritable *ius ad bellum* in the literal sense of the phrase: it did little but acknowledge a state's right to resort to force and war. This opposition, while highlighting the revolutionary impact of the changes wrought in the first half of the twentieth century, has also led students of the subject to consider the rise of the *ius contra bellum* to have taken place within a virtual juridical vacuum. In consequence, they acknowledge the achievements of The Hague, the Covenant, the Pact of Paris and the United Nations Charter on their own merits, or in relation to each other, but rarely in relation to the use of force law existent before 1900.

From the 1950s on, more careful students came to the uneasy conclusion that the doctrines and practices of the nineteenth century were more sophisticated.[8] Recently, a few scholars have struck out at the view that nineteenth-century *ius ad bellum* was an empty box. In his seminal legal history of warfare, Stephen Neff argued for the thickness of nineteenth-century doctrines of 'measures short of war' and for the resilience of traditional 'just war' doctrine therein.[9] In a 2014 article, Agatha Verdebout claimed that the view that international law did not impose any restrictions on recourse to war was not mainstream opinion in 1900 and that it was shared by only a few international legal scholars including Dionisio Anzilotti, Thomas J. Lawrence, Lassa Oppenheim and John Westlake. She further held that it was not reflected in state practice.[10]

This chapter argues that international law at the turn of the nineteenth century encompassed quite sophisticated rules concerning the use of force. These rules were deeply imbedded in a long tradition of thought and practice of *ius ad bellum* with roots in the Late Middle Ages' theological, canonistic and civilian literature. The rules were further developed during the early modern age (1500–1800). Although the nineteenth century wrought important changes to the *ius ad bellum*, a true understanding of use of force law is not possible without some insight into its historical tradition. This chapter contends that international law at the turn of the twentieth century acknowledged that states had a right to resort to force or war, but that this right was conditional and restricted. Taking this as its point of departure, the chapter offers an analysis of The Hague's work in relation to the pacific settlement of disputes. The major thrust of the proponents of pacific settlement at The Hague was to promote arbitration as a means to dent a state's right to resort to force and war and thus take a step towards moving from an *ius ad bellum* to an *ius contra bellum*. This chapter addresses the question of how this concept of international law related to and impacted on existing use of force law.

The 'peace through law' movement, arbitration and the *ius ad bellum* tradition

The wars of the 1860s and early 1870s threw the international peace movement into crisis. The 1870s and 1880s saw its reconstitution and revival. This time, the debate which had plagued the movement during the first half of the nineteenth century—between radical utopians who rejected war under all circumstances and moderate reformers who proposed a step-by-step limitation of war and warfare—was largely resolved to the advantage of the latter.[11] Their work and ideas were abetted by international lawyers' growing contribution.[12] By the 1890s, the international peace movement embraced a programme that put its trust in international law to limit both the chances of war as well as the devastation they wrought. The 'peace through law' programme was the loose amalgam of five major ideas: arms limitation and disarmament through binding treaties, codifying international law, humanising warfare through codifying the laws and customs of war, collective security and settling disputes through arbitration and other pacific means.[13] The last two points, while not mutually exclusive, represented different sensitivities and were at times upheld and defended by opposing groups within the movement. The idea of arbitration—the most legalised solution to the riddle of banning war—was spearheaded by the Anglo-American peace movement. Its European counterpart looked more closely at collective security in the framework of European federation, an idea that had its roots in the old tradition of European peace plans.[14] By the late 1890s, arbitration's proponents had won out.[15] Thanks to the success of the *Alabama* arbitration between Great Britain and the United States in the early 1870s and the peace movements' constant lobbying, arbitration also became an important point on the political agendas of the United States, Great Britain and other countries, including in Latin America.[16]

The arbitration movement's main objective was to offer an alternative way of settling disputes between states. The movement aspired to impose upon states an obligation to attempt to solve their disputes through arbitration before they resorted to force or war. Recourse to war would still be possible in case the arbitration attempt failed or in case one of the parties refused to implement the arbitral award. As most of the 'peace through law' movement proponents realised that introducing a general obligation would prove illusive, they advocated instead for a careful and gradual approach.[17] The movement's major ambition was to convince governments to make bilateral arbitration treaties wherein they committed themselves to submit all their disputes, or at least certain categories of disputes, to arbitration (or other pacific means of dispute settlement) before resorting to force.

Ian Brownlie (1963), one of the more thoughtful scholars on the subject, suggests that the nineteenth century's use of force doctrine was disorganised, unsystematised and inadequate in covering states' practice.[18] In truth, nineteenth-century doctrine should be considered the shambles of a historical tradition that was left after the bombshell of positivism blew natural law to the fringes. In order to make any sense of the confusion that was late-nineteenth-century use of force law, one needs first to return to the classical early modern *ius ad bellum*.

Europe's seventeenth- and eighteenth-century classical law of nations entailed a sophisticated *ius ad bellum*, which was constructed on two different conceptions of war. On the one hand, was the medieval tradition of 'just war'. On the other, was formal or legal war, with roots in thirteenth- and fourteenth-century civilian literature. Hugo Grotius (1583–1645) recycled these two traditions and gave them a place in his dualist theory of the law of nature and of nations. According to Grotius, just war pertained to natural law while legal war referred to the positivist, man-made law of nations. Whereas natural law applied only in conscience, the positive law of nations created rights and obligations in the sphere of external relations among princes and states. Mainstream doctrine after Grotius adopted this systematisation of just and legal war.[19]

A just war is a form of self-help mobilised by one sovereign against another sovereign to enforce an existing right that has been violated. It discriminates between an unjust side, which has committed injury, and a just side, whose right has been injured. In subsequent practice, this discrimination extends to both the *ius in bello*—the laws of war covering belligerent rights and duties—as well the *ius post bellum*—the rules about terminating war and restoring peace. Under the just war doctrine, only the just side may benefit from the laws of war and derive rights—such as the right to conquest, booty or ransom—from its provisions. At the end of a just war comes a just peace, whereby justice is done—regardless of the war's outcome. The just belligerent receives recognition of his contested right and has a claim to compensation for all the damages and costs of the war.[20]

Legal war is a way to settle disputes about legal claims between sovereigns in the absence of a higher authority capable of deciding the matter in an objective and neutral fashion. It grants equal rights under the laws of war to both sides as, unlike just war doctrine, it recognises both belligerents' right to fight the war. The outcome of the war, or of subsequent peace negotiations, determines the dispute's outcome. The victor is granted title to the contested right.[21] Whereas, to use Alberico Gentili's (1552–1608) metaphor, legal war is similar to judgement in a civil court, just war is similar to a bailiff enforcing a pre-existing right.[22]

Under the early modern European dualist doctrine of the laws of nature and of nations, both conceptions of war had their own field of application but were also inextricably linked. The civilians who introduced the notion of legal war acknowledged that the conception of legal was made necessary because of human inability to differentiate between two equal sovereigns where both claimed to be waging a just war.[23] Whereas just war, which pertained to natural law, dictated to the conscience of sovereigns that they should only go to war for a just cause, legal war acknowledged that in the external relations between sovereigns both had a right to resort to war to settle a dispute and were treated equally under the—positive—laws of war and peace-making. While a just war required a just cause (the violation of an existing right), for a war to be legal, it was sufficient that the belligerents were sovereign powers and that the war had been formally declared. But, under this latter formalistic condition and in the connection between legal and just war, lurked another condition: namely that, for a war to be legal and the belligerents to benefit from the protection of the laws of war, a belligerent still had to claim just cause. This claim did not have to be certain, but neither could it be manifestly unjust. If it was absent or if the war was manifestly unjust, there was no reason to consider both states as equally justified in taking up arms.[24] In sum, for a war to be legal, all belligerents had stake a claim that they were waging a just war.

To the modern observer, the early modern law of nations seems devoid of all restraining value since justice in war (as a prescript of natural law) was said to apply only in conscience. However, this assessment comes from too secular a reading of war's normative framework from the sixteenth to early nineteenth centuries. Whereas natural law itself became secularised to some extent, the notion of obligation in conscience did not. To the modern international lawyer, a natural obligation means an unenforceable obligation. However, to many scholars, rulers and diplomats of the sixteenth to early nineteenth centuries, violating natural law equalled sin. From this perspective, natural obligation was very much enforceable: by the supreme judge at the Final Judgement. By reconnecting natural law to the normative frameworks of theology and in some cases canon law, the early modern *ius ad bellum* retained strong normative value for any Christian believer. It remained a relevant determinant of behaviour and fostered intricate attempts at justifying war well into the nineteenth century. Indeed, throughout the early modern age, princes and governments took great care to explicitly justify their resort to force or war. They did so using the discourse of just war.[25]

The secularisation of international relations in the nineteenth century disconnected natural law from Christian religion and undermined much of the extant laws of nature and nations' normative strength.[26] Whereas the discourse of natural law remained resilient well into the nineteenth century, by the century's final decades, positivism had become ascendant and broken international law's dualist structure.[27] It seems logical that the ostracism of natural law from the realm of international law led to the demise of the just war component of the old *ius ad bellum*'s dualist logic, thus leaving only the recognition of a state's right to settle its disputes by force and war. Nevertheless, as Verdebout argued, only a very few positivist international lawyers from around 1900 on took this position.[28] The majority of nineteenth- and early twentieth-century writers retained much of the logic of just war in their legal reasoning. They recycled just war logic into their positive international law, dissolving the distinction between the justice and legality of war in the process.[29]

What major moves did mainstream writers of international law make during the nineteenth century in relation to use of force and war? First, as explained above, natural law receded into the background, and with its shift the distinction between just and legal war collapsed. Elements from both historic conceptions endured and fed into a newly unified concept of war's legality. Second, whereas detaching natural law from religion undid its normative power, many authors introduced a new brake on a sovereign state's right to resort to force and war: statehood itself. The rights of existence, sovereignty, independence, equality and dignity—which were among the fundamental rights considered inherent to statehood—prohibited the use of force against another state for it constituted a major infringement of the same. This relegated force and war to being an opposing right which remained inherent to statehood but could only be resorted to by violating another state's fundamental rights.[30] To most authors, with the exception of the few 'deniers', such violations required justification. In short, a state's right to resort to force and war was conditional and restricted.

Mainstream doctrine provided two legitimations for force and war. First, war was considered a legitimate way to settle disputes. The collapse of just and legal war into one another meant that authors could not fine-tune the distinction between war as law enforcement and war as dispute settlement.

Without the context of the dualism between natural and positive law, the distinction was irrelevant. Many doctrinal writers counselled that war could only be used as a final resort after peaceful means had proven ineffective. Second, self-preservation allowed for recourse to force or war. In nineteenth-century doctrine, self-preservation grew to encompass conceptions of both natural self-defence and defensive warfare from the classical law of nations.[31] It expanded to the point where self-preservation covered any instance of using force or war to ward off unwarranted attack or an imminent threat of attack. The justification held not only in the case of an armed attack but also when a right, the loss of which would endanger national security or independence, was violated. In this way, much of the just war tradition of war as sanction against prior injury of right was recycled into positive international law. This was as true for war itself as for measures short of war, such as self-defence, measures of necessity, intervention or reprisal. Furthermore, the notion of self-preservation was relaxed to encompass violations of vital interests or national honour.[32] Any resort to force that was not based on one of these two arguments—war as dispute settlement or as an action to ward off an unjust enemy attack—was considered illicit. In these cases, the term 'aggression' was loosely but increasingly applied by rulers, diplomats and lawyers alike.

The general state practice of the nineteenth century showed a growing nonchalance towards the requirement under traditional law for a formal declaration of war, but this did not imply that governments became more flippant about justifying their actions. The rise of public opinion in international relations actually necessitated the opposite. A general survey of just war discourses remained remarkably resilient in European state practice during the century before the First World War. States generally included arguments along the lines of an extended notion of self-preservation of a state's security, rights, interests and honour in their explanations for justifying war. They also tended, as if to compensate for the weakness of an argument emanating from the relaxed notion of self-preservation, to claim that the enemy had used force first.[33]

Nevertheless, by the final decades of the nineteenth century, international lawyers became more critical and sceptical about the existing doctrine and practice of *ius ad bellum*. Secularisation and the demise of natural law had removed much of its normative strength and left it in some disarray. Authors like Anzilotti, Lawrence, Oppenheim and Westlake reacted by throwing in the towel and declaring that the law was silent in the face of the free arbiter of resort to war.[34] Many turned to the peace movement and sought alternatives to war. The peace movement's main alternatives to war were collective security and arbitration. Although they were often played out against one another by their respective proponents in the peace movement and in governments, the concepts were actually complementary. Whereas arbitration proposed an alternative to war as a means of dispute settlement, collective security primarily (albeit not exclusively) proposed an alternative to force and war through self-preservation.

Collective security presupposed the establishment of some kind of international community, organisation or federation which through collective action would guarantee states' vital interests and national honour against unwarranted attack or violation. Most plans for collective security provided for a joint decision-making body which would settle differences between states and indicate the aggressor in case of conflict. As such, schemes for collective security often included proposals for a dispute settlement mechanism of a political or legal nature (or both) and covered both categories of legitimate war.

Arbitration plans were more limited in their aspirations inasmuch as limiting the right to wage war was concerned. First, arbitration was generally only put forward as an alternative to war to settle disputes of a legal nature and was thus only relevant for one of the two categories of war. Arbitration treaties and clauses reflected this because they generally applied to certain categories of disputes only. Arbitration plans either distinguished between legal and political differences, with arbitration only applying to the former case, or excluded arbitration for concerning vital interests and national honour.

Second, arbitration schemes were accommodating towards the principle of state sovereignty on which international order and its law were premised. Mainstream proponents of the 'peace through law' movement sought to regulate rather than abolish the right to wage war. With arbitration, the peace movement worked within the confines of traditional just and legal war doctrines which already constructed war as a last resort. The peace movement's hopes rested on states agreeing to an obligation to submit some or all of their future disputes to arbitration before resorting to war. However, such agreements did not exclude resort to force or war if arbitration failed or if one of the parties violated the arbitral award. This in fact buttressed the idea of 'war as a right of last resort' as much as it aspired to limit its necessity. By the time of the first Hague Peace Conference, the states of Europe and America had entered into numerous commitments imposing a duty to resort to arbitration for certain types of conflicts. This was done either through specific arbitration clauses in bilateral or multilateral treaties—which required arbitration for issues relating to those treaties' interpretation and execution—or through special arbitration treaties which committed them to arbitration for whole categories of differences.[35] Such general commitments had only proven feasible at the bilateral level. After the failure of the 1889 Pan-American Convention (only Brazil had ratified the agreement), a more general, multilateral convention remained a pipedream of the 'peace through law' movement.[36]

The 1899 Hague Peace Conference

After the first Hague Peace Conference opened on 18 May 1899, the delegates set about organising the conference's work. The eight points on the agenda set by the Russian government in its second circular of 11 February 1899 were divided among three commissions. Point 8, 'the use of good offices, mediation and voluntary arbitration in cases where they are available, with the purpose of preventing armed conflicts between nations', was entrusted to the Third Commission.[37] This point had been added to the agenda between the Tsar's original call for a conference on 24 August 1898 and the second circular. Professor Fyodor Martens (1845–1909), a renowned international lawyer and adviser to the Russian Foreign Ministry, himself a delegate at The Hague, had been crucial in facilitating this addition.[38] To many of the leading figures in the international peace movement, some of whom had turned up at The Hague, the Third Commission's work was the nucleus of their hopes and expectations for the conference. They hoped to advance the agenda of arbitration as an alternative for war. The same went for the many delegates who were members of the international institutions which comprised the 'peace through law' movement, including the *Institut de Droit International* and the Inter-Parliamentary Union.

Many of the plenary delegates as well as the international lawyers present at the conference sat on the Third Commission. The Commission's second meeting on 26 May 1899 decided to create a restricted Committee of Examination which would examine and discuss in detail the different proposals on the table and report to the Third Commission. This committee became the true battleground of the whole conference. The committee's agenda and composition—it was mainly staffed with lawyers, some of whom had only a loose connection to their governments—allowed freedom to push the agenda of the 'peace through law' movement and arbitration and to go, in some cases, beyond the scope of their instructions.[39] On the one hand, this explains the intensity of the long-drawn-out debates of the committee about far-reaching points, such as compulsory arbitration. On the other hand, it explains how some of these ideas crumbled against some delegations' reluctance to surrender any of their state's sovereignty.

The Committee of Examination's work centred around four proposals tabled by the American, British and Russian delegations. The main document was a Russian draft for a convention concerning the pacific settlement of disputes, often referred to as the 'Draft arbitral code'. The other three documents were proposals from the same three powers suggesting the establishment of a permanent arbitration tribunal.[40] Taken together, these four proposals aimed to standardise, generalise and institutionalise arbitration and other means of pacific dispute settlement. The hope was that standardising these mechanisms of dispute settlement would facilitate their use and promote them to governments locked in a conflict. Every element or aspect of a procedure which could be regulated in advance, rather than *ad hoc* when the dispute had already emerged, was one less point of negotiation between the contestants and one less stumbling block to using such a mechanism.

A major purpose of the Russian proposal was to distinguish between and define the different means of pacific dispute settlement. When the international peace movement adopted arbitration and forwarded it as the spearhead of its endeavours, the concept of arbitration was somewhat opaque. As one critic, Hans Wehberg, put it, arbitration in the nineteenth century had little to do with rendering a verdict on the basis of a strict application of international law. According to him, during the first half of the nineteenth century, the term 'international arbitration' was loosely used to denote a variety of dispute settlement mechanisms. It referred both to a compromise between sovereigns imposed by a third sovereign and to mixed commissions consisting of diplomats and jurists from both sides which acted as commissions of inquiry to detail the facts of a dispute and negotiate towards a compromise. During the late nineteenth century, when proper arbitration panels with neutral individual members were used, these acted on the basis of equity rather than of law and did not hesitate to bend the law so as to assure compromise.[41] Even if Wehberg overstated somewhat in his desire to argue for the necessity of a dedicated international court of arbitration, he was right that there existed extensive confusion about what exactly arbitration entailed. The Convention for the Pacific Settlement of Disputes of 29 July 1899, which the Third Commission produced on the basis of the Russian proposal, provided much-needed clarification.[42]

Article 15 included a definition of international arbitration, which has been considered its standard meaning ever since:

> International arbitration has for its object the settlement of differences between States by judges of their own choice, and on the basis of respect for the law.[43]

Article 16 labelled arbitration 'the most effective, and at the same time most equitable, means of settling disputes [for] questions of a legal nature'.[44] Hereby, the convention adhered to the idea that only legal disputes were suitable for solution on the basis of law. This was an acknowledgment that international law was an incomplete system consisting only of rules states had themselves accepted.[45] Article 9's definition of commissions of inquiry confirmed the limitation of arbitration to legal disputes. It stipulated that commissions of inquiry were considered suitable for differences 'arising from a difference of opinion on points of fact' rather than law.

The convention's title on arbitration did not specifically exclude matters touching on states' vital interests or national honour; doing so was unnecessary because the convention did not impose submission to arbitration.[46] The committee and commission's discussions made clear that there was scant support for the idea that all differences were suitable for arbitration. Whatever some delegates' personal inclinations, there was a broad consensus that states would never agree to submit differences concerning their vital interests or national honour to neutral panels of arbitrators. Article 15's definition also demarcated arbitration from adjudication, a distinction which would become far more relevant in later years when proposals for a true international court were debated. Whereas arbitration involved the free *ad hoc* selection of arbiters by the parties, a court has a fixed bench of independent pre-appointed judges who sit in different cases.

One of the first Hague Peace Conference's greatest achievements was the convention's chapter 'On Arbitral Procedure'. In 28 articles, the convention set out standard rules of procedure for arbitration panels. These rules were optional to the extent that parties to an arbitration could decide to divert from them and set their own rules.[47] But they offered the chance to dispense with the detailed negotiations which were generally necessary whenever rules of arbitration had to be established *ad hoc*. The convention's procedure did not apply to arbitration by a head of state.[48]

Second, the first Hague Peace Conference carried the hope of the 'peace through law' movement that a major step forward could be taken towards making arbitration mandatory for certain categories of disputes. Many in the peace movement considered this generalisation of arbitration the logical next step now that numerous states had been committing themselves to arbitration in specific treaties. The Third Commission took note of this progress through a study by Baron Edouard Descamps (1847–1933) from Belgium on recent arbitration clauses and treaties.[49]

The original Russian proposal had included a whole range of distinctions between categories of disputes which could, should or had to be submitted to arbitration. Article 7 called arbitration 'the most effective and at the same time most equitable means for the friendly settlement' of disputes 'concerning legal questions, and especially with regard to those concerning the interpretation and application of treaties in force'.[50] Article 8 involved a commitment to submit these disputes to arbitration except if they concerned 'the vital interest or national honour' of the parties. This fell, however, short of a real obligation as Article 9 made the belligerents responsible for the decision about whether or not a dispute was effectively submitted to arbitration. Obligatory arbitration would only apply to a very limited set of disputes. These were listed in draft Article 10, again under the exemption for vital interests and national honour. The list included disputes relating 'to pecuniary damages suffered by a state, or its nationals, as a consequence of illegal actions or negligence on the part of another state or its nationals' as well as disputes about interpreting and applying certain categories of treaties, including those covering postal and telegraphic infrastructure and services, navigation on the seas and on international rivers and interoceanic canals, intellectual property, money and measures, sanitation and veterinary surgery, phylloxera, inheritance, exchange of prisoners, reciprocal assistance in administering justice and technical issues relating to boundary demarcation. In early June, Professor Tobias Asser from the Netherlands submitted an extended version of Article 10, which he had prepared with other delegates.[51] Article 12 stressed that for all other matters, arbitration was strictly voluntary and had to be agreed to by all parties to the dispute.

The Russian move towards a limited form of obligatory arbitration received support from some other delegations, particularly the United States' delegates, whose instructions had included supporting the principle of obligatory arbitration.[52] Nevertheless, the proposal never stood a serious chance. Although the German member of the Committee of Examination, Professor Philip Karl Ludwig Zorn, offered little resistance during the initial discussions in late May and early June, during its meeting on 4 July he vetoed Articles 9 and 10. He stated that the principle of general compulsory arbitration was unacceptable to the German government. It could agree with obligatory arbitration through special conventions and would maintain its commitment to existing conventions of that nature, but could go no further. Zorn argued that the proposed Permanent Court of Arbitration's establishment would render new experience with arbitration and that it was wise to await this before new steps were taken. He appealed for support on the grounds of the need for consent and unanimity in making arbitration obligatory.

To the German government any proposal for obligatory arbitration was taboo as it seemed to limit their sovereignty. Moreover, it clashed with German military doctrine which dictated that Germany needed to reserve its right for quick military action in case of conflict, as it could mobilise faster than its opponents and had built its strategy on this advantage.[53] At the time of Zorn's rebuttal, Germany and the United States had already reached an understanding to abandon obligatory arbitration and instead establish a permanent tribunal. From the very beginning of the conference, the American delegation realised that obligatory arbitration had little actual value. Moreover, neither the Russian nor the Asser list was considered worth fighting for as it mainly listed issues of small importance that were unlikely to lead to war. In the words of the French delegate Baron Henri Balluet d'Estournelles de Constant (1852–1924), the conference was in danger of creating 'institutions to prevent war [...] except when war is threatened'.[54] Moreover, the American delegates had been among the first to dispute the Russian list in the Committee when they made a move to exclude navigation on international rivers and canals, a matter which they marked as an issue of vital interest.[55]

The end result of this and related discussions on Article 1 was a watered-down text which underscored the voluntary nature of pacific dispute settlement. Article 1 of the convention went no further than expressing a commitment by states to 'use their best efforts to insure the pacific settlement of international differences'.[56] The term 'differences' was elected to indicate all kinds of conflicts and disputes, whatever their nature. With this article the signatory states silently affirmed the right of states to resort to war, but also confirmed the traditional notion that force and war were a last resort. The convention was a list of pointers and measures to stimulate as well as facilitate the use of pacific means to settle disputes. Article 16 indicated arbitration as the appropriate means for disputes of a legal nature. Although the phrase was barred from the final text, it was clear from the voluntary nature of arbitration that the intention was to exclude disputes touching upon states' vital interests and national honour.

With regard to mediation, the Convention moved beyond the mere recognition of the voluntary nature of arbitration and shifted the balance between state sovereignty and the international community's common interests. After intense discussions, the committee and commission included a phrase in the convention recognising that third powers could offer good offices or mediation before, or even during, hostilities. Article 3 ruled that such an offer could never be regarded as an unfriendly act. This article, as the discussions leading to it betrayed, gave voice to the idea that war was not just a mechanism for two states to resolve a dispute but also affected the rights and interests of other states. Although the article did not restrict a state's right to resort to war, it carried the seeds of its condemnation.[57]

Third, the Convention for the Pacific Settlement of Disputes provided for the establishment of a permanent tribunal of arbitration. This became the most cherished project of the 'peace through law' agenda's stauncher proponents. Sir Julian Pauncefote (1828–1902) from the United Kingdom first tabled the idea. Russia and the United States also submitted drafts endorsing the idea. To the American delegation and other proponents of 'peace through law', it quickly became clear that the tribunal was the best they could hope for. Although many realised that its jurisdiction could only be voluntary and thus the tribunal would be nothing but yet another measure facilitating arbitration, it would be a highly visible and marketable result of the conference and held promise for further institutionalisation. As with obligatory arbitration, Germany was opposed. The German government feared that such a court would gain authority to propose arbitration and thus jeopardise its military strategy by delaying resort to force in case of crisis.[58] In the end, through the endeavours of the American delegation leader, Andrew White (1832–1918), Germany was brought to cede. While the argument that Germany would be held accountable for the conference's failure by the court of public opinion did impress the German delegation at The Hague, the German government itself was more worried about its relationship with Russia.[59]

Discussions on the different drafts for a permanent tribunal centred on the question of to what extent it would resemble a regular court. The American proposal went the farthest in that direction with the Russian the least and the British taking the middle ground. The American proposal that judges be appointed by the high courts of participating countries received little support. Articles 23 and 24 of the Convention for the Pacific Settlement of International Disputes explained the final compromise—largely based on the British draft—about the court's composition. The Convention stipulated that each member state would appoint four persons to the court. From this list, the parties in a conflict would select names to compose the particular tribunal that would arbitrate the case. At Germany's request, the name 'tribunal' was replaced by 'court' as the former was felt to indicate a particular panel in session and the latter was felt to be the more generic term.[60] A later German motion to bar 'court' as well was not carried.[61] Thus, the name Permanent Court of Arbitration was accepted.

A small victory for the proponents of arbitration was the carrying of the French motion that the states would consider it their 'duty' to remind parties to a dispute of the option to use the Permanent Court. Article 27, which stipulated this, stated that such a move was a friendly action. As with the mediation clause in the same vein, the reference to duty indicated a fundamental discontent with the idea that war was a sovereign right of singular states on the grounds that it impacted the rights and interests of all.[62]

The 1907 Hague Peace Conference

The calling of the second Hague Peace Conference eight years after the first was a triumph for the international peace movement. Its lobbying had induced the American President Theodore Roosevelt (1858–1919) to suggest a second conference, and had led to a second initiative by the Russian government.[63] The conference's programme included 'improvements to be made in the provisions of the Convention for the pacific settlement of international disputes as regards the Court of Arbitration and international commission of inquiry'.[64] At the conference, the major issues regarding arbitration were delegated to the First Commission and its First Sub-Commission.[65]

The discussions on arbitration pivoted on two major issues. First, there was the American proposal to establish a new international court with a fixed bench next to the existing Permanent Court of Arbitration. The 'peace through law' movement saw the American proposal as the conference's primary programmatic point. The idea gained support but in the end foundered on the impossibility of the great and smaller powers agreeing on the bench's composition. The conference's Final Act included a resolution recommending adopting the draft Convention for the Creation of a Court of Arbitral Justice and trying to reach an agreement on the bench.[66] The Court's name was apt since its jurisdiction was voluntary.[67] As with the International Prize Court, which the second Hague Peace Conference also discussed, the states failed to reach an agreement in the following years and the Court of Arbitral Justice never materialised. The Permanent Court of International Justice established through the Covenant of the League of Nations after the First World War was, however, largely based on the 1907 proposal.

Second, the conference returned to discussion of obligatory arbitration. As in 1899, the delegates focused on debating a list of disputes considered suitable for obligatory arbitration. While the discussions were much more elaborate and detailed than eight years previously, the idea failed in a way quite similar to 1899. Again, German opposition caused the conference to shelve the idea. This time, the German delegation took even more care than before to explain that it did not oppose obligatory arbitration—on the contrary, it claimed to favour it—but only the means which were proposed. According to its spokesman in the First Commission, it was impractical to try and attain obligatory arbitration through a universal treaty. It would be impossible to catalogue the myriad possible cases and to demarcate legal from political cases *in abstracto*. Therefore, Germany held to the gradual advance of obligatory arbitration through bilateral treaties. In this way, states' experiences could be taken into account to see which cases were suitable for arbitration and which were not. In the end, the concern with unanimity carried the day and obligatory arbitration was not written into the new Convention for the Pacific Settlement of International Disputes of 18 October 1907.[68] But all was not lost this time. The conference's Final Act endorsed the 'principle of obligatory arbitration'. The statement's vagueness allowed both for the universal as well as the bilateral route.[69] Nevertheless, the text constituted a conceptual step towards modulating the right to resort to force and war under positive international law and thus truly making it a last resort. Beyond this statement, however, the second Hague Peace Conference did not make any significant progress in denting a state's right to resort to force and war through the agenda of pacific dispute settlement. It continued on the road of facilitation and only made some small gains in relation to standardisation. Its attempts at institutionalisation and generalisation failed, except in one single respect.

Following up on a resolution passed at the 1906 Pan-American Conference in Rio de Janeiro, the United States submitted a proposal on the settlement of disputes concerning public debts.[70] This included contract debts between governments as well as governments' contract debts to foreign nationals. The proposal, made by General Horace Porter (1837–1921), was a variation on the so-called Drago Doctrine which the then Argentinian Minister of Foreign Affairs, Luis Maria Drago (1859–1921), forwarded in 1902. The doctrine, which Drago had expounded at the time in reaction to European navies' armed action against Venezuela, prohibited the use of force because of public debt. More generally, the Drago Doctrine reacted against a widespread European practice of using forcible reprisal against Latin American, Asian, Middle Eastern and African states for violations of their rights by these latter states or their subjects. In fact, reprisal was a powerful instrument European states used to impose their will worldwide.[71]

The first American proposal both expanded and relaxed the Drago Doctrine. It imposed a resort to arbitration for international conflicts about all kinds of public debt, both state to state—which Drago had aimed at— as well as state debts to foreign nationals. But it also relaxed the Drago Doctrine's prohibition against using force in pursuance of public debt. It stated that force could be used if an offer of arbitration was refused or went unanswered by the debtor, or if the debtor did not comply with the arbitral award.[72] The First Commission and First Sub-Commission hotly debated the Porter proposal. Several states, including Argentina through its delegate Drago, opposed mandatory arbitration for state debts to private persons, invoking national sovereignty. But, above all, Drago took offence at the fact that the American proposal acknowledged the ulterior right to resort to force (his doctrine excluded force altogether). In the end, the conference accepted an amended version of the American proposal, which became known as the Porter Convention, but the two major bones of contention remained.[73] The Porter Convention stated that it did not apply in cases where arbitration was refused or when the award was not complied with, but did not state directly that force would then be allowed. It was, however, the logical consequence when read against the backdrop of the existing *ius ad bellum*. Many states made reservations to these two points.[74] Nevertheless, the Porter Convention was a major conceptual breakthrough as it imposed upon a creditor state a legal obligation to offer arbitration before resorting to force or war. Failing to do so would make use of force or war illegal under positive international law. It brought what was a vaguely defined obligation to exhaust pacific means of dispute settlement under the just war doctrine into the realm of positive international law and transformed it into a concrete, enforceable legal obligation.

The second Hague Peace Conference directly addressed *ius ad bellum* in one other major instance. In the Second Commission a proposal was discussed and accepted to impose on belligerents a duty to declare war upon their enemies and announce it to third powers before hostilities could be opened. The resulting Convention Relative to the Opening of Hostilities of 18 October 1907 thereby confirmed a state's right to resort to war but also pointed to the fact that reasons had to be given.[75]

Conclusion

From the moment news of the Tsar's invitation to a disarmament conference spread in the autumn of 1898, the international 'peace through law' movement reacted with—albeit guarded—enthusiasm and started to try and appropriate the initiative. The agenda's expansion and the inclusion of arbitration in the second Russian circular note of 11 February 1899 allowed hopes and expectations to grow. In the end, the Hague conferences hovered between the 'peace through law' movement's idealism, which was well represented through the important place international lawyers had in the delegations, and the realism of statesmen who had to work in a world where sovereignty was jealously guarded and formed the foundation on which the whole international order rested. To the peace movement, the conferences' outcome could never be anything but ambivalent: disappointing for now but promising for the future.

The answer to the question of how the Hague Peace Conferences contributed to a 'revolution' in use of force law from *ius ad bellum* to *ius contra bellum* is likewise ambivalent. On the one hand, the conferences stayed largely within the confines of a traditional doctrine and practice which recognised a qualified right to resort to force and war. They confirmed this right through the Convention Relative to the Opening of Hostilities and did not allow the drive for arbitration to impose any concrete duties to stop or delay states from resorting to force and war—except in case of public debt—by insisting on the voluntary nature of arbitration and of any other form of pacific dispute settlement. The conferences walked the way of facilitation rather than imposition.

But, on the other hand, the conferences also exploited and concretised the restrictions of the traditional doctrines of just and legal war. The Hague conferences went a long way in bringing them closer to the realm of positive international law and towards slipping in some concrete obligations. The duty to offer arbitration in case of conflict concerning public debt was the most specific and imposing one, but there was also the duty to draw attention to the Permanent Court of Arbitration, the right to offer mediation and, at the second conference, the acceptance of the principle of obligatory arbitration. There was, therefore, reason to hope that the conferences were a beginning. Many discussions—such as the recurrent hints that a sanction was needed to enforce compliance with arbitral awards—showed that the potential existed to overturn the right to resort to force and war in more fundamental ways.

Finally, the often-repeated view that the Covenant of the League of Nations largely abandoned the route of The Hague and marginalised arbitration for collective security's benefit does not fit a reading of The Hague from the perspective of the past and traditional use of force law. The arbitration agenda, as it was moulded before and at The Hague, consciously addressed only half of the *ius ad bellum*—war as dispute resolution—and not war as self-preservation. The idea of collective security addressed the latter. In fact, the 1919 compromise between the British and French (who focused on the former) and the Americans (who focused on the latter) brought the two concepts together in Articles 10 to 16 of the Covenant. These articles imposed an enforceable and concrete obligation to exhaust pacific means, provided for a well-defined, cool-off period and opened the door to sanctions.[76] These were all next logical steps to the work at The Hague and most of them had been lurking behind discussions at The Hague. Elihu Root, a great proponent of the 'peace through law' agenda, was right when he predicted in 1912 that everything already attained was a staging post in a long line of progress. His hunch was shared by one of the 'peace through law' agenda's great opponents, one who would find himself at the losing side of its history in 1919. 'It should not matter to me. But what are these childish dreams', the German Emperor Wilhelm II (1859–1941) scribbled in the margin of a report on the first Hague Peace Conference's discussions on arbitration and a permanent tribunal. He pondered: 'What will it come to as time goes on[?]', thus giving voice to his deeper concern.[77] Childish dreams could, indeed, become reality.

Notes

1 First Hague Peace Conference, Plenary Meeting of 29 July 1899. In: J.B. Scott, ed. (1920). *The Proceedings of the Hague Peace Conferences*. New York: Oxford University Press. Vol. 1. *The Conference of 1899*, pp.224–225.
2 The phrase 'peace through law' indicates the dominance of international law and lawyers in the international peace movement. Some leading national peace associations, such as the French or Dutch, adopted it for their name; D. Laqua. (2013). *The Age of Internationalism and Belgium, 1880–1930. Peace, Progress and Prestige*. Manchester: Manchester University Press, p.148.
3 Scott, *Conference of 1899*, vol. 1, p.225.
4 Quoted in P.C. Jessup. (1938). *Elihu Root*. Vol. 2, New York: Dodd, Mead & Cie., p.74.
5 E.g. G. Abi-Saab. (2008). Evolution dans le Règlement Pacifique des Différends Economiques depuis la Convention Drago–Porter. In: Y. Daudet, ed., *Actualité de la Conférence de La Haye de 1907. Deuxième Conférence de la Paix/ Topicality of the 1907 Hague Conference, the Second Peace Conference*. Leiden and London: Martinus Nijhoff, pp.177–196, at p.179; I. Brownlie. (1963). *International Law and the Use of Force by States*. Oxford: Clarendon Press, pp.23–25.
6 Brownlie, pp.51–129; S.C. Neff. (2005). *War and the Law of Nations. A General History*. Cambridge: Cambridge University Press, pp.285–296, 314–322.
7 D. Cortright. (2008). *Peace. A History of Movements and Ideas*. Cambridge: Cambridge University Press, pp.49–57; F.H. Hinsley. (1963). *Power and the Pursuit of Peace. Theory and Practice in the History of Relations between States*. Cambridge: Cambridge University Press, pp.114–149; M. Koskenniemi. (2008). The Ideology of International Adjudication and the 1907 Hague Conference. In: Daudet, *Actualité*, pp.127–152.
8 Brownlie, pp.49–50.
9 Neff, pp.215–249.
10 A. Verdebout. (2014). The Contemporary Discourse on the Use of Force in the Nineteenth Century: A Diachronic and Critical Analysis. *Journal on the Use of Force and International Law*, 1(2), pp.223–246.
11 Cortright, pp.25–54; C. Lynch. (2012). Peace Movements, Civil Society, and the Development of International Law. In: B. Fassbender and A. Peters, eds., *Oxford Handbook of the History of International Law*. Oxford: Oxford University Press, pp.198–221, at pp.203–214.
12 M. Koskenniemi. (2001). *The Gentle Civilizer of Nations. The Rise and Fall of International Law 1870–1960*. Cambridge: Cambridge University Press, pp.11–97.
13 R. Lesaffer. (2013). The Temple of Peace. The Hague Peace Conferences, Andrew Carnegie and the Building of the Peace Palace (1898–1913). *Mededelingen van de Koninklijke Nederlandse Vereniging voor Internationaal Recht*, 140, pp.1–38, at pp.14–22.
14 B. Arcidiacono. (2011). *Cinq types de paix. Une histoire des plans de pacification perpétuelle (XVIIè–XXè siècles)*. Paris: Presses Universitaires de France; Hinsley, pp.13–91; K. von Raumer. (1953). *Ewiger Friede. Friedensrufe und Friedenspläne seit der Renaissance*. Freiburg and Munich: Karl Alber.
15 See note 8; also Hinsley, pp.94–99; W.F. Kuehl. (1969). *Seeking World Order. The United States and International Organization to 1920*. Nashville: Vanderbilt University Press, pp.50–55.
16 C.G. Roelofsen. (2012). International Arbitration and Courts. In: Fassbender and Peters, eds, pp.145–169, at pp.162–166.
17 For a list of important projects and their texts, see A. von Daehne van Varick, ed. (1921). *Documents Relating to the Program of the First Hague Conference*

Laid before the Conference by the Netherland Government. Oxford/London: Clarendon Press/Humphrey Milford, pp.73–112.
18   Brownlie, pp.23–50.
19   H. Grotius. (1625, text of 1646, ed. 1925). *De Iure Belli ac Pacis Libri Tres. Classics of International Law.* Oxford/London: Clarendon Press/Humphrey Milford, sections 1.3.4.1, 3.3.4–5 and 3.3.12–3.
20   On the just war, P. Haggenmacher. (1983). *Grotius et la Doctrine de la Guerre Juste.* Paris: Presses Universitaires de France; Neff, pp.45–68; F.H. Russell (1975). *The Just War in the Middle Ages.* Cambridge: Cambridge University Press. One of the clearest expositions of mainstream just war doctrine and its consequences from the Early Modern Age comes from E. de Vattel (1758, ed. 1916). *Le Droit des Gens ou Principes de la Loi Naturelle.* Classics of International Law. Oxford/London: Clarendon Press/Humphrey Milford 1916, esp. section 4.2.18.
21   J.Q. Whitman. (2012). *The Verdict of Battle. The Law of Victory and the Making of Modern War.* Cambridge, MA and London: Harvard University Press.
22   A. Gentili (1598, text of 1612, edn. 1933). *De Iure Belli Libri Tres. Classics of International Law.* Oxford/London: Clarendon Press/Humphrey Milford, section 1.6.47–52.
23   Gentili, 1.6.47–52; see also Vattel, 3.3.40.
24   W. Rech. (2013). *Enemies of Mankind. Vattel's Theory of Collective Security.* Leiden and Boston: Martinus Nijhoff.
25   B. Klesmann. (2007). *Bellum Solemne. Formen und Funktionen europäischer Kriegserklärungen des 17. Jahrhunderts*; Mainz: Philipp von Zabern; A. Tischer. (2012). *Offizielle Kriegsbegründungen in der frühen Neuzeit. Hersscherkommunikation in Europa zwischen Souveränität und korporativem Selbstverständniss.* Berlin: LIT Verlag.
26   H. Steiger. (2001). From the International Law of Christianity to the International Law of the World Citizen: Reflections on the Formation of the Epochs of the History of International Law. *Journal of the History of International Law,* 3(2), pp.180–193.
27   M. Koskenniemi. (2005). *From Apology to Utopia. The Structure of International Legal Argument.* 2nd ed. Cambridge: Cambridge University Press, pp.122–157; C. Sylvest. (2004). International Law in Nineteenth-Century Britain. *British Yearbook of International Law,* 75, pp.9–70.
28   Verdebout, p.224.
29   The analysis of nineteenth- and early twentieth-century doctrine is based on the reading of over 40 textbooks of international law from the period.
30   E.g. J.L. Klüber. (1861). *Droit des Gens Moderne de l'Europe avec un Supplément Contenant une Bibliothèque Choisie du Droit des Gens,* ed. M.A. Ott. Paris: Librairie de Guillaumin et Cie.
31   Self-defence was a natural right to use proportional force to stop an unjust armed attack. Defensive war was a full war which was justified by the enemy's unjust armed attack. Neff, pp.126–130.
32   Brownlie, pp.40–52; Neff, pp.215–249; Verdebout, pp.227–234.
33   Russian declaration of war against the Ottoman Empire of 26 April 1828. In: (1842). *British Foreign and State Papers.* Vol. 15, London: HMSO, pp.656–662; declaration of Queen Victoria announcing the war against Russia on 27 March 1854, no. 44. In: *British Foreign and State Papers,* p.110; also see for the First World War, (1915). *Collected Diplomatic Documents Relating to the Outbreak of the European War.* London: Foreign Office.
34   D. Anzilotti. (1912). *Corso di Diritto Internationale.* Rome: Athenaeum; T.J. Lawrence. (1895). *The Principles of International Law.* Boston: Heath; L. Oppenheim. (1905). *International Law: A Treatise.* London and New York:

Longmans, Green and Co.; J. Westlake (1907–1910). *International Law.* 2 Vols. 2nd ed. Cambridge: Cambridge University Press.
35 A list was tabled at the first Hague Peace Conference, General Survey of the Clauses of Mediation and Arbitration Affecting the Powers Represented at the Conference. In: Scott, *Conference of 1899*, vol. 1, pp.191–206.
36 Hinsley, pp.267–268.
37 Russian Circular Note Proposing the Programme of the First Conference, 11 February 1899. In: Shabtai Rosenne, ed. (2001). *The Hague Peace Conferences of 1899 and 1907 and International Arbitration. Reports and Documents.* The Hague: Asser Press, pp.24–26, at p.25.
38 V.V. Pustogarov. (2000). *Our Martens. F.F. Martens, International Lawyer and Architect of Peace.* The Hague, London and Boston: Kluwer Law International, pp.162–167.
39 For the debates and decisions of the Conference, C. Davis. (1962). *The United States and the First Hague Peace Conference.* Ithaca, NY: Cornell University Press; A. Eyffinger (1999). *The 1899 Hague Peace Conference. 'The Parliament of Man, the Federation of the World.* The Hague, London and Boston: Kluwer Law International; F.W. Holls. (1914). *The Peace Conference at The Hague and its Bearings on International Law and Policy.* London: Macmillan; Scott, *Conference of 1899*, vol. 1; A.D. White. (1905). *Autobiography of Andrew Dickson White with Portraits.* Vol. 2. London: Macmillan & Co.
40 For the text of these documents, see the Report of the Third Commission to the Plenary Conference, 25 July 1899. In: Scott, *Conference of 1899.* Vol. 1, pp.106–206, at pp. 166–189.
41 H. Wehberg. (1918). *The Problem of an International Court of Justice.* Oxford/London: Clarendon Press/Humphrey Milford, pp.13–22.
42 For the text of the Convention, Clive Parry, ed. (1969–1981). *The Consolidated Treaty Series.* Vol. 184, Dobbs Ferry: Oceana Press, p. 410 (hereafter 184 CTS 410).
43 184 CTS 410.
44 184 CTS 410.
45 H. Lauterpacht. (1933). *The Function of Law in the International Community;* Oxford: Clarendon Press.
46 Art. 17.
47 Art. 30.
48 Art. 33.
49 First meeting of the Third Commission of 23 May 1899. In: Scott *Conference of 1899*, vol. 1, pp.581–582.
50 Scott, *Conference of 1899*, vol. 1, p.167.
51 See fifth meeting of the Committee of 7 June 1899. In: Scott, *Conference of 1899*, vol. 1, p.705.
52 Davis, *First Hague Peace Conference*, p.137.
53 E. T. S. Dugdale, ed. (1930). *German Diplomatic Documents 1871–1914.* Vol. 3, London: Methuen & Co, esp. pp.74–81. The military argument surfaced in the discussion whether mediation would delay mobilisation. See Art. 7 of the Convention for the Pacific Settlement of International Disputes; third meeting of the Committee, 31 May 1899, amendment by Italy. In: Scott, *Conference of 1899*, vol. 1, p.696. Also see White, vol. 2, p.265.
54 Thirteenth Meeting of the Committee, 3 July 1899. In: Scott, *Conference of 1899*, vol. 1, p.760.
55 Fourth meeting of the Committee, 3 June 1899. In: Scott, *Conference of 1899*, vol. 1, p.702; Davis, *First Hague Peace Conference,* pp.137–160; Holls, p.228; White, vol. 2, pp.265–328.

56 184 CTS 410.
57 Second meeting of the Committee, 29 May 1899. In Scott, *Conference of 1899*, vol. 1, pp.688–694.
58 Count Münster to German Chancellor, 12 June 1899. In: Dugdale, vol. 3, p.76.
59 Dugdale, vol. 3, pp.74–81.
60 Twelfth meeting of the Committee, 1 July 1899. In: Scott, *Conference of 1899*, vol. 1, p.755.
61 Fifteenth meeting of the Committee, 15 July 1899. In: Scott, *Conference of 1899*, vol. 1, pp.775–777.
62 Thirteenth meeting of the Committee, 3 July 1899. In: Scott, *Conference of 1899*, vol. 1, pp.759–764.
63 C. Davis. (1975). *The United States and the Second Hague Peace Conference. American Diplomacy and International Organization 1899–1914*. Durham, NC: Duke University Press; A. Eyffinger. (2007). *The 1907 Hague Peace Conference. 'The Conscience of the Civilized World'*. The Hague: JuciCap, pp.62–80; Kuehl, pp.59–97.
64 Letter of the Russian ambassador to the US Secretary of State, 3 April 1906. In: Rosenne, p.147.
65 For the proceedings and documents, see J.B. Scott. (1920–1921). *The Proceedings of the Hague Peace Conferences. Translation of the Official Texts, The Conference of 1907*. 3 vols, Oxford: Oxford University Press; for the First Commission, vol. 2 (1921).
66 Final Act of the Second International Peace Conference, 18 October 1907. In: Scott, *Conference of 1907*, vol. 1, pp.679–690, at p.689; Draft Convention Relative to the Creation of a Court of Arbitral Justice, in idem, vol. 1, pp.690–696.
67 Art. 17 of the Draft Convention.
68 205 CTS 233.
69 Davis, *Second Hague Peace Conference*, pp.251–257.
70 J.W. Gantenbein (1950). *The Evolution of our Latin-American Policy. A Documentary Record*. New York: Columbia University Press, pp.717–718; Jessup, *Root*, vol. 2, pp.68–75.
71 W. Benedek. (2012). Drago–Porter Convention. In: R. Wolfrum, ed., *Max Planck Encyclopedia of Public International Law*. Vol. 3, Oxford: Oxford University Press, pp.234–236; Neff; pp.225–239. On the Drago Doctrine, A. Hershey. (1907). The Calvo and Drago Doctrines. *American Journal of International Law*, 1(1), pp.26–45.
72 Scott, *Conference of 1907*, vol. 2, p.906.
73 Convention respecting the Limitation of the Employment of Force for Contract Debts, 18 October 1907, 205 CTS 250.
74 Scott, *Conference of 1907*, vol. 2, pp.137–142, 226–231, 300–310.
75 205 CTS 263; Davis, *Second Hague Peace Conference*, pp.202–211.
76 R. Kolb, ed. (2015). *Commentaires sur le Pacte de la Société des Nations*. Brussels: Bruylant; P.J. Yearwood. (2009). *Guarantee of Peace. The League of Nations in British Policy 1914–1925*. Oxford: Oxford University Press, pp.7–137; A. Zimmern. (1939). *The League of Nations and the Rule of Law 1918–1935*, 2nd ed. London: Macmillan, pp.138–253.
77 Foreign Minister to Emperor, 21 June 1899. In Dugdale, vol. 3, p.80.

3 Muddied waters

The influence of the first Hague conference on the evolution of the Geneva Conventions of 1864 and 1906

Neville Wylie[1]

Tuesday 17 January 1899 was not a good day for Gustave Moynier. Unfolding his copy of the *Journal de Genève* that morning, the 72-year-old president of the International Committee of the Red Cross (ICRC) was astounded to discover that Russian plans for the proposed 'disarmament conference', announced the previous summer, included two items that lay close to his heart: the neutralisation of rescue ships and the extension of the 1864 Geneva Convention to maritime conflicts. As is clear from a letter dispatched to the secretary of the Swiss foreign ministry that same day, Moynier was appalled at the thought of the convention being dragged into the maelstrom of great power politics and sullied by its association with a conference so patently designed to serve Russian strategic interests and indulge the Tsar's ego.[2] It was not the first occasion on which Moynier felt ambushed by the Russians. A strikingly similar situation occurred in 1874, when the Brussels Conference, convened at the behest of Tsar Alexander II, only refrained from revising the Geneva Convention after Moynier pledged to consider the matter in a separate conference. This time, Moynier's hand was forced: ten articles applying the Geneva Convention to maritime conflicts were brought together as the third Hague Convention of 1899, and figured again, in a slightly updated form, as the tenth Hague Convention of 1907.

Scholars have paid little attention to how the Hague conferences shaped the development of the Geneva Convention. The decision to include the maritime regulations in the 1899 Hague Peace Conference is usually seen as part of Fyodor Martens' adroit pre-conference manoeuvring and his attempt to insure against the conference breaking up without result by stacking the agenda with less contentious 'legal' issues.[3] If true, the Russians were not to be disappointed at the Hague conference. It took the delegates little over a month to conclude their discussions on the maritime convention, giving them a 'quick win' before settling down to the more substantive and taxing matters of arms limitation, arbitration and the laws of war. Moreover, as Arthur Eyffinger rightly points out, 'in terms of humanitarian precepts', the conference at The Hague

> achieved more than all Red Cross conferences, meetings of the Institute [of International Law] or of the Inter Parliamentary Union up to

then taken together. It effectively moulded precepts into conventions which were at the core of subsequent developments in the sphere of Genevan Law.[4]

As this chapter argues though, 'The Hague' and 'Geneva' were even more intertwined than Eyffinger implies. In determining that its conference should tackle the maritime code, St Petersburg essentially compelled the ICRC and its Swiss backers into agreeing to update the 25-year-old convention at a time when neither was firmly committed to pursuing such a course. The distinction between what would become 'Hague law'—the law of armed conflict—and 'Geneva law'—the international humanitarian law—was not clearly defined in the 1890s.[5] But St Petersburg's actions at the turn of the century triggered a process that anticipated this result: provoking a revival of Swiss interest in the Geneva Convention and in those elements of the Convention that would set it apart from the growing corpus of law governing the conduct of warfare.

The maritime convention

As with all the other items on Mouraviev's agenda in January 1899, discussions on a maritime convention did not begin from a blank slate. Although naval warfare was overlooked in the first Geneva Convention concluded in August 1864, the high loss of life at the battle of Lissa in July 1866 encouraged the Italian government to raise the question of a naval code with the Swiss federal council in May 1867 and champion the cause at the Red Cross conference at Paris later that summer. Italian sponsorship of the project was important because not everyone shared Rome's enthusiasm for renegotiating a treaty of such recent vintage. The French government was particularly wary of reopening discussions, while Moynier and his colleagues in Geneva found the whole idea of tampering with the 1864 Convention 'repugnant'.[6] Nevertheless, beyond the glaring absence of articles dealing with maritime conflicts, the Schleswig-Holstein War of 1864 and Austro-Prussian War of 1866 had pointed to weaknesses in the Geneva Convention. In inviting the signatories to Geneva in October 1868, therefore, the Swiss federal council was mindful to dampen expectations for a full revision of the treaty, circulating to the powers only a synopsis of opinions, not a full draft convention.[7]

Notwithstanding the narrow scope of the 1868 conference's ambitions, this first attempt at 'humanising' naval warfare proved disappointing. Berne's invitation failed to excite much interest amongst the European powers. Only 13 countries heeded the call. Important maritime powers such as Russia, Spain and Portugal stayed away, while the Ottoman delegation only reached the conference in time for the final session. Only the British, Dutch, Prussian, French and Italian delegations included serving naval personnel and, when these officers came together to explore the matter, they found it impossible to steer clear of 'all the most delicate questions of the maritime law of nations'. As a consequence, their debates were 'beset with difficulties' and gave rise to a draft set of articles which bore a markedly military rather than humanitarian imprint.[8] No sooner had they presented their eight draft articles to the plenary meeting, than they were forced to adjourn for a week to respond to fresh instructions from their governments. The net effect was that the articles' humanitarian character was further eroded.[9] Thus, military hospital ships, initially designated as neutral, were to be left open to seizure by enemy forces on the grounds that to do otherwise would allow unscrupulous commanders to assign hospital-ship status to damaged warships and thereby prevent their interception by enemy forces *en route* to the repair yards. Hospital ships could, therefore, be captured and their equipment seized. The final draft also included an article allowing the convention to be suspended on the mere suspicion ('strong presumption') that one side might be guilty of abusing its privileges.

The conference's laconic *procès-verbaux* suggest that at its close, many of those present doubted the value of their labours. The British delegate, for instance, reported that the articles should be taken as merely 'a series of propositions' to which his government was 'in no way pledged'.[10] When Berne circulated the text to the signatory powers, instead of securing ratifications, as was hoped, the exercise merely generated further controversy. The British, French and Russian governments all tabled amendments or 'opinions', which ultimately compounded the lingering sense of uncertainty over the status of the maritime articles. As early as mid-1869, the federal council and the international committee in Geneva felt it wise to limit debate on the maritime clauses and avoid any action that might discourage their ratification.[11] The onset of the Franco-Prussian War brought some relief in that both belligerents pronounced their willingness to comply with the additional articles (even if, in practice, their application left much to be desired).[12]

But it was clear that the powers felt uncomfortable with the results of the 1868 conference. When the British made inquiries in Paris and Berlin in late 1869, they found little enthusiasm amongst military quarters for the additional articles or indeed the 1864 Convention. The French were particularly dismissive, but even in Prussia, where the Red Cross idea had struck a chord, officers were prepared to 'encourage and use [the articles] to the fullest extent but to publish and lay down as a rule as little as possible'.[13] These views were born out in practice. Berlin agreed to apply the additional articles in its war with France the following year, but thereafter declined to formally adhere to the articles or respond to inquiries from Berne or elsewhere.[14] Britain's military authorities were equally sceptical, and even sympathisers of the Red Cross, such as the head of the British military hospital, Professor Thomas Longmore, admitted that the maritime articles presented 'almost insuperable difficulties in practice'.[15] The Admiralty took a distinctly self-serving view of the initiative, applauding the steps taken to regularise the conduct of military hospital ships but disparaging the encouragement given to volunteer or neutral services.[16] At base, though, the 1868 initiative fell victim to Britain's determination to avoid any extension of the laws governing maritime warfare for fear of restricting its operational freedom or limiting the writ of the Admiralty's prize courts.[17] It was principally with an eye to its rights under prize law that London insisted that the 'additional article' 10 be read in such a way as to compel neutral vessels who rescued shipwrecked sailors to subject their cargoes to belligerent inspection. The Admiralty remained hypersensitive towards any questions bearing on prize law over the latter half of the century, especially in light of the increasingly vocal support for private property rights in the United States and amongst some business circles in Britain.[18]

In such circumstances, support for the additional articles quickly faded. Berne managed to resolve some of the disagreements left over from 1868 and the international committee remained committed to humanising naval conflicts. But both lacked the necessary expertise to inject much purpose into the discussions. When the committee produced a revised draft of the Convention in 1885, its section on maritime warfare merely replicated the pertinent articles from 1868. Ultimately, though, the lack of interest shown by the great powers, coupled, perhaps, with the absence of major naval engagements after 1866, discouraged further work on the issue. By the mid-1880s, with the revision process running out of steam, Berne and Geneva took steps to distance the 1864 Convention from the 'failed' initiative of 1868. The federal council even went so far as to refuse to commit to a 'definitive text' of the additional articles.[19]

It was not until the early 1890s that interest in the subject resurfaced. As before, the Italians championed the issue first, taking advantage of the 1892 Red Cross conference in Rome to promote the cause of hospital-ship immunity. On 12 May 1897, Rome approached the federal council offering to host a conference. As we will see below, Rome's appeal coincided with a resurgence of interest in updating the 1864 Convention, the appearance of Alfred Thayer Mahan's seminal work *The Influence of Sea Power upon History* in 1890 and the return of major fleet actions in the Sino-Japanese War of 1894 and Spanish–American War of 1898. Technological developments, especially in the design of torpedoes, also added to the sense of urgency, in making commanders more wary of tolerating the approach of 'rescue boats' lest their presence be used to mask an attack. This partially accounted for the high loss of life at the Sino-Japanese encounter on the Yalu River on 17 September 1894, when fear of Chinese torpedo boats meant that 'the Japanese were not able to give any assistance to the unhappy crews of the *Tchen Yang*, *Chih Yuen* or *King Yuen*, whose shrieks ... could be plainly heard in the lulls of the firing'.[20] Nine months earlier, the French Navy's senior medical officer, Dr Auffret, published the fullest account to date of the negotiations for a 'maritime code' and appealed to the powers to remedy this deficiency.[21] Yet while state practice clearly reflected some elements of the 1868 additional articles, especially regarding the designation of named hospital ships, it is questionable whether Geneva or Berne were ever fully persuaded of the advisability of submitting a 'maritime code' to a diplomatic conference or mixing maritime issues into a general revision of the Geneva Convention.[22] In Swiss circles, there was clearly something rather 'toxic' about the maritime articles.[23] The pervading opinion was summed up by the Swiss foreign minister, less than a month before the opening of the Hague conference, when he remarked:

> If we ask ourselves whether the present moment offers a good opportunity to conclude an agreement over the extension of the Geneva Convention to naval warfare, we have to admit that it is difficult to hold out any great hope in this regard. The concerns of the naval powers, and discussions over whether to expand or restrict so-called prize law, are still entirely unresolved … An agreement with the current powers still looks very doubtful.[24]

It is important to recognise, then, that in turning to the maritime convention in 1898 and 1899, the Russian foreign ministry was not plucking 'low hung fruit' to fill The Hague's basket. Russian diplomats were well aware of the prevailing mood and the soul-searching going on in Switzerland and elsewhere over the issue.[25] While few questioned the need to humanise naval warfare by this date, no one intimately involved with the issue was under any illusion about the difficulty of securing international agreement on the subject.

Revising the Geneva Convention

Moynier's alarm in reading Mouraviev's circular in January 1899 went beyond fussing over the maritime articles' fate. What really concerned him was how the Tsar's proposals might affect the status of the 1864 Geneva Convention. Despite the obvious weaknesses of the Convention, the demise of the 1868 additional articles dampened enthusiasm for revising the treaty within the ICRC.[26] The committee's reluctance to address the issue and its decision, instead, to direct its energies towards building up the national societies and encouraging research on battlefield medicine and ambulance design has yet to be fully explored.[27] There is little doubt, though, that its hesitation stemmed in large measure from anxiety over where any revision of the treaty might lead. This had been the lesson drawn from the Brussels Conference in 1874, when those present only agreed to leave the Geneva Convention intact on the understanding that a record be made of the opinions of the military delegates present.[28] The resulting discussion made unpleasant listening for the Swiss delegates. As Prussia's General Voigts-Rhetz caustically noted, 'had, at the time when the Convention was concluded, been as many military men present as there were doctors, it would have been drawn up differently'.[29] Fear of what might be left of the convention's humanitarian bedrock if its redrafting was left to the likes of Voigts-Rhetz explains why, as late as 1896, the committee admitted that 'for a long time it had serious grounds for believing there was more to lose than gain in convening a new conference, which might result in calling into question the very existence of the convention itself'.[30]

Military officers were not the only people under-represented at the 1864 conference: lawyers were too. As a founding member of the Institute of International Law in 1874, Gustav Moynier was certainly sympathetic to the ambitions and liberal internationalism espoused by the legal community. He was, notably, the moving spirit behind the Institute's draft code of the laws of war, the 1880 Oxford Manual, and he and his ICRC colleagues largely welcomed the growing scholarship on the Geneva Convention.[31] Carl Lüder's *Die Genfer Konvention* (1866) won the coveted Princess Augusta prize. The committee paid for the book's translation into French, and acknowledged its value for shaping any future revision of the treaty.[32] The committee did not, however, view the sight of legal scholars picking over the convention with undiluted pleasure. There was, for instance, a worrying sense of *déjà vu* in the remark made by the celebrated scholar, J.K. Bluntschli, when he attributed the weaknesses of the convention to the sparseness of legal opinion around the conference table in 1864.[33] The legal community's growing success in asserting international law's relevance to inter-state relations meant that it became progressively harder for the ICRC to insist on the special, medical character of the Geneva Convention. It was likewise difficult to reject the right of lawyers to revise the convention on the grounds that they lacked the necessary expertise. It was precisely the convention's 'technical' character that had justified its removal from the agenda in Brussels in 1874. Yet when Eduoard Odier, the head of the Swiss delegation, tried the same reasoning in 1899, Tobias Asser, the Dutch delegate and jurist, affirmed the right of lawyers to pass judgement on the Geneva Convention by drawing a distinction between 'competency in fact and competency in law':

> It is true that... the [Conference] is not competent in fact to pass on questions of a medical and sanitary nature, however... the [Conference] ought [not] to consider itself limited so narrowly.... An exchange of views along these lines appears... to be within the competency of the [Conference] and might, in a form to be determined by the [Conference], serve to call the attention of the Governments to the points which have been taken into consideration.[34]

The ICRC was not wholly averse to the idea of revising the Convention. By the early 1890s, it had made no fewer than five attempts to redraft the text. In every case, however, the committee was effectively prodded into action by the pressure of external events. Three drafts were written in response to the 1874 conference and St Petersburg's efforts to continue negotiations on the Brussels code in subsequent years. The most expansive draft convention, composed by Moynier in 1885, emerged from the committee's musings on a project tabled by the German Red Cross society.[35] Much of the early thinking in Geneva focused not so much on revising the text itself as on creating mechanisms to buttress its operation. The most prominent initiative in this vein was Moynier's 1872 proposal for a permanent court to try infractions of the Geneva Convention. He had earlier explored the idea of creating 'battlefield police' to protect the dead and wounded.[36] Faced with such vacillation, it is hardly surprising that frustration at the committee's apparent foot-dragging was to be heard in the Red Cross conferences and came to frame attitudes towards Switzerland's guardianship of the convention.

It is open to question whether the international committee or, more importantly, the Swiss federal authorities, would have grasped the nettle and agreed to revise the Geneva Convention had Mouraviev's announcement of the Hague agenda not landed on their desks in early January 1899. Of the two, it was the international committee who showed the most interest. Studies conducted by the Swiss military in 1892 resulted in a set of proposals that seemed capable of reconciling 'the requirements of the principle of humanity and the purpose of the war' and finding favour amongst military authorities abroad.[37] The studies' positive reception in German academic circles was particularly heartening, given Berlin's spurning of the 1868 revision and growing affection for the 'mantra' of military necessity in all areas of military conduct.[38] The ICRC broached the subject of treaty revision with the federal authorities in March 1894 and December 1896, and did so again in 1898. Inquiries were also made to gauge the principal national Red Cross societies' opinions. In the summer of 1898, the committee elected to publish a complete draft of a revised Convention. This was the first time it had engaged so openly and publicly in the revision debate. Moynier's last letter to Berne before Mouraviev's circular, sent on 27 July 1898, urged the federal council to take advantage of the imminent conclusion of the Spanish–American War to re-engage with the revision process.[39]

Berne's response was scarcely what Moynier would have wished for, though probably what he had anticipated. Throughout the decade, the federal political department viewed the whole question of treaty revision with the 'the greatest circumspection'.[40] Discouraged by the failure to secure ratifications of the 1868 additional articles, the federal authorities were reluctant to devote the necessary time or effort to develop a coherent policy on the issue. The problem was partly structural. With the exception of a brief period between 1887 and 1896, responsibility for foreign affairs rotated between the country's federal councillors annually. Expertise on international relations thus tended to reside in the nascent diplomatic service, principally its long-serving ambassadors in Paris and Berlin. All attempts to professionalise Swiss foreign policy-making failed to make headway or overcome the public's ingrained dislike for any foreign entanglements. Switzerland's growing appeal as a base for international organisations and a venue for international conferences at this time had little to do with any central direction from Berne.[41] The problem was also a matter of priorities. Although happy to trumpet Switzerland's status as the birth-place of the Geneva Convention, Berne paid scant attention to its custodial duties. In 1895 it even considered passing responsibility for revising the convention over to the Institute of International Law.[42] It was not the convention that consumed Berne's attention in the months prior to the publication of Mouraviev's circular, but rather the burgeoning menace of international anarchism, brought home by the assassination of Empress Elizabeth of Austria in Geneva in September 1898 and the convening of a conference on the issue in Rome later that year. Moynier's call to arms in July 1898 was thus left unanswered, and it was only in January 1899, when the Convention became embroiled in Russia's preparations for the 'disarmament' conference, that Swiss officials turned their attention to the matter at hand.[43]

The Hague Conference, 1899

Swiss officials felt equally affronted by Russian presumptuousness in including the Geneva Convention in their proposed 'peace' conference. Despite lacking a diplomatic mission in St Petersburg, as depository power for the Geneva Convention the Swiss could rightly expect to have been consulted before Russia made its intentions known. They too were sceptical of Russia's humanitarian credentials and worried by the resurrection of the 1874 Brussels' code on the law of war, a code which Berne (together with Europe's other small powers) had been pleased to see the back of 25 years before.[44] Where official thinking differed from the ICRC's was in the willingness to take a pragmatic, even opportunistic, approach to Mouraviev's proposal. Instead of seeking to deflect Russian interest in the Convention, as Moynier clearly wished, the federal government seized upon the Hague conference as an opportunity to revise the treaty. With Russian prestige riding on a successful outcome and doubts growing over the chances of securing agreement on the headline items, there was every possibility, Berne surmised, that pressure to clinch a deal over the Geneva Convention would override any concerns governments might have about individual aspects of the new treaty.[45] This approach was all the more appealing given the difficulties they expected to face in negotiating a maritime code.

In retrospect, it is ironic that Berne's attempt to tether the Geneva Convention to the Tsar's coattails was undone by the very man heralded as the architect of The Hague's success, the Russian lawyer and diplomat Fyodor Martens. As chairman of the Second Commission, it was Martens who led discussion on the issue and, in turn, presented the case against the Swiss proposition. The stated rationale for declining Berne's request was largely technical (the dearth of medically qualified delegates and the absence of some of Geneva's signatory powers), but Martens' reluctance to depart from Mouraviev's agenda was also motivated by the desire to avoid giving licence to other delegations to table their own, potentially embarrassing, proposals. He may also, though, have had other reasons for being ill-disposed. From the outset, Martens appears to have had qualms about including matters relating to the sick and wounded at The Hague. No mention was made of the Geneva Convention in the programme he proposed to the Russian foreign ministry in October 1898, and he probably viewed including the maritime code as an unnecessary distraction from the conference's core business.[46] In any event, it is unlikely that the Swiss delegation pressed Berne's case with much vigour. The chief delegate Edouard Odier (secretary to the ICRC) shared Moynier's views, and had already sought, unsuccessfully, to dissuade Berne from its proposed course of action. He was quietly delighted, therefore, to see Berne's proposal fall to Martens' objections.[47]

Martens' action is doubly ironic in light of subsequent Russian efforts to secure control of the revision process for themselves. In this respect, Martens' rejection of the Swiss proposal represented a lost opportunity for Russian diplomacy. For the remainder of the conference, Berne's principal objective lay in securing support for Switzerland to host a conference on the 1864 Geneva Convention, and to obtain the conference's implicit acknowledgement that it was the Swiss, and nobody else, who held the keys to Geneva's revision. Berne also wanted to capitalise on the headwind generated at The Hague to ease the passage of treaty revision when delegates finally assembled in Geneva. This was no easy task. Italian sponsorship of a maritime code in the 1860s and early 1890s implied that Swiss 'ownership' of the Geneva Convention could not be assumed: a point that Odier conceded through gritted teeth. When discussion turned to the subject of a follow-up conference to revise the 1864 convention, the Swiss had to work furiously to beat off rival bids. Reflecting on the episode four years later, the French delegate, Louis Renault, recalled the Swiss having to overcome the

> sensitivities and jealousies existing between the national societies and the ICRC, the ill will of several states, notably Russia, or certain Russian delegates, and the manoeuvres of the Belgians and the Dutch to prise from Switzerland the 'grandes affaires internationales' and exploit the [anti-Republican] prejudices of the monarchical powers.[48]

The chief threat came from Tobias Asser, the Dutch delegate, who mounted a concerted and initially successful campaign against the Swiss position. This resulted in a Romanian proposal, conferring responsibility on Berne to convene the revision conference, being put to a vote twice before a majority found in Berne's favour.[49] Asser's biographer claims he secretly cherished the 'aspiration to haul this major catch to the Netherlands', but the Swiss delegates clearly found him 'overly preoccupied to please the Russians' and considered him merely a stalking horse for Russian ambitions.[50] The interventions of Asser and Martens in the debate were suspiciously well-choreographed. Although prepared to keep the Geneva Convention off the agenda in 1899, Martens saw no reason to deny Russia the chance of bringing the issue under its purview in the future. On this issue at least, Martens preferred the cloak of a Russian diplomat to the gown of an international jurist.[51] Even after the vote, therefore, the Swiss delegation took the precaution of avoiding any action that might antagonise their Russian hosts or revive Russia's predatory interest in the Convention.[52]

On the face of it, the tensions provoked by discussion over the land convention's fate were absent from the debates that gave rise to the third Hague Convention 'for the adaptation to maritime warfare of the principles of the Geneva Convention of August 22, 1864'.[53] The apparent ease with which agreement was reached on the maritime code was due in part to the template provided by the drafters of the 1868 additional articles and Auffret's writings earlier in the decade. The third Hague Convention differed in certain respects from the earlier articles: it left hospital ships, whether of the regular navy, in neutral service or provided by private relief societies, exempt from capture. Yet the two texts bear a striking similarity. It would be wrong, though, to assume that a consensus on the issues was easily reached or maintained. The original 1864 Convention was so obsolete by 1899 that it was difficult to translate its spirit into the new naval code while ignoring its many and obvious drawbacks. Frustrated at being unable to rule on these shortcomings, the conference had to satisfy itself by making reference to the Geneva Convention (twice) and issuing a *voeu* that its revision be not long delayed. Moreover, the consensus only held because the scope of the new code was deliberately narrow. Repeated efforts by the Americans to have the conference take a view on the immunity of private property at sea were resisted. For the maritime articles this meant that neutral merchantmen coming to the assistance of shipwrecked sailors remained 'liable to capture for any violation of neutrality they may have committed'.[54] The only tacit nod to American wishes was the right granted to medical staff to retain 'the objects and surgical instruments which are their own private property' upon falling into enemy hands.[55] A belated attempt by the United States' naval delegate, the celebrated Captain Mahan, to insert articles dealing with the status of servicemen rescued by neutral merchantmen, was likewise firmly rebuffed. To the Americans the issue's importance was self-evident: in June 1864, Captain Semmes of the Confederate ship *Alabama* had evaded capture by seeking refuge on a British steam yacht. But to Martens and the drafting commission, Mahan's attempt to expand the remit of the convention threatened to undo all the work previously accomplished. It was not simply a matter of tinkering with an agreed text, but rather a question of opening up a new angle of discussion that might 'imperil the unanimity' which had brought discussions to the point of closure.[56] Mahan was ultimately persuaded to withdraw his proposal. However, his ideas were included in the United States' naval regulations drawn up the following year and returned to the negotiating table at the 1907 Hague Peace Conference where they received universal assent.[57]

The difficulties the Swiss delegation encountered at The Hague were replicated in the early years of the new century as Berne sought to convene a conference to revise the 1864 Convention. Both the opening of a legation in St Petersburg in 1902 and the selection of Edouard Odier as Switzerland's first minister were driven in part by a concern to ease relations with Russia over the Geneva Convention. Plans for hosting a conference were initially delayed by the outbreak of fighting in South Africa. A date was set for September 1903 but when, by July, replies from St Petersburg and Berlin were still outstanding, the federal council felt compelled to adjourn the conference until a more opportune moment. The onset of the Russo-Japanese War in February 1904 put pay to convening a conference that spring and the council reluctantly postponed it again until the cessation of hostilities. If anything, events in the Far East only intensified Russian determination to control the revision process. St Petersburg's intentions were made abundantly clear over the winter of 1905 when, with Vienna's support, it tried to pre-empt Berne's call for a fresh conference by formally recommending that discussion on the Geneva Convention be reserved for the second Hague conference.[58] When Berne refused, St Petersburg mischievously insisted that the timing of the Swiss conference not conflict with the forward planning for the second 'peace' conference and then declared its intention to withhold committing to any decisions taken in Switzerland until they had been confirmed by delegates at The Hague.[59] As a well-informed British observer noted, 'the Russians have all along thrown every obstacle in their power in the way of the Swiss convening the Geneva Red Cross Revision Conference'.[60] In the circumstances, it was no small feat for the Swiss to stand up to Russian intimidation and hold fast to their right to oversee the revision process.

Russian machinations did not end with the opening of the Geneva Conference on 11 June 1906. True to their pre-conference rhetoric, the large Russian delegation set out to subordinate the new convention to The Hague's rules. They insisted that the revised code make direct reference to the 1899 regulations, that it conform to the principles enshrined in the maritime convention and that any disagreement over the reading of the new convention be adjudicated by the Permanent Court of Arbitration at The Hague. Russian interventions were directed not so much at amending the content of the revised Geneva Convention as ensuring that the Convention was situated in a framework that had the Hague regulations at its apex.

In the end, Russian efforts were to no avail. Several of the signatory powers at Geneva had not ratified the Hague regulations or, like Switzerland, had been selective in those it had accepted These states could hardly embrace a revised Geneva Convention behoved to a treaty to which they were not parties. Perhaps the biggest advance in 1906 was the recognition accorded to private relief societies. Although relief societies had been integral to the operation of the Geneva Convention since its inception, they had been omitted from the original treaty in 1864 and had only first made an appearance in the maritime articles of 1868. Their first formal expression had to wait until the third Hague Convention of 1899. Moreover, instead of referring to the Hague rules, the Geneva conference agreed to keep the new convention entirely distinct. So while the Hague rules made reference to Geneva, the new Geneva Convention deliberately avoided any explicit cross-referencing. The Hague's echo in the 1906 Convention was, of course, unmistakable, but the essence of the revised Geneva Convention lay elsewhere. What ultimately distinguished it from the nineteenth-century codes were the lessons derived from the recent fighting in South Africa and the Far East and from the impetus provided by the British government's renewed interest in international legal codification. Far from the Hague regulations setting the tone for discussions at Geneva as the Russians had assumed, it was the revised and enlarged Geneva Convention of July 1906 that established the humanitarian baseline for all future discussion. The ideas crafted at the 'technical' conference in Geneva in 1906 compelled the Russians to revise the 1899 maritime convention and return it to The Hague in 1907.

Conclusion

The 1899 Hague Peace Conference played a facilitative, even catalytic, role in the process of updating the 1864 Geneva Convention and in translating its provisions into naval warfare. Its contribution to the development of what would become the centre piece of international humanitarian law could arguably be considered one of its most profound legacies. Yet, as we have seen, the relationship between the two conferences was by no means unproblematic. It was the challenge, rather than the encouragement, provided by the Russian initiative that ultimately shaped the 1864 Convention's revision. The experiences at the 1899 Hague Peace Conference and 1906 Geneva conference had a marked effect on Swiss attitudes towards the Geneva Convention. Historians usually date Berne's 'interest' in the Geneva Convention to 1867, when Franco-Prussian discussions over Luxembourg's fate underscored the limits of small state sovereignty under the new power constellation on the continent. There is no question that the Swiss were proud of the waxing appeal of the Red Cross movement, the prestige of the international committee and Switzerland's position as 'cradle of the Geneva Convention'.[61] Yet it was not until delegates assembled at The Hague in 1899 that the Swiss fully grasped the tenuousness of their custodianship of the Convention or the extent to which their success had provoked the jealousy and ambitions of some of their European partners. In this era of great power politics, it was all too easy to overlook the convention's provenance. In 1887, the eminent jurist Henry Sumner Maine glibly wrote of the Geneva Convention as part of the 'period of humanitarian progress and voluntary codification which deserve[s] to be identified with the name of the Emperor Alexander II of Russia'.[62] If the revised Geneva Convention was not to be identified with the name of the latest Russian tsar, the Swiss would clearly need to pay more heed in exercising their proprietary rights over the convention.

It was also in the wake of the Hague and Geneva conferences of 1899 and 1906 that the international committee began the process of differentiating between the humanitarian provisions of the Geneva Convention and the broader agenda pursued under the Hague rules. Of course, the two threads were closely connected: sailors and hospital-ship crews looked to the 1899 and 1907 regulations, while any battlefield sick and wounded who fell into the hands of their enemies were first and foremost 'prisoners of war' and governed by The Hague's stipulations. But the challenge posed by the existence of the Hague rules provided the urgency needed for serious reflection on the distinctiveness of the Geneva Convention. It was no longer appropriate to consider it as merely a technical convention rooted in a fusion of medical ethics and humanitarianism. Henceforth, it came to be seen as a set of articles dedicated to protecting the victims of war and not a convention whose purpose was to shape the conduct of war itself. Some of Moynier's earlier writings had hinted at the distinction, but it took the Hague conference of 1899 to bring the matter centre-stage.[63] The 1899 conference, in this sense, *created* a historical moment by eliciting a process of treaty revision, which had been stalled for three decades, and by forcing the architects and custodians of the Geneva Convention to clarify what it was that made their convention distinctive and worthy of special attention. Begun at The Hague, this process was accelerated by the events of the First World War: the widespread infractions of the maritime and land conventions, the abuse of the Red Cross emblem and, in particular, the exaction of reprisals against prisoners of war for alleged attacks on hospital ships.[64] Instead of retreating to their original mandate when the guns fell silent, the international committee consciously, and boldly, redefined the subject of humanitarian action. The results of its endeavours—in extending humanitarian protection to new categories of war victims, first prisoners of war and then civilians—are still with us today.

Notes

1 The author would like to thank James Crossland, Lindsey Cameron and the editorial team for their comments on this chapter.
2 G. Moynier (ICRC) to G. Graffina (Secretary, Federal Political Department (FPD), Berne), 17 January 1899, no. 288. In: (1994). *Documents Diplomatiques Suisse (DDS)*. Vol. 4. Berne: Benteli Verlag. For Russia's commitment to international law, P. Holquist. (2004). *The Russian Empire as a "civilized state". International Law as Principle and Practice in Imperial Russia, 1874–1878*. [online]. University Center for International Studies University of Pittsburgh. Available at: https://www.ucis.pitt.edu/nceeer/2004_818-06g_Holquist.pdf [Accessed 23 June 2016].
3 A. Eyffinger. (1999). *The 1899 Hague Peace Conference. 'The Parliament of Man, the Federation of the World'*. The Hague: Kluwer, p.38; J. Dülffer. (1981). *Regeln gegen den Krieg? Die Haager Friedenskonferenzen von 1899 und 1907 in der internationalen Politik*. Berlin: Ullstein.
4 Eyffinger. *1899 Hague Peace Conference*, p.5.
5 F. Bugnion. (2001). Droit de Genève et droit de La Haye. *International Review of the Red Cross*, 83(884), pp.901–922.

6 See discussion on 30 May 1868. In: J.-F. Pitteloud, ed., (1999). *Procès-verbaux des séances du Comité international de la Croix-Rouge, 17 février 1863–28 août 1914*. Geneva: Société Henry Dunant, p.56.
 7 In addition to the maritime articles, the conference sought to strengthen the neutrality of the sick, wounded and medical personnel and to clarify the position of civilians offering aid.
 8 'Proceedings of the International Conference held in October 1868. Draft of additional articles to the Convention of August 12th 1864 for the mitigation of the lot of wounded soldiers in armies in the field'. Meetings 13 and 19 October 1868, Records Relating to the Red Cross Conferences. General Records, vol. 1, pp.42, 44, RG43, National Archive and Management Administration (NARA), College Park, Maryland.
 9 'Proceedings', meeting 19 October 1868, p.46.
10 Admiral Yelverton to the Secretary to the Admiralty, 15 October 1868, RAMC/1139/LP/22/25, Longmore Papers, Wellcome Institute Archive, London.
11 22 May 1869. In: Pitteloud, p.79.
12 J. Dubs (Swiss President) to signatories to the Geneva Convention, 22 July 1870, no. 257. In: *DDS*, vol. 2.
13 Report by British military attaché in Berlin, cited in B. Oliver. (1966). *The British Red Cross in Action*. London: Faber & Faber, p.111. For French and German attitudes, see M. Schultz. (2016). Dilemmas of 'Geneva' Humanitarian Internationalism: The International Committee of the Red Cross and the Red Cross Movement, 1863–1918. In: J. Paulmann, ed., *Dilemmas of Humanitarian Aid in the Twentieth Century*. Oxford: Oxford University Press, pp.42–46. For state adherence, see: M. Finnemore. (1999). Rules of War and Wars of Rules. The International Red Cross and the Restraint of State Violence. In: J. Boli and G.M. Thomas, eds., *Constructing World Culture: INGOs since 1875*. Stanford: Stanford University Press, pp.149–165.
14 G.E. March (Foreign Office), 'Memo. on Additional Articles to the Geneva Convention of 1864, for ameliorating the Condition of Sick and Wounded in time of War', 23 June 1873, FO881/7137, The National Archives of the United Kingdom (TNA).
15 Sir Thomas Longmore to the Director Geneva of the War Office, 14 May 1869, RAMC/1139/LP/22/25. The conference proposed the use of yellow flags to signal vessels in distress. See 'Résultats de la Conférence Internationale des Délégués des Haut Gouvernements qui ont adhere à la Convention de Genève et des Sociétés de Secours aux Militaires Blessés et Malades, qui a eu lieu à Berlin du 22 au 27 avril, 1869', no. 43, FO881/7137, TNA.
16 C.J. Burgess (London) to G. Moynier (ICRC), 9 May 1869, AF 8, 3 08/02/41, ICRC Archives.
17 On the 1856 Paris Declaration: J.M. Lemnitzer. (2014). *Power, Law and the End of Privateering*. London: Palgrave.
18 Admiralty, 'Memo. On the Effect on Ocean Commerce of an Anglo-Continental War', M0190/91 February 1892, ADM1/7422B, TNA.
19 J.K.E. Schenk (Swiss President) to Sir Francis Adams (British minister, Berne), 12 May 1885, FO881/7137, TNA.
20 *Pall Mall Gazette*, 26 January 1897, p.6.
21 Dr. Auffret. (1894). Les Secours aux blessés et aux naufragés des guerres maritimes. *Revue Maritime et Coloniale*, 120(1), pp.66–115, 279–389; Prof. D'Espine. (1894). Les Secours aux blesses et aux naufragés des guerres maritimes, d'après le Dr. Auffret. *Bulletin International des Societies de la Croix-Rouge*, 99, pp.152–157.
22 Minutes of the Federal Council, 8 June 1897, no. 214. In: *DDS*, vol. 4.
23 Washington and Madrid agreed to adhere to the additional articles at the start of the Spanish–American War in 1898: US State Department. (1898). *Foreign*

Relations of the United States. Washington: US Government Printing Office, pp.1148–1182.
24 Proposition by E. Müller (President and Head, FPD) to the Federal Council, 27 April 1899, no. 306. In: *DDS*, vol. 4.
25 For Russian views, see Prof. Martens to Col. Ziegler (Chef Medical Officer, Swiss federal army) 18 February 1896, no. 201/1. In: *DDS*, vol. 4.
26 The Convention was widely abused in the Franco-Prussian War: B. Taithe. (1984). The Red Cross Flag in the Franco-Prussian War: civilians, humanitarians and war in the 'modern age'. In: R. Cooter, M. Harrison and S. Sturdy, eds., *War, Medicine and Modernity*, London: Stutton, pp.22–47.
27 P. Boissier. (1984). *From Solferino to Tsushima: History of the International Committee of the Red Cross.* Geneva: Henri Dunant Institute, *passim*, for an overview.
28 D. Bujard. (1974). The Geneva Convention of 1864 and the Brussels Conference of 1874. *International Review of the Red Cross.* Vol. 56, no. 670, pp.527–537 (Part 1); Vol. 56, no. 671, pp.639–649 (Part 2).
29 Actes de la Conférence Réunie à Bruxelles, du 27 juillet au 27 août 1874, pour régler les lois et coutumes de la guerre.In: C. Samwer and J. Hopf, eds. (1879). *Nouveau Recueil général de traités.* 2nd series, Vol. iv, Gottingen: Dieterich, p.67.
30 E. Odier (ICRC Secretary) to A. Lachenal (President and Head, FPD), 12 December 1896, no. 227. In: *DDS*, vol. 4.
31 For Moynier's involvement in the institute, see: J. de Senarclans. (2000). *Gustave Moynier: Le bâtisseur.* Geneva: Slatkine, pp.221–233; and in broader debates, D.M. Segesser. (2016). Humanitarian intervention and the issue of state sovereignty in the discourse of legal experts between the 1830s and the First World War. In: F. Klose, ed. *The Emergence of Humanitarian Intervention.* Cambridge: Cambridge University Press, pp.56–72.
32 Comment by E. Odier, 14 January 1876. In: Pitteloud, p.376. C.J.F.L Lueder. (1876). *Die Genfer Konvention.* Erlanden: Eduard Besold.
33 Bluntschi was Voigts-Rhetz' legal adviser in 1874. E. Müller (President and Head, FPD) to E. Odier (National Councillor and head, Swiss delegation to the Hague conference) 12 May 1899, no. 312. In: *DDS*, vol. 4.
34 J.B. Scott. (1907). *The Proceedings of the Hague Peace Conferences.* The Hague: Carnegie Endowment for Peace, p.386.
35 V. Harouel. (1999). Les projets genevois de revision de la Convention de Genève du 22 août 1864, 1868–1898. *International Review of the Red Cross*, 81(834), pp.365–386; Pitteloud, sessions of 9, 16, 23 and 30 March, 8 June 1885.
36 G. Moynier. (1872). Note sur la Création d'une Institution Judiciare Internationale proper à prévenir et à réprimer les Infractions à la Convention de Genève. *Bulletin International des Sociétés de Secours aux Militaires Blessés*, 11, pp.122–131; Pitteloud, p.74. C.K. Hall. (1998). Première proposition de creation d'une cour criminelle international permanente. *International Review of the Red Cross*, 80(829), pp.59–78.
37 E. Odier (ICRC Secretary) to A. Lachenal (President and Head, FPD), 12 December 1896, no. 227. In: *DDS*, vol. 4; H. Bircher. (1893) *Die Revision der Genfer-Konvention.* Aarau: H. R. Sauerländer.
38 For German attitudes see I. Hull. (2014). *A Scrap of Paper: Breaking and Making International Law during the Great War.* Ithaca: Cornell University Press, esp. pp.67–88; G. Best. (1984). *Humanity in Warfare. Modern History of the International Law of Armed Conflict.* London: Methuen, esp. pp.47–49; H. Triepel. (1894). *Die neuesten Fortschritte auf dem Gebiete des Kriegsrechts.* Leipzig: Hirschfeld.
39 G. Moynier. (1898). *La révision de la Convention de Genève: étude historique et critique suivie d'un Projet de Convention revise.* Geneva: ICRC. This was based

on the study by the head of the Swiss military medical service, Col. Dr. Ziegler. (3 December 1896). Zur Revision der Genfer Konvention vom 22 August 1864. Memorial des eidgenössischen Oberfeldartzes. Moynier (ICRC) to E. Ruffy (President and Head, FPD), 27 July 1898, no. 267. In: *DDS,* vol. 4.
40 FPD to Moynier (ICRC) 20 March 1884, cited in Harouel, p.374.
41 See M. Herren. (2000). *Hintertüren zur Macht. Internationalismus und modernierungsorientierte Außenpolitik in Belgien, der Schweiz und den USA, 1865–1914.* Munich: Oldenbourg, pp.219–245; C. Altermatt. (2008). On Special Mission: Switzerland and its Diplomatic System. In: M. Möpplang and T. Riotte eds, *The Diplomat's World. A cultural history of diplomacy, 1815–1914.* Oxford: Oxford University Press, pp.317–344; and C. Altermatt (1990). *Les débuts de la diplomatie professionnelle en suisse 1848–1914.* Fribourg: Presse universitaire Fribourg.
42 E. Frey (Head of Swiss Military Department) to A. Lachenal (Head of FPD), 4 November 1895, no. 186. In: *DDS,* vol. 4.
43 R.B. Jensen. (1981). The International Anti-Anarchist Conference of 1898 and the Origins of Interpol. *Journal of Contemporary History,* 16(2), pp.323–347. The assassination removed Geneva as a potential venue for the conference. A.V. Ignatyev. (1993). Russia, the Netherlands and the First Hague Peace Conference of 1899. *Baltic Studies,* 2, pp.207–214.
44 For the 1874 conference, see: K. Nabulsi. (1999). *Traditions of War. Occupation, Resistance and the Law.* Oxford: Oxford University Press, pp.4–12; and J. de Bruecker. (1974). La Déclaration de Bruxelles de 1874 concernant les lois et coutumes de la guerre. *Chronique de politique étrangère,* 27, pp.3–87.
45 The Swiss position is given in Müller's letter to Odier 12 May 1899, no. 312. In: *DDS,* vol. 4. For the context, see: A. Durand. (1999). Le Comité international de la Croix-Rouge à l'époque de la première Conférence de la Haye (1899). *International Review of the Red Cross,* 81(834), pp.353–364.
46 V.V. Pustogarov. (2000). *Our Martens: F. F. Martens, international lawyer and architect of peace,* The Hague: Kluwer, pp.162–172.
47 E. Odier to E. Müller (President and Head, FPD) 9 May 1899, no. 312/1. In: *DDS* vol. 4. For Moyner's 'quelque inquiétude' over Swiss intentions, see: G. Moynier (ICRC) to E. Müller (President and Head, FPD), 7 February 1899, AF 8, 4, ICRC Archives.
48 C. Lardy (Swiss minister, Paris) to A. Deucher (President and Head, FPD) 5 March 1903, no. 425. In: *DDS,* vol. 4.
49 See W.D. White. (1905). *The Autobiography of Andrew Dickson White.* Vol. 2. New York: Century Press, entries for 30 June, 1, 5 July 1899.
50 A. Eyffinger. (2011). *Dreaming the Ideal, Living the Attainable. T. M. C. Asset. Founder of the Hague Tradition.* The Hague: T.M.C. Asser Press, p.51. E. Odier (Swiss delegation to the Hague conference) to E. Müller (President and Head, FPD) 15 June 1899, no. 315. In: *DDS,* vol. 4.
51 Martens' biographer is in two minds over Martens objectivity, see: Pustogarov, pp.191–192, 276–280.
52 A. Roth (Swiss delegation to the Hague conference) to E. Müller (President and Head, FPD) 18 July 1899, no. 322. In: *DDS,* vol. 4. Scott, pp.393–394, 408–409.
53 Available at: http://avalon.law.yale.edu/19th_century/hague993.asp [Accessed August 2016].
54 Article 6.
55 Article 7.
56 Report by Captain A. T. Mahan to the Commission of the USA to the International Conference at The Hague, 26 July 1899, Box 1 Entry 23, RG43, NARA.

57 C.H. Stockton. (1900). *The Laws and Usage of War at Sea. A Naval War Code*. Washington: Government Printing Office. This was withdrawn four years later to leave America with a free hand at the 1907 Hague Conference. J. B. Hattendorf. (1994). Maritime Conflict. In M. Howard, G.J. Andreopoulos and M.R. Shulman eds., *The Laws of War. Constraints on Warfare in the Western World*. New Haven: Yale University Press, pp.110–111.
58 See memoranda communicated by M. Sazonow (Russian ambassador, London) 17 November 1905, and Count Mensdorff (Austro-Hungarian ambassador, London) 6 December 1905, FO881/9056, TNA.
59 Note communicated by M. Sazonov (Russian ambassador, London), 22 March 1906, FO881/9056, TNA.
60 Note by Lt. Col. W. G. Macpherson, 19 March 1906, FO881/9056, TNA.
61 Minutes of Federal Council, 8 June 1897, no. 241. In: *DDS*, vol. 4.
62 H.S. Maine. (1915, first published 1887). *International Law*. 2nd ed., London: John Murray, lecture 7.
63 The experience of the Franco-Prussian War appears to have influenced Moynier: G. Moynier. (1870). *Etude sur la convention de Genève pour l'amélioration du sort des militaires blessés dans les armées en champagne*. Paris. J. Cherbuliez., pp.25–26.
64 A. Durand. (1984). *From Sarajevo to Hiroshima: History of the International Committee of the Red Cross*. Geneva: Henri Dunant Institute, pp. 48–82; L. Cameron. (2016). The ICRC in the First World War: Unwavering belief in the power of law? *International Review of the Red Cross*, 97, pp.353–364.

4 Reconsidering disarmament at the Hague Peace Conference of 1899, and after

Andrew Webster

The 1899 Hague Peace Conference marks the opening of the modern era of efforts towards international disarmament. It is worth reconsidering precisely why it should be seen in that light. Summoned at Tsar Nicholas II's behest with the declared ambition of checking the steady growth of land armaments and armies, it failed utterly in its proclaimed goal and ultimately produced only three very limited 'prohibitory' declarations: on poison gas, bombing from balloons and expanding bullets. Contemporaries certainly considered these to be paltry results, given the extent of their hopes for what might have been achieved. Yet even such narrow agreements were a triumph, for they constituted the first voluntary renunciation by states of the right to use certain types of weaponry. It was a critical first step that could not be taken back: disarmament negotiation had become a legitimate topic in international diplomacy. But this perspective, while important, is limited by its sole focus upon the conference's outcomes rather than the processes which produced them. Historians and legal commentators almost always present the three declarations as stand-alone items, with no relation to the political context or actual debates of the conference itself.[1] They are therefore unable to link the 1899 conference's work in any direct way with the era of disarmament it purportedly opened, particularly the far more extensive international disarmament process—overseen by the League of Nations—that followed the conclusion of the First World War.

In this chapter, I explore two other ways in which the first Hague Peace Conference's context and work as a whole, and not merely its slim results, shaped the international politics of disarmament for the following half century. The first is the relationship between the attitudes of the participating governments and the wider global peace movement. The same basic tension existed for both the 1899 meeting (also to a lesser extent the 1907 Hague Peace Conference) and for the disarmament process of the 1920s and early 1930s. Policymakers across all the major powers, and many of the minor ones also, wished to avoid the issue. They perceived even discussing measures that might limit their absolute sovereignty over the means of defence as a risk to national security. Yet the weight of public opinion forced governments to confront that very question as a core item of international diplomacy. Willingly or not, disarmament had to be discussed. The second aspect concerns the close relationship between the specific proposals put forward during the Hague conference's discussions and the ideas that dominated the League of Nations' negotiations in Geneva during the interwar years. The disarmament debates at The Hague were far more wide-ranging and ambitious than the mere three agreed declarations would indicate. They covered an array of approaches—from limiting specific weapons types, to freezing the size of armies, to verification of compliance with any agreement—all presented and debated for the first time at a multilateral governmental conference. The debates that would follow in Geneva two decades later turned back to all of these ideas, often couched in precisely the same language. In 1899, such proposals verged on the fantastic. In the vastly changed context of the post-war world, they seemed for a time eminently possible.

The disarmament issue did not arise spontaneously in 1899. The European peace movement had called for arms reductions for decades, yet policymakers had paid only lip service to their ideals.[2] Other than some desultory and unformed proposals offered sporadically by the occasional leader across the nineteenth century, the sole achievement was the 1868 declaration at St Petersburg renouncing the use of light explosive projectiles (below 400 grams) in any war amongst the signatory powers. But the final decades of the century saw a step-change in national expenditure on arms, backed by the technological capacity for their industrial mass production. From the 1880s through the early 1900s, new inventions included the magazine-loading small-bore rifle, improved machine guns, smokeless gunpowder, quick-firing field artillery and, at sea, the torpedo, the mine, the submarine and finally the all-big-gun battleship. Political leaders as well as the nascent peace movement appreciated modern war's expanding destructive capacity. The British Prime Minister, Lord Salisbury, in his 9 November 1897 speech at the Guildhall, spoke in this vein:

> You notice that on all sides the instruments of destruction, the piling up of arms, are becoming larger and larger. The powers of concentration are becoming greater, the instruments of death more active and more numerous, and are improved with every year; and each nation is bound, for its own safety's sake, to take part in this competition.[3]

Although no idealist of peace, Salisbury recognised the inherent threat posed by an arms race. However, in his view, international disarmament was not the solution. In his reply accepting the Russian invitation to the peace conference, Salisbury argued that advances in armaments in fact contributed to Europe's stability. The perfection of modern weapons, he insisted, 'and the horrible carnage and destruction which would ensue from their employment on a large scale, have acted no doubt as a serious deterrent from war'. The burden imposed by their enormous financial costs and the consequent 'unrest and discontent' among European populations was what made them so dangerous to 'internal and external tranquillity', he concluded.[4] Other commentators also believed disarmament was detrimental to peace, arguing that it was impossible to implement in practice or indeed actively dangerous to both international security and the very vitality of the human spirit.[5]

The story of the first Hague Peace Conference's summoning by Tsar Nicholas II is well known. At the 24 August 1898 weekly reception at the Ministry for Foreign Affairs for the diplomatic corps of St Petersburg, Count Mouraviev (the Russian Minister of Foreign Affairs) presented the assembled representatives with the Tsar's memorandum calling for the convening of an international conference to consider the 'grave problem' created by the unprecedented growth in armaments. The Tsar's note had as its opening contention:

> The maintenance of general peace and a possible reduction of the excessive armaments which weigh upon all nations present themselves, in the existing condition of the whole world, as the ideal towards which the endeavours of all Governments should be directed.[6]

There was much more, of course, but the proclaimed objective was clear: disarmament. All the European diplomatic establishments were taken by surprise. Their responses varied, mixing suspicion with excitement. From the politicians, diplomats and soldiers of Europe: could Russia be trusted? From the wider public, articulated by the peace societies that had sprung up across the globe since the mid-nineteenth century: could this be the chance at last to bring a halt to the terrifying militarisation of the world? As Barbara Tuchman noted in her still suggestive narrative, phrases such as 'a new epoch in civilisation', 'dawn of a new era', and 'omen for the new century', appeared in press reports worldwide.[7] The *New York Times* indeed called it 'the beginning of the most momentous and beneficent movement of modern history—indeed, of all history'.[8]

In the lead-up to the conference, the disarmament question generated the greatest public and diplomatic interest. Yet most of the invited governments considered the idea of arms limitation unwelcome, unrealistic and potentially highly dangerous. Salisbury remarked, with some understatement, that 'it will be a very arduous task [to arrive at a formula which] would command the assent of all the European Powers'.[9] The initial British reaction was thus cautious and stalling, couched in inquiries for more information. When Salisbury wrote to the ambassador in St Petersburg, he raised in a series of questions the same key issues that would resonate with every subsequent discussion of disarmament during the ensuing decades:

> Is the Congress to be allowed at the instance of one or of a majority of the Powers to discuss existing causes which might lead to hostilities, e.g., Alsace-Lorraine, Constantinople, Afghanistan, Egypt? Are armaments

> to be fixed according to area, population, or wealth, or all three? Is the defensibility of a country or the reverse to be taken into account and if so who is to be the judge of it? If any country refuses to disarm, are the other countries to go to war with her in the interests of peace?[10]

The sharp tongue of the young Foreign Office official Eyre Crowe contained no such reserve: he lashed out at 'the silly rubbish' in the Tsar's note.[11]

As to the motives prompting the Tsar's move, the most common view among the foreign ministries in Europe was that it was flowery and idealised language used to cover a cynical attempt to reduce the financial strain on Russia caused by the swelling arms race. In Berlin, Kaiser Wilhelm II considered the proposal to be no more than an attempt to circumvent the enormous expense required for Russia to develop and equip itself with new quick-firing artillery. He noted dismissively on the letter from his foreign minister, Bernhard von Bülow, that: 'The whole lucubration seems to me to come from Russia's grim necessity of escaping from her financial mess'.[12] As the Germans themselves predicted, the most ambivalent reaction came from Paris. France was Russia's ally, yet had only been informed a few hours before the announcement. When the British ambassador called on foreign minister Théophile Delcassé on 29 August, he noted in astonishment that 'it seems almost incredible that a step of such a nature should have been taken at St Petersburg without preliminary consultation with the professed ally at Paris'.[13] In a world without established mechanisms for negotiating substantial changes to the international system or territorial boundaries, espousing disarmament implied an acceptance of the status quo. Given that France remained utterly unreconciled to its loss of Alsace and Lorraine to Germany, there was little support among policymakers in Paris for the Tsar's proposal.[14]

Despite all the reservations, however, the Russian initiative could not be ignored: it had to be addressed by governments because it came from the Tsar directly. Public and diplomatic necessities required at the very least non-committal applause for the lofty ideals put forward.[15] As to international public opinion, the call for a 'Disarmament Conference' by the Tsar of Russia attracted vehement interest. Some was unreflexively positive, expecting unobtainable results; other commentary was sceptical and suspicious of Russian motives, proposing all sorts of hidden agendas. The key feature for most was that, this time, the call for action on disarmament had been initiated by one of the great powers; surely, something now *had* to be done. The Austrian peace activist, Baroness Bertha von Suttner, recorded her initial astonishment and then happiness at seeing the contents of the Russian note in the newspaper: 'I recollect that hour which, after receiving these tidings ... My Own [husband] and I spent together discussing the marvellous event from all sides; it was one of the loveliest hours of our lives'.[16] The months before the conference saw widespread and unceasing campaigning by peace activists in multiple countries, particularly the chief

European powers. Women's groups in particular agitated for whole-hearted support of the conference's aims and for genuine engagement by governments. In France, a petition sponsored by the *Ligue des Femmes pour le Désarmement International* in favour of the Tsar's proposal garnered over one million signatures. In Britain, the journalist W.T. Stead influenced the high public profile of the approaching conference, calling for a 'pilgrimage of peace' to pressure reluctant governments to engage with its aims. During the four months following the Tsar's manifesto, over 750 resolutions from public groups were received in the Foreign Office welcoming the idea and calling for British efforts to make it succeed, with over 650 more appearing in 1899. Even in Germany there was controlled excitement: indeed, the spring leading up to the opening of the conference was the only time during the *Kaiserreich* that the German peace movement held mass meetings in several large cities.[17]

Faced with the swirling mix of reactions, it is perhaps unsurprising that Mouraviev so quickly sought to clarify and circumscribe the initial Russian proposal's meaning. Out of the blue once again, in January 1899, the Russian government distributed a second circular. It involved a considerable shift from the original note's contents and tone and instead laid out eight more specific points that would compromise the conference's programme. The generalised call for disarmament was now reduced to a single, opening point:

> An understanding stipulating the non-augmentation, for a term to be agreed upon, of the present effective land and sea forces, as well as the war budgets pertaining to them; preliminary study of the ways in which even a reduction of the aforesaid effectives and budgets could be realized in future.[18]

Points two to four concerned prohibiting new land and naval firearms, new types of more powerful explosive (especially if thrown from balloons), the use of submarines in war and the future construction of warships armed with rams. However, the remaining points also introduced two additional topics: the laws of war and the principle of international arbitration to settle disputes between states. These new ideas redirected the conference's focus, in an implicit admission that the original intentions had been abandoned. When Mouraviev toured several of the capitals in Europe to explain more fully the revised nature of Russian intentions, he hardly met a warm welcome. Trying to prepare the way for the approaching meeting, he proposed that the powers might agree to impose a limit of a fixed percentage of their populations that might be called to arms, thus enabling a great reduction in the size of standing armies while still leaving the basic proportions and military balance unchanged. 'Idiot', scribbled Kaiser Wilhelm II in the margins of this memorandum.[19] Peace advocates, meanwhile, resented most of the topics in the second Russian note because these aimed merely to modify or alleviate the practice of war; they saw the task as abolishing war itself.

It is hardly surprising that substantial confusion reigned. The approaching conference was taking place in a void, without true diplomatic precedents. It lacked clear agreement even upon the nature of the specific problem to be tackled: was it to end war (motivated by nineteenth-century notions of a new reign of peace), to alleviate economic burdens (caused by growing arms expenditure), to draft new means of settling disputes in pacific fashion (in keeping with the growing trend towards international arbitration), to advance international law (through codification of widely accepted state practices in war) or even to deal with internal social unrest (addressing popular discontent over service in mass armies and the tax burden required to maintain them)? Continuing governmental reluctance was aptly captured in the leading article in *The Times* commenting upon the British delegation's departure for The Hague. In common with many observers during these months, the paper viewed the conference and its meaning from the perspective of Russian motivations, rather than as a multilateral conference joined to consider common goals of peace:

> The idea of general disarmament seems never to have been seriously regarded as feasible even by the Russian Emperor himself. The idea of an arrest of armaments ... is universally abandoned. ... The wisest thing for statesmen and diplomatists to do is to adopt [Prince Bismarck's] advice and leave such matters 'to the peace societies'.[20]

As the conference prepared to meet, therefore, the gap between cautious governments and newly energised peace communities was all too evident. 'I will go to this conference comedy', the all-too-quotable Kaiser scribbled, 'but I will dance the waltz with a sword by my side'.[21]

The essential problem confronting the conference's First Commission, which addressed the disarmament issue, was that governments had never before tackled the idea through multilateral negotiation in peace time.[22] Daunted by the task, the delegates started considering the second Russian circular's points two to four. This quickly led them into a maze of specialised technical arguments about land and sea weapons. The complexities confounded quick solutions. Indeed, they found it difficult at times even to clarify basic terminology or to agree upon the essential nature of the questions they were asking. With such a short timeframe, it was hopeless to expect too much from this first ever systematic consideration of disarmament as a global issue. It was only after more than a month that the commission turned to address the general aspects of arms limitation contained in the opening point of the Russian note. Progress here proved similarly elusive. Yet the critical point remains that even these abortive discussions were of enormous value as the first steps along a very long road. The conference debates represented the first efforts to flesh out the issues confronting states in negotiating disarmament agreements. They were wide-ranging and revealed much regarding the conceptions and possibilities envisioned for international disarmament. If the ideas were still too unfamiliar to be acceptable, or indeed for some delegates to perceive as worthy of serious consideration, they nonetheless opened a conversation on specific approaches to international disarmament that continues to this day.

The work on disarmament at the 1899 conference can be divided analytically into six main aspects, although these aspects overlapped during the several weeks of discussion and were neither perceived nor treated as coherent categories by the delegates themselves. The consistent theme among them, however, was not reductions to existing armaments levels but rather a pause in the ongoing arms competition. All the main proposals aimed primarily to halt matters where they stood, whether in terms of national expenditure, the development of more powerful weapons, or numbers of men under arms. The implication, for those powers that supported these initiatives, was that the existing status quo constituted a reasonable equilibrium for armaments among the major and minor states.

The first form of disarmament considered was via the prohibition of the development of new, more advanced types of specific classes of weapons. A set of similar Russian and Dutch proposals called for a five-year moratorium during which the small arms currently in service with all national armies would not be replaced by any new models. Improvements were to be permitted, provided that the fundamental type was not changed. The overarching intent was to limit any further increase in the destructiveness of these weapons but also to reduce costs by halting the incessant rearmament of land forces with newer models. Objections came from several directions. Military officers insisted that it was impossible to determine at what point incremental improvements in fact evolved into a fundamentally new type of weapon. More specific propositions to limit guns, either by weight, calibre, muzzle velocity or rate of fire, all foundered because of an inability to agree upon terms. Several delegates also argued that none of these characteristics could be used as the basis for a workable agreement as they were impossible to separate, nor would restricting any of them lead to an overall reduction in destructiveness or inhumanity. The Russians also proposed a three-year moratorium on the development of new types of naval guns and fixing a maximum size of naval gun calibre. These provoked similar objections regarding the impossibility of defining 'new' versions of existing weapons and how the interdependence of weaponry meant that any control of gun calibres would be useless without also drafting controls for armour plating, shell weight, initial gun velocity and so on.

Second was an effort to limit troop numbers via imposing a 'freeze' at current levels. In effect, it was a call to halt the expansion of the new mass armies. The Russian proposal was for a 'non-augmentation' to existing troop numbers in the motherland (i.e. excluding the colonies) in time of peace for a five-year trial period. The plan avoided actual reductions to current forces, although it did provide for further discussion of setting agreed maximum numbers of soldiers for each state (again not including colonial troops) once the idea of a freeze was accepted. Future conferences could take on the task of discussing reducing troop numbers. Again, the idea was rejected: on the basis that it was too difficult to fix troop numbers, even only for five years, without at the same time regulating too many other elements of national defence to be practicable.

Third, and directly linked to the second aspect, was the limitation of armed forces through the imposition of caps on total national spending. The Russian delegates proposed a five-year hold on increases to existing military budgets, matched by a three-year 'halting period' on naval budgets. The Russian conference president, Baron de Staal, insisted:

> What we are hoping for is to attain a limitation—a halt in the ascending course of armaments and expenses. We propose this with the conviction that if such agreement is established, progress in other directions will be made—slowly perhaps, but surely. Immobility is an impossibility in history, and if we shall only be able for some years to provide for a certain stability, everything points to the belief that a tendency toward a diminution of military charges will be able to grow and develop.[23]

It was the single most cogent expression throughout the conference of the idea that once a halt to armaments growth had been established, confidence in the legitimacy of such a voluntary control regime would steadily build over time and real reductions could ultimately follow. There was great reluctance all round, but most particularly from the naval delegates. They argued that the matter of budgets was in the sole competence of national parliaments, that serious constitutional issues might arise in countries with a requirement to pledge the budgetary vote in advance, that national budgetary years did not coincide and that naval and colonial budgets were very hard to differentiate. Furthermore, because Russia's arguments were framed in terms of the beneficial savings that would result in burdensome peace time armaments expenditure, many responses did not address this indirect form of budgetary limitation's efficacy but rather (as in the controversial reply by Germany's Colonel von Schwarzhoff) insisted that armaments did not in fact leave their peoples 'crushed beneath the weight of expenditures and taxes'.[24] Once again, an ambitious new idea was stalled.

Fourth was the critical issue of verification: how were participating states to ensure that all signatories kept to their commitments under any disarmament agreement? The Dutch delegate argued that control would come through mutual trust: states would abide by the agreements they made because of their own sense of their 'nation's honour'.[25] The Russian delegate similarly asserted that the best guarantee 'resides in the good faith of the contracting parties, in the control of public opinion'—an ironic position coming from perhaps the most autocratic state in Europe.[26] Yet, as Schwarzhoff noted in the debate on the issue of the proposed moratorium on new types of guns, it was not only an issue of policing potential violations.

It was also about independent assessment of what constituted allowable or disallowable conduct under any agreement.

> It would be very difficult to determine what improvements could be adopted without constituting as a whole a new type of gun. What changes should be permitted? Where is the authority who would decide these questions? In case of doubt it would be necessary, in order honestly to carry out the clauses of the Convention, to make the new model known to the other Powers and ask them for their consent before adopting it. As this is hardly possible, he regrets having to vote against the proposition.[27]

Neither notions of honour, mutual trust nor the power of public opinion were persuasive as effective checks upon state behaviour. It seemed impossible to many delegates to envisage any limitation at all upon a state's complete freedom of action in an area so vital to national security. When the three-year moratorium on new naval guns was proposed, several delegates noted that this would require an inspection system in order to work. But, as the British naval delegate Admiral Sir John Fisher objected, 'would the nations not consider such a "control" as an assault on their sovereignty'?[28]

Fifth were proposals for the exchange of information: facilitating disarmament through the development of subsidiary confidence-building measures. Here the Russian proposal, advanced in conjunction with their proposed three-year freeze on naval budgets, was for all states to publish during that period the figures for the total tonnage of warships which they planned for construction (without defining the types of ships themselves), their current numbers of naval officers and men and their current expenses for all coast fortifications. The intention was to create some transparency and basis for open comparison. Unsurprisingly, perhaps, it too was rejected as being open to abuse as well as an infringement on sovereignty.

Sixth, and finally, came the well-known proscription of specific weapons—the only area where concrete outcomes were ultimately obtained. The first prohibition, on bombardment from balloons for a five-year term, was widely accepted without substantial demure. The key issue here was a lack of clarity about how this form of warfare might develop—it was four years before the Wright brothers' first flight—hence the decision to impose the ban for five years only. The second prohibition, on the use of projectiles intended to diffuse 'asphyxiating or deleterious gases', passed with near unanimity. The potential for gas to be used as an instrument of mass destruction in war was not yet envisaged.[29] The third prohibition, on the use of expanding ('dum-dum') bullets, that were seen as essentially inhumane weapons which inflicted superfluous injury, generated by far the most debate and ultimately also received near unanimous agreement. The primary objections came from the British delegates, who defended their country's right to retain use of weapons considered by others to be 'barbarous' due to the challenges of policing their imperial holdings. The British military delegate Sir John Ardagh's arguments regarding military necessity were bluntly racist:

> In civilized war a soldier penetrated by a small projectile is wounded, withdraws to the ambulance, and does not advance any further. It is very different with a savage. Even though pierced two or three times, he does not cease to march forward, does not call upon the hospital attendants, but continues on, and before anyone has time to explain to him that he is flagrantly violating the decisions of the Hague Conference, he cuts off your head.[30]

Ultimately the declaration passed, despite British and American refusals. It was easy for others to ban something they did not use and to enjoy criticising Britain in the process.[31]

But, there also were discussions on prohibiting several other weapons that did not succeed. The banning of submarine torpedoes and of warships with rams were both raised. Interestingly, smaller states resisted in this case on the basis that they were cheap and affordable ways for lesser powers to defend their coasts and thus served (in the words of a Dutch delegate) as 'weapons of the weak'.[32] This was in keeping with a trend present throughout all discussions: smaller states insisted that they not be disadvantaged by any agreement. Whether in refitting their armies with the most up-to-date guns or their navies with newer ships, they needed to be allowed to catch up with the larger powers (in terms of modern weapons types, not actual numbers) before any moratorium on further changes could be fairly imposed. In addition, the fact that there was debate at all, however brief, on the future significance of electricity and chemistry in warfare was remarkable, even if it was quickly adjourned as being too speculative. As in other areas of the debates, there was resistance to sweeping prohibitions on new developments regarding future means of warfare (particularly through technological advances) on the basis that these could in fact be both substantially more humane than existing means, and also far less expensive.

As a means to provide some cover for the gap between the great prior expectations on disarmament and the very limited concrete gains that ultimately emerged—the successes over international law and arbitration notwithstanding—the French delegate Léon Bourgeois proposed that the conference at least agree to a general expression that 'the limitation of armaments would be a benefit to humanity'.[33] As his delegation reported back to Paris, 'it appeared vital to us that the labours of the First Commission were not closed on an entirely negative note, with a declaration of impotence and near ill will'.[34] As a consequence, the conference's Final Act included a resolution recording the unanimous opinion 'that the restriction of military charges, which are at present a heavy burden on the world, is extremely desirable for the increase of the material and moral welfare of mankind'. It also concluded in two *voeux* (essentially statements of future hopes) that governments should further study the technical challenges of limiting specific weapons and the general problem of limiting armed forces or military budgets.[35] These diplomatic wishes were not entirely insubstantial. In referring the problems of disarmament for further study, the delegates ensured that the issue did not evaporate. None of the ideas raised at the 1899 conference had ever been tackled directly before and none had yet matured sufficiently to be considered by any major government. It was too much to expect that specific mechanisms for arms control, which would necessarily demand derogations of sovereignty, were going to follow from discussions lasting only a matter of weeks. But at these meetings' end, the issue was not dismissed as intractable and unceremoniously shelved. On the contrary, and in no small part as a response to the public expectations now surrounding the issue, debate and discussion on disarmament within the diplomatic framework was institutionalised.

The 'failure' of progress on disarmament was widely and predictably criticised at the end of the conference by voices within the peace movement and the popular press, though this was mitigated by the unexpected and popular success of the arbitration measures. The British lead delegate, Sir Julian Pauncefote, was convinced that peace advocates need not feel defeated by the failure of disarmament discussions. He told Suttner on 30 June:

> I can assure you ... the Conference is doing a great work, and other conferences will follow. To be sure, the limitation clause was voted down, yet with the general declaration that it must be taken up later.[36]

Though it would be in vastly different circumstances than he could have predicted, Pauncefote's prediction proved correct. The issue remained prominent over the following 15 years, not least because of the acceleration of the armaments race in Europe. Though most states refused the chance to reopen the disarmament debates at the 1907 Hague Peace Conference, despite some British efforts to do so, it took considerable diplomatic effort to side-track the issue. The divisive potential of arms-control talks was perceived as likely only to exacerbate the state of international relations.[37]

The terrors of the cataclysm of 1914–1918 were needed for policymakers to join public peace advocates in a common belief that disarmament was a critical condition of ensuring peace. The pre-war notion had been that armaments created stability, as a typical article in *The Times* in May 1899 had insisted: 'An undoubted effect of perfecting armament is to restrict war; it is still true that efficient preparation is the best security for peace and that weakness invites attack'.[38] Such an assertion was by 1918 untenable as a publicly defensible proposition; instead many blamed the arms race itself for the catastrophic war. The former British Foreign Secretary, Sir Edward Grey, most famously encapsulated this view in his memoirs, writing in 1925 that 'the enormous growth of armaments in Europe, the sense of insecurity and fear caused by them—it was these that made war inevitable'.[39]

As ambitious and idealistic hopes for large-scale international disarmament captured the public imagination, popular opinion worldwide seized upon the prospect that international peace would be found through reducing national armaments, thus making disarmament's success a test of the new League of Nations' worth and indeed a shorthand expression for a guarantee of lasting peace. Article 8 of the League Covenant enshrined disarmament as an integral part of the new organisation's purpose. It stipulated that member states 'recognise that the maintenance of peace requires the reduction of national armaments to the lowest point consistent with national safety' and directed the League Council to 'formulate plans for such reduction'.[40] Member states were now required to engage with disarmament, including even the possibility of a final settlement being imposed upon them. The culmination of a twisting and often dead-ended road was the great World Disarmament Conference which opened in Geneva in February 1932. The combined membership of the pro-disarmament organisations that made presentations at its opening session was perhaps 200 million people, approximately ten per cent of the world's population at the time.[41]

Between 1920 and the mid-1930s, the League oversaw a series of determined attempts to implement substantive disarmament by international agreement.[42] Many of the specific ideas that interwar policymakers grappled with were the same as those faced by the delegates in 1899. But, crucially, the context had shifted, not only regarding armaments' relationship to war but also in the existence of new concepts of international organisation and state obligations that made disarmament agreements more feasible (at least in theory). Where the earlier efforts had concluded only with the three declarations prohibiting highly specific weapons types, the main thrust of the interwar initiatives was towards the other approaches which had failed: in particular, the political acceptance of quantitative limits on the number of 'effectives' (trained men currently under arms) in armed forces and on weapons which were acknowledged as legal and acceptable.

The first aspect, limiting armaments by controls on weapons types, formed one core of the major negotiations of the 1920s. The tonnage and gun-calibre restrictions for capital ships agreed at the naval conference held in Washington in 1921–1922, and for cruisers at the naval conference in London in 1930—though it is true that neither was actually part of the League's process—both took direct limitation as their main approach. Still, the League's disarmament talks in the later 1920s also constantly debated varying proposals for direct limitation of armaments. For example, discussions considered the number of military aircraft each state was to be permitted, though in the end no agreement could be reached and the talks turned to indirect approaches instead. At the World Disarmament Conference a final, if largely unenthusiastic attempt came in the 1933 British 'MacDonald plan', the first to include suggested figures for each nation's armaments levels. It failed amidst the general crisis of the conference resulting from Adolf Hitler's accession to power in Germany two months earlier. The second aspect, limiting troop numbers through a freeze at current levels, was reflected in arguments throughout the 1920s about how to impose specific caps on the quantity of effectives in each state's land, sea and air forces. The Treaty of Versailles set the baseline by limiting the German army to 100,000 officers and men. Leaving aside the German refusal to accept any permanent inferiority in numbers, what blocked any agreement among the former victorious powers was the issue of 'trained reserves' (civilians who had received military training and could be recalled into the armed forces at short notice). The British and Americans, with small, all-volunteer land forces, wanted to place limits upon the number of a state's trained reservists as well as its serving soldiers by imposing limits on the size of annual contingents that could be called up for compulsory military service. The French, Japanese and other continental European states employing conscription, determined to maintain the overall numerical strength of their armies (including both serving soldiers and reserves), demanded that reserves be excluded from limitation.

The third aspect was the indirect approach of 'budgetary limitation'. Its strength was perceived to be its generalised nature, for it avoided the problem of managing specific limits on multiple individual weapons types. The League pursued attempts between 1921 and 1924 to place agreed upper limits on national military budgets via a freeze on all member states' military estimates. However, they foundered on the resistance of almost all participating states. Yet the idea of a freeze reappeared as a central element in the draft disarmament treaty of 1930, prepared for the upcoming World Disarmament Conference, though never adopted. Meanwhile, the 1931 League Assembly accepted an Italian initiative for a year-long 'armaments truce' under which states pledged (though were not formally bound) to refrain from any measures involving an increase in armaments. The intention was to create, echoing Baron de Staal's 1899 plea, 'a psychological and political atmosphere of greater calm and confidence' in the lead-up to the following year's disarmament conference.[43] The fourth issue of verification formed a critical component of the League's work towards a disarmament agreement. What was different was the existence of the League itself, precisely that supra-national body able to carry out the supervisory role that Schwarzhoff and Fisher had decried at The Hague. Here the French were adamant that there had to be an effective inspection system—a permanent body of experts to monitor any disarmament agreement—in order to provide confidence that states (specifically Germany) were abiding by their disarmament obligations. In contrast, the British and Americans would never agree to any form of truly substantive and institutionalised international control.

The fifth aspect was the exchange of information. Influenced by the new post-war demands for transparency and 'open diplomacy', Article 8 of the Covenant specifically called for member states to exchange 'full and frank information' on the scale of their armaments, military programmes and industrial production. This resulted, after some arguments over the extent of the project's intrusiveness, in the annual publication from 1924 to 1940 of a League *Armaments Year-Book* compiling information from open sources on key aspects of all national armed forces. Meanwhile the failed approach of budgetary limitation was, in the mid-1930s, eventually combined with the pursuit of transparency via proposals to adopt the even more indirect method of 'publicity of defence expenditure'. It was one of the few ideas to survive the World Disarmament Conference's 1934 collapse, with a draft convention on the subject discussed at the 1938 Assembly.

The sixth and final aspect was the prohibition of specific weapons. While this approach was in fact atypical for the interwar disarmament process, it nonetheless delivered the period's greatest triumph: the Protocol for the Prohibition of the Use in War of Asphyxiating, Poisonous or Other Gases, concluded in 1925. Based on the experiences with gas during the war, chemical weapons were singled out and banned as fundamentally cruel. The interwar period also saw impassioned debates over the possibility of banning military aircraft or alternatively restricting their use through a prohibition of aerial bombing. Debates over banning aerial bombing paralleled the earlier Hague arguments over the use of weapons considered as inhumane. As they had over dum-dum bullets, British representatives argued for the right to retain a practice widely considered to be barbarous for purposes of imperial policing in its remote colonial possessions.[44]

In 1899, nearly all informed observers considered disarmament to be premature; by the mid-1920s, no one felt that the idea's time had not yet come. But that did not make the problems or challenges any easier to solve. Achieving meaningful disarmament is hard. As the twentieth century's mixed record of success and more often failure makes all too clear, it takes enormous effort, good timing and no small degree of luck. During the four decades from 1899 to 1939, some disarmament attempts worked, some did not, and most of the talks came to no resolution at all. Those years certainly gave little indication that the ideal and pursuit of disarmament led to a wider expansion of moral development or belief in peace and common humanity. Rather, the point is that disarmament and arms control agreements are not ends in themselves: the ends are in fact the reduction of both the likelihood of war and the violence and inhumanity of the wars that do take place. As Richard Dean Burns argued in his classic 1977 overview on arms control:

> It is clear, by definition and by historical experience, that these mechanisms can greatly assist in the construction of a stable, peaceful international community, but that arms control and disarmament agreements cannot, by themselves, solve the political, economic, social, and moral problems that lie at the heart of the world's ills.[45]

This view stands in melancholy contrast to the views of those peace campaigners of a century before who believed that universal disarmament could achieve precisely those larger ends.

Notes

1. For one example among many, see D.F. Vagts. (2000). The Hague Conventions and Arms Control. *American Journal of International Law*, 94(1), pp.31–41.
2. There is an extensive literature on nineteenth-century peace movements. Still among the most useful studies are A.C.F. Beales. (1931). *A History of Peace: A Short Account of the Organised Movements for International Peace*. London: G. Bell & Sons; F.S. Lyons. (1963). *Internationalism in Europe, 1815–1914*. Leiden: A.W. Sijthoff; S.E. Cooper. (1991). *Patriotic Pacifism: Waging War on War in Europe, 1815–1914*. Oxford: Oxford University Press.
3. Salisbury speech, Guildhall, quoted in *The Times* (London), 10 November 1897, p.6.
4. Salisbury to Scott (St Petersburg), 24 October 1898, no. 269. In: (1927). *British Documents on the Origins of the War, 1898–1914*. Vol. 1, London: HMSO.
5. The most famous soldier of the day, Field Marshal von Moltke, in an open letter published in the *Revue de droit international* (1881), insisted: 'War is an element of the divine order of the world. In it are developed the noblest virtues of man: courage and self-denial, fidelity to duty and the spirit of sacrifice ... Without war, the world would stagnate and lose itself in materialism.'
6. Russian first circular note, 24 August 1898. In: J.B. Scott, ed., (1918). *The Hague Conventions and Declarations of 1899 and 1907*. 3rd ed., New York: Oxford University Press, pp.xv–xvi.
7. B.W. Tuchman. (1966). *The Proud Tower: A Portrait of the World before the War, 1890–1914*. London: Hamish Hamilton, p.230.
8. Quoted in *The Times* (London), 30 August 1898, p.3.
9. Salisbury to Scott (St Petersburg), 14 February 1899, quoted in D. Hucker. (2015). British Peace Activism and 'New' Diplomacy: Revisiting the 1899 Hague Peace Conference. *Diplomacy & Statecraft*, 26(3), p.408.
10. Salisbury to Scott (St Petersburg), 30 August 1898, no. 261. In: *British Documents on Origins of War*, vol. 1.
11. Crowe to his mother, 1 September 1898, quoted in Hucker, p.408.
12. Bülow to Wilhelm II, 28 August 1898. In: E.T.S. Dugdale, ed., (1930). *German Diplomatic Documents, 1871–1914*. Vol. 3, London: Methuen, p.74.
13. Monson (Paris) to Salisbury, 1 September 1898, no. 262. In: *British Documents on the Origins of the War*. Vol. 1.
14. Nos. 306–309. In: (1957). *Documents Diplomatiques Français Relatifs aux Origines de la Guerre de 1914*. Vol. 14, Paris: Imprimerie nationale.
15. On other international reactions, including from Austria–Hungary, Italy, Turkey, Japan and the United States, see A. Eyffinger. (1999). *The 1899 Hague Peace Conference: 'The Parliament of Man, the Federation of the World'*. The Hague: Kluwer Law International, pp.28–29.
16. B. von Suttner. (1910). *Memoirs: The Records of an Eventful Life*. Vol. 2, Boston and London: Ginn & Co., pp.187–189.
17. S.E. Cooper (2011). French Feminists and Pacifism, 1889–1914: The Evolution of New Visions. *Peace & Change*, 36(1), pp.12–13; Hucker, pp.409–415; J. Dülffer. (1988). Citizens and Diplomats: The Debate on the First Hague Conference (1899) in Germany. In: C. Chatfield and P. van den Dungen, eds., *Peace Movements and Political Cultures*. Knoxville: University of Tennessee Press, pp.23–39. For a sharper view on the contribution made by Stead, see A. Higgins' chapter in this collection.
18. Russian second circular note, 11 January 1899. In: Scott, *Hague Conventions*, pp.xvii–xix.
19. 22 December 1899, no. 4233. In: (1924). *Die Grosse Politik der Europäischen Kabinette, 1871–1914*. Vol. 15, Berlin: DVFPG.

20 *The Times* (London), 16 May 1899, p.11.
21 15 May 1899, no. 4257. In: *Die Grosse Politik*. Vol. 15.
22 For the full record of the disarmament debates: J.B. Scott, ed., (1920). *The Proceedings of the Hague Peace Conferences: The Conference of 1899*. New York: Oxford University Press, pp.271–380. The discussion which follows is taken from Scott; I have only provided specific references for direct quotations. For the best historical accounts addressing the disarmament debates: M. Tate. (1942). *The Disarmament Illusion: The Movement for a Limitation of Armaments to 1907*. New York: Macmillan; C. Davis. (1962). *The United States and the First Hague Peace Conference*. Ithaca: Cornell University Press; J. Dülffer (1981). *Regeln Gegen den Krieg? Die Haager Friedenskonferenzen von 1899 und 1907 in der Internationalen Politik*. Frankfurt, Berlin and Vienna: Ullstein Verlag; D.J. Bettez. (1988). Unfulfilled Initiative: Disarmament Negotiations and the Hague Peace Conferences of 1899 and 1907. *RUSI Journal*, 133(3), pp.57–62; S.A. Keefer. (2006). Building the Palace of Peace: The Hague Conference of 1899 and Arms Control in the Progressive Era. *Journal of the History of International Law*, 8, pp.1–17.
23 Staal (Russia), First Commission, 4th meeting, 23 June 1899. In: Scott, *Proceedings*, p.301.
24 Schwarzhoff (Germany), First Commission, 5th meeting, 25 June 1899. In: Scott, *Proceedings*, p.309.
25 Poortugael (Netherlands), First Commission: First Sub-Commission, 4th meeting, 7 June 1899. In: Scott, *Proceedings*, p.351.
26 Raffalovich (Russia), First Commission: First Sub-Commission, 4th meeting, 7 June 1899. In: Scott, *Proceedings*, p.353.
27 Schwarzhoff (Germany), First Commission: First Sub-Commission, 3rd meeting, 31 May 1899. In: Scott, *Proceedings*, p.345.
28 Fisher (Britain), First Commission: Second Sub-Commission, 1st meeting, 26 May 1899. In: Scott, *Proceedings*, p.360.
29 See the chapter by M. Dorsey in this collection.
30 Ardagh (Britain), First Commission: First Sub-Commission, 3rd meeting, 31 May 1899. In: Scott, *Proceedings*, p.343.
31 S. Keefer. (2014). 'Explosive missals': International Law, Technology, and Security in Nineteenth-Century Disarmament Conferences. *War in History*, 21(4), pp.445–464.
32 Tadema (Netherlands), First Commission: Second Sub-Commission, 3rd meeting, 31 May 1899. In: Scott, *Proceedings*, p.367.
33 Bourgeois (France), First Commission, 6th meeting, 30 June 1899. In: Scott, *Proceedings*, p.318.
34 French delegation (Hague) to Delcassé, 2 July 1899, no. 228. In: (1959) *Documents Diplomatiques Français Relatifs aux Origines de la Guerre de 1914*. (1959). Vol. 15, Paris: Imprimerie Nationale.
35 Final Act of the International Peace Conference, The Hague, 29 July 1899. In: Scott, *Hague Conventions*, pp.28–29.
36 Suttner, *Memoirs*. Vol. 2, p.309.
37 D. Stevenson. (1996). *Armaments and the Coming of War: Europe, 1904–1914*. Oxford: Oxford University Press, pp.105–111.
38 *The Times*, 16 May 1899, p.6.
39 Lord Grey of Fallodon. [Sir Edward Grey] (1925). *Twenty-Five Years, 1892–1916*. Vol. 1, London: Hodder and Stoughton, p.90.
40 The Avalon Project at Yale Law School. *The Covenant of the League of Nations*. [online] Available at: www.avalon.law.yale.edu/20th_century/leagcov.asp [Accessed 22 June 2016].

41 T.R. Davies. (2007). *The Possibilities of Transnational Activism: The Campaign for Disarmament between the Two World Wars*. Leiden and Boston: Martinus Nijhoff, p.159. See also P.M.H. Bell. (2003). Peace movements. In: R. Boyce and J.A. Maiolo, eds., *The Origins of World War Two: The Debate Continues*, Basingstoke: Palgrave Macmillan, pp.273–285.
42 The following discussion of the interwar disarmament process is drawn from: A. Webster. (2005). The Transnational Dream: Politicians, Diplomats and Soldiers in the League of Nations' Pursuit of International Disarmament, 1920–1938. *Contemporary European History*, 14(4), pp.493–518; idem. (2005). Making Disarmament Work: The Implementation of The International Disarmament Provisions in the League of Nations Covenant, 1919–1925. *Diplomacy & Statecraft*, 16(3), pp.551–570; and idem. (2006). From Versailles to Geneva: The Many Forms of Interwar Disarmament. *Journal of Strategic Studies*, 29(2), pp.225–246. See also the very useful R.D. Burns. (2009). *The Evolution of Arms Control: From Antiquity to the Nuclear Age*. Santa Barbara: ABC-Clio.
43 Grandi (Italy), 8 September 1931. In: League of Nations. (1931). *Official Journal*, special supplement 93, Geneva, pp.38–42.
44 See D.E. Omissi. (1990). *Air Power and Colonial Control: The Royal Air Force, 1919–1939*. Manchester: Manchester University Press; P. Satia. (2006). The Defense of Inhumanity: Air control and the British idea of Arabia. *American Historical Review*, 111(1), pp.16–51.
45 R.D. Burns. (1977). *Arms Control and Disarmament: A Bibliography*. Santa Barbara: ABC-Clio, p.6.

5 More than just a taboo

The legacy of the chemical warfare prohibitions of the 1899 and 1907 Hague Conferences

M. Girard Dorsey[1]

In 2012, US President Barack Obama drew a 'red line' for Syria's government by suggesting that, if it used chemical weapons in its civil war, the United States might intervene militarily.[2] Similarly, in 1991, reacting to fears that Saddam Hussein might use weapons of mass destruction on coalition troops in the First Gulf War, President George H.W. Bush had warned Iraq that the United States 'will not tolerate the use of chemical or biological weapons ... The American people would demand the strongest possible response'.[3] Earlier still, during the Second World War, British Prime Minister Winston Churchill and the US President Franklin Roosevelt had broadcast explicit ultimatums to the Axis powers about what would happen if they used chemical weapons.[4] In each conflict, the message has been clear: chemical weapons were beyond the pale of regular warfare, regardless of how devastating the conflict had become.

Governments felt compelled to issue warnings against the use of chemical weapons, even though diplomacy intended to prevent such use goes back to the nineteenth century. The foundational treaties in this area, the 1899 and 1907 Hague Conventions, were the first in a line of arms control efforts to limit or ban poison gas as a weapon of war. In 1899, the language was quite specific: Declaration II prohibited 'the use of projectiles the sole object of which is the diffusion of asphyxiating or deleterious gases'.[5] The 1899 Convention also outlawed 'poison or poisoned weapons'. The 1907 Hague Convention reiterated and reinforced the latter ban and also rejected arms that caused 'unnecessary suffering'.[6] Both of these phrases could describe chemical weapons.

Nevertheless, in 1915 Germany used poison gas on the Western Front, introducing modern chemical warfare to the world.[7] On the surface, therefore, the Hague treaties failed to prevent chemical warfare. The German deployment of gas, and the subsequent Allied retaliation in kind, certainly violated the spirit of the Hague agreements. While some argue that Germany did not break the technical letter of the Hague laws, the public and historical perception is that they did.[8] Thus the first legacy of The Hague's anti-gas clauses is an historical judgement that the treaties failed. However, the use of gas in 1915 is but one way of gauging the success or failure of the Hague Convention.

I argue, as does Richard Price, that by prohibiting the use of chemical weapons, the 1899 Hague Peace Conference's Declaration II provided the foundation for a new international norm: chemical weapons should be taboo among nations because they were 'uncivilised'. Declaration II was unique and is an important legacy of the Hague conferences because it made the use of chemical weapons illegal, even before such weapons had actually been invented.[9] Given that arms control, and particularly chemical-weapons arms control, is still an important international issue today, it is worth recognising that The Hague's legacies both helped and hindered future efforts to proscribe chemical weapons. Positive legacies include the actual efforts at prohibiting the use of asphyxiating gas in wartime, as well as the shift towards incorporating scientific expertise in drafting and implementing treaties to eradicate technical loopholes in agreements. However, some of the legacies are also negative, such as the enhancing of the sense of distrust and vilification of Germany, during the First World War and through the Second, which hindered the chemical-arms control process during that period. This chapter examines the circumstances surrounding the three main anti-chemical warfare treaties following the Hague agreements, namely the 1922 Washington Naval Conference, the 1925 Geneva Gas Protocol and the 1993 Chemical Weapons Convention.[10] In so doing, it demonstrates that The Hague's ban on chemical warfare had a long-reaching impact on chemical-weapons control that went well beyond its failure to prevent the gas attacks of the First World War. A broken arms-control agreement is not necessarily useless or ignorable.

Defining poison gas

Regardless of the range of compounds and the variety of damage they cause, the popular and official understandings of treaties outlawing chemical weapons is that they ban *all* wartime chemical weapons in spirit. This is true even if the letter of any particular law contains loopholes technically permitting some chemicals or deployment mechanisms. Poison gas, an early term for modern chemical weapons, covers a wide range of toxins. While experts quibble over certain elements of the definition, chemical weapons are lethal, damaging or irritating chemical compounds—whether solid, liquid or gaseous—deployed to injure humans. Traditionally, defoliants, incendiaries and germs were not defined as chemicals weapons. However, in recent decades, the definition of chemical weapons has widened to encompass these weapons and others.[11] Depending upon the molecular make-up of a toxic compound, chemical weapons can cause wide-ranging damage to their victims, including suffocation, blindness, serious burns, a weakened respiratory system and even cardiac arrest.[12] Chlorine, the first gas used in 1915, suffocated soldiers, while mustard gas—the toxin most commonly associated with the conflict and used even in the twenty-first century in the Middle East—can cause temporary blindness, blistered skin and mangled lungs.

Nevertheless, while chemical warfare continued as a feature of modern warfare, gas is not (and never has been) a mainstream weapon. Bans, such as those in the Hague conventions, helped to define chemical weapons from their inception as morally unacceptable and, except during the First World War, as marginal weapons in practice. Fear of their widespread use remained real throughout most of the twentieth century until the 1993 Chemical Weapons Convention. During the 1930s and 1940s, empires used chemical weapons occasionally in colonial conflicts against an adversary who was considered weaker and 'uncivilised', such as Italy's deployment of mustard gas in the Second Italian–Abyssinian War (1935–1936).[13] Both Allied and Axis forces largely avoided the use of chemical weapons on the battlefield during the Second World War, although the Japanese utilised and experimented with chemical agents in Chinese population centres during the first years of the Sino–Japanese War (1936–1945).[14] The Holocaust is a much more complex example, since the Nazis imprisoned their victims before gassing them; it was not an instance of chemical weapons being deployed on the battlefield by an attacking military. After 1945, chemical warfare tended to be wielded only by 'rogue states'.[15] Although the frequency and extent of its use has significantly decreased, lethal gas has thus remained in the arsenals of many states, such as Syria, despite successful efforts to eradicate it from most others, such as the United States.

Outlawing chemical warfare at The Hague

The 1899 Hague Peace Conference introduced chemical weapons to the moral and international law arena, providing the first major instance in which diplomats, military officers and jurists were able to debate the nature and role of poison gas in war. The conference reflected a broader concern regarding how and whether to include scientific expertise in the diplomacy of arms control. Beginning in the closing decades of the nineteenth century, many modernised societies—particularly Germany—transformed their chemical industries through new discoveries, increased production and varied applications of chemical products. The German revolution, for instance, yielded many positive changes including the development of aspirin and modern dyes.[16] Other developments had more destructive and harmful implications that would complicate the ideas and methods of fighting war in the near future by enabling chemical warfare. In particular, scientists discovered new toxic combinations such as xylol bromide (a type of tear gas) and experimented with existing compounds such as chlorine.

However, when the Hague conference convened in 1899, poison gas was only hypothetical.[17] In fact, the second circular Russia sent to potential attendees in January 1899 proposed studying a range of military issues, including projectiles or explosives from balloons and submarines, but did not include gas.[18] The rescript did make it clear that one of the conference's goals was to make war more humane, thus creating the opportunity for delegates to add poison gas to their agenda.[19] Even in 1899, delegates debated whether gas was in fact inhumane or even a poison. There was some speculation by the Dutch delegate plenipotentiary, A.P.C. van Karnebeek, that gas could 'endanger the existence of a large number of non-combatants, for instance, in the case of a siege', and thus be inhumane.[20] In contrast, Captain Alfred Thayer Mahan, the American naval delegate, rejected the idea. He argued that gas 'might even be considered as more humane than those which kill or cripple in a much more cruel manner, by tearing the body with pieces of metal.'[21] Delegates discussed more specifically whether gas was poison, an old and already taboo weapon of war tainted with associations of being uncivilised.[22] A Russian delegate, Captain Scheine, explicitly likened the use of poison gas to the practice of fouling rivers with poison.[23] Mahan, however, refuted Scheine's conceptualisation of gas and criticised the proposed declaration against its use. He argued that any potential gas weapon 'would involve neither useless cruelty nor bad faith, as exists in the case of poisoning waters'.[24] For Mahan, gas was a weapon that had to be deployed openly. Unlike poison, its release could neither be sneaky nor secret.

Although gas was not clearly a poison, it was also not simply a variation on existing explosives. Delegates considered gas to be a new kind of weapon. In fact, Scheine specifically rejected the opportunity to prohibit 'new explosives'. If the delegates thought that gas should be banned and that it was merely an updated explosive, then prohibiting 'new explosives' would be the appropriate course of action. Instead Scheine asked to outlaw a 'new *kind* [my italics] of explosive, the invention of which seems possible ... [specifically] the use of projectiles loaded with explosives which spread asphyxiating and deleterious gases'. In fact, the delegates crafted a proposal 'whose *purpose* was to distinguish chemical weapons, tools whose goal was to emit toxins, from currently existing explosives, armaments that emitted gas as an incidental byproduct'.[25] Still, it is important to note that delegates imagined gas would be launched in well-known, if modern, weapons: artillery shells. It makes sense to think that a new kind of weapon would utilise the most advanced form of deployment mechanisms then known, but that assumption limited their ability to conceive of all the ways a future gas weapon could be deployed. In turn, this inhibited delegates' ability to draft language that would ban all potential gas weapons.[26]

Yet delegates did not outlaw all new weapons; gas made the list, but submarines did not, despite extensive discussion.[27] Chemical weapons were completely new and possibly inhumane. Even Mahan had not argued that they were civilised in nature. He merely believed that 'it was no more cruel to asphyxiate one's enemies by means of deleterious gases than ... by drowning them, as happens when a vessel is sunk' by a submarine.[28] Van Karnebeek captured what the other delegates ultimately believed about poison gas: 'a fairly clear idea may already be formed of it; it is therefore easy to pass [judgement] on the subject' of its prohibition.[29] In contrast, there was no consensus reached about submarines. Some delegates wanted more time to consider submarines, others wanted to preserve the freedom to use them and one even doubted they could be effectively banned.[30] In essence, the delegates decided that they could predict the impact of an imaginary weapon but not one that had been the subject of experimental use since the 1770s.[31]

Hence delegates in 1899 treated gas differently from other weapons, both in their assumptions about it and in their characterisations of it.[32] The delegates at The Hague banned only what diplomats could imagine: 'projectiles whose sole object was asphyxiation'.[33] This precise language left loopholes if other weapons emerged, which is what happened in the First World War. Furthermore, the 1907 Hague Peace Conference did not rectify the vulnerability in the 1899 treaty. It condemned weapons causing 'unnecessary suffering' and 'poison', but did not define such weapons unambiguously.[34] Ambiguity also characterised the role of scientists at the Hague conferences. On the one hand, they were not invited to lend their expertise, leaving laymen to imagine how chemical weapons might evolve in more threatening ways (a task at which they failed miserably). On the other, their new technology had created a brave new world of weaponry that had caught the delegates' attention. While it is impossible to know, the presence of a range of chemists at either meeting might have yielded a more imaginative convention.

The First World War

Once the Germans introduced chlorine to the battlefield at Ypres on 22 April 1915, the genie was out of the bottle. Belligerents on both sides deployed gas repeatedly. As a result, they created an arms race to produce more devastating chemical weapons during the course of the war. As scholar Kim Coleman reported, 110,000 tonnes of gases killed 91,000 individuals and wounded approximately 1.3 million others during the war.[35] The widest impact from the gas war did not, however, come from the number of casualties or from the necessity of changing army routines so as to be prepared for a gas attack, but rather from the post-war consensus that Germany had done a terrible thing by unleashing chemical weapons. Over the course of the conflict, newspapers, veterans and even poets reported the horrors of gas globally. After the First World War, public and legal resistance to gas grew worldwide. The British reaction serves as a useful case study because the nation was a vocal enemy of Germany and a core belligerent in the war.

The uproar began as soon as the Allies recognised what Germany had done at Ypres. Fritz Haber, a German scientist so well renowned that he received a Nobel Prize after the war for his work on ammonia, became known as the father of chemical warfare for figuring out how to weaponise chlorine. His creation was not what the 1899 Hague delegates imagined. Instead of using shells, the German army released 150 tonnes of chlorine gas from canisters to drift on the wind over the lines of two French colonial divisions.[36] Approximately 10,000 Allied soldiers were subject to the gas attack and half died within the space of ten minutes, choking on clouds of pea-green fog.[37] Some Canadians nearby also suffered, although enough stayed at their posts that the lines held. The Germans did not have sufficient reinforcements prepared to break the Allied lines, advance across No Man's Land and thus break the stalemate on the Western Front, probably because the Army did not believe that gas would be so effective.[38]

This opened the door for public and political discourse about gas use and about Germany's role in it. These conversations addressed emotional as well as legal issues, perhaps because the emotional impact of a surprise weapon that suffocates victims inspired fear. For instance, the British public widely perceived Germany as cruel and as guilty of violating the Hague conventions by using gas. It was easy to imagine Germany as guilty, given that it had violated international law by invading neutral Belgium in 1914, been accused of atrocities in Belgium, killed more than 1,200 civilians by sinking *Lusitania* and executed captured nurse Edith Cavell.[39] The use of gas, therefore, provided one more reason to see Germany as an uncivilised, barbaric nation.

It could be argued that gas violated the generic bans in the 1899 and 1907 conventions. Whether gas caused 'unnecessary suffering' or was 'poison' was really in the eye of the beholder. Contemporary accounts of the gas attacks and the suffering they caused victims seem to support the assertion that they were indeed cruel and caused unnecessary suffering. However, critics did not necessarily make explicit connections to the 1907 Hague language; some condemnations were emotional, not legal, in tone. British sergeant Wilgrid Cotton, a month after the first attack, described men 'overcome with the gas ... green and blue, tongues hanging out and eyes staring ... some were coughing up green froth from their lungs'.[40] Perhaps Wilfrid Owen, a famous British poet writing about the First World War, described gas in the most haunting way in 'Dulce et Decorum Est' when he wrote about the suffering of a victim 'guttering, choking, drowning ... the blood ... gargling from the froth-corrupted lungs'.[41] Others used official platforms to respond. Lord Robert Cecil's speech in Parliament, soon after the Ypres attack, harshly condemned Germany's overall conduct during the war. Drawing on a number of questionable German actions, including the sinking of *Lusitania* on 7 May 1915 as well as the use of poison gas, he proclaimed 'we have no right to assume that they will act as ordinary human beings'.[42]

German words, as well as actions, provided fodder for condemnation. On 11 June 1915, for instance, *The Times* reported that Professor Wegener, a German war correspondent, said, 'I am not going into the silly chatter about our new weapon of attack'. He compared it to other weapons in the war and dismissed the notion that gas was any more inhumane. Still, he acknowledged that chemical weapons violated the Hague treaties, by asking: '[So] What if it [gas] were "poisonous" and killed? What is "law" any longer in this most immoral ... of all wars of modern times[?]'.[43] Wegener argued that Germany did break the treaties because laws that attempted to civilise warfare were obsolete in this modern conflict. From *The Times'* perspective, Wegener represented general German thinking, and the newspaper used the war correspondent's own words to demonstrate a connection between Germany's contempt for international law and its use of gas.

On 18 May 1915, Member of Parliament Harold Tennant made the link even more explicit. He dismissed any loopholes in the letter of Declaration II in the House of Commons. He stated flatly that 'Obviously the diffusion of the gases was the object of [the 1899 Hague prohibition] rather than the means by which they were diffused'.[44] Even before they lost the war, the Germans were losing the public relations battle over chemical weapons. Their defeat further undermined the argument that using chemical weapons had been legal.

Thus, even while the British Prime Minister Herbert Asquith noted privately to the king that the Germans had not technically broken the law, public opinion and many officials concluded otherwise.[45] This understanding complicated British desires to retaliate in kind. The British press and government had worked hard to blacken Germany's image in the world, perhaps to enhance their own citizens' morale and sway neutral nations to their side. Thus, prior to launching their own gas attacks, British officials, as well as the popular press, went to great lengths to justify the use of gas on legal and moral levels. Bernard Partridge conveyed this clearly in 'Retribution', a cartoon published in the widely read *Punch* in July of 1915. In it a dark, ominous cloud of gas labelled 'retribution' chases a chastened and hunched-over Kaiser Wilhelm II.[46] The Secretary of State for War, Lord Kitchener, three weeks later, offered an official explanation for the British decision to take the offensive. He emphasised that the use of poison gas arose from the practical exigencies of war, while at the same time having a clear moral purpose, arguing:

> The enemy employed vast quantities of poisonous gases in defiance of the recognised rules of war and of their pledged word ... Full accounts have been published in the newspapers of the effect of the gas and the agonising death which it produces ... His Majesty's Government, no less than the French Government, feel that our troops must be adequately protected by the employment of similar methods so as to remove the enormous and unjustifiable disadvantage which must exist for them if we take no steps to meet on his own ground the enemy who is responsible for the introduction of this pernicious practice.[47]

By choosing to describe Germany's actions as 'pernicious', Kitchener invoked morality to validate retaliation in kind. In the same sentence, he provided a practical rationale for British gas use: it would erase the 'enormous and unjustifiable' handicap that British soldiers suffered if it was only Germany that wielded chemical weapons. Britain had to protect its soldiers, not just with anti-gas equipment like respirators, but also with offensive tools like chemical weapons themselves, but only after it could distinguish the situation in which Britain would be using gas from the one in which Germany introduced it. In this way, Britain could avoid the very condemnation its government had heaped upon the enemy. Considering the death toll and the stalemate in the war, each and every possible tool had to be utilised, and now gas was one of those implements. After this point, both sides escalated the chemical war by using new gases (for example, mustard gas), new means of deploying them (such as shells, which actually did violate the letter of the treaty) and new tactics.[48] Nevertheless, gas failed to break the stalemate.

The interwar period and the Second World War

Even after the war, Germany's 1915 introduction of gas warfare influenced other nations' perceptions of the nation's conduct and doubts about the power of legal gas prohibitions. The Treaty of Versailles prohibited Germany, specifically, from 'the manufacture, storage and use' as well as the 'importation' of gas. Germany, after all, had not only caused the war, but also it had been a world leader in chemistry.[49] The language the diplomats chose, however, shows that the ban was not meant as one of the Treaty of Versailles' many punishments. The clause also served as a reminder that the sentiments behind the poison gas ban at the Hague conferences remained. Clause 171 of the Treaty of Versailles justified the new ban because Declaration II clearly prohibited gas use in war. What was new, though, was the language describing gas. Rather than banning projectiles the new clauses prohibited 'asphyxiating, poisonous or other gases, and all analogous liquids, materials or devices'.[50] After the First World War, therefore, it seems that diplomats learned from Germany's attempts to use chemical weapons that did not violate the strict letter of the law, even if they did ignore the spirit of it. In Clause 171 the diplomats tried to insert language that was as broad as possible, thus ensuring that any toxic chemical or chemical weapon created, whether visualised at the time of drafting or not, would be included.

Efforts to ban gas effectively and to learn from The Hague's narrow phrasing continued throughout the interwar period. The interwar period was an age in which global public pressure encouraged arms control efforts for conventional weapons. There was also a terrifying conviction that future wars would be rife with gas. Britain, a powerful nation in the interwar period, again serves as an illustrative case study to understand interwar attitudes and behaviours towards gas. For example, when the British Prime Minister Stanley Baldwin warned that the 'bomber would always get through', he said it would be carrying gas to drop on civilians.[51] Lord Halsbury, a layman with a particularly loud voice and vivid message, argued that gas could destroy whole cities and even civilisation itself.[52]

This kind of fear—especially since there was a rational basis to the belief that nations would be unlikely to abandon a weapon that had featured so prominently in the First World War—created challenges beyond the need for treaty language that would encompass future kinds of chemical weapons. In light of Germany's actions in the First World War, many in the British government wondered if anti-gas treaties could ever be shields strong enough to eliminate signatory nations' needs to prepare offensively and defensively to fight future gas wars. After all, Germany had disregarded the Hague treaties, and it followed that any nation potentially could do the same in the future. This belief inspired British reluctance to ratify later chemical warfare treaties, even before the international aggression and politically extreme governments of the 1930s meant that distrust of other nations was inevitable.

The concerns about binding a state to a treaty that did not effectively bind others arose during the 1920s. Britain was not the only nation to express concern about the limits of diplomatically imposed restraints. During the 1922 Washington Naval Conference, while delegates focused mainly on the Pacific Ocean, there were multilateral discussions about whether to include anti-gas clauses to bind all signatories more explicitly than had Declaration II. The relevant subcommittee eventually came to a decision, declaring '[n]o nation would dare agree to render itself unprepared for gas warfare if the possibility existed that an unscrupulous enemy might break an agreement for its own advantage'.[53] The group also drafted a gas ban utilising the language in the Treaty of Versailles and thus updated the Hague conventions.[54] Beyond preventing the use of gas, the new treaty permitted research, production and storage. In the end, the Washington gas ban failed. While the five most powerful nations at the conference signed the ban, France failed to ratify the agreement because of its concerns about other parts of the convention regarding submarines.[55]

However, this was not the end of the story. The next chemical weapons treaty, negotiated under the auspices of the League of Nations in 1925, sought to bind more than just the great powers who participated in the Washington Conference, and to make the ban even broader in terms of the weapons and actions it proscribed. The resulting treaty, the Geneva Gas Protocol (a stand-alone treaty, despite the term 'Protocol' in its name), used the same language as the Washington agreement as a base but also added 'bacteriological methods of warfare' to the list of outlawed weapons.[56] There was an effort, in other words, to extend coverage to biological weapons—the next logical development with such a type of armament—as well as to include almost any means of preparing and delivering chemical weaponry.[57] Thirty-seven nations signed immediately. Thirty-nine had ratified or acceded to it by 1939.[58]

British leadership had procrastinated over ratifying the Washington Naval Conference's gas ban and the later Geneva Gas Protocol because it did not believe that either would stop a foe, such as Germany, effectively. It felt public pressure to acquiesce to the agreements, but this was juxtaposed with the distrust generated during the First World War regarding whether a treaty would stop an enemy from using a banned substance. For example, in 1926, the Secretary of State for War offered the Committee of Imperial Defence (CID) a memorandum stating that there could never be any certainty that all signatories would observe the Geneva Protocol. In lieu of such guarantees, it emphasised 'there must inevitably be a danger that if we proclaim our readiness to abstain from using gas, our research work and general preparedness for gas warfare will suffer'.[59] If Britain could not trust in other nations to abide by chemical weapons treaties, it must be prepared to retaliate. Hence, it would have to continue to invest in research and development of offensive chemical weapons and defensive equipment during a time of economic frugality.[60] There seemed to be no way to save the budget, assuage public fear of future gas wars and protect the nation. In the end, Britain ratified the Geneva Gas Protocol, although it did include a reservation stating that it reserved the right of retaliation in kind.[61]

The Geneva Gas Protocol was not perfect. Some might argue it was too broad. The author of the 1926 CID memo mentioned above was accurate when he wrote: 'it is hardly to be expected that public opinion would countenance our using even non-lethal gas in small wars', such as those in the colonies where tear gas might prove a safer tool than guns to put down riots or fight native inhabitants.[62] Because of moral obligations arising from signing past gas treaties, the publicly embraced taboo and the lesson—learned from the German experience—that vilification was the cost of breaking a ban, the government hesitated to use even non-lethal tear gases in situations where doing so may have prevented more serious causalities (including flushing out barricaded criminals in the empire).[63]

On the other hand, the protocol was certainly too narrow. It failed to describe biological weapons broadly—they were merely 'bacteriological' ones. Broader language would have included phrases such as 'viral and bacteriological', or even 'organisms that threatened bodies'. While diplomats theoretically had recourse to both biological and chemical expertise, they focused instead upon those weapons of which they had previous knowledge, which at this point was only chemical weapons. Perhaps this explains why they failed to endorse a broad definition of biological weapons or to imagine future developments in these armaments beyond those based upon the most commonly known germs, bacteria. Regardless, the same flaw that appeared in the Hague language regarding chemical weapons now appeared in the Geneva Gas Protocol—diplomats had not learned to be wary of all hypothetical weapons yet.

Even though the Geneva Protocol barred the use of gas weapons and despite the fact that global public opinion was against their use, Britain remained doubtful even though Germany reassured Britain a week after the Second World War began that they would observe the Geneva Protocol.[64] The British were convinced Germany would use gas as soon as it was at all profitable to do so. Sir John Dill, then Chief of the Imperial General Staff, wrote to Major General Hastings Ismay on 2 July 1940 stressing: 'we are not justified in anticipating that by refraining from using gas ourselves we shall prevent the Germans using it, should they judge it to be expedient'.[65] Since the extensive use of gas in the Holocaust death camps was unknown by the Allies during much of the war, that itself did not increase distrust. Nevertheless, German ruthlessness during the interwar period and the Second World War provided a wider context of suspicion. While concern about the likelihood of Germany using gas ebbed and flowed during the war in Britain, intelligence reports drafted in the last year of the conflict repeatedly addressed the fear that gas would be used. Most of these reports speculated that Hitler might employ it 'as a last desperate resort and without regard to military or humanitarian considerations'.[66] Of course, for reasons that are complex and irrelevant for this story, Germany did not use lethal gas on the battlefield against international foes. Regardless, the experiences of the 1915–1945 period meant that Britain and her allies believed it necessary to expend time, energy, money and manpower preparing for a gas war that never eventuated.

Post-war and beyond

During the Cold War, nations looked for a better tool than the Geneva Gas Protocol for shielding nations from both gas attacks and the need to prepare for them. One approach was visible in its successor treaty, the Chemical Weapons Convention (CWC), which now has more than 100 signatories. This agreement came into force in 1997, 28 years after negotiations began, and four years after it opened for signatures.[67] The CWC is a more sophisticated treaty, requiring inspections and permitting updates to try to ensure compliance and to make sure new scientific developments do not make the agreement obsolete.[68] The core remains a statement of prohibition. Signatories must destroy stockpiles and they cannot 'develop, produce, otherwise acquire, stockpile or retain chemical weapons, or transfer, directly or indirectly, chemical weapons to anyone'.[69] Such a complex document almost certainly could not have emerged without the learning experiences and experimentation regarding gas bans that began with the Hague conferences.

The CWC is by no means perfect. It contains ambiguities, as Treasa Dunworth notes. In particular, she argues that the loophole permitting use of 'non-lethal' chemical weapons (such as tear gas) by police is dangerous. Because a chemical is labelled as non-lethal does not mean that fatalities may not arise in unusual circumstances, such as if it is used (or misused) on particularly vulnerable people. Regardless, allowing any kind of gas to be used leaves gaps in the CWC, which weakens the agreement as a gas ban, 'putting the treaty as a whole in danger'.[70]

The innovations in the CWC are not limited to the language in the treaty. Unlike the Hague, Washington and Geneva anti-gas treaties, diplomats drafted the CWC with the technical assistance of scientists. In addition, the CWC created the Organisation for the Prohibition of Chemical Weapons

(OPCW) to monitor and implement the treaty. It supported the formation of a Scientific Advisory Board (SAB) under the OPCW, composed of 'independent' scientists who meet regularly and propose updates.[71] Its work is vital. As scholars Beatrice Maneshi and Jonathan Forman conclude, the SAB fills 'a critical need for sound assessments of new science and technology'.[72] It sought to respond to the reality, understood by those who drafted Declaration II and later agreements, that scientists will develop new chemicals and weapons in the future that cannot be envisioned in the present. It is also challenging to recognise the threat posed by some chemicals and chemical processes. For example, chlorine can be a weaponised gas but it can also be diluted to sanitise swimming pools. The SAB responds to such challenges. In one case it generated a protocol for managing potentially dangerous by-products, such as variations on mustard gas, of otherwise innocuous chemical mixtures.[73] Unlike Declaration II, the CWC is a living, evolving treaty. Still, it owes its roots to work begun in 1899, namely by codifying the original ban on poison gas and by providing a framework in which to interpret gas use and abuse in the future. It also owes its rigorous structure to the recognition of the importance of scientific expertise and to the hard, historical lessons learned about the potential ineffectiveness of vague or narrow treaty terms.[74]

The anti-gas provisions of the Hague conventions influenced the crises of the next decades, especially through the interwar period, and linger today. The 1899 conference brought chemical weapons themselves, as well as debates about whether and how to outlaw them, into the international law arena. While Declaration II, the explicit declaration against poison gas shells, failed on one level because Germany (and other nations) did use gas in the First World War, the treaty's long-term legacies were mixed. Declaration II provided the foundation for the taboo that exists today. It was also the foundational treaty dealing with arms that have become known as weapons of mass destruction. As the first effort to ban chemical weapons, it provided the base on which diplomats have built improved gas treaties incorporating more inclusive descriptions of chemical weapons and (in the most recent version, the CWC) appointing scientists to ensure that known and potential weaponry will be covered. While Germany must take responsibility for introducing chemical weapons to the battlefield, Declaration II's failure to consider different means of using gas gave them an opening. It is not surprising that the first attempt to ban a new kind of weaponry was imperfect, but the cost of its lack of efficacy was high. Experience with gas in the First World War, as well as vilification and distrust of Germany, enhanced wariness of interbellum diplomatic ability to eradicate chemical weapons and darkened Germany's reputation for decades. The Hague conventions' chemical warfare clauses cannot be relegated to the footnotes of history. They are broad ranging and remain relevant today. Their legacies show that arms control treaties can have unintended impacts for decades, long outlasting the lives of the treaties themselves.

Notes

1 Thank you to the organisers and sponsors of the 'War, Peace and International Order? The Legacies of the Hague Conferences of 1899 and 1907' conference held on 19 April 2016, including the Faculty of Arts at the University of Auckland; The New Zealand Centre for Human Rights Law, Policy and Practice; Associate Professor Maartje Abbenhuis; Annalise Higgins; Christopher Barber and Thomas Munro. I am also grateful for inspiring conversations, talks and papers offered by the participants and audience. I am particularly thankful to Andrew Webster, Neville Wylie, Treasa Dunworth, Mary Jo Nye and Andrei Mamolea for ideas and conversations that continue to stimulate my thoughts on this topic.
2 B. Obama. (2012). *Remarks by the President to the White House Press Corps, 20 August 2012*. [online] The White House. Available at: https://www.whitehouse.gov/the-press-office/2012/08/20/remarks-president-white-house-press-corps. [Accessed 9 April 2016].
3 G.H.W. Bush and B. Scowcroft. (1998). *A World Transformed*. New York: Knopf, pp.441–442.
4 J. Tucker. (2006). *War of Nerves: Chemical Warfare from World War I to al-Qaeda*. New York: Pantheon, pp.64–65.
5 J.B. Scott (ed.). (1899). *The Proceedings of The Hague Peace Conferences, Translation of Official Texts*. New York: Oxford University Press, p.266. It is worth noting that some translations omit 'sole', such as the Avalon Project at Yale Law School. (1899). *Declaration II: Declaration on the Use of Projectiles the Object of which is the Diffusion of Asphyxiating or Deleterious Gases*. [online] Available at: http://avalon.law.yale.edu/19th_century/dec99-02.asp [Accessed 30 April 2016]. However, discussions among the delegates imply that the 'sole' is indeed important. Scott, pp.328, 366.
6 Avalon Project at Yale Law School. (1899). *Laws and Customs of War on Land (Declaration II), Article 23a*. [online] Available at: http://avalon.law.yale.edu/19th_century/hague02.asp#art23 [Accessed 7 April 2016] states 'it is especially prohibited:-- to employ poison or poisoned arms'. Also, see Avalon Project at Yale Law School. (1907). *Laws and Customs of War on Land (Hague IV), Article 23a*. [online] Available at: http://avalon.law.yale.edu/20th_century/hague04.asp#art23 [Accessed 7 April, 2016] states that 'it is especially forbidden – to employ poison or poisoned weapons … [or weapons that] cause unnecessary suffering'.
7 The Battle of Ypres (1915) is generally considered to be where gas was first used, and it is the first major as well as first recognised deployment. Germans had previously used gas on the Russian front, but the cold made the gas so ineffective that no one noticed. The French had considered using tear gas earlier, too. U. Trumpeter. (1975). The Road to Ypres: The Beginnings of Gas Warfare in World War I. *The Journal of Modern History*, 47(3), pp.462–463, 469.
8 An in-depth discussion of the language of the anti-gas laws and whether Germany technically broke them appears below. Ulf Schmidt even argues that Britain was the first to break the laws, but this is not a common view. U. Schmidt. (2015). *Secret Science: A Century of Poison Warfare and Human Experiments*. Oxford: Oxford University Press, pp.28–29.
9 R. Price (1997). *The Chemical Weapons Taboo*. Ithaca, NY: Cornell University Press, pp.11–12 argues this most explicitly as part of his study of the taboo's evolution. In addition, Price and Brown are two of the few who give substantial weight to the chemical weapons laws and their implications. Price, pp.109, 119 and 133 explains the general views of experts in the field and endorses

Brown's perspective. F. Brown. (1968). *Chemical Warfare: A Study in Restraints.* Westport, CT: Greenwood Press, Publishers, p.293.

10 The dates given for these treaties are the dates when they were signed. The first never entered into force, the second became active in 1928 and the third became effective in 1997.

11 K. Coleman. (2005). *A History of Chemical Warfare.* Houndsmill, Hampshire: Palgrave, p.3 also discusses the idea that targets should be human.

12 A. Prentiss. (1937). *Chemicals in War: A Treatise on Chemical Warfare.* New York: McGraw-Hill contains detailed descriptions of many First World War chemicals.

13 Hesketh Bell's letter in *The Times* expresses the common European view that the Abyssinians were 'uncivilized'. *The Times* (London), 30 March 1936, p.13.

14 *Boston Globe*, 15 June 1984, p.24.

15 It is worth noting that scholars debate how many times gas has been used on the battlefield since the First World War. Factors such as credibility of evidence, and differing definitions of chemical weapons, can help explain the varying lists. V. Utgoff. (1991). *The Challenge of Chemical Weapons: An American Perspective.* New York: St Martin's Press, pp.69–87 offers a set of examples. Coleman offers another, for instance, pp.80–130.

16 W. Sneader. (23 December 2000). The Discovery of Aspirin: A Reappraisal. *British Medical Journal.* [online] Vol. 321(7276), pp. 1591–1594. Available at: http://www.ncbi.nlm.nih.gov/pmc/articles/PMC1119266/ [Accessed 7 April 2016] and E. Croddy et al. (2002). *Chemical and Biological Warfare: A Comprehensive Survey for the Concerned Citizen.* New York: Copernicus, pp.134–135. Mary Jo Nye's history of modern developments in chemistry and physics contains a more detailed account of the discoveries in chemistry in the late nineteenth century. M.J. Nye. (1996). *Before Big Science: The Pursuit of Modern Chemistry and Physics, 1800–1940.* New York: Twayne Publishers.

17 Hague II, 1899, Article 23a and Hague IV, 1907, Article 23a. Also, see Avalon Project at Yale Law School. (1899). *Declaration of the Use of Bullets which Expand or Flatten Easily in the Human Body (Declaration III).* [online] Available at: http://avalon.law.yale.edu/19th_century/dec99-03.asp [Accessed 7 April 2016].

18 Count Mouravieff, (1899) *Russian Circular. Peace Conference at The Hague.* [online] Avalon Project at Yale Law School. Available at: http://avalon.law.yale.edu/19th_century/hag99-02.asp [Accessed 9 April 2016].

19 The invitation makes it clear that one goal is 'to put a stop to the progressive development of the present armaments … [a] humanitarian scheme'.

20 Scott, p.283. Thank you to A. Mamolea for reminding me of this statement.

21 Scott, p.366.

22 Price, pp.31–32, emphasises the interest of the delegates in limiting gas because it was an explosive, even if a novel one. He distinguishes this from the idea that poison gas was rejected simply because it was a poison. I argue that the connections between both explosives and poison are important, but so is the idea that gas is a novel kind of weapon, rather than a new type of explosive or poison.

23 Scott, p.296.

24 Scott, p.366.

25 Scott, pp.365–366.

26 Scott, pp.266, 366.

27 Scott, p.367, for example.

28 Scott, p.283. Note that Mahan used the phrase 'torpedo-boat' instead of submarine. The delegates at The Hague used these terms, and divers, as nearly synonymous. Scott, p.275.

29 Scott, p.283.
30 Scott, pp.367–368
31 Turtle sailed in 1776. J.H. Leinhard. *No. 381 Civil War Submarine.* [online] The Engines of Our Ingenuity. Available at: http://www.uh.edu/engines/epi381.htm [Accessed 19 July 2016].
32 The concept of weapons of mass destruction (WMD) has a murky beginning, but most agree that it did not arise until after the advent of nuclear weapons. Thus, while chemical weapons were seen as unusual—and to many, particularly awful—from the beginning, they were not WMDs as we understand them today.
33 Scott, p.266.
34 Avalon Project at Yale Law School. (1907). *Laws and Customs of War on Land (Hague IV), Article 23a.* [online] Available at: http://avalon.law.yale.edu/20th_century/hague04.asp#art23 [Accessed 7 April, 2016].
35 Coleman, p.xv. Even so, it produced fewer casualties than more conventional weapons.
36 Nobelprize.org. *The Nobel Prize in Chemistry 1918.* [online] Available at: http://www.nobelprize.org/nobel_prizes/chemistry/laureates/1918/ [Accessed 9 April 2016]. Note that the 1918 prize-winner was selected in 1919, which is when Haber received the award.
37 Also, see FirstWorldWar.com. *Battle—The Second Battle of Ypres, 1915.* [online] Available at: http://www.firstworldwar.com/battles/ypres2.htm [Accessed 9 April 2016].
38 T. Cook. (1999). *No Place to Run: The Canadian Corps and Gas Warfare in the First World War.* Vancouver: UBC Press, pp.18–24, offers an excellent overview of the battle.
39 The Bryce Report contains the record of the British investigation into allegations of German brutality in Belgium. V. Bryce, et al. (1915). *Report of the Committee on Alleged German Outrages.* [online] Avalon Project at Yale Law School. Available at http://avalon.law.yale.edu/20th_century/brycere.asp [Accessed 18 July 2016]. J. Keegan. (1998) *The First World War.* Toronto: Key Porter Books, p.265, offers some background on *Lusitania*. See how Cavell's execution is still commemorated today. Cavell Nurses Trust. *Who was Edith Cavell?* [online] Available at: https://www.cavellnursestrust.org/edith-cavell [Accessed 5 August 2016].
40 E. Cotton (24 May 1915). *Diary*, Imperial War Museum Document Collection, Imperial War Museum.
41 W. Owen. *Dulce et Decorum Est.* [online] Poetry Foundation. Available at: http://www.poetryfoundation.org/poems-and-poets/poems/detail/46560 [Accessed 28 April 2016].
42 R. Cecil. (13 May 1915). *House of Commons Debates.* Hansard Milbanks, Vol. 71 c. 1848. [online] Available at: http://hansard.millbanksystems.com/commons/1915/may/13/statement-by-prime-minister#S5CV0071P0_19150513_HOC_313 [Accessed 29 April 2016].
43 *The Times*, 11 June 1915, p.7.
44 H. Tennant. (18 May 1915). *House of Commons Debates.* Hansard Milbanks, vol. 71, cc. 2119–2120. [online] Available at: http://hansard.millbanksystems.com/commons/1915/may/18/asphyxiating-gases-hague-convention [Accessed 30 April 2016].
45 H. Asquith to King George V, 27 April 1915, CAB 37/127/40, also listed as CAB 41/36/18, The National Archives of the United Kingdom [hereinafter TNA], Kew, UK.
46 Bernard Partridge, *Punch*, 7 July 1915, p.1.

47 H. Kitchener. (18 May 1915). *House of Lords Debates*. Hansard Milbanks, vol. 18, cc.1017–1018. [online] Available at: http://hansard.millbanksystems.com/lords/1915/may/18/the-war [Accessed 30 April 2016].
48 A. Palazzo. (2000). *Seeking Victory on the Western Front: The British Army and Chemical Warfare in World War I*. Lincoln, Nebraska: University of Nebraska Press.
49 Avalon Project at Yale Law School. (1919). *The Versailles Treaty, Article 171*. [online] Available at: http://avalon.law.yale.edu/imt/partv.asp [Accessed 7 April 2016].
50 *The Versailles Treaty*.
51 S. Baldwin in: *The Times*, 11 November 1932, p.7.
52 See M. Girard. (2008). *A Strange and Formidable Weapon: British Responses to World War I Poison Gas*. Lincoln: University of Nebraska Press, pp.192–194 for a more complete discussion of this topic.
53 Admiral de Bon of France, as cited by Price, p.76. It is worth acknowledging that this concern applies to weapons besides gas. However, since this article is about chemical weapons, and since nations make decisions about whether to use banned armaments on a case-by-case basis, this issue will not be discussed in more detail here.
54 International Committee of the Red Cross. (1922). *Treaty relating to the Use of Submarines and Noxious Gases in Warfare, Article 5*. [online] Available at: https://www.icrc.org/applic/ihl/ihl.nsf/ART/270-360006?OpenDocument [Accessed 7 April 2016].
55 The United States, Britain, France, Japan and Italy drafted and signed the treaty in Washington. International Committee of the Red Cross. (1922). *Treaty relating to the Use of Submarines and Noxious Gases in Warfare, Preamble*. [online] Available at: https://www.icrc.org/applic/ihl/ihl.nsf/ART/270-360001?OpenDocument and https://www.icrc.org/ihl/INTRO/270?OpenDocument [Accessed 18 July 2016].
56 This was drafted at the Conference for the Supervision of the International Trade in Arms and Ammunition, but the Protocol was the only successful product of the conference; the rest did not enter into force. International Committee of the Red Cross. (1925). *Treaties, State Parties, and Commentaries*. [online] Available at: https://www.icrc.org/ihl/INTRO/280?OpenDocument [Accessed 13 April 2016].
57 Treaties do not cover all weapons of mass destruction, such as radiological weapons. W. Potter and J. Lewis. (17 February 2014). *The World Needs an Agreement to Ban Radiological Weapons*. [online] nuclear-news. Available at: http://nuclear-news.net/2014/02/19/the-world-needs-an-agreement-to-ban-radiological-weapons/ [Accessed 7 April 2016].
58 International Committee of the Red Cross. *Treaties, State Parties, and Commentaries*. [online] Available at: https://www.icrc.org/ihl/INTRO/280?OpenDocument [Accessed 18 July 2016].
59 Chemical Warfare Policy, 723-B, Memorandum for the Committee of Imperial Defence, 8 October 1926, CHAR 22/102, Churchill Archives Centre.
60 The fact that major countries like the United States and Japan did not sign the Geneva Gas Protocol before the Second World War added to the treaty's weakness as a shield.
61 Britain withdrew the reservation in 1991. US State Department. (1925). *Protocol for the Prohibition of the Use in War of Asphyxiating, Poisonous or Other Gases, and of Bacteriological Methods of Warfare (Geneva Protocol)*. [online] Available at http://www.state.gov/t/isn/4784.htm#states [Accessed 18 July 2016].
62 Chemical Warfare Policy, 723-B, CHAR 22/102.

63 See, for example, Memorandum for the Cabinet, 10 July 1922, WO 188/144, NA, and L. Worthington-Evan, The Use of Gas in the Suppression of Civil Disturbances, 12 July 1928, CAB 24/196/28, also known as C.P. 228 (28), TNA. Even before the inception of the Geneva Gas Protocol, since Britain had signed the Washington ban, the government felt honour-bound to uphold it despite the fact that the treaty never came into force.
64 Swiss Legation, Use of Poison Gas in Warfare: Corres. With Allied and Foreign Govts. Correspondence to Foreign Office, 8 September 1939, HO 186/2846, TNA.
65 J. Dill to Major General H. L. Ismay, 2 July 1942, CAB 120/775, TNA.
66 Joint Intelligence Sub-Committee, Use of Chemical Warfare by the Germans, 12 February 1945, CAB 121/102, TNA.
67 Organisation for the Prohibition of Chemical Weapons [hereinafter OCPW]. *Genesis and Historical Development of the Chemical Warfare Convention.* [online] Available at: https://www.opcw.org/chemical-weapons-convention/genesis-and-historical-development/ [Accessed 7 April 2016].
68 OPCW, *Genesis and Historical Development.*
69 OPCW, *Article I, Chemical Weapons Convention.* [online] Available at: https://www.opcw.org/chemical-weapons-convention/articles/article-i-general-obligations/ [Accessed 29 April 2016].
70 T. Dunworth. (2012). The Silent Killer: Toxic Chemicals for Law Enforcement and the Chemical Weapons Convention. *New Zealand Yearbook of International Law*, (10), pp.4, 6.
71 OPCW. *Scientific Advisory Board.* [online] Available at: https://www.opcw.org/about-opcw/subsidiary-bodies/scientific-advisory-board/ [Accessed 20 July 2016].
72 B. Maneshi and J. Forman. (21 September 2015). *The Intersection of Science and Chemical Disarmament.* [online] Science and Diplomacy. Available at: http://www.sciencediplomacy.org/perspective/2015/intersection-science-and-chemical-disarmament. [Accessed 13 April 2016].
73 Maneshi and Forman.
74 This development is reflective of a broader trend in arms control. For example, the Biological Weapons Convention acknowledges that scientists are required to raise issues of changes in biological knowledge and threats as well as to enable the 'economic cooperation and development' set out in the agreement. J. Hart and R. Trapp. (2 October 2012). *Science, Technology, and the Biological Weapons Convention.* [online] Arms Control Association. Available at: https://www.armscontrol.org/act/2012_10/Science-Technology-and-the-Biological-Weapons-Convention [Accessed 13 April 2016].

6 *Sub silentio*

The sexual assault of women in international law

Sarah Gendron

Sub silentio: *adv.*, In silence; without express mention or notice; (also) without objection. Freq. in legal contexts in *to pass sub silentio*.[1]
   Precedents that pass *sub silentio are of little or no authority*.[2]
   A decision passes *sub silentio* ... when the particular point of law involved in the decision *is not perceived by the court or present to its mind*.[3]
   Silent uniform course of practice, uninterrupted though *not supported by legal decisions*.[4]

Patricia Viseur Sellers' 2009 'The Prosecution of Sexual Violence in Conflict' is an expertly written report on the regulation of wartime rape.[5] However, in this 41-page study, she assigns only a passing reference to the Hague Conventions of 1899 and 1907 and to their influence on the prohibition of rape in contemporary international humanitarian law (IHL), or law governing conduct in conflict situations. Categorising them as examples of the 'modest' progress of the codification of sex crimes from the late nineteenth to the early twentieth centuries, she limits her discussion of the Hague conventions to two of their articles. The first is Article 1 of both conventions which cautions belligerents to, quite generally, 'conduct their operations in accordance with the laws and customs of war'.[6] The second is Article 46, again of both conventions: the sole article to expressly address the situation of women in war. It specifies that occupying powers must respect the 'Family honours and rights' of civilians.[7] The only analysis that Sellers provides for either article is a statement which reads that the 'laws and customs of war' referenced in Article 1 encompass '*sub silentio*' all conventional war crimes, 'including rape'. In other words, following the first definition of *sub silentio* as listed above, the conventional war crimes 'including rape' of which she speaks are 'without express mention' in the first Article. Yet since they are covered elsewhere in the Convention documents, one can assume that they are understood as 'the laws and customs of war' that Article 1 mandates need be observed. Interestingly, although it substantiates her claim to the very 'modest' influence of the Hague conventions on women's protections under IHL, she does not signal that the prohibition of rape is never actually directly stated in Article 46. Similar to Article 1, it is only referenced *sub silentio,* again in the spirit of the first definition above, as a call to 'respect' 'family honour'. Apart from the description of Article 1 and the mention of Article 46, there is no further reference to the Hague conventions or the expression *sub silentio* in her report.

The above points are raised not to disparage Sellers' excellent study. Rather they illustrate the complex way in which the Hague conventions influenced the evolution of gender-based violence law in IHL. Granted, only one article alludes to the regulation of rape in war, and it does so 'without express mention'. However, given the era in which the conventions were signed, it is not unusual that issues primarily affecting women would figure little in law. Indeed, women were not mentioned in any way in the conference proceedings. Nor is it surprising that the diplomatic language of an international treaty at the turn of the century would be driven by a sense of linguistic delicacy and propriety that might make naming rape unthinkable. Even if drafted *sub silentio*, the inclusion of women as a protected group at all in documents of such import at that time represents a major milestone in women's rights. Sadly, it would take almost a century of progress of social change and ever increasing brutality to women in war for the practice of international law to coincide with the letter of the law. Or rather, it would take almost 100 years before international military tribunals would end the practice of regarding wartime rape itself as a *sub silentio* category; meaning, as a category of law that is, as described above, 'of little or no authority', 'not perceived by the court or present to its mind' and, thus, 'not supported by legal decisions'. Despite the seemingly 'modest' beginnings of this trajectory, the Hague conventions would play a crucial role in inaugurating an era in which sexual violence to women in war would ultimately be condemned internationally in both the drafting and the enforcement of the law.

The Hague Conventions of 1899 and 1907 are commonly thought to signal the dawn of contemporary IHL. At a time of growing concern regarding increased military expansion and a desire for peaceful resolutions for international conflicts, representatives of the world powers came together to draft laws that would govern international wartime conduct, or *jus in bello*. Although the impetus for the Hague conventions was ostensibly dedicated to military and political questions, they also focused on the entitlements and security of the individual. This is particularly evident in the Regulations Respecting the Laws and Customs of War on Land, which Betsy Baker describes as 'the most important source of twentieth- and early twenty-first-century humanitarian law'.[8] At the core of the associated deliberations were issues that would later inform the most significant human rights instruments and discourses of the twentieth century, namely, the gestures of defining and legislating the human subject.

Importantly, the Hague conventions were not the first humanitarian protections scripted in military codes of conduct. Religious texts from the Koran to the Old Testament and 'just war' theories dating back to ancient Rome all extolled the virtues of implementing behavioural codes for soldiers and granting clemency to the non-combatants.[9] However, whereas the Hague regulations seem to have been motivated—like the 1864 Geneva Conventions before them—by the nascent concern for the individual *qua* 'human' that would become the mainstay of modern human rights discourses, ancient prescriptions for mercy were often driven by practical interests of guaranteeing the smooth functioning of society.[10] After all, as unlikely as it seems, there were actual provisions for the tolerance of barbarity when necessity demanded a swift victory.[11] With respect to women civilians, it was as if necessity always demanded such provisions. To quote Sellers, although the very same religious texts, philosophical tracts and customary laws that regulated brutality against males also forbade sexual violence towards females *de jure*, 'the *de facto* situation attested to utter disregard of sexual assault prohibitions'.[12] Garthine Walker fleshes out this broad view with staggering statistics regarding the prosecution of such crimes:

> Between 1562 and 1695, tribunals in Frankfurt dealt with only two rape trials, while those in Geneva heard no more than two or three each decade. In seventeenth-century Delft and Rotterdam, a mere fourteen men were prosecuted for rape or sexual assault and only eight for rape in Amsterdam in the seventeenth and eighteenth centuries. In Ireland, about twelve rape cases were tried each year, grand juries having already thrown out over half of those initiated. The *Parlement de Paris*, with jurisdiction as a court of appeal over one half of the land mass and population of France, heard fewer than three every ten years during the sixteenth and seventeenth centuries.[13]

The wholesale devaluation of sexual violence against women was likely the product of long-held beliefs that women's bodies fell within the domain of legitimate plunder of war. The etymology of the term reinforces this interpretation, with the French *rap* and Latin *rapum* signalling 'the act of taking something by force; *esp.* the seizure of property by violent means; robbery, plundering'.[14] In contrast, the act of sexual violation originated from the Latin *suprare* and *constuprate*, 'to violate, ravish, deflower'.[15] From the perspective of the former term, rape could be perceived as a male-on-male act—a property or honour crime—if criminal at all. Articles 44 and 47 of Section II of the 1863 Lieber Code mark the first explicit references to the term 'rape' in customary law. However, although the code dictates that the crime carries a capital punishment, few of the 450 indictments of Union soldiers (Confederate records were destroyed) yielded anything more than a ten-year sentence. Many convictions were later dismissed or reduced to several months.[16] It took another 36 years before the crime of rape was codified for the first time in a multilateral treaty during the 1899 Hague Peace Conference. It was presented, *sub silentio*, as part of Article 46 of the Regulations Respecting the Laws and Customs of War on Land.

While the admonishment of sexual assault in the 1899 Hague Convention marked a momentous step forward regarding the normative prohibition of rape in IHL, it was also a step backwards in the abstruse description of the act. In contrast to the Lieber Code, the Hague delegates referenced the crime as a violation of 'family honour and rights', or the right to 'private property'.[17] Undoubtedly, the Hague conventions of 1899 and 1907 created an atmosphere of hope for many that, despite cultural and ideological differences, there would be shared rules of conduct between states that would bind them along fundamentally moral lines. History would reveal—sooner rather than later—that the ties that bind, even those that are signed and ratified in treaties, are easily transgressed in power politics. Even less problematic to eschew were those rules inscribed *sub silentio*. Never truly stated to begin with (at least in a legal sense), as the above epitaphs suggest, such regulations could remain virtually invisible to the courts and thus carried little legal authority. This legal and moral loophole would be exploited throughout much of the twentieth century, to the detriment of innumerable women. In the decade following the 1907 Hague Peace Conference, the First World War unleashed unimaginable horrors on the world. The most extensive documentation on sexual assault during the First World War details the thousands of incidents of rape and torture of women and girls that took place in Belgium and France.[18] However, many cases were also reported in Poland and Italy. The earliest took place at the hands of the Cossacks, but there were also rape accusations against the German and Austro-Hungarian troops in the final years of the war.[19] Although retrospectively treated as a relative blip on the screen of history compared to the number and severity of mass rapes in subsequent conflicts, sexual assault was sufficiently widespread during the First World War as to feature prominently in atrocity inquiries undertaken by belligerent parties. No doubt in response to the agreements made at The Hague, these inquiries were prepared in order to document the extent to which various parties violated international law. Both the French *Les Atrocités Allemandes en France* and the English Bryce Report describe the extensive use of rape in the campaign of terror waged by the German military.[20] The French report went one step further by declaring in the opening paragraphs that the severity and frequency of the German assaults on women and young girls was 'unprecedented' and was illustrative of an 'astonishing regression of the German mentality since 1870'.[21]

At the 1919 Peace Conference, the Peace Commission presented an inventory of 32 war crimes committed by Axis parties. Rape and forced prostitution figured on the record as numbers five and six. In closing, the drafters of the report voiced guarded optimism about the consequences of naming the crimes so that they could be prosecuted:

> Our function is ended when we have stated what the evidence establishes, but we may be permitted to express our belief that these disclosures will not have been made in vain if they *touch and rouse the*

conscience of mankind and we venture to hope that as soon as the present war is over the nations of the world in council will consider what means can be provided and sanctions devised to prevent the recurrence of such horrors as our generation is now witnessing.[22]

While the reports of vicious mass rapes may well have helped persuade neutral countries to enter into the war (and if not, certainly made great fodder for anti-German propaganda), once the war ended they ultimately failed to 'touch and rouse the conscience of mankind' enough to effect legal action or political discussion. Bierzanek notes that of the 901 people indicted for war crimes, only 13 were ever charged. The penalties ranged from six months to four years of incarceration. The remaining 888 criminals were either never brought to trial or they were acquitted or otherwise discharged.[23] No one was charged for rape or forced prostitution.

There are possible reasons for this lack of attention to sexual assault during the war crimes trials, despite the ample attention they gained in official narratives and popular culture during the war. The most salient is that—with the exception of the militarily sanctioned rapes and murders of Armenians and Serbians by the Turks and Bulgarians, which failed to capture the attention of the international community—there was little evidence to suggest that assaults committed by the Axis powers were systematically employed as part of a war strategy.[24] Despite the brutality of such attacks, actions taken by individuals while ostensibly not under orders could only constitute a minor war crime that would likely allow perpetrators to evade costly prosecution. After the First World War, it was also the case that the sexual assault of women was not deemed important 'enough' to demand criminal prosecution. It was not important enough because it happened primarily to women. It was not criminal enough because, despite the fact that it was often accompanied by mutilation and murder, it smacked of what one might think of today as 'bad-boy behaviour'; a lack of discipline, the natural outcome of the heady cocktail of intoxicants and trauma served up regularly in war. Disturbingly, the Bryce Report reinforces this interpretation, stating that 'drunken soldiers cannot be trusted to observe the rules or decencies of war', and that rape may be 'the inevitable result of the system of terror deliberately adopted in certain regions'.[25] Infinitely more unsettling are the intimations in the report that the excessive brutality demonstrated by naked, bayonetted or hung women's bodies occurred as a result of 'provocation'. As if to further prove the point, the report goes on to suggest that while it might be conceivable that 'grown-up women' might do something that would merit such wrath, there could be no justifiable cause for shooting, mutilating and bayonetting small children, for, the report assumed, that unlike adult women, 'there can be no possible defence for the murder of children'.[26]

The report of the War Crimes Commission for the Peace Conference also intimated that sexual assaults of women and girls were not terribly serious crimes by placing rape lower than torture on the list of war crimes; at numbers five and three respectively. A strong case can be made that rape is indeed a form of torture, even in the legal sense of the term,[27] although elsewhere in the report it was described as 'lust'.[28] In many ways, it is not terribly surprising that ten years after the Paris Peace Conference, the 1929 Geneva Convention relegated women's protections to a parenthetical remark. Article 3, the only article to reference women directly, states quite unceremoniously that 'women shall be treated with all the regard due to their sex'.[29] More than two decades after the 1907 Hague conventions and at a time when women's suffrage was gaining ground around the world, little had changed with regards to sexual assault in conflict situations or in the language of the laws that governed military conduct.[30]

The same disjunction between evolving understandings of gender relations outside of war and increasing gender-based violence during war continued throughout the 1930s and 1940s. On the home front, gender roles evolved as women entered the workforce in unprecedented numbers. In war zones, they were still subjected to unspeakable acts of sexual violence. The veiled language of the 1929 Geneva Convention certainly did little to curb rampant rape during the Second World War. It also did little to oblige Allied powers to prosecute for such crimes once the war had ended. Similar to the First World War, prosecution of rape was almost non-existent in the war crime trials of the Second World War. Neither the London nor the Tokyo charter referenced rape as a crime against humanity. None of the Nuremberg defendants were charged with rape as a war crime, and no one in the Japanese Imperial Army was indicted for the enslavement and coercion of 'comfort women'. Despite these grim outcomes, there were several notable moments regarding the prosecution of sexual violence in the trials following the Second World War. One of the more significant achievements was the inclusion of rape as a crime against humanity in the charter of the Control Council Law.[31] In addition, seven high-ranking officers of the Japanese Imperial Army were sentenced to death for war crimes during the Rape of Nanking, although none were charged with the crime of rape itself.[32] Finally, General Tomoyuki Yamishita was indicted for mass rape and murder in the Philippines, which represented the first time someone would be prosecuted for rapes that were not committed by himself but by those under his control.[33] This virtual impunity granted almost across the board to perpetrators of rape during world conflict attests to what the language of rape laws already implied; that sexual assault of women and girls was simply not considered an actual crime.

While social change on the home front failed to produce lasting change in legal protections, the barbarism experienced during the Second World War (in general) and the Holocaust (in particular) focussed the international community's attention back on the issue at the core of the Hague conventions: that of human rights. With renewed urgency, world nations came together in the interest of conceptualising and securing a universal set of rights and protections. Out of these deliberations came the Convention on the Prevention and Punishment of the Crime of Genocide in 1948 (CPPCG) and the 1949 Geneva Convention. Both documents ostensibly sought to formally establish the ideological principles that would guarantee the safety of all human beings. But again, the language of the CPPCG and the 1949 Geneva Convention left significant room for interpretation when it came to the rights of women. Although the CPPCG levelled prohibitions against inflicting 'serious bodily or mental harm' on, or 'imposing measures intended to prevent births' within specific groups, gender identity was never included as a 'group' to be protected. Only national, ethnic, racial and religious groups were incorporated in the definition of genocide. As for the Geneva Convention of the following year, the discrete language of the 1929 Convention remained somewhat unchanged in the 1949 iteration. Article 27—the only article to name rape directly—describes it as an example of 'an attack on honour'. Moreover, this article carries with it a familiar proviso: 'the Parties to the conflict may take such measures of control and security in regard to protected persons as may be necessary as a result of the war'.[34] None of the four Geneva conventions list rape within the realm of 'grave breaches', and the common Article 12 (of the first and second Geneva conventions) and Article 14 of the fourth fall back on the same language employed in the 1929 Convention: namely, that 'women shall be treated with all consideration due to their sex'.[35] If the almost total omission of gendered sex crimes in the conventions is any indication, apparently women were due little consideration at all. Certainly, the First and Second Additional Protocols to the Geneva Conventions did prohibit rape explicitly, whether in international or national conflicts. A further ratification of the Protocols by the International Committee of the Red Cross (*The Aide-memoire*) also clarified the past opacity of Article 147 of the Geneva Convention by stating that the breach of wilfully causing great suffering or serious injury to someone 'obviously covers ... rape'.[36] However, the first ratification occurred in 1997, almost 30 years after the 1949 Geneva Conventions, the second occurring in 1992.

As the number of women participants in international relations increased, so too did official attention to the myriad ways in which women—despite changes in the letter of the law—were still underrepresented in the international arena with regards to basic human rights. In an attempt to rectify this rather glaring disconnect, splinter committees were formed under the auspices of the United Nations (UN). One of the earliest documents to issue from these discussions was the 1967 Declaration of the Convention on the Elimination of All Forms of Discrimination against Women (CEDAW), adopted by the UN in 1967.[37] While it addressed economic, social and political inequities within states, it did not reference the treatment of women in times of conflict and, with the exception of proscriptions against child marriage, sex trafficking and exploitation of prostitution, no reference was made to rape, sexual assault or sexual violence. Even still, it took twelve years before the CEDAW became a legally binding treaty.

Between the mid-1970s and the mid-1990s, the UN sponsored four World Conferences on Women meant to identify further sites of gender specific human rights violations and to periodically review progress towards conference goals. The first conference was held in Mexico in 1975, the United Nation's self-proclaimed 'International Women's Year'. The conference report referred only twice to rape. The 28th principle explicitly named it at the head of the list of infractions against women and girls to be prevented.[38] The second reference appears in a note particular to Bangladesh in the appendix.[39] In an effort to keep the attention of the international community trained on women's rights concerns after the conference, the report further advocated for the UN Assembly to pronounce 1975–1985 the 'United Nations Decade for Women and Development'.[40] The ensuing World Conferences on Women in Copenhagen and Nairobi would slowly and sparingly expand the focus from sexual assaults committed against women in private to those in the public sphere, but the general lack of their prominence in the reports clearly suggests that even here they were not of primary importance.

The distinction between humans and persons in international law

Increased efforts to highlight worldwide human rights violations in theory did little to prevent them in practice. In the period between the Second World War and the late 1980s, when human rights discourses were gaining almost universal currency (at least in principle), the world witnessed unprecedented numbers of wartime systematic rapes of women and girls in Pakistan, Guatemala, Cambodia, Indonesia and East Timor. With each occurrence, all of which went virtually unchecked by international military or legal measures in this supposed age of women's rights, gender-specific assault became increasingly and obscenely mundane. The epidemic reached catastrophic proportions in the 1990s during conflicts in Sierra Leone, the former Yugoslavia and Rwanda. When the international community turned a blind eye to early reports of exploiting rape as a weapon of war and ethnic cleansing in those war zones, legal scholar Catherine MacKinnon brilliantly questioned whether women were in fact 'human', and not only before the law but also before the eyes of the world:

> Her suffering has the dignity and her death the honor, of a crime against humanity ... But when a woman is tortured ... humanity is not violated. Here, she is a woman—but *only* a woman. Her violation outrages the conscience of few beyond her friends. What is done to women is either too specific to women to be seen as human or too generic to human beings to be seen as specific to women. Atrocities committed against

women are either too human to fit the notion of female or too female to fit the notion of human. 'Human' and 'female' are mutually exclusive by definition: you cannot be a woman and a human being at the same time.[41]

MacKinnon's palpable exasperation is not without justification. Despite the proliferation of human rights discourses after the Second World War, nothing was being done to stop the escalation in the number and severity of sexual assaults in war. Even as far back as the Hague conventions, the ostensible reason behind the human rights project was to better protect both civilian and non-civilians during conflict situations. However, implicit in such a project is the need to better control the human subject. The efficacy of human rights legislation depends on it. But decisions that pass *sub silentio* leave room for interpretation and are thus less likely to be enforced than those stated directly. That this was still in practice almost 100 years after the 1907 Hague Convention, and following enormous strides in our understanding of gender relations in society, was frankly unbelievable. The message seems to have been that even when rape happened against one's will, it was the product of urges and so was natural, although perhaps unfortunate. Even when it was actualised as a weapon of war, it was still sex. Even when it was acted out on hundreds of thousands of people in public—under command, by gangs, frequently accompanied by the mutilation of breasts, buttocks and genitalia, and often followed by death—it was treated as belonging to the murky, intimate and thus understandably under-regulated private sphere of 'women's matters'.

MacKinnon's assertion that '[one] cannot be a woman and a human being at the same time' is clearly hyperbolic, but the error—if one can even call it that—is semantic alone. Although women obviously belong to the human species, when MacKinnon wrote those words in the early 1990s, women may not have been 'persons', at least in the legal sense, despite the fact that the Vienna Declaration and Program of Action emanating from the 1993 World Conference on Human Rights affirmed for the first time that the rights of women and girls were 'declared to be part of [universal] human rights'.[42] The difference seems to be one of understanding human rights and international humanitarian law as natural law—thus available to all human beings, in theory—or positive law, for which one must earn enfranchisement, otherwise understood as 'personhood'. Joseph Slaughter argues—and MacKinnon would certainly concur—that despite the misnomer, it is the latter that informs the human rights project, whether articulated in literature or the law. To adapt the phrasing of Simone de Beauvoir, one is not born a person; one becomes one. In his exceptional *Human Rights, Inc.*, Slaughter explores this type of Deleuzian 'being-of-becoming' as it manifests in human rights law and its literary analogue, the *Bildungsroman*. His aim is to demonstrate how cultural objects—here, a type of literary text—reflect society on one hand and exert social pressure on the other. For Slaughter, both the discourse of human rights law and that of the *Bildungsroman* articulate a particular form of 'personification'. In human rights law, this is expressed as legal empowerment in the passage from human being to world citizen. In the *Bildungsroman*, it is carried out through the 'coming of age' trope endemic to the genre.

However, not all human beings are created equal before these (heavily invested) discursive practices. Building on the words of René Cassin, Slaughter notes that 'like the cultural institution of the novel' human rights law 'legitimates particular forms and subjects of history and subjugates or erases others'.[43] More precisely, it is *by* legitimating or affirming particular subjects as representatives of the universal to the exclusion of others that human rights discourses negate the potential for the personification of said others. For while human rights narratives 'speak the language of universalism and absolutes' (by stating that such rights simply and inherently belong to 'all human beings' and 'everyone'), the plain truth is that even today not every human is able to realise (cognitively or circumstantially) such 'simple facts ... in a concrete, practicable, or justiciable way'.[44] Ironically, the justification for women's effacement in human rights law was further exacerbated by the intensified emphasis on women's experience as one of alterity. Although necessitated by the absence of attention to women's issues in what were supposedly gender-neutral UN factions, the creation of women-specific splinter groups and conferences served to underscore their marginality in the international arena. As off-shoots of 'standard' divisions of the UN, women's rights could be legitimately perceived as belonging to a special branch of human rights whilst simultaneously not comprising its organic constituents. More alarming still—and this speaks volumes about the co-mingling of the ostensibly liberal human rights project with capitalist ideology—although not all humans are permitted 'incorporation' in international human rights law, corporations almost universally enjoy 'personification'.

Following the reasoning of political philosopher John Locke, James McHugh explains the relative legal status of the 'human' versus that of 'person' by comparing it to the substantive difference between human rights and civil rights. The first term designates the necessity driven rights to which one is entitled by virtue of being a human being and 'possessing the human desire to achieve full potential and dignity as a human individual'.[45] The second stands for those rights to which one is entitled by dint of being a citizen which are entrenched in Locke's concept of private property. In contrast to the recipient of human rights whose desires circulate in the realm of self-actualisation, the citizen's desires focus on his ability 'to enjoy formal access to the potential benefits of, and participation within, civil society' so that 'participation within the political society, as one of its members, becomes crucial for [his] preservation and self-fulfilment'.[46] Either way, if history is any indication, women do not appear to fit into the equation. While they may very well 'desire' to achieve full potential and dignity, laws governing sexual violence in war (or otherwise) do not allow them to do so. They are certainly not 'citizens' of the international community, if the measure of membership is one's ability to 'influence the state, determine its composition and protect [oneself] against its encroachments'.[47]

To be fair, the universalising language of human rights narratives (their 'textual logic') is not intended to be reflective. It is not meant to state the reality of what *is*. Instead, it is 'aspirational' and actualising.[48] In other words, human rights discourse strives to effect *what should be* by declaring that 'what should be' *already is*. For example:

> human rights aspires to convince the individual to regard its projected legal image as real rather than artificial. That is, the trope of incorporation endeavours to naturalize the ideological *persona ficta* of the international human rights person so that the legal image of the person might come to be seen as coextensive with the actual human being.[49]

Despite the best intentions, the 'transitive grammar' at the heart of such narratives ends up crippling the human rights project by instead illuminating the abyss that still exists between what international humanitarian and human rights laws *might mean* (under interpretation) and what they *actually state*. Likewise, human rights law is severely impaired by the discrepancy between what it claims to demand and its power to execute such mandates: the legal exigencies placed on signatories, for example, versus the extent to which the conduct of nations will be policed during conflict and punished after the fact. Admittedly, this last discrepancy is due in part to the incommensurability of international law's grand scope and its comparatively paltry financial and structural resources. But, as William Mulligan brilliantly details, IHL is also routinely betrayed by its very signatories who create justification for opting out of ratified treaties when interests of the state conflict with those of international community.[50] War crimes committed during the First World War demonstrate that this was true with respect to the Hague conventions as well. Such situations represent a refusal on the part of certain states to accept that to be a subject *in* and *of* the law (a scripter and agent of, and an actor within) entails being subject *to* the law, bound by its terms.

For Slaughter, where strong-arm retributive gestures associated with law fail the human rights endeavour in their impotency—feigned or otherwise—'consensus' gained by way of literature can help it to succeed. Here, the *Bildungsroman* acts as both a 'cultural surrogate for the missing warrant and executive sanction of human rights law' and an agent for the human rights message, supplying 'a culturally symbolic legitimacy for the authority of human rights law and the imagination of an international human rights order' that might one day come to pass.[51] While this might well have accounted for the rapid dissemination and increased acceptance of the human rights message following the Second World War and through the end of the twentieth century, it had little effect on governments when state interests were at stake, and almost no effect on the prevention and punishment of sexual assault in conflict situations throughout the mid-1990s. It was all yet more, apparently necessary, collateral damage.

Final thoughts: attention and the letter of the law

> What we cannot speak about we must pass over in silence.
> Ludwig Wittgenstein[52]

The above epitaph is lifted from Wittgenstein's seminal *Tractuatus Logico-Philosophicus*, something of a 'defense and illustration' of logical positivism.[53] In these final words of the text, Wittgenstein offers the only reasonable solution to the problem of attempting to articulate what lies outside of 'reality'. In other words, what we cannot speak about formally (mathematically, for example) or empirically, we must pass over in silence. Although written specifically about the relationship between language and reality as it pertains to philosophy, taken aphoristically this concluding remark could also be read as an eloquent description of the situation of women in armed conflict in IHL throughout most of the twentieth century. Admittedly, the codification of rape in the Hague conventions represented a milestone in jurisprudence pertaining to women in conflict. However, the description of rape as an honour or property crime—even if the honour and property are said to be those of the mostly female victims—is clearly a gross misrepresentation of the reality of rape. Like official reports labelling rape as something driven by lust, hormones and intemperance, such descriptions very obviously do not reflect the violent nature of the act from the point of view of the victim. Rather, they expose how rape was conceived of as a mostly sex-related activity in the male imaginary. The scripting of this crime as something that might be open to interpretation (as is suggested in the vague remark that women ought to be treated with 'all consideration due their sex') or as a criminal act but not one worthy of the label 'grave breach' (as in the 1949 Geneva Convention) is troubling, to say the least. When one adds that these laws were followed by a century of wartime mass rape and a scandalously low rate of prosecution for the crime post-war, it becomes all the more disquieting. It also hints to something that ought to be common knowledge: that there is indeed a connection between legal language and social change, or lack thereof. Put another way, 'what we cannot speak about'—accurately, directly or often enough—'we [tend to] pass over in silence'.

In her stunning 'Language, Judgement, and Attention: Writing in the World', Toril Moi opens by relating the details of a terror rampage that took place in Oslo and Utøya, Norway, in July 2011.[54] Recounting how the terrorist's self-styled manifesto was the product of cutting and pasting from a variety of websites, none of which he authored, she described his relationship to language as 'alienated', further stating '[h]e had lost—or maybe he never really had—any sense of the weight of words'.[55] His incapacity to appreciate the importance of language was paralleled by the challenge his monstrous acts presented to those affected by them. They too were at a loss for words.

Though examined in contexts different from those of this essay, Moi's study expresses a similar urgency to address a presumed inability—or unwillingness—to reconcile language with (oftentimes) unpleasant reality. The solution she offers has its roots in the philosophy of attention as expressed by Iris Murdoch, Simone Weil and Cora Diamond. Moi, reading Diamond, asserts that when we have difficulty expressing something clearly it is not because words are inadequate. On the contrary, when we cannot find words 'the problem is not language, it is us'.[56] What Moi advocates to rectify this disparity between reality and our capacity to grasp it is the cultivation of a particular type of attention; that of the 'just and loving gaze'.[57] Despite the sappy connotation one might associate with this expression, what it encourages is simply that one come to the table with little in the way of a predetermined mind-set. It is to do one's 'utmost to see the situation from the other person's point of view'.[58] Far from maintaining a passive position, to be attentive in this way assumes that one 'answers, responds *and takes responsibility*'.[59] For Moi, there is an obvious connection between this type of attentiveness and good writing, a connection that she emphasises by quoting Henry James as stating that to be a great writer one must 'try to be one of the people on whom nothing is lost'.[60] In other words, one's relationship to language must reflect a 'just and loving' attentiveness, where 'every perceptive reflection, every clear formulation, every accurate description' every instance of a 'precise and attentive use of words' becomes both 'an act of resistance' and 'a small victory'.[61] It is precisely this attentiveness that was lacking in the drafting of rape legislation in IHL since The Hague. The consequences were disastrous. The genteel language gave license to view rape as a genteel act and then to treat it as such in law.

In the context of this study, the most extraordinary examples of the radical power of this type of attention and its articulation took place following the unparalleled sexual violence of the Yugoslavian and Rwandan genocides. The first was the decision on the part of the Fourth UN World Conference on Women (Beijing) to dedicate the conference to combatting violence against women. Among the primary 'critical concerns', were those often found in armed conflict: 'systematic rape, sexual slavery, forced pregnancy, forced sterilization and forced abortion'.[62] In her plenary address to the conference, Hillary Rodham Clinton explicitly connected human rights with those of women and enumerated the ways in which those rights were routinely violated. Eliminating the possibility for there to be any confusion, Clinton prefaced each violation habitually practiced against women with the words, 'It is a violation of human rights when ...'.[63]

Contemporaneous with the Beijing Conference were the preliminary investigations of the International Criminal Tribunals of both Yugoslavia and Rwanda (ICTY and ICTR). The convictions that would later come as the result of these tribunals are well known to most. Less so are the circumstances that allowed for the judgements to come about. Sexual violence reached epic proportions in these two conflicts. In the former Yugoslavia, Serbian militia established 'rape camps' in what were once schools, hotels and homes, where women and girls were chained to mattresses and gang raped, and sometimes filmed in the process. In the name of ethnic cleansing, those who survived were forced to carry the subsequent pregnancies to term. In Rwanda, and in less than 100 days, UN Special Rapporteur on Rwanda Rene Degni-Segui estimated that between 200,000 and 500,000 Tutsi and moderate Hutu women and girls were sexually assaulted—often with sticks and machetes—mutilated, and left to bleed out in the streets. Of those who survived, approximately 80 per cent contracted AIDS.[64] These facts were widely circulated in international media, yet little attention was paid to them in the initial phases of the International Criminal Tribunals. Given past legal (in)activity, it would not have been terribly surprising if no attention were paid to them. Yet, in both cases, it was the somewhat unconventional actions of several women judges that would change the course of history. Although it is not typically within the purview of criminal judges to interfere with the prosecutor's indictments, when there were no references to rape in the hearing applications in the opening phases of the ICTY, judges Elizabeth Odio Benito and Gabrielle MacDonald initiated the process by directly asking the prosecutor whether rape had been investigated at all.[65] Knowledge about this case would also influence the outcome of one of the most significant trials of the ICTR. Jean-Paul Akayesu, the mayor of the Taba commune at the time of the Rwandan genocide, was charged with incitement to commit genocide and crimes against humanity. When presiding justice Navanethem Pillay saw that there were initially no charges of rape in the indictment despite a wealth of evidence, she and several other judges began questioning the witnesses directly about sexual assaults they had either experienced or witnessed.[66] The resultant convictions that issued from these tribunals were ground-breaking. Not only was rape defined in international law for the first time from the victim's perspective, these cases also presented the first judgements for rape as a crime against humanity and a crime constituting genocide.

Admittedly, it took cataclysmic levels of violence before the international community would take legal notice and responsibility. Admittedly again, despite these momentous decisions mass rape during armed conflict is still ubiquitous and largely tolerated. One need only look to the international 'response' to what is currently taking place in the Democratic Republic of the Congo—which UN Special Representative Margo Wallstrom has called the 'rape capital of the world'—to see that this continues to be the case.[67] The same could be argued about the lack of 'response' to the activities of Boko Haram or to Sudan's Janjaweed militia. Nonetheless, it does not diminish the significance of the very direct language of the Beijing Conference, the newly imagined legal protocols for dealing with rape developed at the ICTY and ICTR, or the victories achieved through the 'just and loving attention' of several women judges. Such achievements would later inform the Rome

Statute for the newly established International Criminal Court. Here, provisions were made for the first time for the legal obligation to view systematic rape and associated sexual violations as crimes against humanity (Article 7) and war crimes (Article 8). The stipulation that these obligations would apply whether the conflict was of an international character or not also represented the first time that international human rights law and international humanitarian law would come together in the service of women's rights.[68]

Hillary Rodham Clinton's speech at the Beijing World Conference on Women began by stating that historic ambivalence about human rights abuses against women has been pervasive because 'the history of women has been a history of silence'.[69] It is a history of silence masking the blood-soaked truth of what many, many men have allowed themselves to do to women when enraged. It is also the truth of how they have permitted themselves to get away with it post-conflict. This did not happen not because representatives of state, lawmakers and diplomats were suffering from a linguistic deficit, but rather because they appear not to have seen the need to understand what took place by effecting 'just and loving' attention. Conceivably, this is because, in order to do so they would have to—at least provisionally—place themselves in what might seem to be the passive and subjected position traditionally associated with women in love, law and war. In the words of Simone Weil, they would need to be 'empty, waiting, not seeking anything, but ready to receive in its naked truth the object that is to penetrate it'.[70] If unable to do so, how could they be blamed for not better articulating women's experience of sexual violation in war and thus regulating it in law. For what we choose not to see, we describe poorly. What we cannot speak about we must pass over in silence.

The legacy of the Hague Conventions of 1899 and 1907 on the regulation of sexual violence in wartime is complicated and messy, making it easy to overlook or willingly sidestep. The *sub silentio* admonishment of rape in Article 46 and the gross misrepresentation of the nature of the act in some senses allowed for, and even authorised, the transgression of the prohibition of rape in both war and in war crime tribunals. In spite of new understandings of gender relations and advancements in women's rights on the home front, nearly a century of violent sexual assaults took place before the language and practice of law would coincide with the reality of war. However, it is also necessary to acknowledge the debt owed to the Hague conventions as one of the primary inaugurators of the human rights project that ultimately allowed for the realisation of accurately scripted gender-based violence laws in IHL and in their enforcement.

Notes

1 My emphasis. Oxford English Dictionary. *Definition: Sub Silentio.* [online] Available at: http://www.oed.com/ view/Entry/301650?redirectedFrom=sub+silentio#eid [Accessed 1 May 2016].

2 My emphasis. THELAW.com Dictionary. *Precedents Sub Silentio*. [online] Available at: http://dictionary.thelaw.com/precedents-sub-silentio/ [Accessed 24 August 2016].
3 My emphasis. (2010). *Wharton's Pocket Law Dictionary*. New Delhi: Universal Law Publishing Co., p.731.
4 My emphasis. See Calton v. Bragg, 15 East 226; Thompson v. Musser, 1 Dall. 464, 1 L. Ed. 222.
5 P. Viseur Sellers. (2009). The Prosecution of Sexual Violence in conflict: The Importance of Human Rights as Means of Interpretation. [online] *Special Report for the Office of The United Nations High Commissioner of Human Rights*. Available at: http://www.ohchr.org/Documents/Issues/Women/WRGS/Paper_Prosecution_of_Sexual_Violence.pdf [Accessed 15 May 2016].
6 Article I of the Annex to the 1899 Convention and Article I of the 1907 Convention. Both cited in Sellers, p.7.
7 Although she notes only Article 46 of the 1907 Hague Convention, it first appeared as Article 46 in the Annex of the 1899 Convention with only slight modifications in the language.
8 B. Baker. (2009). Hague Peace Conferences: 1899 and 1907. *Oxford Public International Law* [online]. Available at: http://opil.ouplaw.com/view/10.1093/law:epil/9780199231690/law-9780199231690-e305 [Accessed 3 August 2016].
9 See: K. Draper. (2015). *War and Individual Rights: The Foundations of Just War Theory*. Oxford: Oxford University Press.
10 S. Brownmiller. (1975). *Against Our Will: Men, Women and Rape*. New York: Bantam Books.
11 Sellers.
12 Sellers.
13 G. Walker. (2013). Sexual Violence and Rape in Europe 1500–1750. In: S. Toulalan and K. Fisher, eds, *The Routledge History of Sex and the Body: 1500 to the Present*. New York: Routledge, pp.429–443.
14 Oxford English Dictionary. *Definition: Rape*. [online] Available at: http://0-www.oed.com.libus.csd.mu.edu/search?searchType=dictionary&q=rape&_searchBtn=Search. [Accessed 28 July 2016].
15 Oxford English Dictionary, *Definition: Rape*.
16 The Avalon Project at Yale Law School. (1863). *General Orders No. 100: Lieber Code*. [online] Available at: http://avalon.law.yale.edu/19th_century/lieber.asp#sec2 [Accessed 7 May 2016]. See also C. Feimster. (2013). Rape and Justice in the Civil War. [online] *New York Times*. Available at: http://opinionator.blogs.nytimes.com/2013/04/25/rape-and-justice-in-the-civil-war/?_r=0 [Accessed 10 May 2016].
17 Article 46 of the Laws and Customs of War on Land: 'Family honors and rights, individual lives and private property, as well as religious convictions and liberty, must be respected. Private property cannot be confiscated' The Avalon Project at Yale Law School, (1899). *Laws of War: Laws and Customs of War on Land (Hague II)*. [online] Available at: http://avalon.law.yale.edu/19th_century/hague02.asp#art46 [Accessed 24 August 2016].
18 A. Rivière. (2015). Rape. [online] 1914–1918 Online: International Encyclopedia of the First World War. Available at: http://encyclopedia.1914-1918-online.net/article/rape [Accessed 10 May 10 2016].
19 Rivière.
20 M. Leroy. (1915). *Les atrocités Allemandes en France: Reproduction intégrale illustrée des rapports présentés à M. le Président du Conseil par la commission instituée en vue de constater les actes commis par l'ennemi en violation du droit des gens*. Paris: D. A. Longuet; The Avalon Project at Yale Law School, (1915).

The Bryce Report. [online] Available at: http://avalon.law.yale.edu/20th_century/brycere.asp [Accessed 8 August 2016].
21 My translation.
22 My emphasis. S. Glueck. (1944). *War Criminals: Their Prosecution and Punishment.* New York: Alfred A. Knopf, p.68.
23 R. Biezanek. (1973). War Crimes: History and Definition. In: M. Bassiouni. and V. Nanda, eds. *A Treatise on International Criminal Law.* Vol. 1. Springfield: Charles C. Thomas, p.559.
24 A. Mitrović. (2007). *Serbia's Great War, 1914–1918.* West Lafayette: Purdue University Press, p.222.
25 The Avalon Project at Yale Law School, *The Bryce Report*, Part 2, Section 1b.
26 The Avalon Project at Yale Law School, *The Bryce Report.*
27 The United Nations Convention Against Torture and Other Cruel, Inhuman or Degrading Treatment or Punishment identifies torture in the following way: '1) intentional infliction of severe pain or suffering, 2) for a specific purpose, such as to obtain information, as punishment or to intimidate, or for any reason based on discrimination, 3) by or at the instigation of or with the consent or acquiescence of State authorities'. Available at: International Justice Resource Center. *Torture.* [online] Available at: http://www.ijrcenter.org/thematic-research-guides/torture/ [Accessed 7 August 2016].
28 Glueck, p.88.
29 The Avalon Project at Yale Law School. (1929). *Convention Between the United States of America and Other Powers, Relating to Prisoners of War.* [online] Available at: http://avalon.law.yale.edu/20th_century/geneva02.asp#art3 [Accessed 3 May 2016].
30 A partial list of countries where women had the right to vote by 1929 can be accessed at Women Suffrage and Beyond. *The Woman Suffrage Timeline.* [online] Available at: http://womensuffrage.org/?page_id=69. [Accessed 6 August 2016].
31 Number ten, charter of the four occupying powers in Germany.
32 L. Wolfe. (2 May 2014). The Index: Justice for Rape in War. [online] *Women under Siege.* Available at: http://www.womenundersiegeproject.org/blog/entry/the-index-justice-for-crimes-of-rape-in-war [Accessed 1 August 2016].
33 University of Minnesota Human Rights Library. (1998). *Prosecutor v. Akayesu, Case No. ICTR-96-4, Judgment.* [online] Available at: https://www1.umn.edu/humanrts/instree/ICTR/AKAYESU_ICTR-96-4/Judgment_ICTR-96-4-T.html [Accessed 15 May 2016].
34 The Avalon Project at Yale Law School. (1949). *Convention (IV) Relative to the Protection of Civilian Persons in Time of War.* [online] Available at: http://avalon.law.yale.edu/20th_century/geneva07.asp. [Accessed 6 August 2016].
35 The Avalon Project at Yale Law School. (1949). *Geneva Convention (III) Relative to the Treatment of Prisoners of War.* [online] Available at: http://avalon.law.yale.edu/20th_century/geneva03.asp#art14. [Accessed 6 August 2016].
36 Human Rights Watch. *International Protections.* [online] Available at: https://www.hrw.org/legacy/about/projects/womrep/General-24.htm [Accessed 5 August 2016].
37 UN Women. (1979). *Convention on the Elimination of All Forms of Discrimination against Women.* [online] Available at: http://www.un.org/womenwatch/daw/cedaw/ [Accessed 5 August 2016].
38 United Nations. (1976). *Report of the World Conference of the International Women's Year.* [online] Available at: http://www.un.org/womenwatch/daw/beijing/otherconferences/Mexico/Mexico%20conference%20report%20optimized.pdf, p.7 [Accessed 5 May 2016].

39 United Nations, *Report of the World Conference of the International Women's Year*. p.45.
40 United Nations, *Report of the World Conference of the International Women's Year*. p.35.
41 C. MacKinnon. (1994). Rape, Genocide, and Women's Human Rights. *Harvard Women's Law Journal*, 17, p.6.
42 United Nations. *United Nations Work on Violence Against Women: Information Note, Division for the Advancement of Women*. [online]. Available at: http://www.un.org/womenwatch/daw/news/unwvaw.html [Accessed 20 May 2016].
43 J. Slaughter. (2007). *Human Rights, Inc*. New York: Fordham University Press, p.5.
44 Slaughter, p.3.
45 J. McHugh. (1992). What is the Difference between a 'Person' and a 'Human Being' within the Law. *The Review of Politics*, 54(3), p.458.
46 McHugh, p.457.
47 McHugh, p.457.
48 Slaughter, p.26.
49 Slaughter, p.22.
50 See W. Mulligan's chapter in this collection.
51 Slaughter, p.85.
52 L. Wittgenstein. (2001) *Tractacus Logico-Philosophicus*. D.F. Pears and B.F. McGuinness, trans. London: Routledge, p. 89.
53 Here I am evoking Joachim DuBellay's sixteenth-century manifesto of the Pléiade poets, *Défense et Illustration de la Langue Française* (F. Goyet et O. Millet, eds. Paris, Champion, 2003), which also sought to establish the parameters of a particular type of language by both describing and imitating it.
54 T. Moi. (2017). *Revolution of the Ordinary: Literary Studies after Wittgenstein, Austin, and Cavell*. Forthcoming. Chicago: Chicago University Press.
55 Moi, p.1.
56 Moi, p.7.
57 Moi, pp.3–4.
58 Moi, p.4.
59 Moi, p.5.
60 Moi, p.8.
61 Moi, p.13.
62 United Nations, *United Nations Work on Violence Against Women*.
63 H.R. Clinton. (1995). *Remarks to the UN 4th World Conference on Women Plenary Session*. [online] American Rhetoric. Available at: http://www.americanrhetoric.com/speeches/hillaryclintonbeijingspeech.htm [Accessed 31 July 2016].
64 N. Sai. (2012). *Rwanda*. [online] Women Under Siege. Available at: http://www.womenundersiegeproject.org/conflicts/profile/rwanda [Accessed 8 August 2016].
65 Brandeis University. *Navanethem Pillay, South Africa Judge of the International Criminal Court*. [online] Available at: http://lts.brandeis.edu/images/libguides/judges/pillay.pdf [Accessed 25 May 2016].
66 Brandeis University.
67 F. Lloyd Davies. (24 November 2011). *Why Eastern DR Congo is 'Rape Capital of the World*. [online] CNN. Available at: http://www.cnn.com/2011/11/24/world/africa/democratic-congo-rape/ [Accessed 25 July 2016].
68 International Criminal Court. *Rome Statute of the International Criminal Court*. [online] Available at: https://www.icc-cpi.int/iccdocs/PIDS/publications/RomeStatutEng.pdf [Accessed 25 May 2016].
69 H.R. Clinton.
70 Moi, p.4.

7 The duel of honour and the origins of the rules for arms, warfare and arbitration in the Hague conferences

Robert A. Nye

The duel has been a stock subject in literature, drama and film for generations, and an interest of hobbyists, weapons enthusiasts and cranks. Academic historians, however, only began studying it in the 1970s. The duel ended in the British Isles and its empire and in North America around 1850. However, it persisted and flourished virtually everywhere else in continental Europe until after the First World War. Hundreds of duels took place each year in France, Italy, Germany, Austria–Hungary, Russia, Poland and elsewhere. Each country and society had its own duelling preference: the French favoured the *épée*, the Germans and Russians the pistol, the Italians and Austro-Hungarians the sabre, though all these weapons figured everywhere in European duels. Modern duels were not as lethal or numerous as seventeenth-century duels but, until recently, historians have treated the duel as an anachronism, a vestige of fading aristocratic power and its culture of honour.[1]

Nevertheless, honour codes and the protocols that regulated duels played an important role in the development of modern civility, the evolution of professional ethics in all-male professions and in the Hague Peace Conferences of 1899 and 1907. Over the course of the nineteenth century, duelling protocols attained the status of private law and in continental Europe served as a basis for resolving differences between men with minimal violence or loss of reputation. European elites regarded the concept of honour and its practices as a benevolent influence in the expansion of civility to the middling classes, a way of fashioning gentlemen. It is not surprising, therefore, that western statesmen and the international lawyers and activists who were the moving forces in the continuing efforts to codify the laws of war, limit the growth of dangerous arms and embrace procedures for international arbitration believed, in Martti Koskenniemi's words, that the solution lay in applying 'appropriate personal attitudes' to 'the macrocosm of public law'.[2] Following the founding of the Institute of International Law in Ghent, the 'men of 1873' acted 'like so many chivalrous knights, defending the oppressed against aggressors, peace against war', Koskenniemi vividly suggests. These men believed 'states were above all right-holders whose rights were limited by those of others as well as a moral code akin to that between honourable men in bourgeois society'.³

Our historical memories of bloody jousts, the lethal, collective *mêlées* between nobles in seventeenth-century Europe and the futile deaths of writers and politicians like Aleksandr Pushkin and Alexander Hamilton make it difficult for us to appreciate the positive contributions these rituals played in the civilising process in the West. There is continual historiographical debate on the legacy of honour codes in the gradual recession of civil conflict and inter-state violence since medieval times. Pessimism about the real benefit of restraints on violence based on gentlemanly honour is warranted but this ought not to obscure our understanding of the historical efforts at the end of the nineteenth century to implement a new order of world peace on a foundation that attempted to regulate the scale and danger of conflict.

It is useful to follow the debate on the duel and the 'civilising process' to see how inaccurately it is represented in the historical literature. The term 'civilising process' was first coined by Norbert Elias in the late 1930s to describe the recession of violence in the West since the Middle Ages.⁴ Following in the tradition of Elias' argument, numerous other writers suggest that duelling was a reflection of pre-modern attitudes towards violence and lawlessness.⁵ Two recent popular books address honour cultures in ways that perpetuate misunderstandings of the historical role of the duel of honour. Steven Pinker's *The Better Angels of our Nature: Why Violence Has Declined* (2011) presents impressive statistical evidence for the historic decline in homicide, violent crimes, sexual crimes and bloodshed in warfare.⁶ However, Pinker sees honour cultures and the duel as irrational excrescences of an aristocratic order the persistence of which retarded the advance of the civilising process, until, he writes, the duel became 'ridiculous' and 'vanished into thin air' in the mid-nineteenth century. Honour itself was 'the strange commodity that exists because everyone else believes that it exists'. Today, as Pinker argues, '"take ten paces turn and fire" is more likely to call to mind Bugs Bunny and Yosemite Sam than "men of honor"'.⁷

Kwame Anthony Appiah's *The Honor Code: How Moral Revolutions Happen* (2010) discusses the relationship of honour codes to the abolition of slavery, the demise of foot-binding in China and the end of the Anglo-Saxon duel. He argues that the duel ended suddenly in the 1850s when violent honour was mysteriously transmuted into a modern form of mutual respect and personal dignity. Neither of these recent authors understands the historical role duelling and duelling codes played in the civilising process they are at pains to elucidate. The co-evolution of honour codes and violence mitigation was a slow and piecemeal process with few abrupt disjunctions. The men who participated in the Hague conferences saw themselves at an historical endpoint of the civilising process, when the practices that had developed to contain and regulate individual conflict might be justifiably expanded to the pacification of international relations.

From late medieval times through to the nineteenth century, European honour cultures flourished in regions where state power was weak and disputes were settled more frequently in personal confrontations than by recourse to legal authority. The number of duels varied according to time and place but they became less dangerous over time with fewer fatalities and serious injuries. The history of the duel reveals that the codes and practices associated with affairs of honour not only diminished the violence of encounters but, more importantly, influenced the structures of male interaction in social and professional life in ways that made unrestrained violence less rather than more likely. A historic function of the duel was to distinguish the men who were eligible to participate in its rituals and thus to perpetuate social hierarchy. However, in the long run, the duel exercised a democratising influence in society by stimulating adaptations in the quasi-legal status of honour codes that appealed to both upwardly mobile men and to women, who successfully prosecuted offenses against their honour in criminal and divorce cases in the second half of the nineteenth century.[8]

Elias' account of the pacification of violence rests on two principal assumptions. The first was that by the nineteenth century the state had essentially monopolised violence, imposing the rule of law over society. This made spontaneous violence more liable to punishment, eliminated the fear of falling under the power of another man and encouraged individuals to exercise greater degrees of self-restraint. The second assumption was the increasing complexity of modernising societies, which not only reinforced these affective changes but made them into widespread societal norms. In the account Elias offers, the shifts from emotional spontaneity to restraint and from vertical to more horizontal social orders occurred in tandem. Elias' model has encouraged many historians to place the duel of honour and the decline of the aristocracy together among the casualties of modernisation. In reality, the codes that disciplined and restrained duellers were integral aspects of civility. The codes complemented, rather than undermined the rule of law, and schooled generations of men in the advantages of civility.[9] The self-command that a man of honour required in a duel was the same trait that allowed him to advance and prosper in the settled worlds of commerce and society.

The rules governing disputes and differences between men developed over hundreds of years from rough-and-ready codes of combat into statutes in the domain of private law, which were designed to contain violence and preserve disputants' honour and personal dignity. These rules held men who aspired to honourability upheld ethical standards understood by everyone in good society and subjected them to scrutiny and to judgements which could offset the legal and cultural privileges they otherwise enjoyed as élite males. However daunting it was to face an opponent's bullet or steel, proper adherence to the rules prescribed by honour protocols shielded men against the far more crushing shame endured by those who either avoided duelling confrontations or who yielded to spontaneous or violent reactions to affronts.

Though duelling codes originated in aristocratic *milieux*, they were in fact available to all worthy aspirants. No man or class of men controlled the codes. Rather, it was the codes that made the men. Class, bloodlines or titles of nobility neither conferred a permanent right to honour nor irrevocably excluded men on the margins. Honour cultures were inherently unstable. Who was in and who was out depended on changing social and economic fortunes and on the credible performance of what contemporaries took to be a right to honour. Most affairs of honour took place on the borders of contested social boundaries where individuals engaged in negotiations over claims or rejections of inclusion. Thus, though it was social mobility that produced occasions for conflict over status, it was social symmetry that established the warrant for resolving them.[10]

Group discipline and the negotiation of honour claims enforced egalitarian codes of civility in two ways: by shaming or expelling group members who brought the group into disrespect through dishonourable behaviour and by sanctioning methods for resolving disputes by ritualistic violence if negotiations failed. When there was sufficient agreement within the greater honour culture on these criteria, there was a smooth cycling of the unworthy out and the newly worthy in, and a minimisation of unpredictable violence or collective disorder. In effect, the social evolution of honour throughout the early modern and modern eras expanded the reach of the honour culture, democratised access to its rituals and introduced an increasing number of people to the belief that unrestrained or spontaneous violence was not an inevitable aspect of social life.

The development of duelling jurisprudence from the sixteenth to the twentieth centuries

The duel originated as a judicial instrument. In France, until the last 'judicial duel' was fought in 1547, noble duels were judged by God, presided over by the sovereign and often ended in death. Henceforth duels would be private affairs between individuals, in which comportment mattered more than outcome.[11] By the late sixteenth century, French monarchs had established a number of institutional procedures that sought to adjudicate differences between noblemen in the general interest of civic order. The act of offering or accepting a challenge was not a public criminal offense, but *lèse-majesté*, a personal offense against the sovereign. A *Tribunal du Point d'Honneur*, staffed by gentlemen of the realm, served as an appellate court through the reign of Louis XIV and, together with lesser arbiters, was successful in reducing the number and violence of private duels.[12]

Honour violence was also constrained in Northern Europe by the spread of sixteenth-century Italian civility books. Baldassare Castiglione's *The Courtier* (1529) and other texts on etiquette and courtly deportment circulated widely, schooling generations of European courtiers well into the next century.[13] Lessons in civility and resort to the duel, far from being incompatible, seemed to be natural qualities of noble gentlemen in this era. In France, young noblemen were taught the rules of civil comportment from an early age by parents who wished them worldly success. In England, contemporaneous Italian *Codes Duello* were regarded as complementary to an education in refined manners, not a contradiction to it. The duelling codes taught courteous behaviour, in which civility was the norm and recourse to the duel limited to certain cases.[14] There was thus no decisive break with a military vocation for this class; honour and the civil virtues of *honnêteté* were equal components in a gentleman's armamentarium.

When a conflict between gentlemen arose, violence was never excluded as an option for settling the matter, but the anger this might provoke in individuals was constrained by rules they acknowledged that governed its expression. Indeed, the obligation to conceal open displays of anger was intrinsic to the negotiation of differences between gentlemen and, should it come to that, their performance in duels. The focus of attention in affairs of honour was on the comportment of the antagonists. Displays of anger or fear were far more important indications of weakness or unworthiness in a man than being bested by one's adversary. The principal goal of duellists was to steel themselves and conceal their feelings from the world, no matter what the outcome.

The foundations of modern duelling jurisprudence were laid in the first half of the nineteenth century and reached a kind of floodtide in the 1880s in Germany, Russia, France, Italy and Austria-Hungary. By the 1820s an *embourgeoisment* of the duel had begun, and modern codes appeared to instruct new men in the rules of affairs of honour. The most important of these modern codes appeared in 1836 and was a model for many subsequent publications: *Essai sur le duel* by the Comte de Chateauvillard. Chateauvillard's code was co-signed by peers of France and other eminent gentlemen and designed for use by 'qualified' men.[15]

Because the Criminal Code did not mention the duel, Chateauvillard believed his code merited legal status 'because honour is no less sacred than governmental law'.[16] In the same year Chateauvillard's code appeared it was cited in an Assizes Court case involving a fatal duel, with the effect of exculpating the survivor who was judged to have adhered to the 'law' of the code. The survivor's lawyer conceded that any duel could become an occasion for premeditated murder but, citing Chateauvillard, insisted that an offender merited the death penalty 'not because he has engaged in a duel but because he has violated the laws of honour on the very terrain he had sworn to defend them'.[17] Subsequently, the codes of Chateauvillard and his successors served as the basis for a 'private' jurisprudence that was regarded in civil and criminal law as the warrant for both punishments and civil fines.

Chateauvillard's code outlawed 'extraordinary' duels, strictly regulated dangerous pistol duels by proposing particular forms and distances and held that sword duels should cease with 'first blood'. It specified that each dueller should choose two seconds. Moreover, the code strictly regulated types of weapons used in duels: only paired, unrifled duelling pistols of antique type were permitted; sabres should have blunt tips to minimise stabbing wounds; and *épées* must be identical pairs. He specified a hierarchy of offenses that might provoke duels, from trivial breaches of etiquette to personal 'insults' and, finally, the physical affront that would earn an offended man's seconds the right to choose the weapons and conditions of combat. The character and qualities of a man's seconds were crucial, since they were responsible for protecting his interests and honour in the preliminary negotiations. The seconds were obliged to settle amongst themselves the conditions of combat, appeal to a duelling expert about details of protocol if they disagreed and serve as legal surrogates for their principal and as judges of the correctness of the ensuing combat.

Over the course of the nineteenth century, a duelling jurisprudence developed throughout Europe. It regulated every detail of the duel from the type of dress to duelling ground comportment. One particular development was the requirement that a doctor be present and that a neutral 'master of combat' inspect the weapons and give the signal to begin. Among the other rules developed, swordsmen were allowed to parry but not grasp an opponent's weapon with the free hand. Combat had to cease either at first blood, when one man had fallen or was disabled or disarmed or after an exchange of shots. The fact that a man who broke these rules was not only dishonoured but also liable to criminal or civil penalty underscores the juridical nature of the proceedings. There was also a burden on a man's seconds to negotiate fair conditions for the duel and to draw up a post-combat *procès-verbal* with his opponent's men, which would subsequently be published in the press and which all parties agreed to have accurately described the duelling ground action. Any failure to accomplish these tasks with precision and integrity imperilled the seconds' own honour and put them at legal risk. Above all, a man's seconds needed to possess the frankness and *savoir-faire* to tell him when his own offenses required his apology or when his opponent's offense did not reach the threshold of a duel-worthy provocation.

Everywhere in Europe, the duel was democratised and its dangers lessened. In Germany, where the *Kaiserreich* continued to promote the prerogatives of the nobility, the ability to give 'satisfaction' to another man (*Satisfaktionfähig*) was expanded to vast numbers of middle-class men who were also reserve army officers or state bureaucrats. In lieu of duelling, German professionals had resort to their own disciplinary courts to resolve personal differences. Difficult cases were submitted to a Supreme Honour Court in Leipzig.[18] Similar institutions served professionals in Great Britain and France where procedures were developed to resolve disputes that were modelled on the point of honour.[19]

New egalitarian political orders also helped spread honour cultures. In newly minted republics like France, Mexico and Argentina, regime loyalists considered eligibility for the duel to be the private dimension of their democratic citizenship and a right to be treated with respect by their social superiors.[20] By the 1870s, the new fluidity of social life produced uncertainty about a man's place in the social hierarchy and thus occasions for disputes about precedence in matters great and small. This very uncertainty encouraged men to mind their words and gestures lest they inadvertently give offense.

The legal apotheosis of duelling regulations was attained in Italy, where incremental democratisation, the perils of regional integration and social mobility combined to make duelling a particularly volatile and frequent phenomenon. Thomas Hughes counts over 22 duelling manuals in print in 1914.[21] The most successful of these, Iacopo Gelli's *Codice cavalleresco italiano* (1892), which resembled the legal tomes it was modelled upon, was regarded as 'a living jurisprudence' of the duel. Gelli's book served as the legal basis for court rulings throughout Italy in which punishments and awards in civil suits were meted out for violation of the 'laws' of the duel. Gelli also helped to establish regional honour courts, crowned by a *Corte permanente d'honore* in Florence, which heard their appeals.[22]

The importance of 'private' duelling jurisprudence was heightened in France, Italy and Germany by the relative weakness of libel laws. Libel laws punished public slander with risibly low fines and did not ordinarily consider the truth of an allegation. This process left unresolved feelings and a cloud of uncertainty over the reputation of a slandered party, who, by bringing legal action, had surrendered his right to 'give the lie' to his antagonist. In any case, the laws of libel and defamation had no jurisdiction over private insults or physical affronts, or over breaches of the protection a man extended to the women in his household.[23]

By the end of the nineteenth century, the rituals and practices of the point of honour, and the formal arbitration of differences between men according to its rules, were firmly established in the private and public law codes of many European states. Many of these laws have served as the basis of the dignity laws that have proliferated in international and national law codes since the Second World War, on the principal that no man or woman should suffer insult or disrespect with impunity or be ineligible for the distribution of honours by states or official agencies.[24] The familiarity of cosmopolitan élites with the ways honourable men could resolve differences or expiate them with a minimum of danger was deeply woven into western national cultures. As a consequence, they also played a central role in the negotiations at The Hague in 1899 and 1907.

Duelling protocols, honour and the internationalisation of honour at The Hague

It was perhaps inevitable that the process of personifying peoples and nations in the nineteenth-century era of nationalism would encourage projections of personal honour onto nation-states. This conflation of personal with national honour led to what Geoffrey Best has called this era's 'nationalization of honour', in which 'what had been a precise code for noblemen became a popular code for patriots'.[25] No doubt reinforced by contemporary notions of race and national fitness, nations were viewed—and viewed themselves—as 'a huge collective self'.[26] Barry O'Neill, a political scientist and game theorist, charts the transformation of the vocabulary of national honour from the late nineteenth century to the present from 'honour, insult, and self-respect' to 'national will, credibility, and reputation'.[27] Our contemporary language may seem less personal, but the underlying link between national honour and self-realised autonomy is intact. The secret dread of both honourable men and of nations was to fall under the influence of a power stronger than themselves.[28]

As students of honour cultures have observed: for honour to serve as a governing principle in social relations, individuals must feel themselves part of a group whose members acknowledge one another's equality, who have similar notions of the objective content of honour and who will serve as an audience to affirm when honour has been affronted and successfully redeemed. The Hague conferences appeared to have assembled such a culture of equals when the 1899 conference accorded 'speaker's rights' and one vote for each of the twenty-six sovereign states, an innovation for international diplomacy that was extended to seventeen more states in the 1907 conference.[29] Great powers and small nations interacted on a terrain of sovereign equality.

The Hague conferences were the crowning moment for a series of late nineteenth-century international agreements beginning with the Paris Declaration of 1856, which recommended dispute mediation through the good offices of a third party. There followed a series of naval agreements and conferences of the European powers at St Petersburg in 1868, and at Brussels in 1874, establishing rules for regulating combat modelled, in part, on the Lieber Code. Lieber was a German immigrant who had fought as a young man in the Napoleonic Wars and hoped to introduce 'a kind of soldier's honour' into the bloody American Civil War aimed at minimising unnecessary and random violence in warfare and establishing the rights and duties of soldiers and civilians under occupation.[30] The European powers eventually moved to elevate this battlefield document into a legal cornerstone in the emerging field of international law. In addition, many European powers adopted versions of the Lieber Code in their codes of military conduct.[31]

The Hague conferences of 1899 and 1907 endorsed these innovations in battlefield comportment, and broadened the peace agenda to include some measure of arms control and support for arbitration. In the interest of economy, I will only address the 1899 Conference here. This conference was initiated by the Russian Tsar Nicholas II, who hoped measures might be adopted to limit the arms race in which Russia was particularly ill-positioned to compete. However, once convened, the Hague delegates found that journalistic and public expectations for tangible results put pressure on them to achieve something meaningful.[32]

The Hague conference established three commissions to report on arms limitations, the rules of war and arbitration. Duelling protocols and considerations of honour influenced the discussions and outcomes in all three commissions, sometimes productively, sometimes leading to *culs-de-sac*, sometimes disruptively. For example, to fulfil the aim of diminishing 'the calamities of war', the First Commission on armaments control began its discussions by considering the prohibition of new weaponry and seeking ways to standardise the size and calibre of cannons and the thickness of armour plating on ships.[33] A model here was the notion of the parity of weaponry in duelling, which assured neither side would have an advantage in weaponry. However, the delegates could not make these initiatives work in light of the existing disparity in armaments between sovereign states, and on account of German resistance to arms-limitation of any kind.[34] The 1899 Conference did, however, ban the use of 'asphyxiating gases', as an uncontrollable and perfidious mode of combat, and the release of bombs from air balloons, which seemed to delegates to be exceedingly random and unpredictable. They also banned 'expanding' or 'dum-dum' bullets, which the British had used in colonial uprisings against native Indians and Africans.[35] In a perfect reflection of the historic western military ethos, one delegate argued, since the bullets now in use 'permit soldiers of exceptional bravery to advance, is it necessary to invent bullets that are more cruel in order to combat these brave men'?[36] In the end, a resolution was adopted which endorsed the goal of finding future ways to limit the growth and expenses of arms and the calibre of guns, but it was only that: a wish.[37]

The Second Commission on the laws and customs of war on land adapted the work of the Brussels and St Petersburg conferences and added measures clarifying the treatment of prisoners of war, spies, non-combatants and prisoner exchanges. There were provisions forbidding the bombardment of towns and villages or undefended harbours, and condemnations of individuals behaving treacherously while under a white flag or conducting negotiations. Capitulations and armistices 'must be in accordance with the rules of military honour', which meant no advantage could be taken of a defenceless enemy.[38] By the same token, poisoned weapons were banned, a subterfuge that had long troubled duellers who were fearful that a desperate opponent might poison the tip of his sword. Weapons that caused 'superfluous injury' were also banned, as was killing or wounding 'treacherously' or declaring that 'no quarter will be given'. Furthermore, one could not 'kill or wound an enemy, who, having laid down arms, or having no longer means of defence, has surrendered at discretion'.[39] All these measures echoed aspects of duelling conventions that presumed the rule of fairness in combat and which established, in the words of one delegate, guarantees against 'the abuse of force in time of war'.[40]

The discussions within the Third Commission on arbitration initially took a conservative direction, lingering on the older practice of mediation, in which one power or sovereign extends its 'good offices' to settle a dispute between two others. But mediation required that disputants agreed on a suitable 'neutral' mediator, and eventually attention turned to another alternative: the concept of arbitration, which had recently been employed between nations in the Americas and whose history roughly paralleled the codification of the modern duel.[41] Before the conference began, the American delegate, Frederick Holls, a cosmopolitan lawyer of German heritage, proposed to his delegation an arbitral procedure based on the principle of 'seconding'.[42] At an opportune moment in the debate, when there seemed no clear path forward, Holls proposed a procedure:

> In analogy to the private sphere, of so-called 'seconds', friendly nations entrusted by the contesting parties, not unlike "witnesses" and good friends by rivaling duelists, to look after their interests and to this end communicate freely with the opposing side without running any risk or taking any responsibilities upon themselves. At moments of crisis, the ancient formula, 'one more step means war' could henceforward be substituted by 'one more step and we will appoint seconds'.[43]

The other delegates warmly greeted the proposal and unanimously approved it in principle. After much wrangling, a formula for utilising arbitration emerged: the Hague delegates set up a Permanent Court of Arbitration (PCA) to which states could send disputes on a voluntary basis.

In a procedure modelled directly on prevailing duelling protocols, each power chose four experienced lawyers/diplomats to serve on the PCA. In the event of a dispute, each state would choose from the list two arbiters who would serve as its agents and who would enjoy 'full diplomatic privileges and immunity'. The four arbiters would then choose an 'umpire' (*surarbitre*) who would break tie votes and ensure correct procedures and transparency. The same formula was applied to the constitution of fact-finding commissions engaged to work out debt obligations, borders and other legal matters.[44] In the 1907 Conference, the mediation of international disputes through the 'good offices' of non-disputant states was resolved by a somewhat less elaborate formula for choosing mediating powers. The 1907 Conference also established a parallel Judicial Arbitration Court, which would meet annually and consider disputes brought before it. All of these arrangements were based in some way on the system of national nomination suggested for the PCA in 1899.[45]

In the final plenary discussions on the arbitration conventions in 1899, several delegates objected to the language that obliged every signatory power to inform two disputing powers about the availability of arbitration on the grounds that this would infringe upon the sovereignty of the disputants. The President of the Third Commission, the French politician Léon Bourgeois, sought to convince these sceptics of the advantages arbitration would bring to weak nations and to the cause of peace:

> In conflicts in strength when it is a question of lining up soldiers of flesh and steel, there are the great and the small, the weak and the strong.

> When swords are thrown into the two trays of the balance, one may be heavier and the other lighter. But, when we throw in ideas and rights, the inequality ceases and the rights of the smallest and weakest weigh equally with those of the greatest.[46]

The measure passed unanimously. In his comments, Bourgeois freely granted that the disparity in military strength amongst states vitiated the duel's model of parity of weaponry and fighting conditions.[47] Nevertheless, he hoped that a system of equal access to a panel of honourable advocates would re-establish that parity in law. The duel and the notion of honourable arbitration were never far from Bourgeois' mind. The success of this system depended on three conditions: the existence of clear, written rules, the presence of reliably honourable arbiters and an acknowledgement by the arbiters that rights trumped power imbalances or national interest. The first two conditions could be met. The last one was more of a rhetorical flourish.

The accomplishment of the Third Commission was not a triumph of law but of procedure, and a voluntary one at that. The 'list' system based on the model of duelling seconds proved to be a workable approach to the resolution of international conflicts and fact-finding commissions.[48] Yet, in spite of the lip service paid to compulsory arbitration as a principle, the great powers still resisted mandatory arbitration or a permanent sitting court as an infringement of their sovereignty. Holls knew they would when he proposed his procedural solution. As he wrote to the German Foreign Secretary Bernhard von Bülow during the early work of the Commission: instruments for arbitration should exist as evidence of 'a most solemn declaration and demonstration in the right direction' but should guarantee that 'the very last trace of any compulsion, moral or otherwise, upon any nation, be it great or small, should disappear'.[49]

Though the Hague arbitration conventions were seldom used before 1914, the League of Nations, the United Nations and the Permanent Court of International Justice adopted similar rules for choosing arbiters based on national nomination.[50] The subsequent histories of disarmament and the laws of war also owe something to the principles of fair fighting and the equalisation of armed force exemplified in the duel. However, a system of ensuring peace and restraint in combat built in part on analogies to affairs of honour was fatally unstable. This was not because arbitration did not closely enough replicate the duel's mechanisms of peaceful resolution but because the conflict resolution procedures themselves, civilised as they appeared to be at the dawn of the twentieth century, were utterly indebted to both historic and contemporary images of fighting prowess and martial masculinity. As Joseph Conrad wrote in 1905:

> Never before has war received so much homage at the lips of men, never has it reigned with less undisputed sway in their minds. [war] has made peace altogether its own; it has modelled peace on its own

image—a martial, overbearing, war-lord sort of peace, with a mailed fist and turned-up moustaches, ringing with the din of grand manoeuvres, eloquent with allusions to glorious feats of arms; it has made peace so magnificent as to be almost as expensive to keep up as itself.[51]

Moreover, men of honour who trusted their friends to arbitrate the differences between them, as Geoffrey Best has pointed out, understood that having recourse to such procedures 'required instant readiness to fight' if they should fail.[52] Moreover, the culture of honour ostensibly shared by the Hague conferees as civilised nations with equal rights to speak and vote, was in fact marked by grotesque asymmetries of power. These imbalances effectively excluded small and neutral states from the superordinate peer group constituted by the great powers, whose obligations of national honour and interest trumped the rights of lesser nations. As Barry O'Neill has written about the imperfect analogy of individual and national honour: in a truly shared honour culture the forcefulness of a challenge will be understood by all, but the 'incompletely shared social constructions' of the honour culture in modern international relations means challenges will be misunderstood by at least some of the principal actors.[53] For the small nations, the autonomy guaranteed by sovereignty was the chief source of their national honour while the great powers still measured honour in terms of populations, arms, territory and historic accomplishments.

Indeed, the precious quality of honour was so well understood by the great powers that there was common agreement during the conferences that matters of national honour or 'vital interests' could not be settled automatically through the arbitration process. Nonetheless, the abiding hope among the delegates who were working most diligently for peace was that most international differences would not rise to a level that would constitute a national insult. Duelling codes recognised a hierarchy of offenses from trivial slights to personal insult, to physical contact. It is likely that some delegations imagined a parallel hierarchy of offenses between nations. But, despite the proximate honour culture shared by the great powers, there were alarming gaps between identity and perception in matters of honour that led to flawed estimations of the seriousness of challenges and the proportionality of responses.

As Isabel Hull shows, during the First World War many of the nineteenth-century conventions on weaponry, the laws of war, arbitration and neutrality which culminated in the Hague conventions were not respected by the belligerents. The greatest offender was Imperial Germany and the armistice, and the punitive treaty that ended the war was a consequence of the Allied belief that Germany had failed to abide by virtually all existing international laws and agreements. The military representatives to the Allied Supreme War Council announced in the month before the end of the war that 'The Government of Germany is in a position peculiar among the nations of Europe in that its word cannot be believed, and that it denies any obligation of honour'.⁵⁴ Instead of a bill of legal particulars indicting Germany's violations of international law, the Allies reflexively relied on a discourse of personal honour and integrity as a collective trait of nations. Honour lingered on as a ghost that continued to haunt international relations throughout the twentieth century, as several recent studies affirm.⁵⁵

In the years immediately following the 1907 Conference, some commentators continued to deplore the failure to make matters of national honour subject to arbitration in language that was critical of the duelling analogy. In 1912, the American political scientist Robert MacIver wrote in the essay 'War and Civilization':

> The impossibility of vindicating honor by the accident of superior swordsmanship applies equally to the international duel ... indeed with greater force. For, indeed, no civilized nation ever insults another. A statesman may, a newspaper editor may, an Admiral may—but a whole people—never.⁵⁶

In his mischaracterisation of the duel of honour, MacIver nonetheless unwittingly put his finger on the greatest problem with the analogy. In the modern duelling culture, the superiority of the swordsman was not the issue; honour was vindicated by two rivals' willingness to engage in combat. International duels, despite efforts to limit arms, apply rules to war and encourage arbitration, were not duels between individuals. Two pistol shots from 30 paces without effect, or a wound on the wrist that drew blood, would not satisfy men who had built war machines geared for absolute destruction.

As did many of his contemporaries, both idealists and militarists, MacIver also misjudged the limits of civilisation and its power to exercise restraint. As Sigmund Freud wrote a year into the war:

> Our disillusionment on account of the uncivilized behaviour of our fellow citizens of the world during the war were unjustified. They were based on an illusion to which we had given way. In reality our fellow-citizens have not sunk so low as we feared because they had never risen so high as we believed.⁵⁷

Notes

1 See V. Kiernan. (1988). *The Duel in European History: Honour and the Reign of Aristocracy*. Oxford: Oxford University Press.
2 M. Koskenniemi. (2001). *The Gentle Civilizer of Nations: The Rise and Fall of International Law, 1870–1960*. Cambridge: Cambridge University Press, p.53.
3 Koskenniemi, pp.79–82. On honour as a 'claim-right' see F. Stewart. (1994). *Honor*. Chicago: University of Chicago Press. Other scholars see the influence of the duel in limiting or abolishing war to be negligible, but this view depends on a misunderstanding of the place of the affair of honour in European society and of the historical relation of duelling and feuding. See J. Parent. (2009). Dueling

and the Abolition of War. *Cambridge Review of International Affairs*, 27(2), pp.281–300.
4   N. Elias. (1982). *Power and Civility: The Civilizing Process*. Vol. 2, trans. Edmund Jephcott, New York: Pantheon Books.
5   Among these see P. Spierenburg. (1991). *The Broken Spell: A Cultural and Anthropological History of Preindustrial Europe*. New Brunswick, NJ: Rutgers University Press; M. Greenshields. (1994). *An Economy of Violence in Early Modern France: Crime and Justice in the Haute Auvergne, 1587–1664*. University Park, PA: Pennsylvania State University Press. Among the books on the history of the duel that have taken this perspective is F. Billacois. (1986). *Le Duel dans la Société Française des XVI–XVIIe siècles*. Paris: Editions de L'École des Hautes Études en Sciences Sociales.
6   For a discussion of Pinker's thesis as it applies to the 'decline of war' see N. Gleditsch, S. Pinker, B. Thayer, J. Levy and W. Thompson. (2013). The Forum: The Decline of War. *International Studies Review*, 15(3), pp.396–419.
7   S. Pinker. (2011). *The Better Angels of Our Nature: Why Violence Has Declined*. New York: Viking, pp.17–18, 23, 67, 83–85, 247–248, 256–257. Pinker systematically misrepresents the aspects of chivalric culture that lessened violence and sees no humanism in Shakespeare's admiration for 'his bloody heroes'. For a decisive refutation of that view see T. Meron. (1998). *Bloody Constraint: War and Chivalry in Shakespeare*. Oxford: Oxford University Press.
8   For these developments see A. Mansker. (2011). *Sex, Honor, and Citizenship in Early Third Republic France*. Basingstoke and New York: Palgrave Macmillan; E. Ferguson. (2010). *Gender and Justice: Violence, Intimacy, and Community in Fin-de-Siècle France*. Baltimore: Johns Hopkins University Press.
9   For a critique of Elias' treatment of violence as it related to honour cultures see G. Schwerhoff. (2002). Criminalized Violence and the Process of Civilization: A Reappraisal. *Crime, History and Societies*, 6(2), pp.103–126.
10 R. Gould. (2003). *Collision of Wills: How Ambiguity About Social Rank Breeds Conflict*. Chicago: University of Chicago Press.
11 E. Jager. (2004). *The Last Duel: A True Story of Crime, Scandal, and Trial by Combat in Medieval France*. New York: Broadway Books, pp.81–84.
12 Billacois, pp.83–93.
13 N. Elias. (1983). *The Court Society*. trans. Edmund Jephcott, New York: Pantheon.
14 J. Dewald. (1993). *Aristocratic Experience and the Origins of Modern Culture, 1570–1715*. Berkeley: University of California Press; M. Peltonen. (2003). *The Duel in Early Modern England: Civility, Politeness, and Honour*. Cambridge: Cambridge University Press.
15 C. Chateauvillard. (1836). *Essai sur le Duel*. Paris: Bohaire.
16 Chateauvillard, p.5.
17 R. Nye. (1993). *Masculinity and Male Codes of Honor in Modern France*. New York: Oxford University Press, pp.140–145. At the turn of the twentieth century, rule-making for team sports followed a similar evolution, in which rudimentary notions of fairness became enforceable rules aimed at containing violence, and earning dishonor for those who broke them. See on this point N. Elias and E. Dunning. (1986). *Quest for Excitement: Sport and Leisure in the Civilizing Process*. Oxford: Basil Blackwell, pp.21, 150–190.
18 U. Frevert. (1995). *Men of Honour*. Cambridge: Polity Press, pp.135–191. Even in Russia, where the duel was more dangerous than elsewhere on the continent (15 deaths in 322 duels between 1894 and 1912), a greater respect evolved for equal conditions and on the grounds of what constituted an affront. See I. Reyfman. (1999). *Ritualized Violence Russian Style: The Duel in Russian Culture and Literature*. Stanford: Stanford University Press.

19 For these examples see R. Nye. (2014). How the Duel of Honour Promoted Civility and Attenuated Violence in Western Europe. In: C. Strange, R. Cribb and C. Forth, eds. *Honour, Violence and Emotions in History*. London: Bloomsbury, pp.191–194.
20 R. Nye. *Masculinity*, pp.150–164; P. Piccato. (2010). *The Tyranny of Opinion: Honor in the Construction of the Mexican Public Sphere*. Durham, NC: Duke University Press.
21 C. Hughes. (2007). *Politics of the Sword: Dueling, Honor, and Masculinity in Modern Italy*. Columbus, OH: Ohio State University Press, pp.177–190.
22 Hughes, pp.190–205.
23 On libel and the duel see Hughes, pp.119–121; Frevert, p.144; Nye, *Masculinity*, pp.173–182.
24 See on these matters N. Oman. (2011). The Honor of Private Law. *Fordham Law Review*, 80(1), pp.31–71; J. Whitman. (2000). Enforcing Civility and respect: Three Societies. *Yale Law Review*, 109, pp.1280–1417; A. Mansker. (2011). *Sex, Honor and Citizenship in the Early Third Republic*. New York: Palgrave Macmillan; A. Goldberg. (2010). *Honour, Politics, and the Law in Imperial Germany*. Cambridge: Cambridge University Press; C. Bailey. (2015). Honor Among Peers? A Comparative History of Honor Practices in Postwar Britain and West Germany. *The Journal of Modern History*, 87(4), pp.809–851.
25 G. Best. (1982). *Honour Among Men and Nations*. Toronto: University of Toronto Press, pp.xii. See also P. Robinson. (2006). *Military Honor and The Conduct of War: From Ancient Greece to Iraq*. New York: Routledge, pp.167–170.
26 Best, *Honour Among Men and Nations*, p. 44. See in general on this point, G. Sluga. (2006). *The Nation, Psychology, and International Politics, 1870–1919*. Basingstoke, Houndsmills: Palgrave Macmillan.
27 B. O'Neill. (1999). *Honor, Symbols and War*. Ann Arbor, MI: University of Michigan Press, p.86.
28 O'Neill., p.88.
29 M. Finnemore and M. Jurkovitch. (2014). Getting a Seat at the Table: The Origins of Participation and Modern Multilateral Conferences. *Global Governance*, 20(3), pp.361–373. The principle of 'equality of speaker rights' first practiced at The Hague in 1899, acknowledged, in effect, that all conference participants were peers disposing of a full quotient of honour, though this was not, as in the case of duel-worthiness, a status extended to 'non-civilised' states. See A. Linklater. (2005). Dialogic Politics and the Civilizing Process. *Review of International Studies*, 31(1), pp.141–154.
30 R. Hartigan. (1983). *Lieber's Code and The Law of War*. Chicago: Precedent, p.5. On the intellectual origins of Lieber's principles see C. Mack and H. Lesesne. (2005). *Francis Lieber and the Culture of the Mind*. Columbia: University of South Carolina Press.
31 A. Roberts and R. Guelff, eds. (1989). *Documents on the Laws of War*. 2nd ed. Oxford: Clarendon Press, p.7.
32 S. Cooper. (1991). Pacifism in France, 1889–1914. *French Historical Studies*, 17(2), pp.355–386; R. Chickering. (1975). *Imperial Germany and a World Without War: The Peace Movement and German Society, 1892–1933*. Princeton: Princeton University Press.
33 See the discussion on these first initiatives in A. Eyffinger. (1999). *The 1899 Hague Peace Conference: 'The Parliament of Man, The Federation of the World'*. The Hague: Kluwer, pp.218–224, 237.
34 Detlef Vagts argues that the significance of the 'qualitative' limitations achieved at The Hague, rather than 'quantitative' ones that would limit armaments

growth is greater than is usually understood, because these did observe the general principle that belligerents did not have an 'unlimited' right to injure the enemy, which provided the 'moral foundation' for later prohibitions, including chemical weapons. On the Hague conferences as the origins of chemical bans see R. Price. (1995). A Genealogy of the Chemical Weapons Taboo. *International Organization,* 49(1), pp.73–103.

35 Unlike the 'Laws of War' Commission, the Commission on arms limitation meant its work to apply to combatants only, not to civilians. On this point see G. Aldrich. (2000). The laws of War on Land. *American Journal of International Law,* 94(1), p.59.
36 The words of Colonel Galinsky, as quoted in Eyffinger, p.251.
37 S. Rosenne, ed. (2001). *The Hague Peace Conferences of 1899 and 1907 and International Arbitration: Reports and Documents.* The Hague: Asser Press, pp.136–137.
38 Rosenne. (2001), pp.137–138.
39 For the full text see 'Respecting the Laws and Customs of War on land' in A. Roberts and R. Guelff, eds., pp.43–61.
40 Aldrich, pp.59–60.
41 On the examples of arbitration agreements before 1899 see M. Abbenhuis. (2014), *An Age of Neutrals: Great Power Politics, 1815–1914.* Cambridge: Cambridge University Press, pp.145–148; D. Caron. (2000), War and International Adjudication: Reflections on the 1899 Peace Conference. *American Journal of International law,* 94(4), pp.4–30.
42 C. Davis. (1962). *The United States and the First Hague Peace Conference.* Ithaca, NY: Cornell University Press, p.77.
43 Rosenne, p.35; Eyffinger, pp.370–371. Geoffrey Best has briefly noted this discussion of the duel. See G. Best. (1999). Peace Conferences and the Century of Total War: The Hague Conferences and What Came After. *International Affairs,* 75(3), p.630.
44 J.B. Scott. (1908). *Texts of the Peace Conferences at The Hague, 1899 and 1907.* Boston: Ginn and Company, pp.21–44; for the amplified version approved in 1907, pp.155–192.
45 Scott, pp.141–168.
46 Rosenne, p.61.
47 In his Nobel Peace Prize lecture of 1920, despite the carnage of the Great War, Bourgeois retained the conceptual analogy between individuals and nations that undergirded many of the discussions at the Hague conferences and upheld the central place of honour, which he praised as the highest of our 'spontaneous attributes' and argued that the task of civilisation was to cultivate honour, sociability and goodness over 'egotism'. The eventual success of 'the laws and policies of nations' must draw upon the clear successes of 'private law'. L. Bourgeois. (2016). *Nobel Lecture.* [online] Nobelprize.org. Available at: http://www.nobelprize.org/nobel_prizes/peace/laureates/1920/bourgeois-lecture.html [Accessed 26 February 2016].
48 On procedural rules as necessary compromise see Caron, pp.28–29.
49 Frederick Holls, as quoted in G. Best. (1980). *Humanity in Warfare.* New York: Columbia University Press, p.140.
50 Davis, pp.146–172, 211–212.
51 J. Conrad. (1905). Autocracy and War. *The North American Review,* 181, p.52.
52 Best, *Honour Among Nations,* p.46.
53 O'Neill, pp.120–121.
54 As quoted in I. Hull. (2013). *A Scrap of Paper: Breaking and Making International Law During the Great War.* Ithaca and London: Cornell University Press, p.327.

55 A. Tsygankov. (2012). *Russia and the West from Alexander to Putin: Honor in International Relations*. Cambridge: Cambridge University Press; R. LeBow. (2010). *Why Nations Fight: Past and Future* New York: Cambridge University Press; J. Levy. (2011). *The Arc of War: Origins, Escalation, and Transformation*. Chicago: University of Chicago Press.
56 R. MacIver, as quoted in D. Spitz, ed. (1969). *Robert M. MacIver: Politics and Society*, New Brunswick, NJ: Transaction Press, p.437.
57 S. Freud. (1939). *Civilization, War and Death: Selection from Three Works*. London: Hogarth Press, p.11.

8 Writing for peace

Reconsidering the British public peace petitioning movement's historical legacies after 1898

Annalise R. Higgins[1]

In his 1916 *Künstlerroman* (artist's novel) *Portrait of the Artist as a Young Man*, James Joyce included a scene set at University College Dublin in 1899. The protagonist, Stephen Dedalus, encounters a petition in favour of Tsar Nicholas II's 1898 proposal for the first Hague peace conference. The petition, 'a long roll of paper bearing an irregular tale of signatures', sits beside two framed photographs.[2] One photograph depicts the Tsar. While the identity of the second frame's inhabitant remains unclear, Dedalus' narration implies that it is the bombastic editor of the *Pall Mall Gazette*, William Thomas Stead. Joyce presented MacCann, the university student pressuring his peers to sign the petition, as an uncritical sycophant guilty of installing the Russian autocrat on a pedestal. In the scene, MacCann speaks 'with fluent energy' and tries to persuade potential petitioners with arguments:

> of the Czar's rescript, of Stead, of general disarmament, arbitration in cases of international disputes, of the signs of the times, of the new humanity and the new gospel of life which would make it the business of the community to secure as cheaply as possible the greatest possible happiness of the greatest possible number.[3]

Joyce painted a vivid picture of Dedalus as a man unconvinced by MacCann's ideas, underlining his annoyance at those who were carried away with the Tsar's impractical appeal. The passage reminds the historical observer that the public messages associated with the rescript were memorable, often emotive and controversial. Joyce's account also foreshadows a trend in the modern historiography by focussing on Stead as a primary force in advancing the cause of peace in Britain. In MacCann's ode to the proposed conference, Stead is second in importance only to the rescript itself. This chapter seeks to question whether the prominence afforded to Stead (at the time and subsequently) has obscured the wider relevance of how the British public engaged with the rescript. While Joyce's alter-ego Dedalus did not sign the petition, a significant number of Britons did raise their hands, pens and voices in support of the Tsar's rescript in 1898 and 1899, often citing the proposal's pragmatic potential to advance the cause of arbitration and the possible maintenance of, as MacCann put it, 'the greatest possible happiness' through avoiding war where possible.

When Tsar Nicholas II issued his proposal calling for a conference addressing 'the maintenance of general peace', many Britons reacted positively.[4] From the rescript's release in August 1898 to the peace conference's opening in May 1899, over 1,400 petitions concerning the proposed conference arrived at the British Foreign Office.[5] The petitions represented a wide range of people who met, often in public, to advocate for the Tsar's message. The petitions bore the names of religious groups, church societies, public town and village meetings, trade union and labour councils. There is ample evidence that W.T. Stead, a well-known sensationalist journalist, was interested in and heavily involved with the 1898-1899 public peace movement in Britain. He proclaimed his involvement with Tsar Nicholas II, and with the proposed conference, loudly and publicly.[6] Stead agitated prominently for public expressions of sympathy with the Tsar's proposal and published a periodical, *War Against War: A Chronicle of the International Crusade of Peace*, to record these attempts to elicit public support for the Tsar's proposal. Crucially, he claimed that his Crusade was unique both because of the breadth of public support that it enjoyed and because it was the first public movement to agitate for a specific and attainable peaceable cause as opposed to peace as a generic principle.[7] In The Hague's historiography, Stead has in many ways become synonymous with the public peace movement in Britain at the turn of the century.[8] The historiographical prominence of his role is problematic not because his enthusiasm for The Hague has been overstated but because the historical record of his participation has been constructed in a way which implicitly limits the agency that can be attributed to a range of other actors.

Joyce's account of Dedalus' encounter with one of Stead's peace petitions thus sets the scene for reconsidering the historical legacies of the British peace petitioning movement by reorienting focus onto an individual's encounter with a petition. Regardless of how loudly or publicly anyone agitated for peace in the months leading up to the first Hague conference, the process of producing a petition required groups and individuals to engage with the call for a petition, consider the issue at hand and then make a decision to overtly support the cause through an action designed to make their opinion known to their government.[9] Although Dedalus chose not to sign and was consequently derided with accusations, such as 'minor poets' being 'above such trivial questions as the question of universal peace', large numbers of Britons signed their names in support of peace or voted to have their support recorded in a resolution forwarded to the British prime minister Lord Salisbury.[10] Investigating how Britons expressed their reasons for petitioning for peace in their covering letters and resolutions offers an opportunity to reconsider the way in which the movement's historiographical legacies are rendered and reorient historical focus from the agents facilitating public agitation onto those who petitioned.

*

Historians have largely treated the historical significance of public engagement with the 1899 and 1907 Hague Peace Conferences as subordinate to broader renderings of the moment's many international meanings.[11] As Maartje Abbenhuis observes, how a historian reads the peace conference's significance and relevance depends on the historiographical tradition informing his or her enquiry.[12] However, the lens focussed on the Hague conferences does more than shape historical renderings of their importance: a historian's perspective influences the apparent significance of different historical evidence and actors. Thus, while recent scholars of international law, statecraft and diplomacy recognise the conferences' many successes, they tend to neglect or ignore the importance of public responses in framing those successes.[13] Nevertheless, as Ian Clark argues, the nature of public pressure surrounding the 1899 Hague Peace Conference was in many ways crucial to shaping the conference, as it would be for the 1907 event as well.[14] Public expectations, Clark suggests, coalesced in the creation of a 'world society' that advanced normative assumptions about legitimate state behaviour in the international arena.[15]

James Thompson contends that in the late nineteenth century, public opinion was more than the sum of various individual opinions expressed in a public forum. Instead, he presents 'public opinion' as a political force that relied on the coalescence of ideas. 'Once brought into such groups', he argues, 'the process by which public opinion emerged from the clash of individual views was widely thought to be one of weighing rather than counting'.[16] Historians note numerous examples of public peace activism from around Europe and from as diverse locations as Japan and New Zealand in response to the Tsar's rescript.[17] Furthermore, in 1898, British leaders overtly acknowledged the pressure brought to bear on their position by the public's activism for the Tsar's calls for disarmament and peace. In his October 1898 reply to the Tsar's proposal the British prime minister Salisbury noted the 'sympathy "strikingly manifested with the Emperor's proposal by the very numerous resolutions passed by public meetings and societies in the United Kingdom"'.[18] In Britain, public proponents of peace succeeded in making known their support for the principle of holding an international conference to discuss what they perceived as threats to European peace.

Branches of the organised peace movement, particularly the Peace Society, International Arbitration and Peace Association and the Arbitration Alliance (all of which were based in London) actively encouraged public responses to the rescript in the immediate aftermath of its publication. As Daniel Hucker suggests, the 'diplomatic gesture ... warmed the hearts of a burgeoning global movement inspired by ideals of peace, disarmament, and international arbitration'.[19] Yet, when historians consider the British public's agitation, they tend to do so through the lens of the organised peace movement and Stead features particularly heavily in their interpretations. Paul Laity, for example, argues that Stead was responsible for selling the merits of the Tsar's peace message to the British public as a single, achievable, step capable of improving their world.[20] Glenda Sluga offers a more balanced interpretation which recognises the existence of competing opinions and the mutability of one actor's role when she argues that the 'international sociability and a specifically internationally minded public opinion' can be attributed 'at least in part' to Stead.[21] Cornelia Knab, in a detailed study of the nuances of Stead's peace activism, insightfully considers how Stead wove himself into moments of public agitation. She further argues that his 'autobiographical character sketch' *The Great Pacifist* (written in 1901 and published in June 1912) highlighted the deliberate nature of his actions and showed 'how much Stead in his later years tried to present the struggle for world peace as one of the principle tasks of his life'.[22] Nevertheless, her history does not consider public reactions to Stead's agitation precisely because her intention is to treat Stead as a case study of how examining one individual's activism 'displays transnationally relevant complex mentalities'.[23]

David Cortright weights his history heavily towards Stead when he explains public engagement with peace by describing how: 'The crusading English editor William T. Stead launched a highly visible campaign to urge that the Hague conference adopt measures to half the build-up of arms in Europe'.[24] Even Martin Ceadel, the doyen of peace research, asserts that Stead was responsible for the movement's intellectual thrust in 1898 and 1899, having convinced the established peace societies that their longer-term cause was not at risk of being 'weakened', and would in fact be promoted, by a public show of unity.[25] He goes so far as to argue that it 'was Stead ... who insisted that the Hague Conference be treated by the British peace movement as a major opportunity'.[26] Similarly, while Hucker offers a nuanced and important account of competing strands of pacifist ideology at play in the British public sphere in a recent article, he also drifts towards Stead, contending that 'much credit for raising the public profile of the Conference belongs to Stead'.[27] Ceadel and Hucker ultimately fall prey to Stead's carefully constructed historical legacy and therefore do not fully consider that the British public responded to the Tsar's call for peace in a much wider context. Nevertheless, it is crucial to recognise that the organised peace movement's success depended on the public choosing to compose the memorials and send them to Salisbury. Histories that gravitate towards Stead's role present incomplete accounts of the British public movement. They deny agency to the members of the organised peace societies in Britain who, as this chapter will demonstrate, actively engaged with the Tsar's proposal well before Stead established his Crusade. They also deny the British public's agency in engaging with the Tsar's rescript and deciding to enter into correspondence in its favour with their government.

While accounts of public peace activism permeate the historical record, historians typically cite the existence of such sources as evidence of public engagement's presence.[28] That is to say, historians think it is important that the petitions existed, and they use them as evidence that the Tsar's proposal had a global impact, but they tend not to treat the petitions themselves as the objects of critical historical enquiry. In this vein, historical enquiries into peace activism usually focus on either individual or organised groups of peace activists. However, recent historiography also recognises that it is inaccurate to suggest that attempts to fan public optimism in response to the Tsar's rescript should be read uncritically as 'stock standard' peace activism.[29] The Tsar's proposal posed questions and raised possibilities that had not previously existed.[30] Both organised peace activists and various sectors of the ever-nebulous public reacted to the apparent novelty of the Tsar's proposal and proved willing to consider that it offered a limited, pragmatic step towards addressing contemporary anxieties about militarism and warfare.[31]

The only historian who has analysed the 1898–1899 British petitioning movement in any detail is Barbara Tuchman. In her seminal work *The Proud Tower: A Portrait of the World Before the War* (1966), Tuchman describes 'over 750 resolutions' received 'in the four months following the Czar's manifesto'.[32] She provides a fair, if rough, representation of the petitioners, but it does not consider what they had to say or why they chose to say it. For Tuchman, the movement's significance lies in the vociferous way in which the public reacted to calls for peace. However, her account—which has underpinned so much of the more recent historiography—is incomplete. The wave of petitions received in the first four months after the Tsar's proposal comprised approximately half of the 1406 petitions, resolutions and memorials received by the Foreign Office in support of the Tsar's proposal.[33] For Tuchman, the petitions' existence, rather than the process of their production, is a primary focus. Furthermore, by turning immediately to a detailed description of Stead's role as instigator of the loud and conspicuous International Crusade of Peace, she implicitly subjugates the petitioners' role in their movement.[34] Given that the petitions survive and can be consulted as historical sources, the construction of the movement's history must be reconsidered.

*

The prominent role afforded to Stead in the historiography thus offers an opportunity to examine how a piece of The Hague's history has come to be told and to consider whether a more complete account can be constructed by considering a broader range of historical actors. Historians should not deny Stead a role in The Hague's story but they should contextualise his importance. As Joyce's focus on Stead's role in the public peace agitation foreshadowed, Stead has achieved particular prominence in a historiography dominated by organised peace activism and major actors. To begin to understand how a single historical actor's legacies have been constructed in relation to the Hague Peace Conferences, it is useful to consider Stead's sensational passing. Stead was one of more than 1,500 individuals who perished when the *RMS Titanic* sank on 14 April 1912. After his death, *The*

Times eulogised him as a 'notable victim' of the tragedy. He was remembered as a man of 'enthusiasm, ... optimism, ... and untiring zeal in all causes which appealed to his sympathies'.³⁵ *The Times* reported that

> Of his political efforts... the most constant was an advocacy of a good understanding with Russia ... In 1898 he again visited Russia in order to have audience of Nicholas II. It was after this talk with the Tsar that Stead embarked on the 'Peace Crusade' which occupied much of his later years. He founded and edited a weekly paper, *War against War*. He attended the Hague Conferences and threw himself into Arbitration propaganda.³⁶

In the aftermath of the *Titanic*'s demise, the *Daily Mirror* went so far as to claim on its front page that the world had lost a man whose 'hatred of war created the Hague Peace Conference'.³⁷

Over time, the canvas of collective memory has come to portray Stead two-dimensionally as an unstoppable public force. While historians critique his inflated sense of self-importance and, in some cases, question his efforts to permeate the historical record as a dedicated and selfless individual who worked tirelessly to champion causes of great concern for humanity, in public remembrances, Stead's three-dimensionality has been erased.³⁸ Even today he is revered and represented as 'the inventor of modern investigative journalism', and a 'pivotal figure at [the] Hague Peace Conference[s], arguing for [an] early version of [the] United Nations'.³⁹ In the forward to his recent biography, W. Sydney Robinson dubbed Stead 'arguably the most important journalist of all time', but admitted that 'he undoubtedly went too far on occasion and had a tendency to exaggerate his [own] influence'.⁴⁰ It is fitting that newspaper reporters so readily remember Stead as an 'angel of peace', as it was through newspapers that Stead built his reputation and his legacies. As a leading journalist, Stead was keenly aware that public perceptions could be influenced through careful presentation of selected information. He also knew how to use his understanding and skills to shape public perception of his own activity. Stead promoted various significant causes and his involvement with a cause was rarely (if ever) private or quiet.⁴¹

Stead's activities during the period between Count Mouraviev's publication of the Tsar's rescript on 24 August 1898 and the 18 May 1899 opening of the first Hague Peace Conference offer a perfect example of Stead's signature personal public spectacle. As Tuchman declares: 'within a month of the first news, Stead was on his way'.⁴² Stead decided that he would travel the world, arousing public support for the Tsar's proposal wherever he went. Along the way he planned to meet with various important personages, ostensibly to ensure that they were made aware of the immense public support for the cause of peace. He christened the movement 'the International Crusade of Peace'.

Stead made sure that information about his involvement in the British and international reactions to the Tsar's proposal was well-publicised and recorded for posterity. He did so primarily through two publications. The first was *War Against War*, a twelve-part series intended to record in minute detail every step of his world-wide pilgrimage. This publication was also designed to draw public attention to the peace cause. If one happened to want to read more on Stead's pilgrimage, one could also purchase his full account as a book. *The United States of Europe On the Eve of the Parliament of Peace* was a 468-page opus, published in 1899, which detailed the minutiae of his earlier 1898 journey around Europe.[43] Stead was never opaque about his intention to win public support for his ideas. In 1899, he wrote to Bertha von Suttner (an influential figure in the peace movement) and enquired: 'may I ask you as to what you think would be the best method of carrying on peace propaganda this winter?'[44] Stead's audacious writing style has undoubtedly secured him a prominent place in The Hague's historiography. He is remembered both for his efforts in raising the public profile of the Hague conferences and for his involvement as part of what Eyffinger terms 'the social entourage' of the events.[45]

Like many historians, some of Stead's contemporaries also fell prey to his gift for self-promotion. For example, the Dutch Foreign Minister, Willem van Beaufort, noted in February 1899 that Britain would send a magnificent group of diplomats to the first Hague peace conference because Stead had initiated a massive public movement in Britain in support.[46] Shortly before the second Hague peace conference opened in 1907, J.P. von Schmidt wrote to Stead to propose establishing an 'International Press-Office' which he thought Stead should, naturally, helm. Schmidt asked if he might 'somewhat contribute to your great journalistic work for the sake of humankind'.[47] His question suggested that Stead's contemporaries were well aware of his ability to create and present the sort of spectacle that could draw public attention to a suitably 'noble' question.

Stead's appeal was not, however, universal. Many European diplomats found the burgeoning sphere of journalism, and particularly Stead's cocksure and sometimes discourteous reporting objectionable. In January 1899, Sir Charles Scott, the British Ambassador to St Petersburg, wrote to Salisbury expressing his concern at Stead's public reports following his meeting with Tsar Nicholas II. Scott discussed how Nicholas had 'himself recently experienced its [the press'] embarrassing influence'.[48] He went on to note that 'he [Tsar Nicholas] credits Mr Stead with the best intentions, but … [he] ought perhaps to have been more careful to remember that, after all, he was a journalist'.[49] Hodgson Pratt's International Arbitration and Peace Association (one of the British peace societies with which Stead worked most closely on the Crusade) admitted to being 'puzzled' by the egregious gentleman.[50]

Peace activists also criticised Stead's proclivity to ingratiate himself with those whom he deemed of significant importance, often without regard to those individual's opinions, beliefs or attitudes.[51] Contributors to the famous magazine *Punch* put their concerns more bluntly in a satirical take on the upcoming conference, writing:

> it would be a pity if a great and beneficent endeavour for the welfare of mankind were made ridiculous, and therefore inoperative, because no one thinks it is his business to put aside a fussy person. There may be something inSTEAD [*sic*.] besides a capacity for self-advertising.[52]

While Hucker reads similar comments from the same article as evidence of public opinion's burgeoning influence on international diplomacy, it is equally important to acknowledge that such comments reflect a contemporary sense of unease about Stead's attempts to involve himself with the conference.[53] This sense of unease should motivate historians to take a more nuanced view of Stead's self-professed centrality to the public peace movement.

*

In a 1909 collection of Madame Novicov's 'reminisces and correspondence', Stead claimed that public interest in the proposed conference had been sorely lacking before he decided to initiate public agitation in its favour. He wrote:

> the response of public opinion to [the Tsar's] appeal was at first so disheartening that by the middle of December the Russian Foreign Office had practically decided to abandon the Conference, substituting for it a series of Commissions to study the subject mentioned in the Rescript. Returning to London from a tour round Europe which I had undertaken to see what support was available for the Imperial proposal, I was dismayed at the general apathy and sceptical indifference of the public. After consulting with some friends, I decided to proclaim a Crusade of Peace. St. James's Hall was placed at my disposal on the afternoon of Peace Sunday.[54]

Stead further purported that his meeting single-handedly saved the Tsar's conference proposal, claiming that Pavel M. Lessar—a Russian representative in London—informed him before the St James Hall meeting that: 'if your crusade if not taken up to-day, there will be no Conference' because the Tsar's proposal had not elicited sufficient public interest.[55] In Britain (where Stead launched his crusade), at least, this claim sits at odds with the 619 petitions and resolutions with which Britons had bombarded their foreign office before Peace Sunday on 18 December 1898.[56]

The existence of hundreds of public petitions sent well before Stead launched his International Crusade of Peace on 'Peace Sunday' highlights that public mobilisation on the rescript's behalf existed well before Stead took 'charge' of the public movement. In practice, the vast majority of the petitions sent between August and December 1898 did not come from meetings organised by the existing peace network but from religious groups, church societies and other social clubs who met on a regular basis. While factions of the organised peace movement supported public discussion and even sometimes travelled to speak to groups of Britons, the organisational impetus was largely local in character.[57] The act of petitioning required that Britons *qua* citizens signed their name to a sheet of paper or agreed by voting (usually by standing during a meeting) that their assent to a resolution be recorded and forwarded to their elected representatives. The first phase of the public movement was thus characterised by petitions passed by smaller local meetings. These groups dedicated time during or after their regular meetings to discuss the rescript and its significance. In particular, many church congregations considered the Tsar's rescript after their weekly worship.[58] The British public peace petitioning movement should, therefore, be divided into two phases: the phase after the organised peace movement (including Stead) took charge and turned peace activism for the Hague conference into a highly public and performative act (from 18 December 1898 onward), and that which came before, in which large numbers of Britons announced their support for the Tsar's appeal and used petitions to mobilise their voices in politically charged ways.[59]

The vast majority of the petitions received between 31 August and 19 December, a total of 500 (out of 619) petitions, were from groups meeting for primarily religious purposes. The ratio was much more equal during the movement's following six months, where 396 petitions were sent by groups meeting for religious purposes and 391 were sent by other groups. The massive increase in petitions from other sources can mostly be attributed to the number of town and public meetings organised, often but not exclusively by Stead's International Crusade of Peace, after December 1898. Of the 246 petitions sent by town and public meetings between August 1898 and May 1899, only 33 were sent before December.

The public movement's first phase drew to a close with a particularly strong bout of petitioning from religious groups on 18 and 19 December 1898. The Peace Society declared 18 December 1898 'Peace Sunday', and urged religious groups to pass special resolutions in honour of the occasion.[60] As the Peace Society's secretary, William Evans Darby had established Peace Sunday in 1889 (after several previous attempts) as a day for 'preaching upon international and universal peace'.[61] Darby hoped it would become an annual event held on the Sunday before Christmas.[62] In the wake of the Tsar's rescript, the event took on a special significance. Hundreds of congregations took up the call to write for peace. Churches throughout the British empire, and particularly in Australia, were similarly encouraged to observe Peace Sunday in 1898 and to cooperate

> in making this day (or one as near to it as possible) a day on which every pulpit shall unite in proclaiming the message of Christianity to the world as one of peace and brotherhood under our common Father.[63]

Many churches, and particularly the nonconformist ones, enthusiastically took up Darby's call. Charles Stevenson wrote to the Editor of the *Manchester Guardian* to explain that 34 special sermons, arranged by the Peace Society, would be held in Manchester alone.[64] In the week from 18 December to 25 December 1898, a total of 232 congregations sent petitions to the Foreign Office.[65] The Peace Sunday petitions constituted the single most concentrated moment of petitioning during the entire period of public agitation. Almost all those who wrote used the Peace Society's text or a close variation.[66] Furthermore, while Anglican congregations largely did not send individual petitions in support of the Tsar's rescript, the Bishop of London, who later chaired the International Crusade of Peace in Britain, invited all clergy of the London diocese to take part in Peace Sunday as follows:

> The present time seems to be one in which the Christian message of 'peace on earth' needs to be enforced on the consciences of men. This may be done without expressing opinions on current politics, but by urging a peaceable temper. I commend the duty of doing so to your consideration.[67]

Altogether, the first phase of petitioning illustrated how politically charged and mobilised many Britons were in response to the Tsar's rescript. Their mobilisation was not predicated on Stead or on other peace organisations' machinations—even those of the Peace Society. With the launch of 'Peace Sunday', however, the organised peace societies hoped to activate even greater public agitation in favour of the rescript and the upcoming peace conference. W.T. Stead did too.

As explained above, Stead formally launched his International Crusade of Peace on 'Peace Sunday'. Unlike the Peace Society's model, which encouraged local consideration of the rescript's significance, Stead's Crusade entered onto the scene with great aplomb at a large public meeting. Its official apogee, a National Convention on 21 March 1899, was also a suitably large spectacle. The launch of the International Crusade of Peace was held at St James' Meeting Hall in London at a meeting called by the Arbitration Alliance.[68] Dr Sinclair, the Archdeacon of London, presided.[69] The meeting appointed a committee to co-ordinate public agitation in favour of peace. It also aimed to appoint an English-speaking deputation that would then 'make the tour of Europe, appealing for the support and co-operation of each country'.[70] In his opening article in *War Against War*—his 'Clarion Call to Duty' which was seeped with religious language—Stead specifically argued that his movement was intended to 'dispel' previous 'apathy' and 'exorcise … indifference'.[71]

The Crusade movement seemed simultaneously aware and unaware of the level of popular support for the Tsar's proposal that had already emerged in Britain and around Europe. The Crusade of Peace was characterised by this ambivalence throughout 1899. On the one hand, the Crusade assumed a level of public sympathy to the cause which was presumably evidenced by the public's willingness to petition before December 1898. On the other, it assumed that existing public sentiment was insufficient in strength and organisation to be capable of making an impact on international diplomacy and thus needed to be appropriately marshalled. Conversely, for the Peace Society in particular, the fact that the public were actively expressing their support through the act of petitioning was sufficient as a performance of their support. Public performance and spectacle were complementary to, not compulsory for the public peace movement. Stead's focus on spectacle, and on the reiteration of that spectacle in print, through both popular newspapers and the dedicated periodical *War Against War*, therefore does help to explain why his involvement has so clearly permeated the historical record. He deliberately constructed himself as a public voice in favour of a conspicuously public movement for peace which presumed a lack of efficacy on the part of any earlier agitations for peace. Historians reading *War Against War* are thus exposed to a source which claims responsibility for all Britons' peace activism. It is no surprise that this source's account of Stead's involvement has found a place even in historically critical renderings of public agitation for peace.

While the historical record paints Stead's movement (and by extension the entire public movement) as a unified front, there clearly existed palpable ideological tensions between the different branches of the peace movement interested in encouraging public participation. Stead pinned his calls for public agitation on the argument that it offered Britons the chance to agitate in favour of the inherently reasonable idea of a pragmatic and non-absolute pacifism for the first time. The International Arbitration and Peace Association took care to explain that, although they valued his 'propagandist writing', they had 'often had to differ with Mr. Stead, and that necessity is likely to recur'.[72] The major point of contention was not Stead's involvement in the peace cause but that, to make his argument, Stead constructed an inaccurate picture of the existing organised peace movement by claiming that they advocated only for the eradication of all war. His claim was objectively inaccurate and vehemently denied by the established peace organisations.[73] While Sandi Cooper and others argue that British peace activists were less pragmatic and more motivated by pacifist idealism than their continental counterparts, when it comes to their public support for the Tsar's rescript there is little evidence to support the claim. Much of the literature circulated by these organisations around Britain in 1898 and 1899 explained the practical promise of the upcoming Hague conference.[74]

Members of the Peace Society were particularly unhappy that, after fulfilling their commitment 'to help' Stead, his Crusade continued to deny the potency of the existing peace message.[75] Unlike Stead's interpretation of them, idealism was never the peace movement's agenda. Most pacifists were pragmatists.[76] The Peace Society painted as 'ludicrous' the way in which 'speakers on every platform guarded themselves from any supposed connection with former advocates of peace'.⁷⁷ That Stead went to such lengths to artificially distance his 'new' peace from the 'old' was more symptomatic of his sensationalist style of prose than of his centrality to the public petitioning movement.⁷⁸

Crucially, while Stead liked to believe he had a unique power to convince the public that peace mattered, his fabricated intellectual divide did not, in the end, permeate the public petitions.⁷⁹ Even after the launch of the International Crusade of Peace in 1898, many petitioners worded their own appeals to the Foreign Office. They did not use the Crusade's recommended texts. Most, in fact, focussed their statements on the 'desirable and humane' ideas expressed in the Tsar's rescript.⁸⁰ While some petitions after December 1898 did mention the International Crusade of Peace directly, the focus was always on what the Tsar's proposal meant for their world.⁸¹ Although the petitioners were diverse and the Tsar's rescript inspired multifarious and often contradictory reactions, the British petitioners raised their voices to convey a remarkably consistent message: the Tsar's proposal mattered for their world and, therefore, it mattered to them that their government supported its aims.

That Stead's constructed divide did not permeate the words Britons put on paper in support of peace can be read as evidence that the public petitioning movement deserves historical attention. The British public's engagement with the peace movement changed qualitatively after December 1898 in that individuals began to deliberately attend larger meetings organised specifically to consider and support the Tsar's proposal, but it did not change quantitatively. After Peace Sunday, Britons still deliberately chose to petition their government and they constructed their petitions in the same terms as their compatriots had before 18 December. The location of public peace agitation changed, but it still rested on a willingness to mobilise one of the public's most traditional forms of demonstrating sentiment to the government.⁸² The story of the British public's support for the Tsar's rescript and the ensuing Hague conference is, therefore, much bigger than any one individual. In fact, the petitioning movement's historical legacies are significant precisely because they offer the opportunity to look at how individuals, all of whom encountered the idea in the context of their own experiences (as did the fictional Stephen Dedalus), responded to the range of peace messages available to them.

*

Although Joyce's character Dedalus was not convinced that the Tsar's proposal offered a legitimate opportunity for international cooperation and change, in 1898 and 1899 many Britons were. In their thousands, they petitioned for the Tsar's rescript and in favour of a conference of peace. Ultimately, the 1898–1899 British public movement for peace relied on momentum generated by audiences assembled on meeting hall's floors rather than what could be orchestrated on a meeting hall's stage. While the

Crusade's campaign rested on the construction of a strict divide between 'old' and 'new' forms of peace activism, Stead's vision was incompatible with the existing peace campaigners' ideologies and with many Britons themselves.[83] The continuities in the ideas expressed in the British petitions throughout the entire petitioning campaign suggests that the end of the movement's first phase in December 1898 did not signify a break in how Britons thought about the rescript's relevance to their world.

Stead has undoubtedly crusaded his way into the Hague conferences' historical legacies. While Stead's historical legacy is interwoven with that of the 1899 Hague Peace Conference, he was, of course, equally interested in the second conference. The historical record would likely benefit from a more detailed analysis of his involvement with the 1907 conference as well. At that time, he undertook a second grand tour, this time of North America, during which he was again critiqued for his signature style of self-promotion.[84] Challenging the primacy afforded to the Crusade of Peace in the British context also invites a more nuanced historical investigation of international public movements in response to the Tsar's 1898 proposal, the 1907 conference, and the proposed third Hague Peace Conference of 1915, which was never held.[85] This assertion could, and should, be extended to the broader transnational movement in support of the Tsar's proposal. Ultimately, Stead was not, unlike Joyce's alter ego Stephen Dedalus, the sole protagonist of the piece.[86]

Notes

1 With thanks to all of the participants at the 'War, Peace and International Order? The Legacies of the Hague Conferences of 1899 and 1907' conference held on 19 April 2016. I am particularly grateful for Glenda Sluga's and Robert Nye's thoughtful comments, and for Maartje Abbenhuis' insightful and challenging questions.
2 J. Joyce. (2000). *A Portrait of the Artist as a Young Man*. New ed., Oxford: Oxford University Press, pp.163–165.
3 Joyce, pp.163–165.
4 'Rescript of the Russian Emperor, August 24 (12), 1898', (English translation uncredited) in J.B. Scott. (1909). *The Hague Peace Conferences of 1899 and 1907: A Series of Lectures Delivered before the Johns Hopkins University in the Year 1908. Volume II: Documents*. Baltimore: Johns Hopkins Press, pp.1–2.
5 Based on a count of the petitions preserved in the National Archives of the United Kingdom, Kew, London [TNA], 'General Correspondence before 1906, Great Britain and General: Disarmament Resolution. Volumes 1–5', Records created or inherited by the Foreign Office [FO], 83/1734-1738; 'Resolutions on various subjects (1898–1899)', FO83/1739; 'Conference on armaments. Various. Volume 1', FO83/1699. For a detailed breakdown see A. Higgins. (2016). *Petitioning for Peace: The British Public Movement in Support of the Proposed first Hague Peace Conference, 1898–1899*. MA. University of Auckland, p.10.
6 C. Scott to Salisbury, 14 January 1899, FO83/1699, TNA.
7 *War Against War: A Chronicle of the International Crusade of Peace (WAW)*, London, 13 January 1899, p.1.

8 For a particularly well-known example, see B. Tuchman. (1996). *The Proud Tower: A Portrait of the World Before the War, 1890–1914*. 1st Ballantine Books ed., New York: Ballantine Books, pp.244–248.
9 H. Miller. (2012). Popular Petitioning and the Corn Laws, 1833–46. *The English Historical Review*, 127(527), p.882.
10 Joyce, pp.165–166. While it is not possible to provide an exact estimate of the number of petitioners, assuming the resolutions contain accurate accounts of the numbers represented, public supporters numbered into the millions in Britain alone. See FO83/1734–1739, TNA.
11 M. Abbenhuis. (2014). '"An Error In World History"? Revisiting the Hague Peace Conferences of 1899 and 1907', paper given at the 26th Annual Conference of the British International History Group, London School of Economics and Political Science, 4–6 September 2014.
12 Abbenhuis, n.p.
13 See, for example, D. Hucker. (2015). British Peace Activism and 'New' Diplomacy: Revisiting the 1899 Hague Peace Conference. *Diplomacy & Statecraft*, 26(3), p.406.
14 I. Clark. (2007). *International Legitimacy and World Society*. Oxford: Oxford University Press, p.77.
15 Clark, p.63.
16 J. Thompson. (2013). *British Political Culture and the Idea of Public Opinion, 1867–1914*. Cambridge: Cambridge University Press, p.86. The question of the relationship between the production of 'public opinion' is a point of great historiographical contention. See, for example, K.G. Robbins. (1977). Public Opinion, the Press and Pressure Groups. In: F.H. Hinsley, ed., *British Foreign Policy under Sir Edward Grey*. Cambridge: Cambridge University Press, pp.73–74; M. Wolff and C. Fox. (1973). Pictures from the Magazines. In: H.J. Dyos and M. Wolff, eds, *The Victorian City: Images and Realities*. Vol. 2, Boston: Routledge & Kegan Paul, 1973, pp.559–560.
17 Clark, p.72; M. Hutching. (1990). *'Turn Back this Tide of Barbarism': New Zealand Women who were Opposed to War, 1896–1919*. MA. University of Auckland, p.17; K. Schlichtmann. (2003). Japan, Germany and the Idea of the Hague Peace Conferences. *Journal of Peace Research* 40(4), p.384.
18 As quoted in the *London Standard*, 30 March 1899, p.2.
19 Hucker, p.407.
20 P. Laity. (2001). *The British Peace Movement, 1871–1914*. Oxford: Clarendon Press, pp.145–150.
21 G. Sluga. (2013). *Internationalism in the Age of Nationalism*. Philadelphia: University of Philadelphia Press, p.13.
22 C. Knab. (2013). Civil Society Diplomacy? W. T. Stead, World Peace, and Transgressive Journalism. *Comparativ: Leipziger Beiträge zur Universalgeschichte und Vergleichenden Gesellschaftsforschung*, 23(6), pp.36–49, quote at p.37.
23 Knab, p.50.
24 D. Cortright (2008). *Peace: A History of Movements and Ideas*. Cambridge: Cambridge University Press, p.41.
25 M. Ceadel. (2011). *Semi-Detached Idealists: The British Peace Movement and International Relations, 1854–1945*. 2nd ed., Oxford: Oxford University Press, p.152.
26 Ceadel, p.152. Ian Clark makes similar assertions: pp.73–75.
27 Hucker, p.409.
28 For examples see Clark, pp.73–75; Hucker, p.407; Tuchman, pp.244–245.
29 See Hucker. C.f. S. Cooper. (1967). *Peace and Internationalism: European ideological movements behind the two Hague Conferences (1889 to 1907)*. PhD. New York University, pp.25–27.

30 As James Brown Scott explained in concluding his 1908 series of lectures to the John Hopkins University on the Hague Peace Conferences of 1899 and 1907, there was 'no single precedent like it in all respects', but the Tsar's proposal could be seen to draw on precedents set by three types of international conference. The first were the familiar peace conferences, starting with the Peace of Westphalia in 1648, called to decide the terms of peace after a period of conflict. The second two types of conferences were, in Scott's opinion, nineteenth-century developments. Conferences in the Geneva tradition after 1864 set the precedent of conferences called in time of peace, although such conferences focused solely on the 'usages and customs of war'. Scott also identified a new 'class' of international conference from the later nineteenth century, commencing with the Congo Conference of 1884–1885, which sought to legislate for preserving peace. The Hague peace conferences were, in his view, novel in design in that they united these three strands of international conference and (particularly in the case of the 1907 conference) that 'legitimate' nations from around the world were represented. See Scott, *Hague Peace Conference*. Vol. 1, pp.731–734.
31 C.f. Hucker, p.408.
32 Tuchman, p.244. My count of the Foreign Office archives suggests that 716 petitions were received between the four months from 24 August 1898 and 24 December 1898.
33 FO83/1734–1739, TNA. Tuchman, pp.244–245 directly referred to FO83/1699, which contained three examples of public correspondence on the Tsar's rescript.
34 Tuchman, pp.246–246; *The Times*, 22 December 1898, p.8. Tuchman chose to end her analysis of the public petitioning movement in December 1898, although Stead's International Crusade of Peace movement (to which she proceeds to dedicate several pages) was not officially inaugurated until 18 December 1898. The Headquarters of the International Crusade of Peace (ICOP) were established at Talbot House on 22 December 1898. See *The Times*, 23 December 1898, p.5.
35 *The Times*, 26 April 1912, p.10.
36 *The Times*, 18 April 1912, p.12.
37 *Daily Mirror*, 18 April 1912, p.1.
38 S. Mitchell. (1988). *Victorian Britain: An Encyclopedia*. New York: Garland, p.756.
39 R. Luckhurst. (10 April 2012). *WT Stead, a Forgotten Victim of Titanic*. [online] Telegraph. Available at: http://www.telegraph.co.uk/history/titanic-anniversary/9195793/WT-Stead-a-forgotten-victim-of-Titanic.html [Accessed 3 August 2014].
40 W.S. Robinson. (2012). *Muckraker: The Scandalous Life and Times of W.T. Stead, Britain's First Investigative Journalist*. London: The Robson Press, p.ix. Also L. Brake, E. King, R. Luckhurst and J. Mussell, eds. (2012). *W.T. Stead: Newspaper Revolutionary*. London: British Library; this strong and wide-ranging collection looks critically at his newspaper career and historical legacies, but does not contain a chapter focussing on his peace activism around The Hague. For Grace Eckley's self-published account of Stead's peace activities: G. Eckley. (2007). *Maiden Tribute, A Life of W.T. Stead*, Philadelphia: Xlibris, pp.269–289.
41 Stead's series of four articles on 'The Maiden Tribute of Modern Babylon', which sought to expose child prostitution, generated public outcry and created a particularly grand spectacle. See A. Robson. (1978). The Significance of "The Maiden Tribute of Modern Babylon". *Victorian Periodicals Newsletter*, 11(2), pp.50–57. On Stead's style of journalism see S. Goldsworthy. (2006). English Nonconformity and the Pioneering of the Modern Newspaper Campaign. *Journalism Studies*, 7(3), pp.387–402. Also Knab, pp.22–51. Stead sought to create a public spectacle of opposition to the second Anglo-Boer War (1899–1902). See D. Mutch, In: Brake, King, Luckhurst and Mussell, pp.133–148.

42 Tuchman, p.248.
43 W.T. Stead. (1899). *The United States of Europe On the Eve of the Parliament of Peace*. London: William Clowes and Sons: p.1.
44 W.T. Stead to Baroness von Suttner, 8 July 1899, Bertha von Suttner Papers, 1843–1914, IPM/FS/BvS, United Nations Office at Geneva Library.
45 A. Eyffinger. (1999). *The 1899 Hague Peace Conference: The Parliament of Man, the Federation of the World*. The Hague: Martinus Nijhoff, p.347. C.f. Knab, p.45 for her discussion of 'shadow conferences'.
46 Willem de Beaufort (1899). *Diplomatic Correspondence, 27 February 1899*. In: C. Smit, ed. (1957). *Bescheiden Betreffende de Buitenlandse Politiek van Nederland, 3de Periode. Eerste Deel, 1899–1903*. The Hague: Martinus Nijhoff, pp.24–25. With thanks to Maartje Abbenhuis.
47 J.P. von Schmidt to W.T. Stead, 1 May 1907, W.T. Stead Papers (STED), 1/64, Churchill Archives Centre (CAC), Cambridge University.
48 Scott to Salisbury, 14 January 1899, FO83/1699, TNA.
49 Scott to Salisbury, 14 January 1899, FO83/1699, TNA.
50 *Concord: The Journal of the International Arbitration and Peace Association*, April 1899, p.57.
51 *Herald of Peace and International Arbitration (HOP)*, April 1899, p.199.
52 *Punch, or the London Charivari*, 24 May 1899, p.250.
53 Hucker, p.41.
54 W.T. Stead, ed. (1909). *The M.P. for Russia. Reminiscences & Correspondence of Madame Olga Novikoff*. London: Andrew Melrose, p.405. Madame Novicov (contemporary transliteration Novikoff) was the wife of the famous Russian peace activist Jacques Novicov and was herself involved with the Crusade of Peace in Britain. For detailed and insightful discussion of Jacques Novicov and the Hague peace conferences, see Cooper.
55 Stead, *M.P. for Russia*, p.5.
56 Based on petitions received on or before 19 December 1898. See FO83/1734–1735, TNA.
57 Members of Britain's peace associations and members of parliament associated with the movement travelled around the country in an attempt to further encourage public participation. See, for example, *Manchester Guardian*, 30 January 1899, p.7 noting that John Morley, MP, spoke in Leeds; 21 February 1899, p.9 noting that G. Harwood, MP, spoke in Southport; 1 March 1899, p.6 noting that Leonard Courtney, MP, spoke in Chelsea. During November 1898 alone William Evans Darby gave speeches in Braintree, Grays, Southwark, Tunbridge Wells, Westbourne Park, Rotherhithe, Acton, South Bromley, Bedford and Streatham Hill, see *HOP*, 1 December 1899, p.145.
58 See, for example, St Leonard on Sea Congregational Church to Salisbury, 6 September 1898, FO83/1734, TNA. The surviving petitions represent only those groups that decided that composing and sending a resolution was a worthwhile use of their time. It is not possible to gain an accurate measure of those who actively chose not to petition for peace.
59 The Foreign Office drew a similar distinction (for pragmatic reasons), by placing the petitions received on or before 19 December 1898 in FO83/1734–1735 and all of those received after 19 December 1898 in FO83/1736–1738, TNA.
60 Resolutions from 'Peace Sunday' are stored in FO 83/1735, TNA. As an example United Methodist Free Church Hill Street (Leicester) to Salisbury, 19 December 1898, FO 83/1735, TNA.
61 Laity, p.116. Also, *The Advertiser* (Adelaide, South Australia), 12 December 1934, p.11; *The Times*, 5 December 1898, p. 6.
62 Laity, p.116; *Daily Mail*, 21 December 1896, p.3; *Daily Mail*, 7 December 1897, p.5.

63 *South Australian Register* (Adelaide), 8 December 1898, p.5; *The Timaru Herald* (New Zealand) printed an excerpt from Stead's 'Peace Sunday' speech in an article entitled 'What the Czar Said', *Timaru Herald*, 7 February 1899, p.4.
64 Chas. Stevenson to the Editor, *Manchester Guardian*, 17 December 1898, p.6.
65 These resolutions can be found in FO83/1735–1736, TNA.
66 Nine congregations modified the resolution to specifically explain that mediation should be conducted by 'neutrals'. See Wood Green Pleasant Sunday Afternoon Association (Middlesex) to Salisbury, 18 December 1898, FO83/1735, TNA.
67 See the Bishop of London, quoted *The Times*, 5 December 1898, p.6; *WAW*, 18 January 1899, p.1. Unlike Tuchman's implication that Anglicans were noticeably absent, they were encouraged to attend Stead's public meetings. See also *Daily Mail*, 28 December 1898, p.3. C.f. Tuchman, p.245 for an argument that Church of England congregations were 'conspicuously absent' in the public resolutions.
68 *Daily Mail*, 19 December 1898, p.5; *Manchester Guardian*, 19 December 1898, p.5.
69 *Observer*, London, England, 18 December 1898, p.7.
70 *The Times*, 22 December 1898, p.8.
71 *WAW*, 13 January 1899, p.1.
72 *Concord*, December 1898, p.193
73 *WAW*, 13 January 1899, p.1; c.f. Cortright, p.11.
74 See, for example, Cooper, pp.7–9.
75 *HOP*, 1 April 1899, pp.200–201.
76 Cortright, p.8; Johnston, p.516.
77 *HOP*, 1 April 1899, pp.200–201.
78 Mitchell, p.756.
79 J. Baylen. (2010). *Stead, William Thomas (1849–1912)*. [online] Oxford Dictionary of National Biography. Available at: doi:10.1093/ref:odnb/36258, [Accessed 3 August 2014]; *The Times*, 18 April 1912, p.12; *The Times*, 26 April 1912, p.10; M. Hampton. (2004). *Visions of the Press in Britain, 1850–1950*. Urbana: University of Illinois Press, p.115.
80 See, for example, the New Barnet P.S.A. to Salisbury, 29 September 1898, FO83/1734, TNA, which explained that they supported the Tsar's proposal precisely because it raised a 'desirable and humane' question.
81 The Macfadyen Memorial Congregational Church to Salisbury, 26 January 1899, FO83/1736, TNA, wrote that the congregation 'rejoices at the inauguration of the Crusade of Peace'.
82 Higgins, pp.48–59.
83 *HOP*, 1 April 1899, pp.200–201; Cooper, pp.24–26.
84 *New York Times*, 5 May 1907, p.SM1.
85 Eyffinger, p.458.
86 Joyce, pp.163–169.

9 The Hague as a framework for British and American newspapers' public presentations of the First World War

Thomas Munro

In August 1914, the pages of the prominent mid-west American newspaper, the *Chicago Daily Tribune*, were filled with news of the war in Europe. The newspaper attempted to make sense of the events in Europe and assess their impact on the United States. Among the articles published on 15 August—discussing responsibility for the war, the German advance in Belgium and the conflict's economic impact on the United States—was an interview with the librarian of the local Chicago County Law Library, who had noticed a decided increase in demand for books on international law and the proceedings of the Hague conferences of 1899 and 1907.[1] Among the volumes in greatest demand, the librarian explained, was William Hull's overview history, *The Two Hague Conferences*, that had been published the previous year.[2] It seemed that Chicago locals sought out information about the Hague conferences and conventions to help them make sense of the war. Across the Atlantic Ocean, in Great Britain, a similar public desire for information on The Hague was evident in the *Manchester Guardian*'s 'Questions and Answers on the War' section. On nine separate occasions in August and September 1914, readers asked specific questions about the Hague conventions and how they applied to the war in which Britain was involved.[3]

British and American newspaper reporting in August and September 1914 demonstrated a significant engagement with the idea of The Hague (conceptualised here as a generic concept that embraced knowledge of the conferences, the Hague conventions of 1899 and 1907 and the internationalist principles they engendered) as a framework for assessing and understanding the war. From the first days of the war, newspapers on both sides of the Atlantic used The Hague as a lens to assess the legality of a wide array of belligerent conduct. References to The Hague in the opening months of the war were so numerous that a *Daily Mail* editorial on 18 December declared that the 'debating habit of flinging articles of The Hague convention' at the enemy should cease'.[4] The newspapers show how The Hague was part of a global conversation about the conduct of the war. Their editorials utilised The Hague as a means to assess the conduct of the war at sea, on land and in the air. It was presented as determining how neutrals, prisoners of war and civilians should be treated by and behave towards belligerents. The Hague was referenced so extensively because their readers in Britain and the United States assessed the war in legal terms from the outset.

In the opening months of the First World War, Britons and Americans were confronted with a conflict that quickly surpassed the scale and destructiveness of any they had previously witnessed. Significantly, they reacted to these events by referencing 'The Hague'. When contemporaries used the words 'The Hague' they usually did so in relation to one of the following prominent issues: disarmament or the reduction of spending on armaments, the development of arbitration for the peaceful settlement of disputes, the value of international organisations for ensuring pacific international relations, the development of international law and the basis it provided for concepts of international justice, and the limits of acceptable conduct for states and their armed forces during wartime. They also used the words 'The Hague' to reference the rather vague concept of 'civilisation'. This term conveyed the idea that states and governments that followed the Hague's rules, principles and conventions were often classified as civilised, while those that broke or did not apply them were not. The city of The Hague itself had become intertwined with many of these ideas, particularly after the erection of the Peace Palace in 1913. Thus, to speak of 'The Hague' in 1914 could entail reference to the legal conventions signed at The Hague or to The Hague as a site for international justice, or a combination of the two.

Most importantly, the idea of 'The Hague', with its myriad meanings, permeated newspaper coverage in the opening weeks of the war in both Britain and the United States. Front-page articles, editorials, published official statements and letters to the editor all made reference to The Hague in a particularly wide range of contexts. These included belligerent powers' use of aircraft, belligerent access to neutral communication networks and the protection of civilians in occupied areas. The Hague's legal mechanisms for international arbitration and mediation were also presented as a possible means of ending the war. Others suggested that a third Hague peace conference could bring the war to a speedy conclusion. For the most part, however, newspapers on both sides of the Atlantic used The Hague to assess the legality of wartime conduct. Furthermore, they promoted The Hague as a means of articulating and strengthening the legitimacy and legality of each country's position—one neutral, the other belligerent—in the conflict.

The outbreak of war generated a multitude of reactions in the United States. Expressions of shock at the scale of the war and the desire to avoid involvement and remain neutral, were common in the American newspapers. The war was also an exciting news event and the causes of the conflict and its conduct were discussed with great enthusiasm. The public response to the war was complicated by the vast number of Americans who had significant ties to one or more of the belligerents. Being born in—or having relatives from—one of the belligerents did not, however, necessarily entail support for that nation's war effort.[5] Indeed, many Americans looked at Europe's 'descent into barbarism' with disdain, with Progressives in particular fearing that the conflict would bring to a halt the preceding half century's social reforms.⁶ American concerns about modern war's destructiveness were coupled with awareness of the conflict's economic opportunities and how neutrality could be used to exploit them.⁷ Articles evaluating whether the United States' and the belligerents' actions adhered to the requirements of neutrality, as dictated by the Hague conventions, appeared frequently in the American newspapers.

A sense of shock that the political crisis on the continent had degenerated into war was also evident in the British newspapers. In the weeks leading up to the British declaration of war, newspapers had largely split down party lines with the conservative papers stressing the need for Britain to stand by France and the liberal and provincial press opposing any British involvement on the continent.⁸ Yet, once Britain went to war with Germany on 4 August 1914, even those newspapers that had promoted British neutrality begrudgingly offered their support.⁹ One of the British government's key justifications for going to war was defending international law, which Germany had violated by invading Belgium, and this framed the public discussion concerning the war's meaning and conduct in British newspapers. Their reports presented Germany's violations of the Hague conventions, real or imagined, as evidence of the illegal manner in which the Kaiser's forces were waging war. The tenor of the discussions helped to establish a rationale for Britain's declaration of war.

This chapter examines the messages about The Hague that appeared in select British and American newspapers in the first two months of the war. It argues that The Hague was embedded in popular understandings of war in Britain and the United States. Well before 1914, the concept of 'The Hague' offered a medium to discuss the conduct of war.¹⁰ The outbreak of the war cemented the importance of the Hague conventions, providing Britons and Americans with a means to measure belligerent conduct and assess the war's impact. While the British government certainly used The Hague for official propaganda purposes, the British press—largely independent of official pressure—also used the Hague conventions to assess belligerent and neutral conduct. This was equally true in the neutral United States, where it had become difficult to discuss the war without referencing the Hague laws. Isabel Hull's contention that, from the war's opening days, 'world public opinion' focussed on belligerent violations of the laws of war is borne out by the newspaper reporting in Britain and the United States.¹¹ To that end, the belligerents' official accusations of their enemy's illegal conduct added to an already existing discussion about the conduct of the war. The Hague was central to these debates.

Newspaper coverage of the war's first months, demonstrated a greater degree of public engagement with the laws of war than historians typically acknowledge. John Horne and Alan Kramer argue that during the war the British governmental, military and intellectual establishment placed more importance on violations of The Hague conventions than did 'ordinary opinion'.[12] However, Hull suggests that The Hague was important to both 'leaders and public opinion' in Britain and that both immediately viewed the First World War as a struggle over law.[13] Despite her claim, Hull's work largely focusses on élite opinion and does not clearly demonstrate the British public's engagement with The Hague. Similarly, Catriona Pennell's excellent book on British reactions to the outbreak of war suggests that the public regarded international law as an important cause, but does not engage extensively with The Hague.[14] The newspapers from Britain and the United States substantiate Pennell and Hull's claims about the importance of international law for the British public in the first months of the war while also demonstrating that a similar sentiment existed in the neutral United States.

Historians have long debated newspapers' role in society and how they can be used for historical study. Mark Hampton claims that commentators on the press in Britain have 'argued about the extent of press influence and whether newspapers shaped or reflected public opinion' since the mid-nineteenth century.[15] That newspaper owners and editors sought to influence the public is undeniable but, as Adrian Gregory points out, their ability to do so was 'constrained by the fact that the vast majority of readers of the national press bought newspapers that reflected their existing political tendencies'.[16] Newspapers, therefore, should not be treated as uncomplicated windows onto public opinion or disregarded as merely the expression of a particular newspaper proprietor's ideas. Newspapers contained a multitude of opinions—those of editors, journalists and members of the public—expressed in a number of different forms, such as editorials, articles and letters to the editor.[17] By critically examining and comparing multiple newspapers, historians are able to identify what issues people thought were important at particular times and how they were discussed. As such, this chapter contends that the prevalence and nature of references to The Hague in four newspapers from Britain and the United States during August and September 1914 offers insight into the ways in which Britons and Americans understood the place of the Hague laws in their world.

Newspaper discussions of The Hague reflected specific national and regional responses to the outbreak of war. The newspapers surveyed in this chapter—the *Manchester Guardian* and *Daily Mail* from Britain, and the *Chicago Tribune* and *Los Angeles Times* from the United States—have been selected because they were prominent and well-read newspapers but had different readerships in a political and geographic sense. The *Daily Mail* in 1914 was the 'true titan' of the daily press in Britain.[18] The newspaper had the largest circulation in Britain and it tended to reflect—its proprietor Lord Northcliffe's—negative views on Germany.[19] The *Manchester Guardian* remained the most important regional newspaper in Britain and was seen as the voice of 'establishment liberalism'.[20] The *Los Angeles Times* was an influential newspaper on the United States' West Coast and was used by its Republican stalwart owner, Harry Chandler, as a vehicle for promoting Los Angeles and to push for particular development ventures.[21] The *Chicago*

Tribune had played a similar role for Joseph Medill who, as publisher of the newspaper in the 1850s, used the newspaper to promote Chicago and the modern Republican Party.[22] By 1914, the *Chicago Tribune* was considered an important newspaper in the Midwest and 'one of the top Republican papers in the country'.[23] These newspapers all engaged with the war in different ways and all four referenced The Hague extensively. Despite one nation's belligerency and the other's neutrality, newspaper reporting from both countries demonstrated a shared perception of The Hague's importance both for understanding the war and for imagining the post-war world.

In the first weeks of August 1914, the Hague conventions gained extensive coverage in Britain and the United States as newspapers discussed their potential to stop the escalating conflict. On 5 August, the *Manchester Guardian* reprinted the Arbitration Society's suggestion that Britain should stay out of the conflict and use 'the machinery of the Hague Conventions' to bring about peace.[24] On the same day, President Wilson offered his services as a mediator under Article 8 of the 1899 pacific dispute settlement convention.[25] All four newspapers reported extensively on Wilson's proposal. They discussed in great detail how the offer was valid under the convention's terms, exactly what the relevant articles entailed and speculated on the likelihood that any of the belligerents would take up Wilson's offer.[26] The American newspapers reported extensively on Wilson's peace initiative, with a front page article in the *Los Angeles Times* and an editorial in the *Chicago Tribune*.[27] While these newspapers did not convey a sense of optimism about mediation being successful—the *Los Angeles Times* even described Wilson's offer as useless at that particular time—they did present it as the appropriate course of action for the United States as a neutral state.[28] Coverage of Wilson's offer of mediation continued in the newspapers through August and September, gaining front page coverage in the *Chicago Tribune* on 13 and 17 September and in the *Los Angeles Times* on 11 September.[29] Even in late September, the *Manchester Guardian* printed an article claiming that a possibility of achieving peace through The Hague's mediation process remained.[30]

The newspapers also discussed the possibility of the third Hague peace conference, scheduled to take place in 1915, convening earlier in an attempt to stop the conflict. On 2 September, for example, the *Manchester Guardian* published a letter to the editor which highlighted that the conflict was the first general European war since the Hague peace conferences. The letter suggested that it was incumbent on those non-belligerent signatories to the Hague conventions to call for another conference in a bid to stop the hostilities.[31] The idea that neutrals should take the initiative to bring about an end to the war was expressed in articles in both the *Manchester Guardian* and the *Chicago Tribune*.[32] The *Manchester Guardian* article called for a conference of neutrals to be convened at The Hague 'without a moment's delay', while the *Chicago Tribune* article suggested that the third peace conference should be held in Washington 'as soon as possible'.[33] A remarkable letter to the editor of the *Los Angeles Times* went a step further, claiming that another Hague conference was the best way of achieving peace and that the conference should form the basis of the re-organisation of the post-war world. According to the correspondent, if all nations contributed armed forces to 'the conference', it would be able to enforce its decisions in the interests of peace. The best way to achieve lasting peace, the letter continued, was to make every man 'take an oath to serve the Hague conference in the interests of justice'.[34]

The Hague's mechanisms and conventions were presented as tools that could prevent conflicts. A number of articles, therefore, criticised European rulers for not using the conventions when the threat of conflict arose or even for intentionally undermining their development in the years since 1899. An article in the *Chicago Tribune* discussed The Hague's potential for preventing war but claimed that Germany and the 'war party' that lead the country had undermined attempts at disarmament and the use of arbitration.[35] An article in the *Los Angeles Times* attributed blame more broadly and argued that many of those involved at The Hague had been disingenuous because they had talked about peace and restraints on conflict whilst continuing to develop instruments of war.[36] Another *Los Angeles Times* article expressed a similar sentiment when it claimed that the governments who attended The Hague had made professions of peace with their mouths, but made monstrous fighting machines with their hands.[37] Articles in the *Daily Mail* and *Manchester Guardian* argued that it was the failure of the international community to place such fighting machines at the The Hague's disposal—so that states could be forced to use the Permanent Court of Arbitration and accept its decisions—which had undermined its ability to prevent war.[38] The newspaper coverage from both countries suggests that the Hague conferences were seen by many as a missed opportunity. Disarmament, the Permanent Court of Arbitration and the commissions of inquiry were ideas and mechanisms which could have prevented war but were undermined at the time by duplicitous leaders.

Despite its failure to prevent the war, it is clear from the newspaper reporting that people in Britain and the United States believed that the Hague's rules continued to represent the civilised way of conducting war. The Hague conferences had attempted to establish means of preventing war but also of humanising war should it occur. The resulting conventions, particularly the 1907 conference's Convention IV Respecting the Laws and Customs of War on Land, sought to regulate military violence and confine it to combatants.[39] All four newspapers discussed the Hague conventions governing the manner in which civilised states treated prisoners of war.[40] Indeed, Convention IV contained 17 articles relating to the treatment of prisoners of war, the most important of which (Article 4) stated that they must be treated humanely. Referencing these articles, the *Manchester Guardian* claimed that the:

> lot of a prisoner of war, whether he be a captured foe or a detained reservist, need not be altogether an unhappy one [as] a number of

chivalrous rules have been made at the Hague for relieving the anxieties of this position, and by these rules all civilised nations are bound.[41]

Two days later, in response to a reader's question, the newspaper explained how belligerents' employment of prisoners of war was determined by the Hague rules.[42] However, the difficulties of interpreting the Hague conventions became apparent in late September when the Dutch government decided to return British sailors rescued after their cruisers had been sunk.[43] The *Manchester Guardian* and the *Los Angeles Times* both printed detailed articles discussing the Dutch government's responsibility with regard to the rescued British sailors.[44] The articles demonstrated that there was some doubt about how the Hague's rules should be interpreted in particular situations but no question of them being the authority on the treatment of prisoners of war.[45]

The difficulty of interpreting the Hague's rules was also evident in the British and American newspapers' coverage of the aerial bombardment of cities. Aeronautical science was still in its infancy during the two Hague conferences, which made attempts to regulate its military application particularly difficult. However, the conference delegates were aware of the potential for aviation to be used against civilians and attempted to prevent this by prohibiting the discharge of projectiles and explosives from balloons. Article 25 of the 1907 conference's Convention IV prohibited the bombardment of undefended towns 'by whatever means'.[46] While contemporaries interpreted 'by whatever means' to include aircraft, defining an undefended town was more problematic. If a town contained a single soldier, was it considered defended? For a town to be a legitimate target for aerial bombardment it not only needed to be defended but, according to Convention IV's Article 26, also required the commanding officer of the attacking forces to 'do all in his power' to warn the town's authorities before a bombardment commenced. When belligerents used aircraft to attack towns in August and September 1914, the newspapers in Britain and the United States engaged with the ambiguous phrasing of the Hague conventions and debated the legality of aerial bombardment.[47]

The Zeppelin raids on Antwerp in late August and the aeroplane raids on Paris in early September inspired a number of articles in all four newspapers.[48] Even before the raids occurred, the *Los Angeles Times* published an extensive commentary that detailed belligerent air force strengths and how the Hague conventions determined how aircraft could be utilised in war.[49] A week after this article, and two days before the Zeppelin raid on Antwerp, the newspaper also published a paragraph in their 'Pen Points' section concerning what the Hague laws allowed in terms of explosives discharged from aircraft.[50] The *Manchester Guardian* and the *Chicago Tribune* also gave aviation and its regulation by the Hague conventions prominent coverage. The *Manchester Guardian* printed an editorial discussing The Hague's provisions for warfare in the air and used them to assess the legalities of Germany's

Zeppelin raid on Antwerp.[51] An editorial in the *Chicago Tribune* analysed the Hague conventions in detail in discussing the Zeppelin raid.[52] Reports on the use of aircraft in August and September implied that aircraft had captured people's imagination and that there was a widespread discussion about how they could be used in war. Crucially, all of these discussions used The Hague as a framework for understanding the aerial attack's legality.

As the war in Europe escalated, the *Chicago Tribune* and *Los Angeles Times* debated how the conflict might affect the United States. Their discussions used The Hague as a framework for predicting how belligerents might treat American shipping. The United States' recent industrial expansion was heavily reliant on exports to Europe in general and to Britain and Germany in particular.[53] In the first week of August, even before all the European powers had made formal declarations of war, the *Chicago Tribune* published articles noting the protection the Hague conventions afforded to neutral shipping.[54] The articles published in early August demonstrated an assumption that belligerents would likely use blockades, but avoid other wartime measures against neutral trade. Their discussion, therefore, focused on freedom of passage for neutral vessels and the likelihood of American ships being stopped and searched for contraband. The articles clearly stated that the Hague conventions determined the rules governing such behaviour and they provided significant description and analysis of the relevant articles and the 1909 Declaration of London's attempts to refine them.[55] That The Hague's language left room for interpretation created concern in the United States over what exactly belligerents would consider contraband and how they would deal with murky issues such as merchant ship conversion and foreign crew registration.[56] Despite these concerns, the *Chicago Tribune*'s coverage demonstrated a belief that The Hague would offer protection to American shipping.

While the *Chicago Tribune* focussed on the issues related to a potential blockade, the *Los Angeles Times* concentrated on naval mines as the bigger threat to American shipping and published a number of articles analysing their legality under the Hague rules. The articles demonstrated an assumption that The Hague governed what types of mines were legal and how they could be used. Belligerents laid mines in an attempt to control the shipping lanes to Europe, and their use became a prominent issue on 9 August 1914 when the *Los Angeles Times* and *Chicago Tribune* printed reports concerning a mine sinking the Norwegian ship *Tysla*.[57] Both newspapers considered the legality of using mines in great detail. The *Chicago Tribune* noted how 'momentous' the problem of agreeing on the issue of mines had been at the Hague conferences and claimed that using the mine in this case was legal.[58] Three days after *Tysla* sank, the *Los Angeles Times* published an extensive article about mines being used in the North Sea, the legality of their use under the Hague's laws and how this affected neutral American shipping.[59] The newspapers demonstrated an acknowledgement that The Hague was the appropriate venue for regulating the use of mines but also anger that the conferences had failed to effectively do so and could not provide adequate protection for neutral trade. A subsequent *Los Angeles Times* article called for 'the next Hague conference' to do something about mines as their current use meant war ruled the seas and business had no place there.[60]

The rules of neutrality and the desire for the United States to remain neutral were common themes in all of the aforementioned articles. The laws of neutrality's codification at the 1907 Hague conference had created 'a much clearer set of expectations of neutrals' in wartime and the newspapers made clear that neutrality's rules need to be treated with respect and care.[61] President Wilson made the link between neutrality and The Hague obvious when he declared American neutrality with reference to the Hague conventions. Fearing that belligerents, if given the excuse, might flout the Hague conventions which protected neutral shipping in times of war, American newspapers stressed the importance of the United States adhering strictly to international law to prevent this possibility. On 8 August, the *Chicago Tribune* emphasised the need for the United States to be perceived as closely following The Hague's rules. The article discussed the Department of Commerce's orders setting out regulations to port authorities. These rules were quickly withdrawn and corrected when it became clear that they were inconsistent with the neutrality regulations embedded in the Hague conventions.[62] A series of articles in the *Los Angeles Times* concerning belligerent use of cable and wireless networks in the Unites States also demonstrated concern about meeting the obligations of neutrality. The articles all referenced The Hague in their discussion of the United States' responsibilities to the belligerents with regard to neutral communication networks.[63] The newspapers suggest an awareness within the United States that The Hague determined neutrals' rights and duties, something which Americans needed to keep in mind as the war progressed.

British newspapers also discussed the need for neutral shipping to be treated in accordance with the Hague regulations. That they did so became particularly important for Britain as it came to define its role in the war as the protector of international law. The *Manchester Guardian* published a number of articles on the protections the Hague rules offered for merchant shipping.[64] These articles, one of which was a response to a reader's question, discussed the relevant Hague convention and its relationship with the Declaration of London (1909), in detail. Prize courts in particular drew British newspapers' attention and elicited discussions in relation to the courts' historical development, current legality and use by the Royal Navy.[65] American concerns about the legality of using naval mines were also mirrored in British newspapers. Two days after Britain declared war, the *Manchester Guardian* printed an extensive article about mines and their legal standing as determined by The Hague.[66] The article described mines as a horror of war and argued that they were still being used because the Hague conventions had failed to effectively ban them.[67] A similar sentiment was expressed in a letter to the *Daily Mail*'s editor, which claimed that using mines was legal under the Hague rules but should not be as they could damage 'harmless neutrals'.[68]

The American newspapers' concern that belligerents might not adhere to the Hague conventions was echoed in the British newspapers, but with particular reference to Germany.[69] The British newspapers printed numerous accusations that Germany had violated the Hague conventions by indiscriminately sowing mines in the North Sea. In so doing, they helped to shape the image of Germany as a rogue state operating outside the bounds of international law. A letter to the *Manchester Guardian*'s editor, furthermore, claimed that Germany's use of mines contravened the Hague conventions by 'poisoning the waters' of the world.[70] A similar sentiment was expressed in a *Daily Mail* article which listed the way Germany had used mines as one of their armed forces' many atrocities.[71] The issue of legality had become a central feature of the war with Britain attempting to discredit Germany's conduct in the war in the eyes of the international community.[72] As these articles demonstrate, attempts to portray Germany as conducting the war in an illegal manner were not restricted to the British government. The *Manchester Guardian* discussed a request made by the town of Grimsby's chamber of commerce that the British government protest to the neutral powers signatory to the Hague conventions about Germany's use of mines.[73] Clearly, some members of the British public were assessing the war in legal terms and understood the importance of winning favour with the international community.

Of all the belligerents' attempts to discredit their enemy's conduct of the war in the eyes of global society, accusations of mistreating civilians were the most controversial.[74] Newspaper coverage of the conflict's first two months demonstrated how people in Britain and the United States recognised the Hague conventions as pivotal in regulating the treatment of civilians in occupied areas. The key regulations for protecting civilians were Articles 25 to 28 in the 1907 conference's Convention IV, which prohibited a range of actions including bombarding undefended towns, unnecessarily destroying civic buildings and pillaging private property. Even before the accusations of German atrocities against civilians came to prominence, the *Los Angeles Times* printed an editorial about the laws of war in which it claimed that civilians in modern warfare were protected by the Hague conventions.[75] When allegations against the German armed forces appeared, in late August, they were discussed primarily with reference to these conventions.[76] Indeed, the *Manchester Guardian* and the *Chicago Tribune* reported that French government protests about German treatment of civilians should be addressed to The Hague's signatories.[77] When German forces were accused of bombarding undefended towns, the *Los Angeles Times* claimed that this was exactly the sort of barbaric act that the Hague conventions were supposed to prevent.[78] A similar point was made in the *Manchester Guardian*, which responded to a reader's question about bombarding towns by discussing the Hague conventions.[79] German violations of The Hague allowed them to be presented as uncivilised by their enemies. The *Daily Mail* claimed that Germany's treatment of civilians was ironic, revealing the cruelty of the soldiers from a nation that 'boasted at the last Hague conference of the humanity and chivalry of the German military'.[80]

Newspapers also discussed German responses to the claims that their soldiers were mistreating civilians and thus demonstrated the public awareness that The Hague determined not only how civilians in occupied territory should be treated, but also how they should behave. Even before prominent incidents such as the sacking of the Belgian university town of Louvain (Leuven) by the German forces occurred in late August 1914, the *Manchester Guardian* responded to a reader's question about the legality of civilian resistance in occupied areas by stating that The Hague determined the relevant rules.[81] As stories of atrocities committed by German troops emerged, Germany claimed their actions were in response to Belgian civilians violating the laws of war.[82] All four newspapers printed articles discussing the German claims that the Belgian civilians in Louvain had violated the Hague conventions by firing on German troops after the town had surrendered.[83] The American newspapers printed a number of articles discussing civilian violations of The Hague in Belgium.[84] The *Los Angeles Times* claimed Belgian civilians were poisoning water supplies and printed a letter to the editor claiming that Belgian civilians were not behaving in accordance with the laws of war.[85] An article in the *Daily Mail*, however, alleged that German civilians were violating The Hague in their behaviour towards Russian troops in East Prussia.[86] The articles all shared an assumption that The Hague determined what acceptable conduct was for civilians in occupied areas. The assertion was reiterated in late September when the *Manchester Guardian* responded to a reader's question about the recognition of belligerents by providing details of The Hague's rules on militia and volunteers.[87] The Hague was thus presented as an appropriate lens through which to assess the legality of civilian conduct in time of war.

From the outbreak of war, the belligerents competed in the 'international public sphere' to present their cause as morally superior.[88] The Hague was hugely important to the belligerent attempts to win global opinion. Its centrality was particularly evident in the debate over using dum-dum bullets. Dum-dum bullets were prohibited in conflicts between civilised powers by the 1899 Hague conventions because of the horrific wounds they inflicted.[89] In many of the conflicts that had occurred subsequent to the 1899 Hague Peace Conference, belligerents had attempted to discredit their enemy in the international community's eyes by accusing each other of using dum-dums. By late August 1914, accusations of dum-dum usage joined the broader debate about the conduct of war. The belligerents made numerous official statements accusing each other of violating The Hague by using dum-dum bullets and these were duly printed in British and American newspapers.[90] Personal accounts from soldiers, doctors and journalists—all of whom provided their opinion on who had been using, possessing or manufacturing dum-dums—supplemented official statements in the newspapers.[91] The newspapers became a site for public engagement with the debate about using dum-dums. Public engagement with these legal ideas was clearly demonstrated by how the British and American public critically evaluated the belligerents' accusations in letters to editors.[92]

The importance belligerents placed on global opinion is evident in the British government's concern with the perception that their armed forces were violating The Hague by using dum-dum bullets. The *Manchester Guardian* covered British parliamentary debates about the issue. During one debate, Liberal MP Sir William Byles directly questioned British use of dum-dum bullets.[93] The government responded by stating that British soldiers were only using ammunition that met The Hague's requirements. The next day, Irish MP John MacNeill asked the government what they were doing to counteract the accusations that Britain was using dum-dums.[94] The British government had, in fact, already taken steps to refute German accusations. The *Daily Mail* and *Chicago Tribune* reproduced a placard, authorised by Sir Edward Grey and distributed throughout the Netherlands, claiming that British and French forces were only using ammunition that was acceptable under the Hague regulations.[95] The questions in the House of Commons and the fact that Grey's placards were distributed in the Netherlands, demonstrates British concern with neutral countries' opinions.

The public in neutral countries such as the United States were well aware of belligerent attempts to win their favour and engaged with the debate about dum-dum bullets in a sophisticated manner. As a prominent target for belligerent propaganda, the United States was sent a number of official protests about the use of dum-dum bullets. Belgium, France and Germany all sent protests to the United States and the newspapers extensively covered the protests' content and how Wilson might reply.[96] American journalists in Europe were also shown dum-dum bullets allegedly found on British and French soldiers by German officials and the *Chicago Tribune* even printed photographs of the alleged bullets.[97] The American press acknowledged that many belligerent accusations about the use of dum-dums were likely fabricated. An editorial in the *Chicago Tribune* noted that such accusations were 'the first to get circulation in any war' and that in trying to determine who was telling the truth 'rational opinion wanders hopelessly afield'.[98] American newspapers also acknowledged that the belligerents were not only trying to win the hearts and minds of neutrals in the present but that they were simultaneously preparing their cases for a hypothetical post-war tribunal seeking to sort out the war's illegalities. The *Los Angeles Times* expressed this idea in an article arguing that the Hague conventions specifically prohibited dum-dums and that by accusing each other of using them, belligerents were placing their cases on record to be sorted out at the end of the war.[99] Clearly, The Hague had come to be considered a permanent feature of international affairs and newspapers expected that their reading publics would understand what it meant to discuss conduct in terms of its rules.

In August and September 1914 Britons and Americans were faced with a conflict unlike any they had previously experienced. Millions of soldiers clashed across vast swathes of Europe as the war began to inexorably draw in nations from across the globe. The belligerents unleashed industrial warfare's destructive power on land, at sea and in the air and it quickly became apparent that non-combatants and neutrals would not be able to avoid the violence. The language of the Hague peace conferences of 1899 and 1907 was widely used to make sense of the war. The understanding that public audiences would use The Hague as a lens on the war was ubiquitously reflected in newspaper reports. The Hague conventions were discussed in front page articles, editorials and letters to the editor. The Hague offered a key framework to assess neutral and belligerent conduct and to imagine ways to prevent such a global conflagration happening again. In the face of what many perceived to be civilisation's collapse, the Hague conventions were seen as more important than ever.

Notes

1 *Chicago Tribune*, 15 August 1914, p.9.
2 *Chicago Tribune*, 15 August 1914, p.9.
3 *Manchester Guardian*, 11 August 1914, p.4; 17 August 1914, p.3; 21 August 1914, p.3; 22 August 1914, p.8; 25 August 1914, p.10; 26 August 1914, p.3; 19 September 1914, p.5; 25 September 1914, p.3. There were two separate questions in relation to The Hague on 25 August 1914.
4 *Daily Mail*, 18 December 1914, p.6.
5 Zieger notes that it is likely, of course, that more sympathy for the Central Powers would be found in the German–American community, but that broad national and ethnic categorisations 'masked powerful crosscurrents of difference, dissent, and perspective'. R. Zieger. (2000). *America's Great War: World War I and the American Experience*. Oxford: Rowman & Littlefield, p.15.
6 Zieger, p.15. Nancy Ford argues that some progressives supported the Allies' war effort but that the many others began to define themselves as pacifists and sought an early end to the war. N. Ford. (2008). *The Great War and America: Civil-Military Relations During World War I*. Westport: Praeger Security International. p.52.
7 P. O'Brien. (2013). The American Press, Public, and the Reaction to the Outbreak of the First World War. *Diplomatic History*, 37(3), pp.456–457.
8 A. Gregory. (2004). A Clash of Cultures: The British Press and the Opening of the Great War. In: T. Paddock, ed., *A Call to Arms: Propaganda, Public Opinion, and Newspapers in the Great War*. Westport: Praeger, pp.19–20.
9 Gregory, p.20.
10 M. Abbenhuis. (2014). *An Age of Neutrals: Great Power Politics, 1815–1914*. Cambridge: Cambridge University Press, pp.178–218.
11 I. Hull. (2014). *A Scrap of Paper: Breaking and Making International Law During the Great War*. Ithaca: Cornell University Press, p.51.
12 J. Horne and A. Kramer. (2001). *German Atrocities, 1914: A History of Denial*. New Haven: Yale University Press, pp.215–216.
13 Hull, p.2.
14 C. Pennell. (2012). *A Kingdom United: Popular Responses to the Outbreak of the First World War in Britain and Ireland*. Oxford: Oxford University Press.

15 M. Hampton. (2004). *Visions of the Press in Britain, 1850–1950*. Urbana: University of Illinois Press, p.25.
16 Gregory, p.19.
17 Pennell, p.6.
18 Gregory, p.16.
19 C. Haste. (1977). *Keep the Home Fires Burning: Propaganda in the First World War*. London: Allen Lane, p.8.
20 Gregory, pp.16–18.
21 A. Wallace. (2005). *Newspapers and the Making of Modern America: A History*, Westport: Greenwood Press, pp.79–81.
22 T. Leonard. (1995). *News for All: America's Coming-of-Age with the Press*. New York: Oxford University Press, p.49.
23 O'Brien, p.459. See also, G. Douglas. (1999). *The Golden Age of the Newspaper*. Westport: Greenwood Press, p.50.
24 *Manchester Guardian*, 5 August 1914, p.3.
25 M. Floyd. (2013). *Abandoning American Neutrality: Woodrow Wilson and the Beginning of the Great War, August 1914 –December 1915*. New York: Palgrave Macmillan, p.11.
26 *Daily Mail*, 6 August 1914, p.6; *Manchester Guardian*, 6 August 1914, p.4; 10 August 1914, p.6; *Chicago Tribune*, 6 August 1914, p.6; *Los Angeles Times*, 6 August 1914, p.I1.
27 *Chicago Tribune*, 6 August 1914, p.6; *Los Angeles Times*, 6 August 1914, p.I1.
28 *Los Angeles Times*, 8 August 1914, p.II4.
29 *Chicago Tribune*, 13 September 1914, p.1; 17 September 1914, p.1; *Los Angeles Times*, 11 September 1914, p.I1.
30 *Manchester Guardian*, 22 September 1914, p.7.
31 *Manchester Guardian*, 2 September 1914, p.3.
32 *Manchester Guardian*, 28 September 1914, p.6. *Chicago Tribune*, 10 September 1914, p.4.
33 *Manchester Guardian*, 28 September 1914, p.6. *Chicago Tribune*, 10 September 1914, p.4.
34 *Los Angeles Times*, 19 September 1914, p.II5.
35 *Chicago Tribune*, 9 September 1914, p.3.
36 *Los Angeles Times*, 21 August 1914, p.II4.
37 *Los Angeles Times*, 7 September 1914, p.II3.
38 *Daily Mail*, 26 August 1914, p.5. *Manchester Guardian*, 25 September 1914, p.10.
39 A. Kramer. (2007). *Dynamic of Destruction: Culture and Mass Killing in the First World War*. Oxford: Oxford University Press, p. 25.
40 *Daily Mail*, 24 September 1914, p.4; *Chicago Tribune*, 23 August 1914, p.1; *Los Angeles Times*, 20 September 1914, p.I12; *Manchester Guardian*, 15 August 1914, p.9.
41 *Manchester Guardian*, 19 August 1914, p.3.
42 *Manchester Guardian*, 21 August 1914, p.3.
43 The rules relating to neutral internment of belligerent sailors were particularly difficult to apply in practice. See M. Abbenhuis. (2006). *The Art of Staying Neutral: The Netherlands in the First World War, 1914–1918*. Amsterdam: Amsterdam University Press, pp.103–112.
44 *Manchester Guardian*, 24 September 1914, p.6; *Los Angeles Times*, 25 September 1914, p.I4.
45 Alan Kramer argues that prisoners of war were not treated in accordance with the Hague conventions by their captives, but that this was usually due to a lack of resources and organisation rather than systematic and deliberate mistreatment. Kramer, p.62.

46 G. Best. (1980). *Humanity in Warfare*. New York: Columbia University Press, pp.262–264.
47 See for example *Chicago Tribune*, 2 September 1914, p.1; *Los Angeles Times*, 27 August 1914, p.I4; *Daily Mail*, 26 August 1914, p.5; *Manchester Guardian*, 26 August 1914, p.5.
48 *Chicago Tribune*, 2 September 1914, p.1; 13 September 1914, p.13; *Los Angeles Times*, 27 August 1914, p.I4; 9 September 1914, p.II4; *Daily Mail*, 26 August 1914, p.5; 2 September 1914, p.5; *Manchester Guardian*, 26 August 1914, p.5; 2 September 1914, p.4.
49 *Los Angeles Times*, 16 August 1914, p.IIIA11.
50 *Los Angeles Times*, 23 August 1914, p.II6.
51 *Manchester Guardian*, 27 August 1914, p.4.
52 *Chicago Tribune*, 13 September 1914, p.A4.
53 Floyd, p.15.
54 *Chicago Tribune*, 1 August 1914, p.7; 3 August 1914, p.10; 5 August 1914, p.5; 5 August 1914, p.7; 6 August 1914, p.3; 7 August 1914, p.7.
55 For informative analysis of the Declaration of London and its connection to The Hague, see C. Davis. (1975). *The United States and the Second Hague Peace Conference: American Diplomacy and International Organization, 1899–1914*. Durham: Duke University Press; and J. Coogan. (1981). *The End of Neutrality: The United States, Britain, and Maritime Rights, 1899–1915*. Ithaca: Cornell University Press.
56 *Chicago Tribune*, 5 August 1914, p.5; 6 August 1914, p.3. There were concerns in the United States about how British authorities would treat American ships with German crew and German vessels that were now registered and sailed by Americans.
57 *Los Angeles Times*, 9 August 1914, p.IV10; *Chicago Tribune*, 9 August 1914, p.3. Both articles started with the Associated Press article giving the basic information regarding the sinking and then provided separate analysis.
58 *Chicago Tribune*, 9 August 1914, p.3.
59 *Los Angeles Times*, 12 August 1914, p.I2.
60 *Los Angeles Times*, 20 August 1914, p.II4.
61 Abbenhuis, *An Age of Neutrals*, p.217.
62 *Chicago Tribune*, 8 August 1914, p.7.
63 *Los Angeles Times*, 12 August 1914, p.I6; 14 August 1914, p.I1; 22 August 1914, p.I3; 26 August 1914, p.I5; 4 September 1914, p.I3.
64 *Manchester Guardian*, 11 August 1914, p.3; 15 August 1914, p.3; 26 August 1914, p.3.
65 *Daily Mail*, 5 September 1914, p.3; *Manchester Guardian*, 15 August 1914, p.3; 26 August 1914, p.3; 5 September 1914, p.6. For more information on the Royal Navy's adherence to Hague and Prize Law during the First World War see N. Lambert. (2012). *Planning Armageddon: British Economic Warfare and the First World War*. Cambridge: Harvard University Press.
66 *Manchester Guardian*, 7 August 1914, p.10.
67 *Manchester Guardian*, 7 August 1914, p.10.
68 *Daily Mail*, 11 September 1914, p.4.
69 *Daily Mail*, 5 September 1914, p.3. *Manchester Guardian*, 5 September 1914, p.6.
70 *Manchester Guardian*, 9 September 1914, p.3.
71 *Daily Mail*, 16 September 1914, p.4.
72 See Pennell, p.64. Hull, p.51.
73 *Manchester Guardian*, 11 September 1914, p.4.
74 This has also proved to be one of the more controversial aspects of First World War historiography. For an excellent survey of the historiography see N. Gullace.

(2011). Allied Propaganda and World War I: Interwar Legacies, Media Studies, and the Politics of War Guilt. *History Compass*, 9(9), pp.686–700.
75 *Los Angeles Times*, 9 August 1914, p.II6.
76 Adrian Gregory argues that the issue first gained real prominence in the British newspapers on 21 August 1914: Gregory, p.28.
77 *Manchester Guardian*, 21 Aug 1914, p.10; *Chicago Tribune*, 26 September 1914, p.3.
78 *Los Angeles Times*, 18 August 1914, p.II6.
79 *Manchester Guardian*, 17 Aug 1914, p.3.
80 *Daily Mail*, 16 September 1914, p.4.
81 *Manchester Guardian*, 11 August 1914, p.4. For more on the sacking of Louvain (Leuven): Gregory, pp.29–31; Horne and Kramer, pp.38–42.
82 Historians have demonstrated that the German claims about an illegal uprising of Belgian civilians, a *franc-tireur* war, are 'as much a myth as the claim that German troops systematically hacked the hands off of Belgian children'. J. Lipkes. (2007). *Rehearsals: The German Army in Belgium, August 1914*. Leuven: Leuven University Press, p.16.
83 *Daily Mail*, 2 September 1914, p.7; *Manchester Guardian*, 4 September 1914, p.10; *Chicago Tribune*, 29 September 1914, p.2; *Los Angeles Times*, 1 September 1914, p.I4.
84 See for example *Chicago Tribune*, 13 September 1914, p.7.
85 *Los Angeles Times*, 10 September 1914, p.I2; 14 September 1914, p.II5.
86 *Daily Mail*, 11 September 1914, p.5.
87 *Manchester Guardian*, 25 September 1914, p.3.
88 Horne & Kramer, p.249.
89 For a history of dum-dum bullets and attempts to prohibit their use, see J. Bourke. (2014). *Deep Violence: Military Violence, War Play, and the Social Life of Weapons*. Berkeley: Counterpoint.
90 *Manchester Guardian*, 22 August 1914, p.4; 24 August 1914, p.6; *Daily Mail*, 9 September 1914, p.6; 17 September 1914, p.5; *Chicago Tribune*, 12 September 1914, p.2; 29 September 1914, p.1; *Los Angeles Times*, 1 September 1914, p.I4; 12 September 1914, p.I2.
91 For an example of a French doctor's claims about German use of dum-dum bullets see *Daily Mail*, 26 September 1914, p.3. For a British soldier's opinion on who was using dum-dums see *Manchester Guardian*, 10 September 1914, p.7. The *Chicago Tribune* contained a number of reports from their own journalists near the Western Front offering their opinion on who was using dum-dum bullets. Examples include: *Chicago Tribune*, 26 September 1914, p.1; 27 September 1914, p.5.
92 *Daily Mail*, 25 September 1914, p.4. *Los Angeles Times*, 14 September 1914, p.II5.
93 *Manchester Guardian*, 16 September 1914, p.7.
94 *Manchester Guardian*, 17 September 1914, p.7.
95 *Daily Mail*, 14 September 1914, p.3; *Chicago Tribune*, 15 September 1914, p.4.
96 *Los Angeles Times*, 26 August 1914, p.I5; *Chicago Tribune*, 29 September 1914, p.1; *Daily Mail*, 10 September 1914, p.5; *Manchester Guardian*, 11 September 1914, p.6. Wilson, whose focus in the first months of the war was to maintain the country's neutrality, did little more than acknowledge the protests and encourage belligerents to adhere to The Hague.
97 *Chicago Tribune*, 26 September 1914, p.1; 27 September 1914, p.5. For the photographs of dum-dum bullets see *Chicago Tribune*, 27 September 1914, p.7.
98 *Chicago Tribune*, 12 September 1914, p.6.
99 *Los Angeles Times*, 10 September 1914, p.I2.

10 Norway's legalistic approach to peace in the aftermath of the First World War

Marta Stachurska-Kounta

In an address to their king in 1890, a group of liberal members of the Norwegian *Storting* proposed concluding arbitration treaties for all kinds of disputes with other countries.[1] The Swedish authorities rejected the initiative claiming that it resulted from 'the lack of contact on the part of Norwegians as to what belongs to the foreign policy sphere'.[2] Sweden's response was certainly paternalistic in form, but it should not be interpreted as primarily directed against the Norwegian parliamentarians. In many ways, it reflected political leaders' conservative and cautious views towards the use of international arbitration in the nineteenth century. It was only at the first Hague Peace Conference, nine years later, that diplomats attempted to entrench and extend the use of arbitration in resolving international disputes.

Although Norway was not an independent country in 1899, two technical delegates from Norway joined the Swedish delegation to the first Hague peace conference.[3] Since only sovereign states exercising control over their own foreign policy could participate in the conference, the Norwegian presence represented special recognition of Norway as a weaker partner in the union with Sweden. After gaining its independence in 1905, Norway sent its own delegation to the second Hague Peace Conference in 1907. The delegation had the express mandate to support 'every effort to make international arbitration more compulsory and more encompassing'.[4] The outbreak of the First World War in 1914 put an end to the third Hague Peace Conference planned for 1915. Prior to its cancellation, however, Norway had already made extensive preparations for the conference, including a proposal for advancing international arbitration. This proposal would come to serve as a guiding document for Norway's position towards the emerging international order at the end of the war and in the wake of the League of Nations' establishment in 1920.

Focusing on the key period between 1918 and 1921, when the postwar order was established, this chapter sheds light on Norway's efforts to strengthen the rule of law in the international system. In keeping with the spirit of the Hague peace conferences, Norway's emphasis on legalism was based on a belief that peace between nations depended on establishing a system of compulsory and binding forms of pacific settlement to resolve international disputes. The Norwegian government was not alone in promoting such ideas. However, the Norwegian approach was characterised—and distinguished from, for example, the ideas promoted by the United States based League to Enforce Peace (LEP)—by not including any proposals regarding how to enforce peaceful settlements. The country's reliance on policies of non-alignment in peace and neutrality in war prevented the government from providing support for an international organisation using coercive measures. It was then in the judicial sphere, notably with the creation of the Permanent Court of International Justice (PCIJ), that the Norwegians hoped to make their mark. In doing so, they invoked the principles and ideas that had imbued the Hague conferences and conventions of the pre-war era.

The Scandinavian proposal for an international judicial organisation

During the war, neutral countries such as Norway faced serious challenges in defending their on-going legitimacy as neutrals in a world beset with war and one in which the concept of collective security gained increasing traction. At a meeting in Kristiania in November 1917, the governments of Norway, Sweden and Denmark decided to set up national study committees for the purpose of establishing a joint position on the issue of a post-war order.[5] In response, the Norwegian government established a committee in March 1918 to examine how to secure the neutral states' mutual interests at the war's end.[6] The Norwegian committee consisted of three former delegates to the second Hague Peace Conference, namely the former conservative prime minister and international legal scholar Francis Hagerup, shipping tycoon and member of the Libertarian Party (*Frisinnende Venstre*) Joachim Grieg and the Secretary General of the Inter-Parliamentary Union (IPU) Christian Lous Lange. The Norwegian government's choice of delegates indicated three main areas of interest: international jurisdiction, shipping and peace advocacy.

With the war's end, the Scandinavian preparatory committees worked out a joint draft in December 1918, which they considered to be their 'contribution to the forging of a "League of Nations"'.[7] The strong legalistic undertones were indicated in the title 'Draft of an International Judicial Organisation'. The draft proposed that the League of Nations should have four components, including: a permanent international court, a council to serve as an organ for international inquiry, an obligation for states to submit disputes either to judicial procedure or to another form of peaceful resolution like international inquiry, and mediation as well as a permanent organisation for international law and peace conferences.[8] The organisation's role would be to provide a venue to promote peace between nations and the development of international law.[9]

At first sight, the Scandinavian 'Draft of an International Judicial Organisation' strongly resembled the legalistic vision of an international organisation promoted by the LEP.[10] However, the LEP also envisaged military means to enforce judicial settlement of disputes. This was not included in the Scandinavian draft. As a result, the Scandinavian draft represented a rather toothless version of the LEP's legalistic scheme centred around an international court instead of a political council. Nevertheless, the most striking similarity between the Scandinavian vision and that championed by the LEP was the notion of a world governed by law rather than politics. The primary aim of a future international organisation for both was to provide peaceful settlement of international disputes and accelerate the development of legal codes.

Another framework within which to consider the Scandinavian draft is its relationship to the wartime peace programme of the Central Organization for a Durable Peace (CODP).[11] The CODP was formed at The Hague in 1915 by representatives from nine European nations and the United States. Lange played a key role in the organisation and it is likely that he wished to influence the committee's work with the ideas promoted by the CODP. Envisaging methods of securing peace between nations after the war's end, the CODP formulated the so-called minimum programme which, apart from peaceful settlement of disputes and means to enforce law, also urged reducing armaments.

Nevertheless, the joint Scandinavian draft did not mention any means of international law enforcement to discipline states that resorted to violent means to settle disputes, nor did it include the question of reducing armaments. The main reason for this was the contradictory positions Hagerup and Lange held on these points. In the report signed by Hagerup and Lange, the Norwegian committee members argued that they did not regard themselves as sufficiently competent to give a well-rounded account on these two issues.[12] Given their mandate, this explanation is not persuasive. In reality, as Lange later admitted, Hagerup left the committee in protest against proposals for including disarmament and equipping the League with the means to enforce law.[13] Therefore, the legalistic character of the December 1918 Scandinavian draft came out of a compromise between Lange's progressive internationalism and Hagerup's more conservative standpoint. It was not a conscious plan to reduce the proposals' scope to deal solely with legal issues. In this context, it is important to note that the differences between Lange and Hagerup were long-standing. They disagreed about similar issues during the 1907 Hague Peace Conference.[14]

Hagerup's resignation from the committee was also important because he was one of three persons who initially dominated the Scandinavian negotiations. The other two were Lange and the Swede Erik Marks von Würtenberg, an expert in international law, and later President of the Swedish Supreme Court (1920–1931) and Minister of Foreign Affairs (1923–1924).[15] According to the Swedish comment on the Scandinavian draft, it was not in the remit of small states to initiate questions on sanctions and reducing armaments in post-war negotiations.[16] The conservative von

Würtenberg and his party shared Hagerup's view of the new organisation's role. Hagerup's sceptical attitude towards certain aspects of the new emerging international order again played a part when he, as a member of the Norwegian Nobel Committee, strongly opposed Wilson's candidacy for the Nobel Peace Prize in 1919. Hagerup even threatened to resign from the committee in protest if the prize were awarded to the American president. Eventually, deputy member Wollert Konow attended in his place when the Nobel Committee took the decisive vote in 1920.[17]

The government reconstituted the Norwegian committee with a resolution of 24 January 1919.[18] The resolution relieved Hagerup of his duties and added Johan L. Mowinckel and Otto Blehr, both from the governing Liberal Party (*Venstre*). In addition, Mikael H. Lie, a lawyer and international law expert, was appointed as the committee's technical advisor and secretary.[19] Both Lange and Grieg stayed on. By reorganising the committee in this way, the government clearly indicated its desire for stronger political control of the process.[20]

Neither Hagerup's nor Lange's standpoint fully reflected the Liberal government's official position. Both Mowinckel and Lie belonged to a minority that voted against Norwegian support for an international association endowed with means of enforcement during one of the Consultative Assembly of the Norwegian IPU's meetings in May 1917.[21] During these meetings to develop a tentative Norwegian position, Lange persuaded the majority of the participating Norwegian parliamentarians to support an international association with means of enforcement.[22] Mowinckel and Lie, as well as Blehr, were more representative of the Liberal government's viewpoint, which was based both on the notion of Norway's policy of non-alignment and reliance on the principles of classic liberalism. Yet, although the committee's new members, unlike Lange, did not sympathise with any form of enforcement mechanism; unlike Hagerup, they supported a general reduction of armaments.

Gram-Skjoldager and Tønnesson consider the December 1918 draft a stepping stone for Scandinavian states towards attaining membership in the League of Nations.[23] They argue that the draft acted as a means to initiate discussions on a future international organisation at a national and inter-Scandinavian level. In the international context, however, the Scandinavian draft did not play a significant role. First of all, the draft did not embody any particularly original ideas. Instead it was mainly based on a collection of pre-existing ideas from the programmes of the IPU and the CODP.[24] Nor did the Scandinavian draft attract much international attention given that the Scandinavian governments were not really given the opportunity to put forward their joint proposals. They appealed jointly to the Allied and Associated Powers for permission to take part in the peace conference in Paris but their request was not granted.[25] The official answer pointed out that neutral states could not join the conference since it was a meeting reserved for the victorious powers.[26] The victors wanted to keep the neutrals at arm's length. The Norwegians, in fact, colluded by not pushing the matter. Tønnesson states that in early February 1919 Lange unsuccessfully asked the Foreign Ministry to send him copies of the Scandinavian Study Committees' reports which he wanted to transmit to Lord Robert Cecil, one of the leading British representatives at the Paris Peace Conference.[27] But the Norwegian government apparently displayed no interest in promoting the Scandinavian committees' work through informal channels either.[28] Yet the draft is nevertheless important for it signalled the Scandinavian countries' firm commitment to the vision of international order based on a legalistic foundation.

Drafting the Permanent Court of International Justice's statute

Despite being kept out of the official peace negotiations, the neutral states' representatives were invited for brief private consultations at the Hotel Crillon on 20–21 March 1919.[29] The representatives were encouraged to express their opinions concerning the draft covenant of the League of Nations published on 14 February 1919. The meeting at Hotel Crillon offered, however, only a modest opportunity to confront the nearly finished draft. In Paris, the Scandinavian states failed to gain general acceptance for their proposal to include a provision for compulsory arbitration in the Covenant of the League. Therefore, as soon as the victorious powers announced that governments would be allowed to submit their own drafts on a permanent international court, the Norwegian Ministry of Foreign Affairs asked the Study Committee to prepare such a proposal.[30] The opportunity to make an impact on shaping international affairs was not lost on the Norwegians.

Although the first Hague Peace Conference succeeded in establishing the Permanent Court of Arbitration (PCA), it was not a court in the proper sense. Instead it was a panel of arbitrators selected by the signatory powers which could nominate up to four persons 'of known competence in questions of international law, of the highest moral reputation, and disposed to accept the duties of arbitrators'.[31] In the case of a dispute, the parties could appoint arbiters from the panel in order to compose an arbitral court. Signatory states were not required to submit disputes to arbitration. In addition, because each arbitral court would have a different composition and the judges were not obliged to reside at the official seat of the PCA, such a court was not in a position to build up a continuous system of jurisprudence. Similarly, the delegates to the second Hague Peace Conference did not manage to reach a compromise on a permanent international court.

However, things looked very different in 1919 when the League of Nations' Covenant provided for the establishment of an International Court. According to Article XIV of the Covenant, the court was 'to hear and determine any dispute of an international character which the parties thereto submit to it'.[32] The Council or the Assembly could also ask the court to issue an advisory opinion if the parties submitted a case to one of these bodies. The article's wording was, however, only the first step towards a fully developed statute of the International Court. Therefore, when the governments received an official invitation to submit their own recommendations for a permanent international court, the Scandinavian Study Committees agreed that the previous joint draft for an international judicial organisation—drawn up in December 1918—was no longer applicable in the new situation and found it necessary to prepare a new proposal. In addition, the Norwegian committee insisted that the Scandinavian states should submit separate proposals in order to highlight national differences.[33] Such a move would supposedly also make the Scandinavian proposals more visible. The Norwegian Study Committee's new draft was ready at the end of August 1919.

The small neutral states' consuming interest in having a say on the International Court's statue became even more evident when the Scandinavian states' representatives, the Netherlands and Switzerland met at The Hague in February 1920 'in order to give every possible assistance to ensure the success of so important an undertaking as that proposed'.[34] The result of the consultations was a new draft reflecting the common ground between the five neutral states' representatives. These states also submitted their own separate drafts to the League's Advisory Committee of Jurists, set up by the Council to prepare a statute for the court. Thus, out of 15 drafts, seven were prepared by the five neutral European states. Their fervent activity was in many ways an attempt to make up for their lack of influence over framing the League of Nations during the Paris Peace Conference. According to the Norwegian Study Committee, these states had 'a special task with regard to creating a secure and just foundation for the future of international relations'.[35] By submitting drafts of the International Court's statute, these five European neutral states acted in tandem with a number of prominent international organisations advocating peace and international law such as the *Union Juridique Internationale* and the IPU.

In the draft developed during the conference in The Hague in February 1920, the five neutral states reached an agreement on four cardinal principles affecting the International Court's nature, composition and organisation.[36] The principles included: equality of states, complete and methodological separation of the notions of justice and arbitration, total exclusion of political influences and total independence of judges as against their own country.[37] The draft was thus based on completely different principles to those of the Covenant of the League, which was, in words of Swiss diplomat and League official William Rappard, 'a compromise between law and politics, between justice theory and tradition and political expediency'.[38] From this perspective, the five neutral states' work represented an attempt to create an institution that would embrace some of the ideals they had hoped to implement in the Covenant of the League.

The members of the Norwegian Study Committee had originally disagreed on the principle of equality of states.[39] In May 1918, Hagerup reported on behalf of the committee that they disagreed on 'whether the smaller states in order to achieve the crucial progress, that the establishment of such a court would be, should renounce a strict assertion of the sovereign state equality principle'.[40] Hagerup had argued as early as 1907 that as a prominent sea power, Norway had interests of a global character, similar to the great powers, and thus should be represented on the proposed permanent court under equal conditions.[41] He then convinced the Norwegian government to let him vote against a plan of a permanent international court dominated by the great powers. This happened although the Norwegian government was, in principle, closer to Lange's standpoint which considered a formal differentiation between the great powers and small states to be acceptable so long as it could contribute to establishing a permanent international court.[42] In this matter, in 1907, the Norwegian Liberal government adopted Hagerup's conservative standpoint as its actual policy.[43]

Therefore, it is significant that the principle of the equality of states also dominated the Norwegian proposal of August 1919 when Hagerup was no longer a member of the Study Committee. However, whereas the original 1918 Scandinavian report dealt with a scheme for an international organisation, the August 1919 Norwegian proposal and that drafted by the five neutral states in February 1920 were exclusively concerned with an international court. The Norwegian Study Committee emphasised that, while it was natural to accept the great powers' preponderant influence in a political body such as the League of Nations, an international court had to be based on the equal rights of all states.[44] In other words, while they were willing to accept the great powers' superior political and military position, they did not find it desirable to formally accept the inequality of states in the sphere of justice. There is no indication that any member of the Norwegian committee disagreed.

The second principle of the five neutral states' plan was expressed as a desire to distinguish between notions of justice and arbitration. This was significant since, in reality, the distinction was blurred. In contrast to mediation or conciliation, for example, states recognised arbitration as a judicial process under the Hague Convention on the Pacific Settlement of International Disputes adopted in 1899.[45] The fundamental difference between arbitration and other methods of peaceful settlement had already been acknowledged in the eighteenth century.[46] Emer de Vattel (1714–1767), for instance, regarded arbitration as the first step in developing an advanced set of procedural rules under existing international law.[47] The recognition of arbitration as a judicial process through the Hague Convention was thus only a confirmation of a generally accepted principle. According to this principle, an arbitral award, in contrast to other methods of peaceful settlement, was binding for the parties involved.

At the same time, arbitration could be carried out either by applying the rules of law or, in a less formal way, by considering what was fair and equitable. In practice, arbitral courts often used their discretion in giving awards instead of strictly applying the law. As a result, as British lawyer Hersch Lauterpacht pointed out:

> there was a tendency to deny the judicial character of arbitration, as it then existed, in order to strengthen the argument for the establishment of a true international court able to develop International Law by the continuity of its pronouncements and the permanency of its personnel.[48]

The status of arbitration as a judicial procedure, although formally recognised, could still be disputed. The five neutral states therefore put forward the principle of separating justice and arbitration in order to distinguish between the two methods of reaching a decision: equity which was often used in arbitration and the strict application of law.[49] It is also important to point out that Articles XII, XIII and XV of the Covenant of the League of Nations operated with the phrase 'arbitration or judicial settlement', thus implying that these two methods were considered distinct.

The five neutral states recognised that arbitration could still be applied by special agreement between states, but they urged at the same time that 'all ideas of arbitration must therefore be excluded from the Statutes of the Court'.[50] This argumentation conformed with the classical realism within legal thought: a perception, widely recognised in the first half of the twentieth century, that neutral courts could settle disputes between states only if it was possible to draw a clear demarcation between law and politics.[51] This view echoed Hagerup's disagreement with Lange's idea—which had marked the Norwegian delegation's performance at the 1907 Hague Peace Conference—that the existence of international institutions and regulations could in itself bring about more peaceful relations between states.[52]

Paradoxically, the August 1919 Norwegian proposal (drafted without Hagerup, but with Lange) stated explicitly that small states would profit from 'a purely judicial decision, unconstrained by any strain of political considerations'.[53] This apparent paradox needs to be considered in a broader context. In 1918, as a head of the Norwegian Study Committee, Hagerup reported to the Ministry of Foreign Affairs that:

> With regard to issues of a primarily legal nature, where political interests are not predominant, we assume that the relationship between great and small powers is not a matter of concern.[54]

This remark implies that Hagerup was willing to formally abandon the principle of the equality of states to a certain degree so long as the competence of an international court would be limited to purely judicial questions. In this sense his support for separating law and politics was directly related to his opposition to an international court dominated by great powers.[55] However Lange, although eager to limit the PCIJ's competence to exclusively judicial questions, also wished to develop a complete system of peaceful settlement for all kinds of international disputes.[56] In this regard, he supported establishing a separate system of conciliation for disputes arising out of conflicts of interests and a special system of arbitration for mixed (i.e. partly judicial and partly political) disputes. The biggest controversy concerned the question of providing a conciliation and inquiry body with the right to take initiative in settling an international dispute. In practice, this would amount to making such solutions compulsory. In 1918, Lange was among those members of the Scandinavian Study Committees who considered it natural for the neutral states to take the lead in promoting this idea. Hagerup, on the other hand, was among those who claimed that 'so far-reaching a proposal presumably may sound scary'.[57] The compulsory system of conciliation and arbitration would imply too powerful an intrusion on the state's sovereignty and could put the legal equality of states on the line.

Thus, the third principle included in the five neutral states' proposal directly related to both the equality of states and the distinction between arbitration and justice. Here, the proposal attempted to exclude any political influence from the International Court since 'politics have nothing in common with law'.[58] However, although the five neutral states' delegates agreed that the International Court should deal chiefly with questions of a legal nature, they were divided on the question of defining the court's sphere of jurisdiction. Since the Covenant failed to establish a clear demarcation between disputes of a legal nature and those generally described as political, the joint draft for the PCIJ listed five issues for the court's compulsory jurisdiction.[59] The first four points coincided with the kinds of disputes mentioned in Article XIII of the Covenant of the League, and included: disputes concerning the interpretation of a treaty, any question of international law, the existence of any fact which if established would constitute a breach of any international obligation and the extent and nature of the preparation to be made for any such breach. The neutral states' draft added to the court's compulsory jurisdiction a category of disputes relating to 'the interpretation of a judgment given by the court'.[60] Significantly, the Norwegian and Danish delegates—as noted in the draft—preferred not to address this question because they were not convinced that the wording of Articles XIII and XIV of the Covenant of the League authorised such a step.

The Norwegian approach was very cautious. This was not due to any uncertainty about the court's compulsory jurisdiction. The real problem lay in preparing a list of subjects of an exclusively legal nature which should always by consequence be submitted to judicial settlement. As Hagerup emphasised it was

> difficult to reach an agreement on the dividing line between issues that may be subject to legal decisions ('justiciable'), and where legal procedures and arbitration may be appropriate, and disagreements of a different character ('non-justiciable'), where investigations and conciliation may be more appropriate.[61]

While the December 1918 Scandinavian joint proposal addressed this problem by including a need for the parties' consent in submitting a dispute to the court's jurisdiction, the following year the reconstituted Norwegian Study Committee found it unsatisfactory.[62] Although the committee argued that it was 'desirable to broaden the court's competence as much as possible', its August 1919 proposal shied away from the issue because of its complexity.[63]

The Hague conventions of 1899 and 1907 had introduced a distinction between legal and non-legal disputes which came to constitute the basis of the so-called doctrine of the inherent limitations of the international judicial process. However, the question of deciding which disputes were exclusively legal in character had proven controversial. Both the extent of international jurisdiction and the countries' consent to it were at stake. During the 1907 Hague Peace Conference, the British and American delegations attempted to set up such a distinction by enumeration (i.e. by providing a list of disputes suitable for submission to compulsory arbitration), but even a modest list failed to secure unanimity.[64] The disagreement also materialised within the Norwegian delegation, as Hagerup and Lange looked at the issue differently.[65] Lange's attempts to position the Norwegian delegation in favour of the most progressive ideas seemed to reflect Norway's official support for widening the scope of compulsory arbitration. However Hagerup, as the head of the delegation, abstained on a proposal to set out common definitions of the types of disputes where states should not be allowed to make reservations against international arbitration. The Study Committee also maintained this position from 1918–1920. Although, the Norwegian government's policy was in favour of widening the scope of the court's compulsory jurisdiction, the Study Committee eventually refrained from addressing this issue in detail.

Furthermore, the court's competence was also specified by the sources of law, which were to form the basis of its decisions. In this regard, the five neutral states' proposal referred to the law of nations as well as conventions and treaties.[66] The diverging Scandinavian opinions also concerned this issue. Accordingly, the December 1918 Scandinavian joint draft included two different suggestions.[67] The first, integrated into the main text, pointed out three sources of law: agreements in force between the parties, the established rules of international law and the general principles of law. The second, presented as an alternative, overlapped with regard to the first two sources but, instead of referring to the general principles of law, postulated that the court could decide what (in its opinion) constituted the rules of international law. The alternative therefore implied moving beyond jurisdiction based exclusively on positive international law. The August 1919 Norwegian draft included only the second of these two alternatives, indicating that at least some of the members of the Norwegian Study Committee strongly favoured this option. In fact, it is plausible to argue that the initiative came from Lange who wished to make the Norwegian proposal as radical as possible. This may be concluded from the fact that the initial work of the Scandinavian committees was dominated by Hagerup, Lange and the Swedish representative von Würtenberg, and of them only Lange contributed to the August 1919 Norwegian draft. Consequently, Lange's influence on the work of the Norwegian Study Committee positioned it as the most progressive among the five neutral states.

The Norwegian proposal to split the preparatory works of the Scandinavian committees and present separate drafts to the PCIJ clearly originated in a desire to take up a distinct position with regard to two questions: the scope of the court's obligatory jurisdiction and the court's power to create law. On the issue of the scope of the court's obligatory jurisdiction, the Norwegian delegates to the February 1920 meeting of the five neutral states in The Hague in effect opted out of the decision-making process. They refrained from making a specific proposal. In addition, since the Norwegian provision addressing the question of the court's power to create law was not included in the joint draft, it seems that the majority of the five neutral states' representatives did not agree with the Norwegian approach.

Eventually, the five neutral states envisaged the total independence of judges. This fourth principle was related to the previous principles since it was based on a desire to exclude any political considerations from the judicial procedure. Consequently, the five neutral states' draft urged the exclusion of any judge who was a citizen of one of the contesting states. It acted as a way to mark a distinction between an arbitral court and the PCIJ, because an arbitral court afforded the parties the right to appoint their own nationals to try the case together with a neutral umpire. The Norwegian Study Committee also proposed providing each of the parties in a case with the power to challenge three of the tribunals' members.[68] The power of challenge was intended to work as a regulatory mechanism enabling the parties to exclude judges they considered potentially biased. Lange was the only committee member not to support this motion. He argued that the judges should perceive themselves as representatives of the principle of law and that the statute of the PCIJ should therefore avoid any provisions emphasising judges' nationalities. Moreover, he claimed, the power of challenge would result in the tribunal's composition constantly changing and in this way hamper the development of the court's own tradition of jurisprudence. In effect, Lange regarded the power of challenge as 'a measure that may undermine the authority of the court and would in principle weaken its legal character'.[69] Clearly, the disagreements about the power of challenge reflected the majority's cautious attitude towards the emerging system, in contrast to Lange's confidence in the internationalist project.

These three drafts, which Norway prepared or helped to prepare, reflected tensions between the two different approaches towards the organisation and the competence of the International Court. Accordingly, they represented two distinct traditions of international law.[70] On the one hand, they reference the impact of the Anglo-Saxon common law tradition. This tradition promoted peaceful settlement of international disputes by arbitration or adjudication. Within this tradition, the judge played a crucial role in guaranteeing peace through law and the court was equipped with a broad competence, including the power to create law. On the other hand, the preparatory works for the PCIJ were also strongly influenced by the tradition closer to the continental civil law system where the court's main task was not to legislate but to apply the law. According to this tradition it was the concept of law itself that was the medium through which peace should be created. Although both traditions regarded international law as the best instrument to enhance peace in the world, the first was more pragmatic and the latter more conceptual.[71] The approach associated with Lange and his efforts to broaden the scope of the International Court's competence is best understood within the first tradition, whereas the approach most notably identified with Hagerup and his focus on the strict application of the principles of law has much in common with the second tradition.[72] As already mentioned, Hagerup's commitment to legal positivism dominated the Norwegian delegation's negotiations at the 1907 Hague Peace Conference, despite the fact that the government favoured a more progressive approach. In 1919 and 1920, on the other hand, Lange set the tone of the Norwegian position towards the peaceful settlement of international disputes. However, this radical Norwegian position was not representative of the Scandinavian states or the five neutrals.

The establishment of the Permanent Court of International Justice

In June and July 1920, the Advisory Committee of Jurists met in The Hague to take over the work of preparing a statute for the Permanent Court. Since Hagerup was one of the Advisory Committee's ten members and the president of its subcommittee, his position had the potential to strengthen the ideas shared by the Norwegian Study Committee. Importantly, the Norwegian government in no way promoted his appointment.[73] Taking into consideration Hagerup's resignation from the Norwegian Study Committee in January 1919, it is highly unlikely that his vision of international order fully reflected the ideas promoted by the Norwegian government. It seems more likely that he was eager to promote international jurisdiction based on the continental civil law tradition. This standpoint was more in tune with the five neutral states' joint draft.

The Advisory Committee of Jurists' proposal for the PCIJ statute provided an acceptable vision of international jurisdiction, though one much less ambitious than the five neutral states desired. First, their proposal established a clear distinction between the notions of justice and arbitration. The court was to apply rules of law. However, it could also—when parties agreed—decide a case *ex aequo et bono*.[74] This implied that the court could use its discretion in giving awards. Consequently, the proposal provided an opening to broaden the court's competence, but made it dependent on the consent of parties to a dispute. Second, the apparently insurmountable problem of the court's composition was solved by laying down that the judges would be elected concurrently but independently and by a majority decision of the Assembly and the Council.[75] The proposal appeared to be a workable solution combining the small states' appeal for applying, on the one hand, the principle of sovereign equality and, on the other, the great powers' privileged status.

Eventually, the Committee of Jurists' proposal specified that the member states would be obliged to submit all kinds of disputes mentioned in Article XIII of the Covenant to the court's jurisdiction. The Council considered this idea to go too far in its interpretation of the Covenant because, as Article XII stated, member states were free to decide whether they wanted to submit disputes to arbitration, to the court or to enquiry by the Council. The crux of the matter was whether a state could bring a dispute before the PCIJ unilaterally without the other party's consent.[76] In the end, the PCIJ's statutes included what came to be known as the Optional Clause, which stated that any state could accept the court's compulsory jurisdiction either unconditionally or on the basis of reciprocity.[77] As a result the PCIJ's efficacy still depended to a considerable degree on ratification of the Optional Clause by as many states as possible, particularly the great powers.[78]

The PCIJ's establishment appeared to be the greatest achievement of the League's first years.[79] Norway was also one of the first states to ratify the Protocol of the Permanent Court of International Justice on 20 August 1921.[80] From the Norwegian perspective, however, the significant disadvantage of this unquestioned achievement was the fact that ratifying the PCIJ did not imply automatic recognition of compulsory international jurisdiction. In addition, the PCIJ's jurisdiction was limited, because the process of codification lagged. To that end, the League of Nations' Council could continue to play a significant role in settling international disputes. As the Norwegian Foreign Ministry pointed out, according to Article XV of the League's Covenant, only disputes likely to develop into an open conflict could be submitted to the Council.[81] This implied that a number of issues could be left to simmer until they approached boiling point. Furthermore, a Council decision with regard to a dispute was not binding. The parties were only obliged to refrain from starting hostilities against each other. Although this provision could hopefully prevent war, it did not secure a real solution to the source of a dispute. Since implementing the Council's decision depended on its unanimity on any particular issue, it was—according to the Ministry—not realistic to expect that Council members would always reach an agreement.

Therefore, as Lange much later emphasised in his 1927 speech in the Assembly, accepting the Optional Clause was only 'the first step on the road to giv[ing] international law a mandatory character'.[82] There were two ways of responding to this challenge. In the first place, international law required codification. This standpoint was related to the legal positivism associated with Hagerup. Shortly before his death in 1921 Hagerup, while emphasising the PCIJ's role in settling international disputes, anticipated that the League's impact would essentially be of a moral nature.[83] Nevertheless, when the PCIJ's establishment became a reality, international law's codification was indeed at such an early stage that doubt was even voiced as to whether a future court would have enough work on its hands.[84]

The second way of responding to the PCIJ's limited jurisdiction was promoting compulsory arbitration. In the face of slow progress in codification work, and several countries' reservations with regard to signing the Optional Clause, compulsory arbitration appeared to be the best alternative. This option was closer to Lange's position. It was also favoured by the Liberal Party, which dominated the political scene in Norway until the mid-1930s. Nevertheless, since the efforts to include provisions to secure compulsory arbitration in the Covenant of the League failed, the Norwegian Foreign Ministry stated in 1922 that 'the establishment of the League does not make the work for the conclusion of arbitration treaties superfluous'.[85] Norway's lack of faith in the impartiality of the great powers dominating the Council prompted the Norwegian policy makers to recognise the League as a crucial arena to promote arbitration and conciliation but not as a central actor in settling disputes. Norwegian advocacy in favour of the principle of compulsory and unconditional arbitration in the 1920s in fact represented an attempt to organise a system of international dispute settlements that functioned independently of the League.

Conclusion

In the first decades of the twentieth century, Norwegian support for peaceful solutions to international disputes contributed to creating a perception at home and abroad that Norway was a prominent champion of arbitration. Norway's promotion of the principle of compulsory and unconditional arbitration in the League of Nations became one of the pillars of the country's assumed peace tradition. In particular, the subsequent Liberal governments advocated the idea that arbitration and reliance on international law principles could eliminate war as an instrument of national policy. The Norwegian government displayed much more enthusiasm for the General Act for the Pacific Settlement of International Disputes, approved by the League's Assembly in 1928, than the Kellogg-Briand Pact signed that same year. Although the latter condemned war as an instrument of national policy, it included no positive obligation or procedure for the pacific settlement of disputes.[86]

Nevertheless, the Norwegian arbitration policy in the 1920s was never an undisputed issue. The discord on the scope of arbitration in the Nordic treaties and in the General Act corresponded to different standpoints across the Norwegian political scene. The disagreements also witnessed a new stage of the clash between proponents of the common law tradition and those who were closer to the continental law tradition. Despite these disagreements, the country's advocacy in 1920s was always in line with the tradition established at the Hague Peace Conferences, which emphasised the peaceful coexistence between nations based on a legalistic foundation. Norwegian efforts to strengthen the rule of law in international relations reflected a small state's efforts to establish a system of peaceful settlement of disputes which would be exempt from the great powers' traditional dominance on the international scene.

Notes

1 F. Hagerup, G. Gade, J. Grieg and Chr. L. Lange. (1913). *Indstilling fra den kongelige commission til forberedelse fra norsk side av den tredje fredskonferanse. Om avlsutning av voldfitstraktater, som omfatter alle tvistemaal.* Kristiania: Det Mallingske Bogtrykkeri, pp.3–5. Also published as an attachment to St. med. (Report to the *Storting*), nr. 7, 1923.
2 St. med., nr. 14, 1925, p.85.
3 C. Schjatvet. (2012). *Fredssak og selvbestemmelse 1890–1909. Folkeretten under unionskonflikten.* Oslo: Akademisk Publisering, pp.18–21.
4 C. Schjatvet, ed. (2002). *Dossier—Norges folkerettsbaserte utenrikspolitikk 1890–1909: noen dokumenter fra Utenriksdepartamentets arkiv.* Vol. 3b, Oslo: Institutt for offentlig rett, p.26. Quoted in C. Schjatvet. (2007). Folkerett og småstatspolitikk—Hagerup om opprettelsen av faste folkerettsdomstoler. In: S. Blandhol and D. Michalsen, eds., *Rettsforsker, Politiker, Internasjonalist: perspektiver på Francis Hagerup.* Oslo: Unipax, p.177.
5 Between 1624 and 1877 Oslo was named Christiania.
6 See St. prp. (Proposition to the *Storting*), nr. 33, supplement 1, 1920, p.7.
7 St. prp., nr. 33, supplement 1, 1920, p.11.
8 For the Norwegian text of the draft see St. prp., nr. 33, supplement 1, 1920, pp.12–26; for the French and English text see Draft of a Convention respecting an international judicial organisation drawn up by the three Commissions appointed by the Danish, Norwegian and Swedish Governments, December 1918, see: Permanent Court of International Justice. Advisory Committee of Jurists. (1920). *Documents Presented to the Committee relating to Existing Plans for the Establishment of a Permanent Court of International Justice*, London: HM Stationary Office Press, pp.210–233.
9 This idea was also included in the earlier 23 May 1918 report, signed by Francis Hagerup. See St. prp., nr. 33, supplement 1, 1920, pp.2–3.
10 S. Wertheim. (2011). The League That Wasn't: American Designs for a Legalist-Sanctionist League of Nations and the Intellectual Origins of International Organization, 1914–1920. *Diplomatic History*, 35(5), pp.797–836; S. Wertheim. (2012). The League of Nations: a Retreat from International Law? *Journal of Global History*, 7(2), pp.210–232.
11 See Ø. Tønnesson. (2013). *With Christian L. Lange as a Prism. A Study of Transnational Peace Politics, 1899–1919.* PhD. University of Oslo, p.347.
12 St. prp., nr. 33, supplement 1, 1920, p.10.
13 Ch. L. Lange. (1922). Francis Hagerup som internasjonalist. *Tidsskrift for Rettsvitenskap*, 35, p.84. Referenced in Schjatvet, Folkerett og småstatspolitikk, pp.189–190.
14 Schjatvet, Folkerett og småstatspolitikk, pp.188–189; Tønnesson, pp.52–53.

15 K. Larsen. (1976). *Forsvar og Folkeforbund. En studie i Venstres og Det konservative Folkepartis forsvarspolitiske meningsdannelse 1918–1922*. Aarhus: Universitetsforlaget i Aarhus, p.195 quoted in K.E. Haug. (2012). *Folkeforbundet og krigens bekjempelse. Norsk utenrikspolitikk mellom realisme og idealisme*. PhD. Norwegian University of Science and Technology, p.90.
16 Explanatory Statement. Extract of the report addressed by the Swedish Commission to the Minister for Foreign Affairs, 21 December 1918. In: Permanent Court of International Justice. Advisory Committee of Jurists, pp.150–167.
17 A. Sveen. (2000). The Nobel Peace Prize. Some aspects of the decision-making process, 1919–31. *The Norwegian Nobel Institute Series*, 1(3), pp.10–13. Note: Wollert Konow (SB) (1845–1924) should be distinguished from Wollert Konow (H) (1847–1932). Both were prominent politicians and members of the *Storting*. The first represented Søndre Bergenhus (SB) region, the latter Hedemarken (H).
18 St. prp., nr. 33, 1920, p.2.
19 M.H. Lie. (1938). In: A.W. Brøgger and E. Jansen, eds., *Norsk Biografisk Leksikon*. Oslo: Aschehoug Forlag. See also M. Stachurska-Kounta. (2014). *Mikael Strøm Henriksen Lie*. [online] Store Norske Leksikon. Available at: https://snl.no/Mikael_Str%C3%B8m_Henriksen_Lie [Accessed 18 May 2016].
20 L. Mjeldheim. (2009). *Johan Ludvig Mowinckel*. [online] *Norsk biografisk leksikon*. Available at: https://nbl.snl.no/Johan_Ludvig_Mowinckel [Accessed 8 November 2013] and K. Gaarder Losnedahl. (2009). Agnes Mowinckel. [online] *Norsk biografisk leksikon*. Available at: https://nbl.snl.no/Agnes_Mowinckel [Accessed 8 November 2013].
21 Tønnesson, pp.349–352.
22 The minority consisted of seven persons, the majority of twelve. Tønnesson, p.351.
23 K. Gram-Skjoldager and Ø. Tønnesson. (2008). Unity and Divergence: Scandinavian Internationalism, 1914–1921. *Contemporary European History*, 17(3), p.318.
24 Lange and Lie could also have been inspired by the ideas promoted by an Austrian jurist Heinrich Lammasch (1852–1920). In the work *Das Völkerrecht nach dem Kriege* (1917) Lammasch argued strongly for international arbitration and mediation, as well for development of international law and not least a duty for the neutral states to cooperate for peace between nations. In the years 1916–1919 Lange nominated him to the Nobel Peace Prize and Lie, in his capacity as a Nobel Committee adviser, wrote analyses of Lammasch. See *Den Norske Nobelskomiteens Redegjørelser for årene 1915–1919* (Norwegian Nobel Committee Reports for the years 1915–1919), Oslo: Norwegian Nobel Institute.
25 St. prp., nr. 33, supplement 1, 1920, p.6.
26 S. Shepard Jones, (1939). *The Scandinavian States and the League of Nations*. Princeton: Princeton University Press, p.49.
27 Compare Tønnesson, p.374.
28 There is no evidence in the archives consulted that the Norwegians discussed the issue of promoting the draft.
29 The other twelve neutral countries invited to the meeting were: Argentina, Chile, Colombia, Denmark, Holland, Paraguay, Persia, El Salvador, Spain, Sweden, Switzerland and Venezuela. See Shepard Jones, pp.47–62.
30 St. prp., nr. 33, supplement 3, 1920, p.44.
31 Permanent Court of Arbitration, (1899). *1899 Convention for the pacific settlement of international disputes*. [online] Permanent Court of Arbitration/Cour Permanente D'Arbitrage. Available at: https://pca-cpa.org/wp-content/uploads/sites/175/2016/01/1899-Convention-for-the-Pacific-Settlement-of-International-Disputes.pdf [Accessed 20 June 2016].

32 For the Covenant of the League of Nations see A.H.M. van Ginneken. (2006). *Historical Dictionary of the League of Nations*. Lanham, Toronto, Oxford: The Scarecrow Press, pp.203–216.
33 Shepard Jones, pp.171–172.
34 Annex to the draft. Memorandum of the Work of the Conference, 27 February 1920. In: Permanent Court of International Justice. Advisory Committee of Jurists, p.325.
35 St. prp., nr. 33, supplement 4, 1920, p.90.
36 K. Gram-Skjoldager. (2012). *Fred og folkeret. Dansk internationalistisk udenrigspolitik 1899–1939*. København: Museum Tusculanum Forlag, p.232.
37 Plan of the five neutral powers. In: Permanent Court of International Justice. Advisory Committee of Jurists, p.327.
38 W. Rappard. (1934). Small States in the League of Nations. *Political Science Quarterly*, 49(4), p.557.
39 Tønnesson, p.52, Schjatvet, *Folkerett og småstatspolitikk*, pp.176–182.
40 St. prp., nr. 33, supplement 1, 1922, p.5.
41 See R. Berg. (1995). *Norge på egen hand 1905–1920*. Oslo: Universitetsforlaget, p.92.
42 Tønnesson, pp.53–59; Schjatvet, *Folkerett og småstatspolitikk*, pp.182–189.
43 Schjatvet, *Folkerett og småstatspolitikk*, p.189.
44 St. prp., nr. 33, supplement 3, 1920, p.45.
45 C.f. Schjatvet, *Fredssak og selvbestemmelse 1890–1909*, p.25.
46 See H. Lauterpacht. (2011, first published 1933). *The Function of Law in the International Community*. New edition, Oxford: Oxford University Press, pp.7–8.
47 M. Koskenniemi. (2011). Introduction. In: Lauterpacht, p.xxi.
48 L. Oppenheim. (1935–1937). *International Law*. Vol. 2, 5th ed., London: Longmans, p.23, note 1. Quoted in O. Spiermann. (2005). *International Legal Argument in the Permanent Court of International Justice. The Rise of the International Judiciary*. Cambridge: Cambridge University Press, p.4.
49 Spiermann, p.4.
50 Tønnesson, pp.52–53, Schjatvet, *Folkerett og småstatspolitikk*, pp.188–189.
51 Schjatvet, *Folkerett og småstatspolitikk*, pp.188–189.
52 Tønnesson, pp.52–53; Schjatvet, *Folkerett og småstatspolitikk*, pp.188–189.
53 St. prp., nr. 33, supplement 3, 1920, p.50.
54 St. prp. nr. 33, supplement 1, 1920, p.5.
55 Schjatvet, *Folkerett og småstatspolitikk*, p.186.
56 St. prp., nr. 33, supplement 3, 1920, p.50.
57 C.f. St. prp., nr. 33, supplement 1, 1920, p.4.
58 Plan of the five neutral powers. In: Permanent Court of International Justice. Advisory Committee of Jurists, p.327.
59 This alleged difference between two kinds of disputes—legal and political (or justiciable and non-justiciable, or disputes as of rights and disputes arising out of conflicts of interests)—was a basis of the doctrine of the limitations of the judicial process in international law. See Lauterpacht, pp.3–6.
60 Plan of the five neutral powers, p.309.
61 St. prp., nr. 33, supplement 1, 1920, p.4.
62 St. prp., nr. 33, supplement 1, 1920, p.16 and St. prp., nr. 33, supplement 3, 1920, p.51. For the English and French versions of the latter report see Report on the Organisation of a Permanent International Tribunal submitted by the Norwegian Committee appointed to enquire into certain questions concerning the League of Nations, 29 August 1919. In: Permanent Court of International Justice. Advisory Committee of Jurists, pp.210–235.
63 St. prp., nr. 33, supplement 3, 1920, p.51.

64 Lauterpacht, pp.192–193.
65 Tønnesson, pp.58–59.
66 Annex to the draft. Memorandum of the Work of the Conference, 27 February 1920. In: Permanent Court of International Justice. Advisory Committee of Jurists, p.329.
67 Draft Scheme of a Convention Concerning an International Judicial Organisation, p.179.
68 St. prp., nr. 33, supplement 3, 1920, pp.49–51.
69 St. prp., nr. 33, supplement 3, 1920, p.51.
70 C.f. M. García-Salmones. (2011). Walther Schücking and the Pacifist Traditions of International Law. *The European Journal of International Law*, 22(3), pp.755–782.
71 García-Salmones, p.756. See also C. Pejovic. (2001). Civil Law and Common Law: Two Different Paths Leading to the Same Goal. *Victoria University of Wellington Law Review*, 32(3), p.820.
72 It is important to add that Lange was not a lawyer himself. His support for compulsory international arbitration has thus to be seen in light of his pragmatic approach to the questions of international peace.
73 Haug, p.265.
74 This was specified in Article 38 of the statute of the PCIJ. *Ex aequo et bono* (Latin for 'according to the right and good' or 'from equity and conscience') is a legal term which, in the context of arbitration, refers to arbiters' power to dispense with consideration of the law and consider solely what they see as fair and equitable in the case at hand. Legal Terms. Definitions and Dictionary. Ex aequo et bono. [online] Available at: http://definitions.uslegal.com/e/ex-aequo-et-bono/ [Accessed 23 May 2016].
75 F. Walters. (1967). *A History of the League of Nations*. London: Oxford University Press, p.125.
76 Spiermann, p.9.
77 Publications of the Permanent Court of International Justice. (1926). *No.1: Statute of the Court: Rules of Court (as Amended on July 31st, 1926)*. Series D, Leyden: A. W. Sijthoff's Publishing Company, pp.19–20.
78 Spiermann, p.11.
79 Walters, p.125.
80 Indst. S. (Recommendation to the *Storting*), LXVI, 1921.
81 St. med., nr 7, 1923, p.3.
82 Quoted in O.B. Fure. (1995). *Mellomkrigstid, 1920–1940*. Oslo: Universitetsforlaget, p.187.
83 St. med., nr 9, 1921, p.7.
84 St. prp., nr. 33, supplement 1, 1920, p.5.
85 St. med., nr. 7, 1923, p.3.
86 C.f. Shepard Jones, p.240.

11 Against the Hague Conventions
Promoting new rules for neutrality in the Cold War

Wolfgang Mueller

The 1907 Hague Conventions Respecting the Rights and Duties of Neutral Powers and Persons in Case of War on Land (V) and of Neutral Powers in Naval War (XII) codified a set of rules for the behaviour of neutrals in wartime. They defined neutrality as a status of not participating in war, treating all belligerents equally and doing nothing that might draw the neutral into a war. According to Convention V, a neutral state could not tolerate belligerents moving troops or convoys through its territory (which was seen as inviolable), establishing telegraphy stations on its territory or recruiting or organising combatants there. All restrictions on the export or transport of goods (military or non-military) or on the use of communication devices had to be applied impartially by the neutral to all belligerents. A neutral would lose its status if it committed hostile acts against a belligerent or, conversely, acted in favour of one.[1]

The Hague Conventions were a product of the pre-First World War international system and of nineteenth-century international law. First, the conventions did not outlaw war outright. Armed conflict was accepted as a natural feature of international relations—not necessarily in a Clausewitzian sense, but nonetheless as a state's right. War, however, should be 'obviated' or tamed as far as some of its consequences were concerned. Therefore, neutral states should be protected from being drawn into conflicts. Private commerce—the conventions were a child of the liberal age—should continue unhindered during wartime. To that end, entrepreneurs from neutral countries were not bound by any restrictions. Neither was public opinion. Secondly, the conventions did not differentiate between 'just' or 'unjust' wars, as many treatises on international law had up until the early modern period. Perhaps the most famous of these, Hugo Grotius' *De Iure Belli ac Pacis* (1625), argued that neutral states should do nothing to weaken a belligerent whose cause was considered just, or to strengthen a belligerent whose cause was unjust. Only in those cases when it was not clear which cause was just and which unjust was a neutral state to treat both sides equally in permitting the passage of troops, supplying them with provisions or rendering assistance. After Grotius, however, the differentiation between 'just' and 'unjust' wars ceased to be made in many works on international law.² The Hague conventions did not do this either. They ruled that neutral states were to treat all belligerents equally.

Fifty years later, some of these and other features of the Hague conventions were critiqued under a new international system and legal tradition. In the intervening years, two developments had done much to change the international political and legal environment. First, the two world wars, the creation of the League of Nations, the Kellogg-Briand Pact and the establishment of the United Nations (UN) contributed not only to outlawing war but also to establishing the principle of collective security. The Covenant of the League of Nations stipulated that any war or threat of war was a concern to all members and obliged them to sever relations with and apply sanctions against aggressors, thus leaving no space for neutrality.³ The Kellogg-Briand Pact of 1928 and the UN Charter prohibited any recourse to war or application of force.⁴ These agreements, combined with the widespread view that the neutrality of some European states during the Second World War benefitted Nazi Germany, largely tainted the image of neutrality. Nevertheless, neutrality was not banned in the UN Charter as some proposed at the time.⁵ However, collective security reduced the neutrals' space to manoeuvre. Under Article 43 of the UN Charter they, like all members of the United Nations, had to agree 'to make available to the Security Council ... armed forces, assistance, and facilities, including rights of passage, necessary for the purpose of maintaining international peace and security'.

The second major development that affected international law in the years after the Hague conferences was the communist takeovers of 1917–1949. The newly established communist regimes created a second set of international law in competition with existing western international law. Their aim was to create the best legal conditions for promoting Soviet interests and the ultimate victory of communism on a global scale. While in the interwar years, only two weak states—the Union of Soviet Socialist Republics (USSR) and Mongolia—had adhered to communist ideology, the Second World War made one of them a superpower. In addition, from East Berlin to Beijing, new communist regimes were created in the war's wake. In the emerging Cold War, communist efforts to change international law were renewed, this time with great energy.⁶

As a result, the Hague conventions regarding the definition and rules of neutrality underwent significance reassessment. This chapter focuses on a communist attempt to change the laws of neutrality during the Cold War period and to formulate guidelines for permanently neutral states in time of peace. The initiative sought to fill a gap that had been left by the Hague conventions, which only focussed on the duties incumbent on neutrals in time of war and not on those of permanent neutrals in a collective security environment. The initiative to revise the law of neutrality was launched by representatives from communist and non-aligned countries and supported by left-wing lawyers in the 1950s and 1960s. Ultimately, it aimed to make neutrality an instrument in waging the Cold War.⁷ Using communist documents, declarations, textbooks and treatises on international law, this chapter analyses how key communist states and actors promoted permanent neutrality and assesses the ideological and political motivations behind their efforts. Beginning with the communist 're-discovery' of neutrality after 1949, the chapter explores why the initiative did not succeed.[8]

The communist 're-discovery' of neutrality

In a note dated 7 March 1955, the USSR formally subscribed to the Hague conventions of 1907 relating to neutrality.[9] Whilst, in the early Cold War, the communist doctrine of 'two camps' had dismissed neutrality between the East and the West as being a disguise for a pro-western posture, in the 1950s the Soviet struggle against the emergence of western alliances such as the North Atlantic Treaty Organisation (NATO), the European Defence Community (EDC) and the Southeast Asia Treaty Organisation (SEATO) relied on a new strategy of promoting permanent neutrality and non-alignment as a tool for preventing other states from joining these blocs.[10] With this aim in mind, in 1952 Stalin offered the reunification of Germany at the price of the country's neutralisation.[11] With a similar aim in mind, Austria was neutralised in 1955.[12] The Soviet re-evaluation of neutrality was also highlighted by its recognition of Finnish neutrality in 1956.[13] When the Norwegian, Danish and Swedish prime ministers visited Moscow in 1955–1956, the USSR proposed transforming northern Europe into a neutralised zone. Similar suggestions were made with regard to West Germany, Italy, Greece, Turkey and Japan.[14] The campaign promoting neutrality reached its high point between 1955 and 1959, when countries in the process of decolonisation were also targeted for neutralisation. The Bandung conference of non-aligned states held in April 1955 opened the door for improving Soviet relations with South Asian regimes.[15] The Kremlin was confident that it might be possible to win the allegiance of the neutrals and non-aligned and thus tilt the international balance in favour of the communist side.[16]

In communist eyes, neutrality was more progressive than capitalism but less progressive than socialism.[17] Through ever-closer political, economic and cultural cooperation with communist states, neutrals were expected to gravitate toward socialism. The combination of the wish to promote neutrality abroad with the wish to stabilise communist rule 'at home' led to a somewhat ambivalent attitude. While in 1955 the Soviet lawyer Lidiia Modzhorian claimed that the USSR 'indiscriminatingly supports all states that strive for maintaining a policy of neutrality', it was soon made clear that permanent neutrality was not deemed appropriate for a communist state.[18] The Soviet refusal to accept Hungary's 1956 declaration of neutrality and the subsequent military crackdown proved that the objective of the communist promotion of neutrality was only to undermine *western* military organisations.[19] Communist lawyers explained the refusal in two ways. First, due to other states' alleged aggressiveness, they claimed that communist states had no choice but to uphold their own military alliance, namely the Warsaw Pact.[20] Second, communist lawyers labelled neutrality a product of bourgeois law, a construct that had been removed in socialist countries.[21]

Throughout the 1960s, communist relations with European neutrals focused on two ends. The first was preventing the neutrals' rapprochement with the European Economic Community (EEC). This policy was due not only to the negative Soviet attitude toward all western political organisations, but also to the fact that the communists wanted the neutrals not to join western groupings but rather to help to undermine them.[22] The second communist aim regarding the European neutrals was encouraging them to act as icebreakers in formally recognising communist states and developing relations with them (in particular the German Democratic Republic (GDR) and the People's Republic of China (PRC)) or in promoting Soviet ideas such as the convening of a European conference designed to legitimise the post-war order. In the Warsaw Pact's Bucharest Declaration of July 1966, neutrals were assured that they 'could play a positive role' in the convocation of a European summit.[23] Communist leaders and diplomats echoed this appeal. In the end it was Finland—against the background of the Warsaw Pact's invasion of Czechoslovakia in 1968 and of growing Soviet pressure—that fulfilled the Soviet Union's wish. In a memorandum issued on 5 May 1969, it called for a European conference.[24]

In the age of *détente*, the communist interest in neutrality and non-alignment declined. This decline did not mean that the Soviet criticism of allegedly improper implementation of neutrality ceased. While Austria, Sweden and Switzerland were criticised by the USSR for not being sufficiently neutral, after 1970 the Kremlin no longer recognised Finland as a neutral country at all.[25] The Soviet tactic of including specific political wishes into an ever-growing list of alleged 'legal obligations' of neutrals also continued. However, the advent of *détente* was accompanied by fewer official statements promoting neutrality and non-alignment. The Communist Party of the Soviet Union congresses in the 1970s did not promote neutrality, and the third edition of the Soviet semi-official *Diplomatic Handbook* published in 1971–1973 reduced the coverage of neutrality significantly.[26] The shift of emphasis accompanied a move in communist understanding of neutrality as well, which heightened the distinction between permanent neutrality and non-alignment. The shift seems to have been linked to three developments. First, once the Eastern bloc had established more friendly relations with the leading western powers and the Conference on Security and Cooperation in Europe (CSCE) had been convened in 1975, the neutrals appeared less crucial as mediators and promoters of communist ideas. The behaviour of the neutrals at the CSCE had not reflected the communists' hopes. Second, in the Third World, the non-aligned movement had not achieved the historic shift of power the Soviet Union expected. Finally, the Prague Spring had demonstrated the danger of diversity for the cohesion of the Eastern bloc. In the aftermath of 1968, the Kremlin perceived any support for neutrality as a risky strategy.

Attempts at reshaping neutrality in the Cold War era

In order to be able to make the best use of the neutral states, the USSR and its satellites aimed at reshaping their behaviour. Communist statements underlined the alleged benefits of neutrality, including prestige, security, friendly relations with all states (including the USSR) and low defence-spending leading to the availability of more resources for welfare.[27] These benefits were contrasted with the alleged disadvantages of membership in the western alliance system, including the threat of nuclear war. In order to influence the behaviour of permanent neutrals, communist propaganda commented on the foreign policy of neutral states. It branded undesirable policies as being at odds with neutrality. If a neutral country behaved 'correctly' (from the Soviet perspective), it was praised and rewarded. If the communist side wished to persuade a neutral to take certain steps, it claimed that neutrality obliged the country to do so. If the neutral did not fulfil communist expectations, however, it was criticised for not living up to its 'obligations' as a neutral, threatened with negative consequences and told what to do.[28]

Furthermore, communist and left-wing lawyers took on the task of formulating a new set of rules in order to turn permanent neutrality into a useful tool for Soviet ambition. The creation of these rules was a top-down process. New positions were publicised through political leaders' statements, moulded by articles published under party control and, finally, elaborated upon in specialised treatises compiled by experts.[29] Brief references to interpretations of peace-time neutrality could be found in the Soviet Union's *Diplomatic Handbook*.[30] A major step toward modifying the norms enshrined by the Hague conventions was made by the Soviet-sponsored International Association of Democratic Lawyers (IADL).[31] At the IADL's seventh conference in Sofia in October 1960, some 350 lawyers, attorneys and legal experts from 47 countries gathered to examine four topics including the 'legal aspects of neutrality'. A special commission comprising about 60 delegates was tasked with discussing the definition of neutrality as well as the rights and obligations of permanently neutral states in peace time. Many speakers claimed that a 'new concept of neutrality' had emerged in recent years that was 'radically different from the traditional view which had prevailed up to the Second World War'.[32] The main reason for this change was seen in the altered attitude toward war in general. In the past, war had been an acceptable feature of international relations. However, the two world wars and changes in international law altered the premise. Accordingly, neutrality, which had been a special feature of international law in times of war, also required modification.

As a point of departure, the introduction to the proceedings of the 1960 conference noted that neutrality should be recognised as a 'form of peaceful coexistence' and that its features had not been sufficiently defined.[33] One delegate proposed preparing a memorandum delineating neutrality and submitting it to the 'competent branches of the United Nations'.[34] Many delegates at the Sofia conference expressed their discontent with the Hague conventions. Their critique focused not only on its legal loopholes, but also on the concept of impartiality in general, which contradicted the Leninist (and, in fact, Grotian) viewpoint. A Hungarian lawyer stated that:

> under the terms of the Hague Convention, neutrality carries with it the duty of impartiality and abstention. Now, according to the Charter [of the United Nations] no member may be impartial, and no member may abstain from certain actions in the event of an international conflict.[35]

A Greek delegate claimed that:

> the Hague Conventions [on neutrality] are now out of date. They deal with wars waged with small caliber rifles, and we are now faced with atom and H[ydrogen] bombs, machines and missiles and weapons of mass destruction.[36]

The discussion was summed up by Modzhorian with the following words:

> Some of the preceding speakers have spoken of the Hague Conventions of 1907 and, in their opinion, the need for their revision, since they conflict with the UN Charter. I myself believe that no attempt should be made to inject the modern concept of neutrality into an outworn body, no longer corresponding to the international relations of the present day.[37]

As Modzhorian explained, a new world war 'would almost certainly be so destructive that the question of neutrality would not even arise'. Therefore, she argued, it was impossible to cling to the traditional understanding of neutrality. In her eyes, a new, a 'modern, legal' concept of neutrality was necessary, a concept that was:

> based on the need to maintain peace and protect national sovereignty, [which is] why in our time the vital question is neutrality in time of peace, taking the form of non-participation in the Cold War.[38]

Her allusions to 'national sovereignty' and 'non-participation in the Cold War' correlated with the USSR's interest in preventing western states from participating in organisations for collective defence. As a new catalogue of rights and duties of neutral states, she proposed:

1 non-participation in military blocs;
2 a ban on the maintenance of foreign military bases or troops on neutral soil and the prohibition of using neutral airspace for espionage purposes (obviously a reference to the recent US overflights over Soviet territory for the purpose of monitoring nuclear weapons);
3 a ban on the possession or production of nuclear weapons;

4 the duty of maintaining good relations with all states without discrimination;
5 a ban on giving aid to an aggressor; and
6 the right to self-defence.³⁹

These proposals, which were later reflected in the conference resolution, combined three groups of elements. The first group drew on the Hague rules for wartime neutrality and extended them to peace-time conditions as well (points 1 and 2). While the Hague convention referred to non-participation in *war* and the prohibition of the maintenance of *belligerent* troops on neutral territory, the Soviet proposal expanded these restrictions to non-participation in military *alliances* and the presence of *foreign* troops on neutral soil in peace time. This was in line with western (e.g. Swiss or Austrian) definitions of peace-time neutrality. The second group was also based on the Hague rules but reformulated them in a restrictive and oppositional sense. While the Hague convention neither differentiated between aggressors and victims nor banned trade with belligerents as long as restrictions were applied equally, point 5 did both, thus referring to the theory of just wars and to one of the main points of the Soviet criticism of the Hague conventions. The third group of rules, on nuclear weapons and good relations (points 3 and 4), did not have any equivalent in the Hague convention. Point 6 on the neutral right or obligation to self-defence already featured in the conventions.

In the subsequent discussion, the Neutrality Commission reached an agreement that the general ban on war affected the right to neutrality. However, no consensus could be achieved on the question of whether neutrality was consistent with the Charter of the United Nations.⁴⁰ The result of the discussions was a draft entitled 'Resolution on the Legal Aspects of Neutrality', which was adopted by the conference plenum. It claimed that the time was 'ripe for a fresh approach to the problem of neutrality' and called for a special commission to prepare a reliable definition of neutrality and aggression. In contrast to the 'traditional concept' of neutrality, which focused on wartime obligations, the 'contemporary legal concept of neutrality' should be based 'on the need to maintain peace and national sovereignty'.⁴¹ Regarding the rights and duties of neutral states, the commission obviously followed the Soviet proposal, adding that neutral airspace must not be used 'for espionage, nuclear war or other hostile purposes' and additionally requiring the 'withdrawal from all pacts creating obligations which are incompatible with those deriving from a neutral status' as per point 6 of the list of duties. The main 'innovation', contained in point 5 of the resolution, was that neutrals should not treat belligerents equally, but instead 'neither offer nor permit on its territory any aid or support, whether direct or indirect, *to an aggressor*'. The Finnish political scientist Harto Hakovirta described the resolution as a *mélange* of:

> traditional Western concepts, adaptation to the realities of the politics of neutrality in today's Europe, and efforts to persuade the

European neutral states to support the 'peace policies' of the socialist camp.⁴²

While the proposed ban on nuclear weapons reduced the neutrals' ability to defend themselves against an assault, the vague but extensive list of banned activities in neutral airspace (e.g. 'other hostile activities') opened up opportunities for third states to accuse neutrals of violating their obligations (as the USSR had done in 1956 toward Austria).

Despite passing the resolution, the Neutrality Commission deemed further discussion necessary. A conference of 25 non-aligned states in Belgrade between 1 and 6 September 1961 adopted a special declaration listing the objectives of the respective countries' peace-time policies, namely:

1 'the active fight for peace',
2 'peaceful coexistence',
3 the liquidation of colonialism,
4 support for countries fighting against the establishment of foreign military bases on their territory, and
5 the final abolition of economic inequality.⁴³

In the following years, anti-colonial demands were increasingly integrated into the communist list of neutral duties. The work of the IADL's Third Commission on neutrality was continued at a meeting in Moscow in July 1962 without, however, being able to achieve a breakthrough. In the meantime, a number of specialised treatises on neutrality were published by communist lawyers, who attempted to extend the neutrals' wartime obligations into peace time, thereby revising the Hague conventions.

New rules for neutrals

Despite communist and left-wing criticism, the Hague conventions served as the starting point for developing the communist canon of neutral duties. The *Diplomatic Handbook* of 1960–1961 referred to them, albeit not without mentioning that 'the content of the rules of neutrality changed in every historical epoch'.⁴⁴ Among the peace-time duties of permanent neutral states, the handbook listed the obligations not to participate in a war or in military alliances and to refrain from policies that might entangle the neutral in a war. It also issued a ban on foreign military bases as well as nuclear weapons (the latter point obviously a reference to Swiss discussions regarding the acquisition of such arms). Similarly, but without reference to nuclear weapons, Modzhorian in 1955 described neutral duties as follows: 'never to start a war, not to participate in a war, but to refrain from a policy that might entangle the neutral into a war'.⁴⁵ A more traditional reference to the Hague conventions was contained in K.A. Baginian's 1956 formulation: in peace time neither to partake in military coalitions, nor to accept the stationing of foreign armed forces on its territory; in wartime not to support any belligerent but to treat them equally.[46] In the event of the Security Council applying sanctions, a neutral, under western and communist international law, had to join UN collective measures since, as Modzhorian stated: 'Participation in the enforcement of sanctions is consequently an act of necessary defence, a lawful reaction to an act of aggression'.[47] This did not rule out the unofficial Soviet viewpoint that, since the Second World War, neutrals should distinguish between just and unjust wars, an issue which the Hague conventions and also Modzhorian and Baginian's 1955–1956 definitions omitted. The 1960 IADL declaration and lawyer F.I. Kozhevnikov even claimed that, in the event of war, a neutral was not to treat the aggressor and the victim equally.[48] While this thesis was a result of the theory of 'just war' it was hardly reconcilable with the Hague convention's concept of neutrality.

Another contradiction to the Hague conventions existed regarding the question of whether neutrals were obliged to defend themselves in the case of war. The question was not unanimously answered by communist and leftwing scholars.[49] Communist lawyers were, however, unanimous in demanding that neutrals' armies be moderate in size and held that the Swedish and Swiss armies exceeded the limits. The possession of nuclear weapons was declared incompatible with neutrality because it would allegedly increase the neutral's dependence on foreign military technology.[50] When Switzerland and Sweden considered introducing a programme of nuclear defence in the late 1950s and 1960s both countries were fiercely attacked by Soviet propaganda and a ban on nuclear weapons was included in the communist catalogue of neutral obligations.[51] With regard to arms trade, Soviet lawyer Oleg Tiunov demanded a general ban on exports of neutral arms and a revision of Article 7 of the Hague convention (which did not ban exports of armaments).[52] But the true reason for the communist concern over nuclear weapons and armies in neutral states was obviously that the USSR did not want western neutrals to increase their defensive capabilities or to change the nuclear balance of power.

While these deviations from the Hague conventions on wartime duties were remarkable, the most significant claims launched by Soviet legal experts had to do with peace-time obligations. Modzhorian, one of the most active communist experts on neutrality, stated in 1964 that:

> it must be admitted that the definitions of the rights and duties [of neutral states] ... vary greatly. The factor common to them all is only the engagement to refrain from participation in military alliances and to develop *friendly relations* with all countries.[53]

Her latter claim, however, was anything but a 'common factor'. In fact, it was a supplement to the Hague conventions and western understanding of peace-time neutral policy. In a similar vein, Soviet lawyers D. Levin and G. Kaliushniaia claimed in 1967 that permanent neutrals were bound 'to permanently maintain neutrality, never to start a war, and to refrain from conducting a policy that might lead to war' and, therefore, 'not to partake in military blocs or groupings, to ban the presence of foreign troops on their soil, and to maintain *friendly relations* with all states'.[54]

Article 3 of the 1899 Hague Convention for the Pacific Settlement of International Disputes (I) recommends 'that one or more Powers, *strangers to the dispute*, should, on their own initiative, and as far as circumstances may allow, offer their good offices or mediation to the States at variance'.[55] While this did not address permanent neutrals explicitly, neutrals had been called upon even before that time to help diffuse tensions. Baltic lawyer Friedrich Fromhold (Fyodor) Martens, a delegate of the Russian Empire whom many considered the 'mastermind' of the Hague conferences,[56] claimed that neutral states:

> had the right and the obligation to prevent, as far as possible, the emergence of war—the right, since the neutrals themselves suffer directly from the military actions of belligerents; —the obligation, since they are members of the international community, a community for which war and peace are not indiscriminate facts.[57]

While this 'obligation' applied to all 'members of the international community', the IADL declaration of 1960 formulated an explicit duty for neutrals to maintain 'good relations with all states', a duty also mentioned in textbooks of international law.[58] The obligation was explained by pointing to the avoidance of any measure that might compel the neutral to join a conflict, including participation in economic embargoes or hostile propaganda against foreign powers. It aimed not only at 'neutralising' western neutrals in the Cold War even further, but also at obliging them to establish contacts with socialist states that were not yet recognised by the West, such as the GDR and the PRC.[59]

In their claims regarding neutrals' peace-time behaviour, communist and left-wing lawyers demanded the maintenance of friendly relations with all states and a 'duty to contribute to general peace'.[60] Some criticised:

> that the permanent neutrality of Switzerland and Austria, and the traditional neutrality of Sweden—in contrast to the active and dynamic Afro-Asian neutralism—is significantly more passive and plays a less positive role in international relations.[61]

In the communist understanding, it was not possible for a neutral to be passively indifferent to all occurrences in the international arena.[62] The active 'struggle for peace' was seen as the highest duty of neutral policy and as 'the main criterion for evaluating it'.[63] Neutrals had to actively contribute to a 'relaxation of tensions', to fight the 'forces of war and imperialism' (i.e. the West) and to support the 'forces of peace' (i.e. the Eastern bloc).[64] In practice, communist theory expected neutral countries to support existing communist initiatives and to condemn western policies. Swiss lawyer Denise Bindschedler-Robert argues that if the USSR proposed a resolution in the United Nations, it expected the neutrals' support.[65] If the General Assembly made a decision that was against the Soviet will, the neutrals were expected to remain 'neutral' and not to follow.

With regard to western military alliances, the lawyers formulated more radical demands that clearly exceeded the Hague consensus. For example, one IADL publication claimed that:

> if military pacts of the respective Power blocs cannot be justified either under Article 51 [of the UN Charter] or as a regional arrangement there seem to be no other provisions within the Charter to support them. The formation of such alliances, indeed in peacetime, amounts to a breach of the obligations under Article 2, § 4.[66]

Therefore, neutrals were called upon to strive for the 'disruption of military alliances' which were accused of 'subjugat[ing] countries'.[67] Yoshitaro Hirano, the vice president of the Association, made the (albeit unsustainable) claim that 'collective self-defence is an outright violation of the principle[s] laid down in the United Nations Charter'.[68] Inconsistent with the Hague conventions was the Soviet assertion that a neutral should join the struggle for decolonisation, a movement that was expected to dismantle western military bases worldwide and disrupt the flow of raw material from the colonies to western Europe.[69]

Communist theory also maintained that permanent neutrals were bound by non-discrimination and economic equidistance between the blocs.[70] Both positions were deduced from The Hague's obligation that neutrals treat both sides in a conflict impartially. As far as economic equidistance was concerned, the communist experts tended to tacitly overlook the fact that many non-aligned states oriented themselves towards the East. This bias was justified in Soviet statements with the claim that the Eastern bloc, by definition, did not abuse economic links by using them to exert pressure. While European neutrals were attacked for their desire to gain associative membership to the EEC, African associates of the same organisation were still recognised as being 'neutral'.[71] Several theses were put forward against the neutrals' rapprochement with the EEC. First, the EEC was allegedly an economic basis for NATO and thus it would be unacceptable for a neutral to join. Second, the EEC's supranational structure would make it impossible to maintain neutrality. Since the EEC treated outsiders differently from members, neutral adhesion was seen as a violation of the Soviet claim that neutrals could not discriminate against third countries.[72]

The issue of freedom of opinion in a neutral state was another debated point. Leaders of neutral states insisted that their status did 'not extend to political convictions'.[73] Indeed, neither the Hague conventions nor peace-time neutrality curbed freedom of opinion. Soviet lawyer Boris Ganiushkin agreed that neutrality obliged the state, not the individual. Nonetheless, he and other communist lawyers insisted on a ban against 'hostile propaganda' and—not without a side blow against western ideas such as 'freedom of the media'—advised the neutrals to take action against such behaviour.[74]

The communist teachings of the late 1950s and early 1960s, therefore, distinguished between permanent neutrality (which was founded either on an international agreement or a national declaration recognised by other states) and 'positive' neutrality (which in the majority of cases was declared unilaterally and often associated with neutralism or non-alignment).[75] Communist politicians and publications stressed that both groups had to conduct a 'neutral policy' in time of peace (one by obligation, the other by free will).[76] Since the peace-time policy of permanently neutral and non-aligned countries was subsumed under 'neutral policy', the differences between the policies of countries as diverse as India, Yugoslavia, Finland, Austria and Switzerland were blurred.[77] Even more importantly, the Soviet claim that in peace time permanent neutrals were legally obliged to follow the same foreign policy as was practiced by the non-aligned states increased the burden laid on the permanent neutrals. The claim was, actually, the key feature of the communist neutrality doctrine in the 1950s and 1960s and its main bone of contention for the western neutrals, whose governments rejected it outright.[78]

According to western interpretations of neutrality, which were shaped by the Hague conventions, if neutrals fulfilled these tasks, they would have abandoned their neutrality. At the very least, such behaviour was considered as 'non-alignment' rather than as 'neutrality'. While communist theory strove to mould the permanent neutrals along the model of the non-aligned, this was unacceptable to western states and neutrals. While most of the communist theory's assertions with regard to the required behaviour of permanently neutral states in time of peace could be dismissed as unofficial postulates without legal basis or international relevance, the growing catalogue of Soviet demands was nonetheless hard to ignore. If unchallenged by the West, the growing corpus of communist expectations of neutrals bore the risk of being transformed into legal precedents exceeding The Hague's consensus.

Conclusion

In communist eyes, the Hague conventions on neutrality were flawed in a double sense. On the one hand, they did not discriminate between just and unjust wars (or what the USSR declared these to be). On the other hand, they did not define the rights and duties of permanently neutral states in peace time, a subject that communists were keen to use as an instrument in the Cold War in the 1950s and 1960s. Since communist lawyers wanted the neutrals to embody and promote a specific approach to neutrality, they attempted to push the neutrals' understanding and practice of neutral policy in the direction envisaged by their works. Neutrality provided the Kremlin with a lever over the neutral states. Communist leaders, lawyers and propaganda consistently claimed the right—by referring to the communist teachings of neutrality—to tell the neutrals what to do and what not to do. Since many western neutrals' policies were not as pro-Soviet or anti-western as the Kremlin wished, they were repeatedly criticised for their behaviour. As neutrality gave the communists a self-defined measuring stick for evaluating neutral politics, any unwanted act was attacked as being at odds with neutrality. Such acts included Switzerland's refusal to ban nuclear weapons, Sweden's maintenance of a strong army and the efforts of Austria, Sweden and Switzerland to reach an association agreement with the EEC. On the other hand, desirable behaviour was encouraged, such as Swedish criticism of American foreign policy, Finnish proposals for nuclear-weapon free zones and efforts to call for an all-European summit.

Neutrality meant different things at different times, and the various communist interpretations of neutrals' obligations were always formulated in accordance with the prevailing Soviet political agenda. While in the 1950s the containment and undermining of western blocs, as well as the forging of an informal alliance of the socialist, neutral and non-aligned countries, seems to have been the main function of neutrality from the Soviet point of view, through the 1960s the neutrals were encouraged to recognise the GDR and promote a European summit. Furthermore, they were to act as scouts for developing East–West trade relationships and providing the Eastern bloc with goods that could not be purchased in other western countries due to lacking economic contacts. Once *détente* was achieved in the 1970s, the neutrals' role in Soviet politics diminished.

The sinking importance of neutrality after 1968–1969 may help to explain why the communist attempts at reformulating the Hague conventions never succeeded. A second reason for the lack of success was most likely that these attempts did not receive enough support in the West. While some features of communist-style neutrality started to enter the discussion in some western neutral countries, this was insufficient for launching a United Nations conference to codify new rules for neutrality and to replace or complement the Hague conventions. For western countries and neutrals, the communist agenda of formulating extensive catalogues of new obligations for permanent neutrals in peace time that exceeded the existing consensus was clearly unacceptable. Inadequate and unbeloved as the Hague conventions on neutrality were among communists, they still reflected a common denominator in the Cold War world.

Notes

1 For the text of the Hague convention, see: The Avalon Project at Yale Law School. (1907). *Laws of War: Rights and Duties of Neutral Powers and Persons in Case of War on Land (Hague V)*. [online] Available at: http://avalon.law.yale.edu/20th_century/hague05.asp [Accessed August 2016].

2 H. Lauterpacht. (1946). The Grotian Tradition in International Law. In: *British Year Book of International Law*. pp.1–53, here p.39. Cf. M.E. O'Connell (2012). Peace and War. In: B. Fassbender and A. Peters, eds, *The Oxford Handbook on the History of International Law*. Oxford: Oxford University Press, pp.272–293. On the history of neutrality, see: S.C. Neff. (2000). *The Rights and Duties of Neutrals: A General History*. Manchester: Manchester University Press; M. Abbenhuis. (2014). *An Age of Neutrals: Great Power Politics 1815–1914*. Cambridge: Cambridge University Press. On twentieth-century neutrality, see: R. Ogley. (1970). *The Theory and Practice of Neutrality in the Twentieth Century*, London: Routledge & Kegan Paul; P. Wrange. (2007). *Impartial or Uninvolved? The Anatomy of 20th Century Doctrine on the Law of Neutrality*. Visby: Juridiska institutionen. Grotius' *De Iure Belli ac Pacis*, book III, chapter 17 reads: 'it is the duty of those, who profess neutrality in a war to do nothing towards increasing the strength of a party maintaining an unjust cause, nor to impede the measures of a power engaged in a just and righteous cause. But in doubtful cases, they ought to shew themselves impartial to both sides, and to give no succour to besieged places, but should allow the troops of each to march through the country, and to purchase forage, and other supplies'. H. Grotius. (2001). *On the Law of War and Peace*. Trans. A.C. Campbell. Kitchener: Batoche, p.336.

3 Article 16 of the Covenant from: The Avalon Project at Yale Law School. (1924). *The Covenant of the League of Nations*. [online] available at: http://avalon.law.yale.edu/20th_century/leagcov.asp [Accessed August 2016].

4 Article 1 and 2 of the Kellogg–Briand Pact: The Avalon Project at Yale Law School. (1928). Kellogg–Briand Pact. [online] Available at: http://avalon.law.yale.edu/20th_century/kbpact.asp [Accessed August 2016]; and Article 2 of the UN Charter: The Avalon Project at Yale Law School. (1945). *Charter of the United Nations*. [online] Available at: http://avalon.law.yale.edu/20th_century/unchart.asp [Accessed August 2016].

5 On the development of international law, 1917–1945, see: K.H. Ziegler. (2007). *Völkerrechtsgeschichte*. Munich: Beck, pp.193–211; P. Krüger. (2012). From the Paris Peace Treaties to the End of the Second World War. In: B. Fassbender and A. Peters, eds, *The Oxford Handbook on the History of International Law*, Oxford: Oxford University Press, pp.679–698; H. Kleinschmidt. (2013). *Geschichte des Völkerrechts in Krieg und Frieden*. Tübingen: Francke, pp.421–452. On the neutrality discourse in this era: Neff, pp.166–217 and Wrange, pp.234–248, 570–590.

6 On the development of the Soviet theory of international law: B. Meissner, ed. (1963). *Sowjetunion und Völkerrecht 1917 bis 1962: Eine bibliographische Dokumentation*. Cologne: Wissenschaft und Politik, pp.40–43; c.f. L. Mälksoo. (2015). *Russian Approaches to International Law*. Oxford: Oxford University Press.

7 Until recently, neutrality was 'one of the less researched topics of the Cold War'. J.M. Hanhimäki. (2006). The Lure of Neutrality: Finland and the Cold War. In: K. Larres and K. Osgood, eds, *The Cold War after Stalin's Death: A Missed Opportunity for Peace?* Lanham: Rowland & Littlefield, p.257; c.f. D. Geppert and U. Wengst, eds, (2005). Neutralität–Chance oder Chimäre? Konzepte des Dritten Weges für Deutschland und die Welt 1945–1990. Munich: Oldenbourg, pp.177–202; S. Bott, J. Hanhimaki, J. Schaufelbuehl and M. Wyss, eds, (2016). *Neutrality and Neutralism in the Global Cold War: Between or Within the Blocs?* London: Routledge.

8 C.f. G. Hafner. (1969). Die permanente Neutralität in der sowjetischen Völkerrechtslehre. Österreichische *Zeitschrift für öffentliches Recht*, 19(2–3), pp.215–258; P.H. Vigor. (1975). *The Soviet View of War, Peace, and Neutrality*. London: Routledge; H. Hakovirta. (1983). The Soviet Union and the Varieties of

Neutrality in Western Europe. *World Politics*, 35(4), pp.563–585; B. Petersson. (1990). *The Soviet Union and Peacetime Neutrality in Europe: A Study of Soviet Political Language*. Stockholm: MH Publishing; V. Zubok. (2000). The Soviet Attitude towards European Neutrals during the Cold War. In: M. Gehler and R. Steininger, eds, *The Neutrals and the European Integration, 1945–1995*. Vienna: Böhlau, pp.29–43; W. Mueller. (2011). *A Good Example of Peaceful Coexistence? The Soviet Union, Austria, and Neutrality, 1955–1991*. Vienna: Verlag der Österreichischen Akademie der Wissenschaften; W. Mueller. (forthcoming). The USSR and Permanent Neutrality in the Cold War. *Journal of Cold War Studies*.
9 F.I. Koschewnikow. (1960). Die Gesetze und Gewohnheiten des Krieges. In: idem, ed., *Völkerrecht*, Hamburg: Hansischer Gildenverlag, pp.458–459.
10 A.A. Komarov. (2003). Politika SSSR po otnosheniiu k Skandinavskim stranam v Khrushchevskii period. In: N.I. Egorova and A.O. Chubar'ian, eds, *Kholodnaia Voina i Politika Razriadki*. Vol. 1, Moscow: Institut vseobshchei istorii, pp.96–98.
11 J. Zarusky, ed. (2002). *Die Stalinnote vom 10. März 1952: Neue Quellen und Analysen*, Munich: Oldenbourg; P. Ruggenthaler, ed. (2007). *Stalins großer Bluff: Die Geschichte der Stalinnote in sowjetischen Dokumenten*, Munich: Oldenbourg. For a different view, see W. Loth. (2008). German Historians and the German Question in the Cold War. In J. Aunesluoma and P. Kettunen, eds, *The Cold War and the Politics of History*. Helsinki: Edita, pp.169–188.
12 G. Stourzh. (2005). *Um Einheit und Freiheit: Staatsvertrag, Neutralität und das Ende der Ost-West-Besetzung Österreichs 1945–1955*, 5th rev. ed. Vienna: Böhlau.
13 N.S. Chrustschow. (1956). *Rechenschaftsbericht des Zentralkomitees der Kommunistischen Partei der Sowjetunion an den XX. Parteitag*, Moskau: Verlag für Fremdsprachige Literatur, p.51.
14 Mueller, *A Good Example*, pp.43–55.
15 On the conference: O.A. Westad. (2005). *The Global Cold War: Third World Interventions and the Making of Our Times*. Cambridge: University Press, pp.99–103.
16 A.A. Gromyko et al., eds. (1960–1964). *Diplomaticheskii slovar'*, 2nd ed., Vol. 2, Moscow: Gospolitizdat, p.394; Programm der Kommunistischen Partei der Sowjetunion, angenommen auf dem XXII. Parteikongress 1961. In: B. Meissner, ed. (1962). *Das Parteiprogramm der KPdSU 1903 bis 1961*, Cologne: Wissenschaft und Politik, p.183.
17 G.I. Tunkin. (1963). *Das Völkerrecht der Gegenwart. Theorie und Praxis*. [Ost-]Berlin: Staatsverlag der DDR, p.25; O.I. Tiunov. (1968). *Neitralitet v Mezhdunarodnom Prave*. Perm: Gosudarstvennyi universitet im. Gor'kogo, p.115.
18 L.A. Modzhorian. (1955). Postoianno neitral'nye gosudarstva i mezhdunarodnoe pravo. *Sovetskoe gosudarstvo i pravo*, (7), p.113. See also E. Korovin. (1958). Proletarian Internationalism in World Relations. *International Affairs*, (2), p.29, as quoted by R. Allison. (1988). *The Soviet Union and the Strategy of Non-Alignment in the Third World*. Cambridge: University Press, p.18.
19 It is true that the Warsaw Treaty would cease to be operative 'should a system of collective security be established in Europe'. V. Mastny and M. Byrne, eds, (2005). *A Cardboard Castle? An Inside History of the Warsaw Pact* XE "Warsaw Pact" *1955–1991*. Budapest: Central European University Press, p.79.
20 Romanian delegation, in International Association of Democratic Lawyers, ed. (1960). *Legal Aspects of Neutrality: Proceedings of the Third Commission*. Brussels: International Association of Democratic Lawyers, pp.105, 109.

21. M.E. Airapetian and V.V. Sukhodeev. (1964). *Novyi tip mezhdunarodnyh otnoshenii*. Moscow: Mysl', p.227, as quoted in Hafner, p.220.
22. K. Timashkova. (1969). Neitral'nye strany v usloviiakh imperialisticheskoi integratsii. In: M.M. Maksimova, ed., *Ekonomicheskie gruppirovki v zapadnoi Evropy*. Moscow, pp.269–280.
23. F. Schramm, W. Riggert, and A. Friedel, eds, (1972). *Sicherheitskonferenz in Europa: Dokumentation 1954–1972: Die Bemühungen um Entspannung und Annäherung im politischen, militärischen, wirtschaftlichen, wissenschaftlich-technologischen und kulturellen Bereich*. Frankfurt am Main: Metzner, pp.425–435, 434.
24. H. Jacobsen, W. Mallmann, and C. Meier, eds. (1973). *Sicherheit und Zusammenarbeit in Europa (KSZE): Analyse und Dokumentation* II/1. Cologne: Wissenschaft und Politik, pp.128–129.
25. Petersson, p.14.
26. (1971). *XXIV. Parteitag der Kommunistischen Partei der Sowjetunion 30. März-9. April 1971: Dokumente*. Moscow: APN; (1976). Rechenschaftsbericht des Zentralkomitees der Kommunistischen Partei der Sowjetunion. Prague: Frieden und Sozialismus; (1971). *Diplomaticheskii slovar'*. 3rd ed., Vol. 2, Moscow: Politizdat, pp.373.
27. N. Khrushchev. (1960). *For Victory in Competition with Capitalism*. New York: Dutton, pp.231–248.
28. For an in-depth study of this issue, see Petersson.
29. For examples: L.A. Modzhorian. (1956). *Politika podlinnogo neitraliteta—vazhnyi factor bor'by narodov za mir i nezavisimost'*. Moscow: Znanie; B.V. Ganiushkin. (1968). *Sovremennyi neitralitet*. Moscow: Institut mezhdunarodnykh otnoshenii; L.A. Modzhorian. (1962). *Politika neitraliteta*. Moscow: Znanie; B. V. Ganiushkin. (1965). *Neitralitet i neprisoedinenie*. Moscow: Mezhdunarodnye otnosheniia; O.I. Tiunov. (1968). *Neitralitet v mezhdunarodnom prave*. Perm: Gosudarstvennyi universitet im. Gor'kogo; L.A. Mojoryan [Modzhorian]. (1969). Neutrality in Present-Day International Law. In: G. Tunkin, ed., *Contemporary International Law: Collection of Articles*. Moscow: Progess, 1969, pp.216–232; I.M. Prusakov. (1972). *Neitralitet v sovremennom mezhdunarodnom prave*. Moscow: Znanie.
30. For examples: G.I. Tunkin. (1956). *Osnovy sovremennogo mezhdunarodnogo prava*. Moscow: Vysshaia partiinaia shkola TsK KPSS; F.I. Koschewnikow, ed. (1960). *Völkerrecht*. Hamburg: Hansischer Gildenverlag; G.I. Tunkin, D.B. Lewin, E. Menzel. (1969). *Drei sowjetische Beiträge zur Völkerrechtslehre*. Hamburg: Hansischer Gildenverlag; V.I. Lisovskii. (1970). *Mezhdunarodnoe pravo*. Moscow: Vysshaia shkola; G.I. Tunkin. (1974). *Theory of International Law*. Cambridge, MA: Harvard University Press. For Western bibliographies, see B. Meissner, *Sowjetunion und Völkerrecht 1917 bis 1962*; B. Meissner, D. Frenzke and E. Chilecki, eds. (1977). *Sowjetunion und Völkerrecht 1962 bis 1973: Bibliographie und Analyse*. Cologne: Wissenschaft und Politik. See also A.I. Vyshinskii, ed. (1948–1950). Diplomaticheskii slovar. 2 vols. Moscow: Gospolitizdat; A.A. Gromyko et al., eds. (1960–1964). *Diplomaticheskii slovar'*, 2nd ed., 3 vols. Moscow: Gospolitizdat; and (1971–1973). 3rd ed., 3 vols. Moscow: Politizdat.
31. International Association of Democratic Lawyers, ed. (1960). *Legal Aspects of Neutrality: Proceedings of the Third Commission*. Brussels: International Association of Democratic Lawyers, pp. 8, 113–114. On the IADL: R.F. Staar. (1991). *Foreign Policies of the Soviet Union*. Stanford: Hoover Press, p.80.
32. (1960). VIIth Congress of the International Association of Democratic Lawyers. *Review of Contemporary Law*, 7(2), pp.135–147.

33 *Legal Aspects of Neutrality*, pp.5–6.
34 *Legal Aspects of Neutrality*, p.104.
35 Gyula Haidu in *Legal Aspects of Neutrality*, p.102.
36 Nicolas Veicopoulos in *Legal Aspects of Neutrality*, p.93.
37 *Legal Aspects of Neutrality*, p.110.
38 *Legal Aspects of Neutrality*, p.110.
39 *Legal Aspects of Neutrality*, pp.111–112.
40 *Legal Aspects of Neutrality*, p.7.
41 *Legal Aspects of Neutrality*, pp.113–114. Emphasis mine.
42 Hakovirta, p.582.
43 L.A. Modjorian [Modzhorian]. (1964). Legal Aspects of Neutrality in the Modern World. *Review of Contemporary Law*, 11(1), p.44.
44 *Diplomaticheskii slovar'*. (1961). Vol. 2, pp.392–393.
45 L.A. Modzhorian. (1955). Postoianno neitral'nye gosudarstva i mezhdunarodnoe pravo. *Sovetskoe gosudarstvo i pravo*, 7, p.109.
46 K.A. Baginian. (1956). Postoiannyi neitralitet, pravo na samooboronu i sistema regionalizma v svete Ustava OON. *Sovetskoe gosudarstvo i pravo*, 6, p.102, as quoted in Hafner, p.234.
47 Modjorian [Modzhorian], Legal Aspects of Neutrality in the Modern World, p.50.
48 Koschewnikow, Die Gesetze und Gewohnheiten des Krieges, p.469; *Legal Aspects of Neutrality*, pp.113–114.
49 While Durdenevskii, Tiunov and Ganiushkin, *Sovremennyi neitralitet*, pp.93–95, support the opinion that a permanently neutral state is obliged to defend itself, Ganiushkin, *Neitralitet i neprisoedinenie*, pp.121–127, casts doubt on whether such obligations were still valid and praises plans for full disarmament.
50 *Diplomaticheskii slovar'*, 2nd ed., vol. 2, p.396; *Legal Aspects of Neutrality*, p.11.
51 D.A. Neval. (2003). *„Mit Atombomben nach Moskau": Gegenseitige Wahrnehmung der Schweiz und des Ostblocks im Kalten Krieg 1945–1968*. Zürich: Chronos, pp.487–496.
52 Hafner, p.242.
53 Modjorian [Modzhorian], Legal Aspects of Neutrality in the Modern World, pp.47–48.
54 D.B. Lewin and G.P. Kaljushnaja, eds. (1967). *Völkerrecht*. Berlin [Ost]: Staatsverlag der DDR, p.112.
55 Article 3 of the 1899 Hague Convention (I): The Avalon Law Project at Yale Law School. (1899). *Laws of War: Pacific Settlement of International Disputes (Hague I)*. [online] Available at: http://avalon.law.yale.edu/19th_century/hague01.asp#art3 [Accessed August 2016].
56 V.V. Pustogarov. (2000). *Our Martens: F. F. Martens, International Lawyer and Architect of Peace*. The Hague: Kluwer, pp. 179–182.
57 F. Martens. (1888). *Sovremennoe mezhdunarodnoe pravo tsivilisovannyh narodov*. vol. 2, St Petersburg: Benke, p.545, as quoted by I.A. Egorov. (1959). Kistorii neitraliteta Shvetsii. *Sovetskoe gosudarstvo i pravo*, 9, pp.72–78.
58 *Legal Aspects of Neutrality*, pp.111–112. D.B. Lewin and G.P. Kaljushnaja, p.112.
59 D.B. Lewin. (1969). Grundprinzipien des modernen Völkerrechts. In: *Drei sowjetische Beiträge zur Völkerrechtslehre*. Hamburg: Hanseatischer Gildenverlag, pp.59–306; Ganiushkin, *Sovremennyi neitralitet*, pp. 83–84; Tiunov, *Neitralitet v mezhdunarodnom prave*, pp. 5–7; *Legal Aspects of Neutrality*, p.13.
60 Modjorian [Modzhorian], Legal Aspects of Neutrality in the Modern World, p.49.
61 Ganiushkin, *Neitralitet i neprisoedinenie*, p.176.
62 Modzhorian, *Politika neitraliteta*, p.5.

63 Ganiushkin, *Sovremennyi neitralitet*, p.8. Mojoryan [Modzhorian], Neutrality in Present-Day International Law, p.219.
64 Mojoryan [Modzhorian], Neutrality in Present-Day International Law, pp.219, 226; E.A. Korovin. (1957). Istoriia mezhdunarodnogo prava. In: F.I. Kozhevnikov, ed., *Mezhdunarodnoe pravo*.Moscow: Iurizdat, pp.24–85.
65 D. Bindschedler-Robert. (1965). Völkerrecht und Neutralität aus sowjetischer Sicht. Österreichische Zeitschrift für Außenpolitik, 5(3), pp.144–163.
66 *Legal Aspects of Neutrality*, p.24.
67 *Legal Aspects of Neutrality*, pp.8–9.
68 *Legal Aspects of Neutrality*, p.13.
69 Tiunov, pp.27–29.
70 *Legal Aspects of Neutrality*, pp.111–112. G. Osnitskaya. (1962). Neutrality and the Common Market. International Affairs, 6, pp.52–55, 54.
71 D. Tarschys. (1971). Neutrality and the Common Market: The Soviet View. *Cooperation and Conflict*, 6(2), pp.65–75.
72 Ganiushkin, *Neitralitet i neprisoedinenie*, pp.168–175.
73 U. Kekkonen. (1982). *A President's View*. London: Heinemann, p.168.
74 Ganiushkin, *Neitralitet i neprisoedinenie*, p.146, Cf. pp.13, 118–120.
75 *Diplomaticheskii slovar'*, 2nd ed. Vol. 2, pp.395–397. C.f. H. Fiedler. (1959). Der sowjetische Neutralitätsbegriff in Theorie und Praxis: Ein Beitrag zum Problem des Disengagement. Cologne: Politik und Wirtschaft, pp.84–89.
76 Ganiushkin, *Sovremennyi neitralitet*, pp.16, 83–84, 86.
77 *Bol'shaia Sovetskaia Entsiklopediia*. (1974). Vol.17, 3rd ed., Moscow: Sovetskaia entsiklopediia, pp.498–499.
78 Hafner, pp.224–225, 234.

12 The neutrals and Spanish neutrality
A legal approach to international peace in constitutional texts

Yolanda Gamarra

The public advocacy of the pacifist and internationalist movements of the late nineteenth century and the work of the Hague Peace Conferences in 1899 and 1907 serve as vital contexts for understanding Spain's neutral position during the First World War and the country's institutionalisation of the renunciation of war during the 1930s. The ideas of these movements and the international legal instruments created at The Hague inspired the Spanish Constitution of 9 December 1931. They also underpinned the current Spanish Constitution of 6 December 1978. Pacifism and neutrality have a long history of inter-connectedness. It was not, then, surprising to find an avowedly neutral state, Spain, presenting a pacifist agenda in the aftermath of the First World War. What is surprising, however, is that the state incorporated the principles of the Hague conventions into their constitutional framework.

This chapter explores how the international legal innovations of the Hague conventions (of 1899 and 1907), the League of Nations Pact (1919) and the Kellogg–Briand Pact (1928) impacted the Spanish legal system. It focuses particularly on the 1931 Spanish Constitution and suggests it was the best-prepared legal pacifist product of the interwar period, offering an extraordinary mandate for the Spanish state to promote the value of international peace.[1] With the overthrow of Primo de Rivera's dictatorship and the end of the Spanish monarchy in the 1930s, politicians and self-proclaimed 'intellectuals' looked to create a progressive Spanish society committed to the principles of democracy, peace and neutrality.[2] The Spanish Constitution of 1931 prohibited Spain from initiating war (Article 6) and required the government to adhere to international law at all times (Article 7). Furthermore, Article 77 also emphasised Spain's commitment to using international arbitration and pacific dispute-settlement mechanisms. These constitutional developments had a fundamental impact on Spain's obligations both as a member of the League of Nations and as a neutral state. In contrast, the 1978 Spanish Constitution invoked the concepts of pacifism and international obligation symbolically, by only noting the country's commitment to international peace in its preamble. The constitutional text included, in Article 63 paragraph 3, an obsolete formula for declaring war that was not subject to the limitations of international law. As a result, in 1978 Spain revoked many of the 1931 articles. In particular, it allowed the government to declare war without international legal restraint. These changes had a significant impact on, and continue to have significance for, Spain's international position.

A commitment to peace

Spain's commitment to peace and pacifist principles was well established by 1931. The Spanish government turned to a position of long-term neutrality after its defeat in the Spanish–American war of 1898–1899 (or, as it is known in Spain, the 'disaster of 98').[3] The adoption of neutrality was a declaration of Spain's powerlessness in the international environment motivated by its ailing economy, an unworkable political system, an inefficient army and an insufficient naval fleet to defend its long coastlines and territories dotted throughout the Atlantic and the Mediterranean.[4] At the same time, a regeneration movement of intellectuals, jurists, politicians and influential figures arose seeking to repair Spain's ability to appear powerful on the international stage.[5] The regeneration movement aimed to integrate Spain into Europe and to demonstrate Spanish adherence to European standards of civilisation.[6]

Spain's neutrality was maintained throughout the war, although not without enduring its own political and economic crises.[7] Because Spain managed to maintain its neutrality which benefitted the Allies during the war, Spain was rewarded with a non-permanent position on the League of Nations' Council along with Belgium, Brazil and Greece.[8] This key position at the heart of the newly established League of Nations proved important in defining much of Spain's interwar foreign policy outlook.[9]

Even after suffering from political problems throughout the 1920s, culminating with Primo De Rivera's dictatorship in 1923, Spain still continued to be a prominent voice in international affairs.[10] However, with De Rivera's overthrow and the establishment of a republic in 1931, the liberal government promoted a stronger relationship with the League of Nations that would institutionalise Spain's self-avowed international commitment to peace.[11] The 1931 Constitution reconfigured Spain's foreign policy outlook. Warmongering and aggressive foreign policies were replaced with a formal acknowledgement of international law and of the need to work within the norms of the League of Nations. The bases for this constitutional adherence to international law were the Hague conventions of 1907, the League of Nations Pact and the Kellogg–Briand Pact. The terms of these agreements were incorporated into the constitution, not only through the adoption of its general principles but also by means of specific regulations for procedures to ensure that the principles were observed.

Of particular interest is Article 6, which established the renunciation of war as 'a general political instrument'.[12] Based on a broad interpretation,

Spain renounced wars defined as 'international political instruments' or, rather, wars conducted as a result of identifiable illicit facts.[13] The pacifist influence of the Hague conventions of 1907, especially the Third Convention, and of the Kellogg–Briand Pact materialised in the constitutional limitations on the possibility of resorting to a declaration of war.[14] Article 1 of the Third Hague Convention of 1907 recognised that hostilities 'must not commence without previous and explicit warning, in the form either of a reasoned declaration of war or of an ultimatum with conditional declaration of war'. Meanwhile, the Kellogg–Briand Pact placed a general prohibition on warfare. Article 1 of the Pact stated that the parties 'solemnly declare ... that they condemn recourse to war for solution of international controversies, and renounce it as an instrument of national policy'.

Article 7 stated that the Spanish state would respect the universal norms of international law, incorporating them as a positive right.[15] According to this article, the constitutional text was subject to the limitations of international law. It stated that: '(t)he Spanish state shall comply with the universal rules of international law, incorporating them into its statutory law'.[16] This clause carried with it the obligatory, though not automatic, adoption of the general rules of international law. The observance of the universal norms of international law was combined in Article 65 with a recognition of the primacy of international treaties over state law.[17] The obligatory nature of publicising the treaties and the illegitimacy of secret agreements was laid down in Article 76, in line with Articles 18–20 of the League of Nations Pact. In particular, the subordination of a declaration of war to the mechanisms of arbitration and conciliation was covered in Article 77, while Article 78 declared that Spain could not withdraw from the League of Nations without the promulgation of a special law voted by an absolute majority in parliament. Therefore, the presidential power to declare war was delegated within the limitations of international law.[18]

The general limitation of presidential power was exacerbated by the fact that any declaration had to be authorised by a law. Article 76 stipulated that the President of the Republic had the right to 'declare war' if, in accordance with Article 77 paragraph 3, he was authorised to sign such a declaration by a specific law. The president's right to declare war was therefore subject to authorisation by the *Cortes Generales*. This limitation on the right to declare war and, in particular, the need for the approval of parliament was a highly significant step and predated Article 2 paragraph 4 of the United Nations Charter of 1945 on the prohibition of the use of force.[19] The constitution did not explicitly renounce war but established a parliamentary procedure to that effect. War retained, as it continues to do today, its character as an international legal institution. The renunciation of war as an instrument of national policy did not imply the rejection of the principle of self-defence either. The only war that could be declared by the President of the Republic, through constitutional imperative, was a lawful war (in accordance with Article 77).

A muted criticism of the international legal principles embedded in the 1931 Constitution was raised at the time.[20] But, by and large, the lack of opposing views to the constitutional development demonstrated the high degree of political consensus regarding the constitution's internationalist outlook. It also demonstrated the general lack of concern for international matters in Spanish society, particularly since many politicians regarded the constitution as more a matter of law than politics. In contrast, in the parliamentary commission's discussions and in the Constituent Parliament's sessions in September 1931, there was a certain degree of opposition expressed to adopting the League of Nations' principles, including by the philosopher-diplomat Salvador de Madariaga (1866–1978), members of the agrarian minority and Antonio Royo Villanova (1869–1958), who disagreed with the renunciation of war appearing in the constitutional text because of the tradition of Spanish neutrality. He extended this opposition to all international law because, as he stated, 'it is stupid, naive, ingenuous and antipatriotic for me to commit myself to anything foreign', and he continued:

> it is fine that in international relations Spain defines its policy, joins the League of Nations and acquires all of the commitments it desires; but committing itself to something is not practical.[21]

The radical politician, Justo Villanueva Gómez (1893–1952), opposed the amendment made by Royo Villanova, his teacher and colleague, instead calling for Articles 6 and 7 of the Constitution to be withdrawn. For Villanueva Gómez, the two principles were inter-connected and already established in the preliminary title of the constitution.[22] Ricardo Gómez Rojí (1881–1936), for his part, branded Article 7 as dangerously vague and imprecise. His conservative position led him to argue that the '*surge*' (in his own words) of international law would eventually kill Spanish law.[23] José Álvarez Buylla y Godino (1881–1954) also criticised the adoption of the League of Nations' principles, especially Articles 76 and 77.[24] Godino suggested that fundamental law represented 'a mosaic featuring the magnificence of European and American constitutions', something 'made of off-cuts', a 'jazz band constitution, without rhythm or harmony'.[25] In other words, Álvarez Buylla y Godino critiqued the excessive 'foreignness' of the constitutional text.

At the end of the day, none of the articles relating to external policy were modified in the consituent debates. The Constitution was approved on 9 December of 1931.[26] The Constitution was curiously pusblished without a preamble.[27] It subjected the declaration of war to the mechanisms of arbitration and conciliation. First, the declaration of war was dependent upon compliance with the conditions provided in the Third Hague Convention regarding the opening of hostilities and the League of Nations Pact. It also required approval from either the Council or the Assembly.[28] Second, it was dependent upon the exhaustion of defensive procedures not of a warlike nature. In other words, Spain was required to engage in alternate uses of force such as retaliations, reprisals, embargos and blockades. Third, it was incumbent upon the both parties to exhaust any legal procedures, such as mediation, conciliation or arbitration procedures, as stipulated in the 1899 Hague Convention before resorting to war. In the words of José Ramón de Orué y Arregui (1894–1953), professor in public and private international law at the University of Valencia, the constitutional procedure for declaring war in fact entailed *a preventive law of war* made up of international research commissions, good practices, mediation, arbitration, conciliation and appeals to the Permanent Court of International Justice.[29] The President's authority to declare war also remained subject to international law. As explained above, a fourth condition was added to this general limitation of presidential authority: any warlike act had to be authorised by a law.

A common opinion expressed by various legal internationalists in the 1930s, in particular by Orué y Arregui, was that the constitutional provisions contained an excessive degree of *Platonism*. Orué considered the articles idealistic and too far removed from contemporary realities. He also saw the constitution as not covering other international legal issues such as *jus ad bellum*.[30] Orué denounced the absence of a principle that included a commitment to respect the so-called 'laws of war' as a collection of valid rules when conflict did occur.[31]

Altogether, the 1931 Constitution went some way towards formalising the ideal of peace and thus marked a new direction in Spanish foreign policy. From a legal point of view, the articles were in harmony with the pre-existing regulations of domestic and international public law. The 1931 Constitution was an *ius gentium pacis*, a 'model and example' to be followed by other states. Many pacifists and internationalists analysed Spain's new approach, lauding its legal innovations on unifying public law.[32] They had good reason to be so optimistic. Not even the comparatively progressive Weimar Constitution of 1919 in Germany had gone so far in unifying constitutional law with international law. In 1932, the Russian jurist Boris Mirkine-Guetzévitch wrote that for the first time in the constitutional history of the modern world, the 1931 Spanish Constitution had brought a state's constitutional text into concordance with its international responsibilities. This represented an important stage in developing a new methodology for peace.[33]

The constitutional text of 1931 represented the most elaborate product of international legal pacifism of the interwar period by imposing limits on national sovereignty based on contracted international obligations. The 1931 Constitution included values, principles and rules of post-classical international law founded in the same democratic principles as the Spanish nation. In practice those values meant incorporating the essential postulates of the League of Nations Pact and the Hague conventions into Spain's domestic law. The outcome was restricting the right of appeal to war to solve disputes.[34] The constitution gave a considerable boost to 1930s internationalist currents that were attempting to promote the peaceful development of relations between nation states by means of institutionalising an international system.

(Re)defining neutrality in a system of collective security in the League of Nations era

Diplomat and professor of international law Fernando María Castiella (1907–1976) argued in the 1960s that Spain's neutrality constitued neither an 'absolute' nor the 'sole purpose' of foreign policy.[35] Instead, it was a 'consciously imposed neutrality in view of certain circumstances'. This circumstantial neutrality was due, in Castiella's words, to 'the conviction that there was no higher reason that would force Spain to take the side of one of the contending parties'.[36] It was precisely this conviction that Spanish republicans rejected. Manuel Azaña (1880–1940), President of the Government (1931–1933) and President of the Republic (1936–1939), defended the idea that in the event of war a state had to adopt a stance consistent with its position during the build-up to war.[37] Based on this abstraction, which was connected to the just war theory of Francisco de Vitoria, some reasoned that any intended 'neutral' was obliged to choose sides in support of its friends.

Spain's neutrality during the First World War was not due to conviction, as the republicans later claimed, but was rather a response to its international weakness and the Spanish monarchy's abandonment of international diplomacy. Between 1914 and 1918, the country did not comply with the requirements of neutrality. It was more of a 'forced'—even imposed and 'fictitious'—neutrality that was based on the insular and isolationist position of Spain in international affairs. As far as the republicans were concerned, Spain's isolationism had to come to an end.

The League of Nations Pact (1919) attempted to prevent the unnecessary outbreak of war by offering a range of institutionalised mechanisms capable of providing peaceful avenues for resolving disputes.[38] Such mechanisms included arbitration, diplomatic negotiations, mediation, good offices and judicial settlement. The League of Nations Pact did not question the fact that states had the right to resort to armed force. However, it distinguished wars of aggression when the aggressor failed to use peaceful avenues first. In the event of such a war, the League of Nations Pact provided for a number of economic, diplomatic and military sanctions at the Council's discretion.[39]

The League of Nations thereby attempted to provide a 'security guarantee' to 'small' and defenceless states such as Spain. Article 10 included the Wilsonian principle guaranteeing the territorial integrity and political independence of states against the threat of external aggression. The purpose of this principle was to associate national interest with a commitment towards peace.[40] The reasoning was impeccable in theory and its establishment meant that Spain, without any military capability to repel aggression and without any material possibility of defending its national independence with its own resources, could only guarantee its security by using international rules.[41]

Of course, membership in the League of Nations for 'small' states such as Spain also entailed a certain degree of obligation.[42] Article 16 of the pact established that:

> should any Member of the League resort to war ..., it shall *ipso facto* be deemed to have committed an act of war against all other Members of the League.[43]

Similarly, each of the members enjoyed the security guarantee provided by other members, but each member was also the co-guarantor of others, undertaking to adopt collective sanctions against aggressor states and, therefore, to support *de iure* and *de facto* the attacked state.

This commitment to collective security had some consequences for Spain as a neutral state. On the one hand, the acceptance of the League of Nations Pact represented a theoretical renunciation of its policy of neutrality. On the other, its participation in the multilateral forum of the League of Nations and the growing interest from European and American nations led it to employ a foreign policy that was increasingly active and vigilant in order to avoid any possibility of confrontation. This tension led many Spanish politicians and legalists to question the future viability of Spain's neutrality in light of its newfound obligation as a member of the League of Nations. As a result, Spain's policy on neutrality was not the same after the First World War. The international legal instruments created at The Hague and Paris did not abolish the institution of neutrality, but had an impact on the regime. Spain managed international law in service of its own (national and international) interests of peace, democracy and rule of law. To that end, Spain could refuse to participate in an illegal war, even if it was condoned by the League, and invoke its neutrality instead.

Yet a contradiction remained in aligning Spanish neutrality within the League's collective security system. On the one hand, Spain was committed to collective security under the League of Nations Pact. On the other, the constitution made clear the republic's intention of defining Spain's foreign policy rationale as one based largely on peace in keeping with the spirit of the Kellogg–Briand Pact. In this context, notions such as 'positive' or 'active' neutrality—understood as 'a permanent effort for the upholding and organisation of peace in the world'—arose.[44] The defence of the institution of 'positive' or 'active' neutrality was justified by a political and juridical approach: it was inspired by a consideration of self-defence and took the illegality of war into account. Still, many republicans, including Salvador de Madariaga, Manuel Azaña and Luís de Zulueta (1878–1964), could not clarify the final objectives of an 'active' policy of neutrality, as the contradiction of neutrality versus the League of Nations Pact was inherent to the system itself.

The contradiction and dichotomy between neutrality and collective security remained throughout the interwar period. It was not only a problem for Spain. In the 1930s, Nicolas Politis, among many other international legal scholars, argued that the acceptance of the modern concept of neutrality represented a return to Francisco de Vitoria's concept of the 'just' war.[45] In other words, he suggested that the classic concept of a neutrality based on abstention and impartiality was superceded by moral imperatives.[46] Manuel Lasala Llanas (1875–1944), professor in public and private international law at the University of Zaragoza, also defended the compatibility between collective security and neutrality.[47] He argued that, given the interdependence of states, it was no longer possible for any neutral to remain on the sidelines. The notion of neutrality had experienced changes in its nature after the establishment of the League of Nations as well as the *jus ad bellum*. He further suggested that the concept of modern neutrality should be of an 'occasional' nature.[48]

Nevertheless, participation in the international system did not presuppose any militaristic intentions. To the contrary, Spain's adoption of the League of Nations' principles required the nation to continuously seek to avoid war. The primary change was Spain's acceptance that, depending on the circumstances of war, abstention could represent a real crime that was similar or equal to providing indirect aid to the transgressor.[49] In the event of a war with a 'just' cause (a lawful war) Spain could, in last instance and in a proportional way, resort to war. This is where the reference by Salvador de Madariaga to Spanish legal tradition in the sixteenth century and to the figure of Francisco de Vitoria makes sense, and that was how it was understood by Spanish liberal republicans.[50]

It also needs to be remembered that legal theory (as expressed by Salvador de Madariaga, Nicholas Politis and others) did not reflect the actual practice of Spanish foreign policy. The discrepancy between theory and reality was not an exclusively Spanish problem. Other 'small' European democracies also had to deal with the contradiction when finding themselves trapped between the loss of their traditional neutrality and the clear risk of war in the 1930s. Both the League of Nations Pact and the Kellogg–Briand Pact effectively made the traditional or classical position of neutrality obsolete. When faced with the 'crime' of war, these treaties effectively put an end to states being able to remain on the sidelines. In other words, in the interwar period, war was defined by morality. It therefore became incumbant on all states to punish and prevent illegal wars. Many weak states agreed to the League of Nations' principles in part because they considered collective security an effective 'instrument for the promotion of peace through justice'. They were thus able to present themselves as the League's most loyal champions, yet keep their connections to the policy of neutrality intact.[51] According to William Rappard, this was due less to their superior virtue and more to their inferior power, given that 'by serving the League of Nations they were not just defending justice, but were also promoting their national interests more effectively'.[52]

In the end, the Spanish Civil War (1936–1939) showed up the ineffectiveness of the League of Nation's collective security system.[53] The republican discourse in the 1930s was as idealistic as the League of Nations' collective security system.[54] The outbreak of war in 1936 began a tragic era in Spanish history that would take it back, under Generalissimo Franco's rule, to the structures and institutions of the nineteenth century. At the beginning of the Second World War (1939–1945), Franco's regime proclaimed Spanish neutrality.[55] One year later, on 12 June 1940, the 'new state' officially adopted, following the path of Italy and Turkey, a position of 'non-belligerence' as opposed to one of neutrality.[56]

The law of war in an age of democracy

The 1978 Spanish Constitution was the result of consensus between the various political groups and social agents supporting democracy, the rule of law and respect for fundamental rights and freedoms in the aftermath of Franco's dictatorship. The drafting of the constitution represented an effort to overcome obstacles both in the dogmatic arena (constitutional principles and fundamental rights) and in the organic area (the division of powers and territorial political organisation). The principles related to war and peace included in the 1978 Constitution bear some similarities to the provisions included in the 1931 Spanish Constitution. However, while the 1931 Constitution recognised the commitment to peace in keeping with international law, the 1978 Constitution did not situate the declaration of war and the commitment to peace as subject to international law.

From a technical legal perspective, this difference is highly significant. The 1931 Constitution represented the unification of public law (both internal and international), while the 1978 Constitution expressed the Spanish legal system's dual nature. In the interwar period, several international legal scholars, philosophers and constitutionalists defended the concept that internal law and international law were the product of the same historical medium. Some argued that the principle of unity of public law lay in the unity of legal awareness and the empirical unity of historical evolution.[57] The 1931 Constitution represented the unity of national and international public law. The 1978 Constitution, on the other hand, represented a dualist moderate and reasonable system; a dualist system because it demanded recognition of international agreements and a moderate and reasonable system because all this reception required was publication in the *Official Journal of the State*, not the creation of a particular law using parliamentary process.[58]

The preamble to the 1978 Constitution confirmed Spain's commitment to peace by mentioning one of its fundamental objectives as being to 'collaborate in the strengthening of peaceful relations and effective co-operation amongst all the peoples of the World'.[59] This constitutional text was also inspired by the pacifist tradition of the Hague and Paris peace conferences. Nevertheless, its peculiarity was giving the King as head of the Spanish state the power to declare war and make peace, subject to the previous authorisation of the *Cortes Generales*.[60] The power to declare war was therefore not constitutionally subject to the constraints placed by international law.[61]

International law puts strict limitations on the use of force. The 1945 United Nations (UN) Charter prohibits the threat or use of force against the territorial integrity or independent policy of any nation-state.[62] The purpose of the charter was to proscribe the role of war and the use of force in international relations.[63] It does however, allow for the use of force under specific circumstances such as self-defence or collective action under the mandate of the Security Council. Outside of this legal framework, any other offensive action is illegal regardless of whether the belligerents regard their conflict as having 'a just cause'.[64] The inclusion contradicts the prohibition of the use of force as laid down by international law.[65]

A more in-depth analysis of the 1978 Constitution reveals that the declaration of war under international law is irrelevant as it is not a condition that a 'state of war' really exists.[66] In the first place, this 'condition' of international law has been rendered obsolete.[67] Second, according to the Geneva Conventions and protocols on international humanitarian law, the concept of 'war' can be substituted with the concept of 'armed conflict'.[68] This 'disappearance' of the concept of war has also taken with it the formulism that required its declaration.[69] Today, international law attempts to regulate inter-state and intra-state conflicts by means of peaceful conflict resolution or by resorting to the system of collective security as instituted in Chapter VII of the UN Charter, so long as there is a threat to peace or an act of aggression.[70] In addition, there exists a set of regulations applicable to armed conflicts in the Geneva Conventions of 1949, the Protocols of 1977 and a whole series of other specific conventions.[71] These instruments introduce rules applicable to any national or international armed conflict.

The 1978 Constitution is therefore out of step with the existing international legal system because it harkens back to traditional notions of international law. The UN Charter provides only two—not universally accepted—exceptions to the prohibition of the use of military force: individual or collective self-defence, and collective measures. Both categories are referenced in Article 51 of the UN Charter and Chapter VII, decided on by the UN Security Council in accordance with Articles 41 and 42. In this context, a response invoking self-defence must be immediate and of a provisional, subsidiary nature until the UN Security Council can take the appropriate measures. In a case of self-defence, the Spanish government would still be obliged to seek the authorisation of the *Cortes Generales* in accordance with the constitution, as well as informing the UN Security Council, so that it may implement the necessary action.

In light of current international law, the declaration of war as written in Article 63 paragraph 3 of the constitution would need not apply given its outdated formulation.[72] It also makes the dualist character of Spanish legislation abundantly clear. The spirit of the 1978 Constitution, which was laid out in the preamble, is very much tied to the notions of collaborating in strengthening peaceful relations between states and maintaining international security. As such, it is contrary for Spain to involve itself in any armed conflict that violates its international obligations.[73] The problem for those political groups that rejected Spain's logistic and humanitarian participation in inter-state or civil wars was that, if the debate was directed—as Javier García Fernández argued—towards the necessity to declare war and therefore subject to parliamentary authorisation, the mission would be hindered and parliamentary control over international military operations would become more difficult.[74] The 1978 Constitution was the result of a political consensus that established a new basis for collective co-existence. The price of this consensus was a certain ambiguity and vagueness.[75]

Conclusions

The Hague Peace Conferences' greatest achievement was how it set up the basis for progressive reform of the international system through law and peace intiatives. Ideas of peace, neutrality, arbitration, disarmament, justice and social progress became part of the international system. The language concerning the law of war and peace was included in the constitutional text of 1931 and recovered in the 1978 Constitution. The Hague conventions (1899 and 1907) and the Paris peace treaties (of 1919 and 1928) represented a new age in international law. All the treaties failed in the task of preventing international conflicts, as the First and Second World Wars demonstrated. However, in the Spanish case, they left their mark.

The new international legal system which arose after the First World War placed Spain amongst civilised nations. The 1931 Constitution represented a definitive break with the precepts put forward in the failed Spanish constitutions of the nineteenth century by redistributing power to the *Cortes Generales*.[76] The constitution redefined the position of the Spanish armed forces in the democratic constitutional system by requiring civil supremacy, military neutrality, demilitarisation of public order, limitation of military authority and above all, a limitation on the employment of force through the mechanisms of the separation of powers within the framework of an effectively representative system.[77]

There is no doubt that the ideas of the pacifist movement in the first decades of the twentieth century had a significant influence on both the 1931 and 1978 constitutions. In the Second Republic, the policy of the Republican Government was (unsuccessfully) based on the democratisation and modernisation of the armed forces.[78] After a number of decades, the 1978 Constitution once more afforded the *Cortes Generales* power in matters of defence, even if these were much more limited than in 1931.

Regardless of the limits and shortcomings of the 1931 Constitution, its international principles were used as a model for the most progressive constitutional texts in the late interwar period and even in later decades. The 1931 Spanish Constitution was original to a certain extent and also influenced the Italian Constitution of 1947, the Portuguese Constitution of 1976 and, particularly, the later Spanish Constitution of 1978. It included typical post-classical international law provisions relating to the observance of international obligations including *pacta sunt servanda* (the transparency of treaties), the end of secret treaties, the prohibition of war and even the recognition of a certain level of protection of fundamental rights, which represented the equality of all Spanish people before the law.[79] With the return to democracy in 1978, high politics recovered the traditions of the Hague Peace Conferences (of 1899 and 1907), albeit in a weaker form. Still, the constitutional text of 1978 is the expression of Spain's international commitment to peace, democracy, the rule of law and human rights.

In the twenty-first century, in its attempts to become fully integrated in international society, Spain has taken on international obligations and encouraged principles of justice, democracy, human rights and the rule of law whilst promoting itself as a peace-loving nation. Within the limits of its economic and political situation, Spain has played a positive role in world events and especially in the creation of a structure to facilitate international peace and security. Spain is a member of the United Nations, the European Union and the North Atlantic Treaty Organisation, among others. Spanish participation in these organisations has laid the basis for the country's return to the top table in terms of those countries that dominate European economics, politics and matters of security. It is today high time to revisit a legacy that some Spanish international legal scholars at the end of 1970s saw as one 'alive with topicality'.[80] In order to contextualise Spain's commitment to international law and peace in the present, it is necessary to consider how the international legal principles at play during the late nineteenth and early twentieth centuries were incorporated into and promulgated through Spanish constitutional texts over the course of the twentieth century.

Notes

1 F. Quintana Navarro. (1993). *España en Europa, 1931–1936. Del compromiso por la paz a la huida de la guerra*. Madrid: Nerea.
2 J.L. Neila Hernández. (2003). El proyecto internacional de la República: democracia, paz y neutralidad. In: J. C. Pereira Castañares, ed. *La política exterior de España (1800–2003)*. Barcelona: Ariel, pp.353–361.
3 See the international legal approach of J.A. Carrillo Salcedo. (1967). Las relaciones exteriores de España. (Del desastre de 1898 al desastre de 1921). *Historia Social de España del siglo XX*. Madrid, pp.355–372.
4 See F. Quintana Navarro. (1991). La política exterior española en la Europa de entreguerras: Cuatro momentos, dos concepciones y una constante impotencia. In: H. de la Torres Gómez, ed. *Portugal, España y Europa. Cien años de desafío (1890–1990). III Jornadas de Estudios Luso-Españoles*. Mérida: UNED, pp.51–74.
5 For more on this regenerationist movement, see A. Niño. (2000). Política de alianzas y compromisos coloniales para la *regeneración* internacional de España, 1898–1914. In: J. Tusell et al., eds. *Política exterior de España en el siglo XX*.

Madrid: Biblioteca Nueva/UNED, pp.31–94; and J.L. Neila Hernández. (2002). *Regeneracionismo y política exterior en el reinado de Alfonso XIII (1902–1931)*. Madrid: CEHRI.
6   One of the leaders of this regeneration movement was Rafael Altamira y Crevea. For more on his ideas of integrating Spain into Europe and demonstrating European standards of civilisation, see Y. Gamarra. (2012). Rafael Altamira y Crevea (1866–1951). The International Judge as 'Gentle Civilizer'. *The Journal of the History of International Law*, 14, pp.1–49.
7   The Conservative Government of Eduardo Dato published a Decree on Spain's neutrality in *Gaceta* on 30 July 1914. See *Gaceta* (of Madrid), 7 August 1914. Five other European neutral countries, Switzerland, Denmark, Sweden, Norway and the Netherlands, followed that step against the 35 belligerents. See more information in J. Matthews. (2015). España neutral: un contraejemplo. In: R. Gerwarth and E. Manela, eds. *Imperios en guerra, 1911–1923*. Madrid: Biblioteca Nueva, pp.411–415, and J. Ponce Marrero. (2007). La política exterior española de 1907 a 1920: entre el regeneracionismo de intenciones y la neutralidad condicionada. *Historia Contemporánea*, 37, pp.93–115.
8   See M. Espadas Burgos. (2000). España y la Primera Guerra Mundial. In: J. Tussel et al., eds. *Política exterior de España en el siglo XX*. Madrid: Biblioteca Nueva/UNED, pp.95–116.
9   See G. Solé. (1976). La incorporación de España a la Sociedad de Naciones. *Hispania. Revsita española de Historia*, 132(36), pp.131–174.
10 Two classic studies on the subject are M. Fernández Almagro. (1986). *Historia del reinado de D. Alfonso XIII*. 2 vols, Madrid: Sarpe (1st ed. Barcelona, Montaner y Simón, 1933); and C. Seco Serrano. (1979). *Alfonso XIII y la crisis de la Restauración*. Madrid: Rialp.
11 The Spanish Constitution of 1931 indicated some of the advances made by international society during the twentieth century, see M.O. Hudson. (1931). The Spanish Constitution of 1931. *The American Journal of International Law*, 26(3), pp.579–582.
12 Spain closely followed the Kellogg-Briand Pact and became a member in 1929. Indeed, as Nicolás Pérez Serrano points out, 'we probably had the honour of being the first to give a constitutional character to the agreements that were almost conceived in the same terms and consecrated in Article 1 of the Kellogg-Briand Pact, signed on 27th August 1928', see N. Pérez Serrano. (1932). La Constitución española de 1931. Antecedentes, texto y comentarios. *Revista de Derecho Privado*, p.73.
13 Article 6 of the Constitution of 1931states that 'Spain renounce war as an instrument of national policy', J. de Esteban. (1981). *Las Constituciones de España*. Madrid: Taurus, p.260.
14 See J.T. Shotwell. (1928–1929). The Pact of Paris with Historical Commentary. *International Conciliation*, 12, pp.447–520; R. O. Paxton. (1975). *Europe in the Twentieth Century*. New York: Harcourt Brace Jovanovich.
15 The language used in this article drew very positive comments from B. Mirkine-Guetzévitch: (1928). Les Tendences Internationales des Nouvelles Constitutions Europeéenes. *L'Esprit Internationale*, 2, p.530; and (1934). *Modernas tendencias del Derecho constitucional*. Trans. Sabino Alvarez Gendin, Madrid: Reus, pp.60–63.
16 Esteban, p.260.
17 L. Pérez Gil. (2001). Análisis de los principios constitucionales y las competencias en las relaciones exteriores de la Constitución española de diciembre de 1931. *Revista Española de Derecho Constitucional*, 63, pp.160–164.
18 See E. Arroyo Lara. (1981). *La no beligerancia. Análisis jurídico*. La Laguna: Universidad de La Laguna, p.199.

19 See J. Oliver Araujo. (1991). *El sistema político de la Constitución española de 1931*. Palma de Mallorca: Universidad de las Islas Baleares.
20 See Y. Gamarra. (2012). Los lenguajes del Derecho internacional en la Constitución española de 1931. In: Y. Gamarra and I. de la Rasilla, eds. *El pensamiento iusinternacionalista español del siglo XX. Estudios*. Vol. 1. Cizur Menor (Pamplona): Thomson Reuters-Aranzadi, pp.269–320.
21 *Journal of the Sessions Courts (Diario de las Sesiones de Cortes) 1931–33*, 4 September 1931, Vol. 41, p.765 and 18 September 1931, Vol. 41, pp. 1027 and 1031.
22 *Journal of the Sessions Courts*, 41, p.1029.
23 *Journal of the Sessions Courts*, 41, p.766.
24 *Journal of the Sessions Courts*, 41, pp.1026–1031, 2094–2098.
25 *Journal of the Sessions Courts*, 30, p.2321.
26 Constitution of the Spanish Republic. *Gaceta* (of Madrid), 10 December 1931, Vol. 344, pp.1578–1588.
27 See the perspective of A. Remiro Brotóns. (1984). *La acción exterior del Estado*. Madrid: Tecnos, p.94.
28 See A.E. Zimmern. (1998). *The League of Nations and the rule of law, 1918–1935*. Holmes Beach: Gaun; and C.H. Howard-Ellis. (2003). *The origin, structure and working of the League of Nations*. Clark, NJ: The Lawbook Exchange.
29 J.R. Orué y Arregui. (1932). Preceptos internacionales en la Constitución de la República española (9 de diciembre de 1931). *Revista General de Legislación y Jurisprudencia*, 4(160), p.405.
30 Orué, p.403.
31 Orué, p.403.
32 Navarro, *España en Europa, 1931–1936*, pp.35–39.
33 B. Mirkine-Guetzévitch. (1932). Ius Gentium Pacis. *Revista de Derecho Público*, 1(9), pp.259–275.
34 A. Remiro Brotóns proposed from a comparative approach the democratizing advance that the Constitution of 1931 meant in foreign policy, see Brotóns, *La acción exterior del Estado*, pp.22–23.
35 F.M. Castiella Maíz. (1960). *Política exterior de España, 1898–1960*. Madrid, p.13.
36 Maíz, pp.13–14.
37 M. Azaña (1990). Los motivos de la germanofilia. Discourse at the Ateneo of Madrid, 25 May 1917. In: *Obras Completas. Mexico: Oasis, 1966–68*. Reed. Vol. 1, Madrid: Giner, pp.145–146.
38 Of clear Catholic roots as stated in F. Yerly. (1996). Les catholiques et la Société des Nations: l'exemple de l'Union Catholique d'Études Internationales. In: G. Cholvy, ed., *L'éveil des catholiques français à la dimension internationale de leur foi, XIXe et XXe siècles*. Montpellier: Centre Regional d'Histoire des Mentalités.
39 See W.G. Grewe. (2000). *The Epochs of International Law*. Trans. and ed. Michael Byers. Berlin/New York: Walter de Guyter, pp.592–598.
40 See B.A. Coates. (2016). *Legalist Empire: International Law and American Foreign Relations in the Early Twentieth Century*. Oxford: Oxford University Press.
41 United Nations Library. (1983). *The League of Nations in retrospect. Proceedings of the Symposium organized by the United Nations Library*. Berlin/New York: Walter de Gruyter.
42 As C. Barcia Trelles understood and expressed in *La Libertad*, 2 November 1932.
43 See Article 16 of the League of Nations Covenant at The Avalon Project at Yale Law School. (1924). The Covenant of the League of Nations. [online] Available

at: http://avalon.law.yale.edu/20th_century/leagcov.asp [Accessed 3 August 2016].
44 Navarro, España en Europa, 1931–1936, p.29.
45 N. Politis. (1935). *La neutralité et la paix*. Paris: Libraire Hachette.
46 P. Fauchille. (1921). *Traité de Droit International public*. Vol. 2, Paris: Libraire Arthur Rousseau, p.653.
47 See M. Lasala Llanas. (1924). El nuevo concepto de neutralidad. *Revue de droit international et de sciencies diplomatiques et soicales*, pp.112–115.
48 Llanas, pp.114- 115.
49 See the approach of T. Boye. (1938). Quelques aspects du développement des règles de la neutralité. *Recueil des Cours de l'Academie de Droit International de la Haye*, 64, pp.157–232.
50 A. del Valle López. (1998). *Aportación bio-bibliográfica a la historia de la ciencia*. Madrid: Narcea Ediciones.
51 W.E. Rappard. (1935). Small States in the League of Nations. In: Geneva Institute of International Relations. *Problems of Peace*. 9th series, London: George Allen & Unwin Ltd, pp.49–51.
52 Rappard, p.50.
53 See the approaches of F. Wilcox. (1938). The League of Nations and the Spanish Civil War. *Annals of the American Academy of Political and Social Science*, 198, pp.65–72. Also, see C.R. Fernández Liesa. (2014). *La guerra civil española y el orden jurídico internacional*. Madrid: Thomson Reuters.
54 See N.A. Graebner. (2011). *The Versailles Treaty and its legacy: the failure of the Wilsonian Vision*. New York: Cambridge University Press.
55 Decree of 4 September of 1939 ordering the strictest neutrality in the European conflict. *Boletín Oficial del Estado*, 15 September 1939, p.4937.
56 Decree of 12 June of 1940 whereby non-belligerency of Spain in the current conflict is resolved. *Boletín Oficial del Estado*, 13 June 1940, p.4068.
57 Mirkine-Guetzévitch, *Modernas tendencias del Derecho constitucional*, p.54.
58 J.A. Pastor Ridruejo. (2015). *Curso de Derecho internacional público y Organizaciones internacionales*. Madrid: Tecnos, p.185.
59 Preamble of the Spanish Constitution of 1978, included in Esteban, p.359.
60 See comments on Article 63 paragraph 3 of the Constitution of 1978 by E. Pérez Vera and A. Rodríguez Carrión. (1997). Artículo 63. Atribuciones del Rey. In: O. Alzaga Villaamil, ed. *La Constitución española de 1978 (comentario sistemático)*. Vol. 5, Madrid, Cortes Generales, pp.274–275; M. Aragón. (1979). El control de constitucionalidad en la Constitución española de 1978. *Revista de Estudios Políticos*, 7, pp.178–179; M. Martínez Cuadrado and F.J.Vanaclocha Bellver. (1981). La jurisdicción constitucional. In: E. García de Enterría and A. Predieri, eds. *La Constitución española de 1978. Un estudio sistemático*. Madrid: Civitas, pp.832–834; F. Garrido Falla. (2001). *Comentarios a la Constitución*. 3rd ed., Madrid: Civitas; S. Ripol Carulla. (2009). Artículo 63. In: Mª E. Casas and M. Rodríguez-Piñero y Braco Ferrer, eds. *Comentarios a la Constitución española. XXX Aniversario*. Madrid: Fundación Wolters Kluwer España, pp.1293–1296.
61 See M. Herrero de Miñón. (1997). Dimensión constitucional de la profesionalización de las Fuerzas Armadas. *Revista de Derecho Político*, 43, pp.11–27.
62 Article 2 paragraph 4 of the United Nations Charter states that 'All Members shall refrain in their international relations from the threat or use of force against the territorial integrity or political independence of any state, or in any other manner inconsistent with the Purposes of the United Nations'. United Nations. (1945). *Charter of the United Nations: Chapter 1*. [online] Available at: http://www.un.org/en/sections/un-charter/chapter-i/index.html [Accessed 5 August 2016].

63 On the evolution of the law of war see R. Lesaffer. (2012). Too much history: From war as a sanction to the sanctioning of war. In: M. Weller, ed. *Oxford Handbook of the Use of Force in International Law*. Oxford: Oxford University Press, pp.35–55.
64 In Vitoria's words, F. De Vitoria. (1999). *Sobre el derecho de la guerra*. Madrid: Tecnos.
65 1978 was when the apparent irrelevance of the prohibition of the use of force in international relations was least obsolete, as defended by P. Vera and R. Carrión, p.275; and more recently J. García Fernández. (2000). Guerra y Derecho Constitucional. *Cuadernos Constitucionales de la Cátedra Furió Ceriol*, 32, pp.44–46; E. Melero Alonso. (2006). *La declaración de guerra en el ordenamiento jurídico español. Un mecanismo para el control jurídico de la participación del Estado español en conflictos armados*. Madrid: Dykinson; J.M. Fernández-Palacios Martínez. (2010). *Rey, Constitución y Política Exterior*. Madrid: Marcial Pons, pp.128–129; and R.I. Rodríguez Magdaleno. (2015). *La participación de las Cortes Generales en la acción exterior del Estado (1979–2011)*. Madrid: Congreso de los Diputados, p.196.
66 Hugo Grotius classified wars as those which were 'declared' and therefore legal, and those which were not declared which were not necessarily illegal. See Chapter 3 of H. Grotius. (1925). *De jure belli ac pacis*. Trans. F.W. Kelsey. Washington: Carnegie Endowment for International Peace. See also P. Haggenmacher. (1983). *Grotius et la Doctrine de la Guerre Juste*. Paris: Presses Universitaires de France.
67 As I. Detter puts it, '(I)n earlier days, declarations of war, depending as they did on the subjective will of States, made clear that war "in a formal sense" existed, i.e. war existed in the "opinion" of one or more of the parties to a conflict. But the formal dichotomy of state of war in a formal sense, relying on subjective criteria, and actual war in the material sense, is now probably obsolete'. I. Detter. (2000). *The Law of War*. Cambridge: Cambridge University Press, p.13. A similar view is expressed by Y. Dinstein. (2011). *War, Agression and Self-Defence*. 5th ed., Cambridge: Cambridge University Press.
68 The term 'armed conflict' has been used since 1949, in the Geneva Conventions of 1949, the Protocols of 1977, and the Convention of 1954 (Article 18). For the differences between 'armed conflict' and 'war' see K.J. Partsch. (1982). Armed Conflict. In: R. Bernhardt, ed. *Encyclopaedia of Public International Law*. Amsterdam/New York/Oxford: North-Holland Publishing Company, pp.25–28; and I. Detter, pp.17–19. See also the definition of armed conflict given by the International Criminal Tribunal for the former Yugoslavia, *The Prosecutor v. Dusko Tadic*, Decision on the Defence Motion for Interlocutory Appeal on Jurisdiction, Case N° IT-94-1-AR72, *International Legal Materials*, 1996, paragraph 70.
69 Pastor Ridruejo. (2015), pp.658–659; J.L. Fernández Flores. (2001). *El derecho de los conflictos armados, de iure belli, el derecho de la guerra, el derecho internacional humanitario, el derecho humanitario bélico*. Madrid: Ministry of Defence; and J.D. González Campos, I.I. Sánchez Rodríguez and P. Andrés Sáenz de Santa María. (2008). *Curso de Derecho internacional público*. 4th ed., Pamplona: Thompson-Civitas, pp.1009–1011.
70 On the value of peaceful solutions to international settlements, see L. Caflisch. (2001). Cent ans de règlement pacifique des différends interétatiques. *Recueil des Cours de l'Academie de Droit International de la Haye*, 288, pp.268–271.
71 For a collection of texts and an introductory study on the control of compliance with international humanitarian law and their efficiency, see E. Orihuela Calatayud. (1998). *Derecho internacional humanitario. Tratados internacionales y otros textos*. Madrid: McGraw Hill.

72 If this were not the situation we would have a case of nullity 'ab initio'. On the differences in international law between an illicit act—responsibility falling on the contravening party—and an invalid act—lack of conditions required for prosecution—see M. Díez de Velasco. (2005). *Instituciones de Derecho internacional público*. Madrid: Tecnos, pp.751–752.

73 A state may not invoke its Constitution or internal laws to avoid the obligations that emanate from international law, as has been consistently argued by, among others, the International Court of Justice (ICJ) in a consultative opinion on the *Applicability of the Obligation to Arbitrate under Section 21 of the United Nations Headquarters Agreements of 26 June 1947*, Advisory Opinion, ICJ, 26th April, 1988. On this doctrine see the contribution of A. Marín López. (1995). Orden jurídico internacional y Constitución española. *Revista de Derecho Político*, 45, pp.35–67; G.M. Quintero Saravia. (1995). Las relaciones entre el Derecho internacional y el Derecho interno: el caso de la Constitución. La Constitución como fuente del Derecho internacional. *Revista de Derecho Político*, 45, pp.69–104, and A. Remiro Brotóns. (1998). La Constitución y el Derecho Internacional. In: *Administraciones Públicas y Constitución, Reflexiones sobre el XX aniversario de la Constitución española de 1978*. Madrid: INAP, pp.227–258.

74 J. García Fernández. (2003). El control político de las misiones militares en el exterior: derecho internacional y derecho interno. *Newsletter*, 9, p.26. See also Melero Alonso; Fernández-Palacios Martínez, p.129; and Rodríguez Magdaleno, p.201.

75 L. Martín Rebollo, ed. (2003). *Constitución Española. Preliminary study*. Pamplona: Aranzadi, p.21.

76 The nineteenth-century constitutional texts may be consulted in Esteban, pp.95–258.

77 See L. Cotino Hueso. (2000). La posición de las Cortes en el ámbito militar y de la defensa (atención particular a la reciente experiencia de la crisis de Kosovo). *Anuario de Derecho parlamentario*, 9, p.261.

78 See F. López Ramón. (1987). *La caracterización jurídica de las Fuerzas Armadas*. Madrid: Centro de Estudios Constitucionales, pp.187–203.

79 An interesting study on the recognition of social rights in the 1931 Spanish Constitution can be found in M. Contreras Casado. (2006). Sobre la Constitución de 1931 y su aportación al constitucionalismo español. In: *II República Española, 75 Aniversario 1931–2006*. Zaragoza: Diputación de Zaragoza, pp.18–20.

80 See A. Remiro Brotóns. (1979). El discreto encanto—y desencanto—de la Revista Española del Derecho Internacional (1948–1978). In: *Estudios de Derecho Internacional. Homenaje al Profesor Miaja de la Muela*. Vol. 1, Madrid: Technos, p.131.

Index

1899 Hague Peace Conference *see* Hague Peace Conference (1899, First)
1907 Hague Peace Conference *see* Hague Peace Conference (1907, Second)

Aehrenthal, Alois von 22–7
aerial warfare 161–2
Alabama arbitration *see* Geneva Arbitration
Alabama crisis 61
Álavarez Buylla y Godino, José 210
Anglo-Boer War (1899–1902, Second) 62
Appiah, Kwame Anthony 122
arbitration 3–4, 34, 38, 177–8; development of 39–40; as dispute resolution mechanism 16, 156, 160, 171, 179, 211; at the 1899 Hague conference 39–43; and The Hague 32, 129–32; at the 1907 Hague conference 44–6, 130; proposal for obligatory arbitration 40–1, 44–6, 179, 184
Arbitration Alliance 147
Arbitration Society 159
Ardagh, Sir John 78
arms limitation *see* disarmament
Asquith, Herbert 15, 92
Asser, Tobias 41–2, 57, 60–1
Austro-Prussian War (1866) 53
Azaña, Manuel 212

Baldwin, Stanley 93
Balkan Wars (1912–3) 27
Bandung Conference of Non-Aligned States (1955) 191
Battle of Ypres (1915) 90–1
Beaufort, Willem de 144
Belgrade Non-Aligned Summit (1961) 196

Bismarck, Otto von 12–13
Blehr, Otto 174
Bluntschli, Johann Kasper 57
Boer War *see* Anglo-Boer War (1899–1902, Second)
Bosnia Crisis (1908) 5, 12, 18, 22–6
Bourgeois, Léon 78, 130–1
Brussels Conference (1874) 52, 56, 59, 128
Bryce Report (1915) 100n39, 106–7
Bucharest Declaration (1966) 192
Bulgarian independence 22–4
Bülow, Bernhard von 17, 20, 26, 72, 131
Bush, George Herbert Walker 86

Castiella, Fernando María 212
Cavell, Edith 91
Ceadel, Martin 141
Cecil, Lord Robert 91, 175
Central Organization for a Durable Peace 173
Chateauvillard, Comte de 125–6
chemical warfare/weapons 6, 77, 86–8, 135n34; fear of 93–4; prohibition of 87, 94; use of 86, 88
Chemical Weapons Convention (1993) 87–8, 96–7
Chicago Daily Tribune 155, 158–66
Churchill, Winston
civilisation 8, 133; 'civilising mission' 21–2, 26; 'civilising process' 122, 124
Clark, Ian 140
Cold War 8–9, 189–201
collective security 32, 34, 38, 190, 213–15
Committee of Examination *see* Hague Peace Conference 1899
Committee of Unity and Progress 22
communist regimes 190–1
Conrad, Joseph 131–2

constitutional text 211–12
cosmopolitanism 16, 127

d'Estournelles de Constant, Henri Balluet 42
Daily Mail 158–66
Darby, William Evans 146–7
De Rivera, Primo 207–8
Declaration of London (1909) 3, 162–3
Delcassé, Théophile 17, 19–21, 72
Descamps, Edouard 41
détente 192
disarmament 6, 16–17, 71, 75–9, 80–2, 160
Drago Doctrine, 45–6
Drago, Luis Maria, 45–6
duelling 7, 121, 123; codes of 124; jurisprudence of 125–7; origin and development of 124–6; protocols of 129–31
dum-dum bullets 2, 77–8, 82, 129, 164–6

Eastern Question 22, 25–6
Elias, Norbert 122–4
Elizabeth of Austria, Empress 59
Entente Cordiale 19
European Defence Community 191
European Economic Community 192, 199
European peace movements 34, 73, 148
Eyffinger, Arthur 52–3, 144

First World War (1914–1918) 8, 13, 18, 79–80, 86–8, 90–3, 106, 132–3, 190; legality of conduct 155–6, 164–5; and public opinion 156–8; and Spain 207–8, 212
Fisher, Sir John 77, 81
Franco-Prussian War (1870–1871) 14

gas (as weapon) 6, 89–90, 129
gas warfare *see* chemical warfare
Gascoyne-Cecil, Robert, Third Marquess of Salisbury 70–1, 139–41
gender roles 7, 108–9
gender-based violence law 7, 104–10, 110–13, 114–17
General Act for the Pacific Settlement of International Disputes 184
Geneva Arbitration 14, 34
Geneva Conference (1906) 62–3
Geneva Convention (1864) 53, 59; proposed revisions of 59–63

Geneva Convention (1929) 108
Geneva Convention (1949) 109
Geneva Gas Protocol (1925) 82, 87, 94–6
genocide 109
Gómez Rojí, Ricardo 210
Grey, Sir Edward 17, 79–80, 166
Grotius, Hugo 34, 189, 222n66

Haber, Fritz 90
Hagerup, Francis 172–5, 176–7, 180, 182–4
Hague conferences in history 32, 150
Hague Conventions (1899) 1–2, 103–4, 167, 180, 194–5, 207; Convention for the adaptation to maritime warfare of the principles of the Geneva Convention 6, 61; Convention for the Pacific Settlement of Disputes 5, 31, 40, 159, 198–9; Convention with respect to the Laws and Customs of War on Land 86, 93, 97, 104–5
Hague Conventions (1907) 3, 103–4, 167, 180, 194–5, 207; Convention Relative to the Opening of Hostilities 46, 209; Convention Respecting the Rights and Duties of Neutral Powers and Persons in Case of War on Land 189; Convention Respecting the Rights and Duties of Neutral Powers in Naval War 18
Hague Peace Conference (1899, First) agenda of the 38–9, 88–9; and disarmament 69, 75–9; calling of the 1, 71–4, 128, 139; First Commission 31, 74–5, 128–9; Second Commission 31, 128–9; Third Commission 31, 39–43, 128–32
Hague Peace Conference (1907, Second) agenda of the 79, 180; calling of the 2, 44, 128, 171; Final Act 44–5; First Commission 44–6; First Sub-Commission 44–6; meeting of the 26–7; popular support for 27; proposals for 62
Hague Peace Conference (1915, Third) 4, 156, 159–60, 171
Hague, The (the city of) 4, 156
Hague, The (the idea of) 4, 5, 8, 155–6, 167
Haldane, Richard 15–6
Hardinge, Charles 24
Holls, Frederick 130–1

Holocaust, The 88, 108–9
Holstein, Friedrich von 19–21
honour cultures or honour codes 7, 121–4, 128, 132
hospital-ship immunity 54–6
Hull, Isabel 13, 132, 157–8
humanitarianism 7, 64, 78, 105, 110–11, 217; *see also* international humanitarian law
human rights 2, 5, 103–5, 108–13, 115, 218
Hungarian uprising (1956) 191

imperialism 22, 198
Institut de droit international 14, 39, 57, 121
Institute of International Law *see Institut de droit international*
International Arbitration and Peace Association 144, 149
International Association of Democratic Lawyers 193, 199
International Committee of the Red Cross 52, 54–9, 64
International Criminal Tribunal of Rwanda 115–17
International Criminal Tribunal of Yugoslavia 115–17
International Crusade of Peace 139, 147–9
international humanitarian law 7, 103–7, 111–13, 164–5
international law: codification of 93, 121–2, 181–2, 189–90, 216; communist conception of 190–1, 193, 197; and diplomacy, 27; effective enforcement of 19–20; and European politics 16–17; historiography of 32; importance of 13, 217; and international legal imaginary 16; interpretation of 161–2; and legal reasoning 36–7; as normative pillar 27; rule of 171–2; use of 18; violation of 28, 160–1
international lawyers 57–8
International Prize Court 3
internationalism 15, 57, 155, 173, 207
Inter-Parliamentary Union 39, 172, 174, 176
Italian-Abyssinian War (1935–6, Second) 88
ius ad bellum 5, 32–3, 34, 46; and dispute resolution 47; and self-preservation 37–8

ius contra bellum 5, 32–3
Izvolksi, Alexander 22, 24, 26

Jackson, Peter 15
Joyce, James 138–9, 149–50
just war 17, 34–6, 47, 104, 189–90

Karnebeek, A. P. C. von 89
Kellogg-Briand Pact (1928) 184, 190, 207, 209, 214
Kitchener, Lord 92–3
Koskenniemi, Marti 121
Kristiania 172

Lange, Christian Louis 172–5, 180, 183–4
law of nations *see* international law
League of Nations 69–70, 80–2, 131, 210; Covenant of 32, 44, 47, 80–2, 175, 179, 190; establishment of 174, 190; Pact 207, 212–14
League to Enforce Peace 172–3
legal war 34–5, 47 *see also* just war
legitimacy 13–14, 172
Lie, Mikael H. 174
Lieber Code (1863) 105–6, 128
Ligue des femmes pour le désarmement international 73
London Naval Conference (1930) 80
Los Angeles Times 158–66
Louvain atrocities (1914, Leuven) 165
Lüder, Carl 57
Lusitania 91

MacDonald, Gabrielle 116
MacDonald Plan 80
MacIver, Robert 133
MacKinnon, Catherine 110–12
Madariaga, Salvador de 210
Madrid Convention (1880) 18, 19, 21
Mahan, Alfred Thayer 55, 61, 89
Manchester Guardian 155, 158–66
Martens, Fyodor 39, 52, 59–60
Martens' Clause 2
mediation 39, 43, 47, 129–30, 156, 159, 211
Modzhorian, Lidiia 191–2, 194, 196–8
Moi, Toril 114–15
Moroccan Crisis (1905, First) 18–22
Mouraviev, Count Mikhail 73
Mowinckel, John L. 174
Moynier, Gustave 14, 52, 57–8

national honour *see* honour cultures
nationality 27
naval mines 162–4
naval warfare 53–6, 63
neutrality 8–9, 54, 156–7, 162–4, 167, 172, 189, 200–1, 207 communist conception of 191–200
newspaper reporting 8, 14, 90, 143, 148, 155–60, 166
Nicholas II of Russia 1, 79, 128, 144
Nobel prizes 90, 136n47, 174
non-alignment 190–2, 200
normative frameworks: in international politics 13–14, 140; for law 36; mechanisms for applying 17
normative restraints 18
normative value 18–19, 21–2
North Atlantic Treaty Organisation 191, 199
North Sea 164
Norwegian independence 171
Nuremberg trials 108

Obama, Barack 86
Odier, Edouard 57–9, 62,
Odio, Elizabeth 116
Owen, Wilfrid 91

pacific settlement of disputes 33, 39–43; *see also* arbitration
Pact of Paris (1928) 32
Pan-American Conference (1906) 45
Paris Peace Conference (1919) 106–8, 175
Pauncefote, Sir Julian 43, 79
Peace Crusade 9
peace movements 34, 37, 44, 80, 140–1, 207, 217
Peace Society 146–9
Peace Sunday 145–7
peace petitions 139, 142, 145–6, 149–50; *see also* petitioning
peace through law movement 33–4, 41, 46
Permanent Court of Arbitration 3, 13, 16, 43–4, 47, 130, 160, 175
Permanent Court of International Justice 8, 44, 131, 172; establishment of 182–4; proposal for 173, 175–82
petitioning 73, 141–2, 146, 149
Pillay, Navanethem 116
Pinker, Stephen 122
Poincaré, Raymond 16

poison 89, 129; *see also* gas, chemical warfare
Porter, Horace, 45–6
power politics 12–13, 21
prisoners of war 41, 64, 129
public opinion 14, 140, 189; in favour of disarmament 69–72, 76, 80; and the Hague peace conferences 155; in international relations 37, 157–8; and justification of foreign policy 17, 165–6; and poison gas 90–1
public sphere 27
Punch 92, 145

Rape of Nanking (1937–8) 108
rape *see* gender-based violence law
Red Cross Conference in Rome (1892) 55
Red Cross movement 63; *see also* International Committee of the Red Cross
rescript *see* Russian Circular (1898, First)
restraint 133
Riezler, Kurt 15–16
Rome Statute 116–17
Roosevelt, Franklin Delano 86
Roosevelt, Theodore 44
Root, Elihu 31–2, 47
Royo Villanova, Antonio 210
Russian Circular (1898, First) 1, 7, 46, 71–2, 88–9, 138–41, 146, 149
Russian Circular (1899, Second) 39, 46, 53, 56, 58–9, 73–4, 88
Russo-Japanese War (1904–5) 62
Russo-Turkish War (1877–8) 22

Saint Petersburg Declaration (1868) 53–5, 70, 128
Salisbury, Lord *see* Gascoyne-Cecil, Robert, Third Marquess of Salisbury
Scheine, Captain 89
Schleswig-Holstein War (1864) 53
Schwarzhoff, Colonel von 76–7
Scott, James Brown 152n30
Scott, Sir Charles 144
Second World War (1939–1945) 88, 108, 190
secularisation 36–7
Sellers, Patricia Viseur 103–5
Sino-Japanese War (1894) 55–6, 88
Slaughter, Joseph 111–14
solidarisme 15

Southeast Asia Treaty Organisation 191
sovereignty 43
Spanish Civil War (1936–9) 214–15
Spanish Constitution (1931) 9, 207–12, 217–18
Spanish Constitution (1978) 9, 207, 215–17
Spanish-American War (1898) 208
Staal, Baron Egor *see* Staal, Georges de
Staal, Georges de 31, 76
Stead, William Thomas 7–8, 73, 139–45, 147–50

Temps, Les 21
torpedoes 55–6, 78
Treaty of Berlin (1878) 18, 22; violation of 23–5
Treaty of Bucharest (1913) 27
Treaty of Geneva (1925) 6
Treaty of London (1871) 14
Treaty of London (1913) 27
Treaty of Paris (1856) 128
Treaty of Paris (1993) 6
Treaty of Versailles (1919) 8, 81, 93
Treaty of Washington (1922) 6
Tuchman, Barbara 71, 142–3
Tysla 162–3

Union Juridique Internationale 176
United Nations 109–10, 131; Charter of 32, 190, 209, 216; establishment of 190
use of force law 32–3, 34–8, 46–7, 129, 216

Vattel, Emer de 49n20, 177
Villanueva Gómez, Justo 210
voeux 2, 78–9

War Against War 139, 147–8
war law *see* use of force law; *ius ad bellum*; *ius contra bellum*; international law
Warsaw Pact 191–2
warships 78
Washington Naval Conference (1921–2) 80, 87, 94–5
weaponry 70
weapons of mass destruction 86, 94, 100fn32, 194
Wegener, Professor 91–2
Wehberg, Hans 40
Wekerle, Sándor 23
White, Andrew 43
Wilhelm II of Germany 19, 47, 73
Wilson, Woodrow 159, 174
Wittgenstein, Ludwig 114
World Conferences on Women 110; Fourth UN Conference on Women (1995) 115–17
World Disarmament Conference (1932) 80–2
Würtenberg, Erik Marks von 173–4

Young Turks 22
Ypres, battle for (1915) 90–1

Zepellin raids 161
Zorn, Philip Karl Ludwig 42